I am heartily ashamed

VOLUME II:
THE REVOLUTIONARY WAR'S FINAL CAMPAIGN
AS WAGED FROM CANADA IN 1782

James Peachey, circa 1784. (Library and Archives Canada, C-002005.)

A west view of Sorel, 1784. This view shows some of the fifty storehouses and barracks built by Haldimand to house a large proportion of the province's military and naval stores and a substantial garrison.

I am heartily ashamed

VOLUME II:
THE REVOLUTIONARY WAR'S FINAL CAMPAIGN
AS WAGED FROM CANADA IN 1782

Gavin K. Watt

with the research assistance of James F. Morrison and William A. Smy

DUNDURN PRESS
TORONTO

Editor: Shannon Whibbs
Designer: Courtney Horner
Printer: Marquis

Library and Archives Canada Cataloguing in Publication

Watt, Gavin K.
          I am heartily ashamed : the Revolutionary War's final campaign as waged
from Canada in 1782 / Gavin K. Watt.

Sequel to: A dirty, trifling, piece of business"
Includes bibliographical references and index.
Contents: "Volume II"
ISBN 978-1-55488-715-6 (v. 2)

          1. Canada--History--1775-1783. 2. United
States--History--Revolution,
1775-1783--Participation, Canadian. 3. United States--History--Revolution,
1775-1783. 4. Haldimand, Frederick, Sir, 1718-1791. I. Title.

FC420.W383 2010   971.02'4   C2009-907474-5

1   2   3   4   5   14   13   12   11   10

  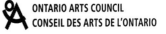

Conseil des Arts du Canada   Canada Council for the Arts   Canadä   ONTARIO ARTS COUNCIL CONSEIL DES ARTS DE L'ONTARIO

We acknowledge the support of the **Canada Council for the Arts** and the **Ontario Arts Council** for our publishing program. We also acknowledge the financial support of the **Government of Canada** through the **Canada Book Fund** and **The Association for the Export of Canadian Books**, and the **Government of Ontario** through the **Ontario Book Publishers Tax Credit** program and the **Ontario Media Development Corporation**.

Printed and bound in Canada
www.dundurn.com

Front cover photograph: John W. Moore
Cover designer: Christopher Armstrong

Dundurn Press	Gazelle Book Services Limited	Dundurn Press
3 Church Street, Suite 500	White Cross Mills	2250 Military Road
Toronto, Ontario, Canada	High Town, Lancaster, England	Tonawanda, NY U.S.A.
M5E 1M2	LA1 4XS	14150

CONTENTS

LIST OF MAPS AND PLANS

INTRODUCTION AND ACKNOWLEDGEMENTS

*A*lthough this book stands on its own merits, it should be recognized as a sequel to Volume I, *A dirty, trifling piece of business*, which describes the Canadian campaign of 1781 against the United States' frontiers. Like the first volume, *I am heartily ashamed* will appeal to students of the American Revolution in Canada and the northern United States.

After closing off the 1781 campaign, Volume II moves through an incredibly fierce Quebec winter during which Governor Haldimand receives alarming reports of a possible Franco-American invasion and spurs his Secret Service into action to measure the risks.

Early in the new year, the sparring between New York and Vermont reaches a critical stage when New Yorkers at Sancoick in the so-called Western Union throw their support behind Vermont and create an uproar that comes extremely close to open warfare.

The 1782 Canadian campaign opens with a resumption of raids against the rebel frontiers, but, unlike the year before, the defence of the Mohawk region falls into disarray when New York's Colonel Marinus Willett jousts for command control with Lieutenant-Colonel George Reid, a New Hampshire Continental.

A major strategic initiative by Haldimand is to repossess Oswego, which his troops accomplish with great secrecy and energy. And, to further keep the rebels off balance, he assigns large elements of the Canadian army to strengthen the fortifications at Isle aux Noix.

Because of Ross's costly expedition of the previous October, the governor contents himself with less ambitious and dangerous ventures, allowing two prominent Mohawk war captains, John Deserontyon and Joseph Brant, to lead large raids into the Mohawk Valley supported by British and Provincial Regulars. The native leaders create great challenges for the rebels by their bold, far ranging assaults.

In mid-summer, the new British ministry suddenly announces a cessation of active operations which is soon followed by news of peace negotiations. As the war draws to a close, far too many issues are left unresolved and the natives and loyalists face a time of great unrest, despair, and upheaval.

———————————————

———————————————

Mohawk Valley expert, James F. Morrison, and Butler's Rangers' specialist, William A. Smy, contributed extensively to this volume. I owe both a great debt of gratitude.

Ken D. Johnson of Fort Plain was very helpful, especially with details of Oswego. Justin Boggess assisted with the analysis of the German troops. Jeff O'Connor of Schoharie, Neil Goodwin of Vermont, and John A. Houlding, the British Army guru, were also most helpful.

John W. Moore and my son Gavin provided extensive service with artwork and photography. Particularly notable was the professional assistance and guidance so freely offered by graphics designer Chris Armstrong with the enhancement of images and maps and, once again, with the design of the book's cover.

Gavin K. Watt
Museum of Applied Military History
King City, Ontario, Canada, 2009

LIST OF ABBREVIATIONS

1KRR	1st Battalion, King's Royal Regiment of New York
2KRR	2nd Battalion, King's Royal Regiment of New York
1NH	1st Regiment, New Hampshire Continental Line
2NH	2nd Regiment, New Hampshire Continental Line
1NY	First Regiment, New York Continental Line
1–5NY	First to Fifth Regiments, New York Continental Line
1RI	1st Regiment, Rhode Island Continental Line
2RI	2nd Regiment, Rhode Island Continental Line
2-I-C	Second-in-Command
6NID	Six Nations' Indian Department
84RHE	84th Regiment, Royal Highland Emigrants
1/84RHE	1st battalion, 84th Regiment
ACM	Albany County Militia
1–17ACM	1st to 17th ACM Regiments
BR	(John Butler's regiment) Butler's Rangers
C-in-C	Commander-in-Chief
CO	Commanding Officer
CT	Connecticut
DQMG	Deputy Quartermaster General
GO	General Orders
HQ	Headquarters
KLA	(Eben Jessup's) King's Loyal Americans
KR	(James Rogers's) 2nd Battalion, King's Rangers

KRR	(Sir John Johnson's) King's Royal Regiment of New York
LR	(Edward Jessup's) Loyal Rangers
MA	Massachusetts
OC	Officer Commanding
pdr	pounder (weight of solid shot capable of being fired from a gun)
QID	Quebec Indian Department
QM	Quartermaster
QMG	Quartermaster General
QLR	(John Peters's) Queen's Loyal Rangers
RHE	(Allan Maclean's) Royal Highland Emigrants
RIR	The Rhode Island Continental Regiment
Royal Yorkers	King's Royal Regiment of New York
RN	Royal Navy
TCM	Tryon County Militia
1–4TCM	First to Fourth TCM Regiments
WL	Willett's Levies

Crown

Bettys, Joseph	Notorious loyalist Secret Service agent
Brant, Joseph	Mohawk War Captain/Captain 6NID
Butler, John	Deputy Superintendent, 6NID; Lieutenant-Colonel, BR
Caldwell, William	Active Captain, BR
Campbell, John	Colonel, QID
Carleton, Guy	Replacement C-in-C America
Chambers, William	Commodore, Lake Champlain squadron
Claus, Daniel	Senior Deputy Superintendent, 6NID
Clinton, Sir Henry	C-in-C America
Crawford, William Redford	Active Captain QID and 2KRR
Crysler, Adam	Lieutenant, 6NID/scourge of Schoharie Valley
DePeyster, Arent	Major, 8th Regiment/Commandant Detroit
Deserontyon, John	Senior Fort Hunter Mohawk War Captain
Fraser, William	Captain, LR/commandant Yamaska Blockhouse
Gray, James	Major-Commandant, 1KRR
Haldimand, Frederick	Captain-General/Governor of Canada
Jessup, Edward	Major-Commandant, LR
Johnson, Guy	Colonel/disgraced Superintendent, 6NID
Johnson, Sir John	Brigadier-General/Superintendent Northern Indian Affairs
Lernoult, Richard	Major/Adjutant General, Quebec

Maclean, Allan	Brigadier-General, Montreal and Niagara Military District
Mathews, Robert	Captain, 8th/Haldimand's military secretary
McAlpin, James	Ensign, 1KRR/dismissed the service
Powell, Henry Watson	Brigadier-General/OC Niagara District
Pritchard, Azariah	Captain, 2KR/active Secret Service agent
Prenties, John Thomas	Lieutenant, 1KRR/bad conduct
Riedesel, Friederich Adolphus	Brunswick Major-General/Haldimand's closest confidant
Robertson, Daniel	Active Captain, 84RHE/OC Oswegatchie
Rogers, James	Major-Commandant, 2KR
Ross, John	Major-Commandant, 2KRR/OC Oswego
St. Leger, Barry	Colonel, 34th/OC St. John's Military District
Sherwood, Justus	Captain, LR/OC Secret Service
Singleton, George	Light Infantry captain, 2KRR
Smyth, Dr. George	2-I-C, Secret Service
Stevens, Roger	Ensign, KR/active Secret Service agent
Sutherland, Walter	Lieutenant, 2KRR/active Secret Service agent
Thompson, John	Volunteer, 1KRR/severely beaten by Canadien
Wasmus, Julius	Surgeon, Prinz Ludwig Dragoon Regiment

Rebel

Allen, Ethan	General/key member, Vermont Council
Allen, Ira	Colonel/key member, Vermont Council
Bayley, Jacob	Militia Brigadier-General, Cöos, Vermont/ opposed Allens
Calkins, Matthew	Light Infantry private, Willett's Levies
Chittenden, Thomas	Governor, Vermont
Clark, George Rogers	Brigadier-General, Virginia/commanded far west
Clinton, George	Governor, New York State
Colonel Louis Atayataghronghta	Continental LCol/ Kahnawake War Chief, rebel Indians
Finck, Andrew	Major, Willett's Levies
Gansevoort, Peter	Brigadier-General, 1st brigade, ACM
Heath, William	Continental Major-General/replaced Washington in the north mid-1781
Johnson, Thomas	Militia Lieutenant-Colonel Cöos/double agent

Klock, Jacob J.	Son of Colonel Klock/ex Ensign, 1NY/traitor
Olney, Jeremiah	Colonel commanding Rhode Island Regiment
Otaawighton, John	Oneida Captain/Willett's guide at Oswego
Reid, George	Lieutenant-Colonel, 2NH; jousted with Willett for command control
Schuyler, Philip	Major-General, Indian Affairs Commissioner
Stark, John	Major-General/OC Northern Frontiers
Stirling, Lord	Major-General/OC Northern Frontiers after Stark
Van Rensselaer, Robert	Brigadier-General, OC, 2nd Brigade, Albany County Militia
Vrooman, Peter	Colonel, 15ACM/OC Schoharie Valley
Washington, George	C-in-C Allied Forces
Willett, Marinus	Colonel, NY State Troops and Levies/OC Mohawk region
Younglove, John	2nd Major, 16ACM/Committee of Sequestration, Albany County

1781

October 26	Another Indian attack at New Dorlach
November 9	Crysler attacks Vroomansland/Utsayantho Lake action
November 29	Sutherland on patrol
December 19	Sutherland on second patrol
December 25	Scout to St. Francis R.; Grand Scout to Hazen's Road

1782

January-March	Raiders at Fairfield, German Flatts, and Walradt's Ferry
January 7	Sutherland, Stevens, and Miller at Crown Point
January 19	Grand Scout to Hazen's Road
January 24	St. Francis River scout
February 2	Tyler's Grand Scout to Hazen's Road
February 28	Stevens back from Vermont scout
Early March	Raiders on Mohawk River and at Cobleskill
March 7	Rebel massacre of Moravian Delawares
March 9	Pritchard back from Vermont scout
March 11	de Monveil on scout to Hazen's Road
March 22	Raiders along Bowman's Creek and at Fort Herkimer
March 23	Hill leads raid on Schoharie
Late March	Bettys, Parker, Miller, Crowfoot, Van Camp on scouts
April 7	Houghton has three scouting parties out of Kahnawake
April 20	Nelles with raid at Pine Creek, Pennsylvania

April 24   War party at Fort Plain
April 30   Pritchard returns from Vermont scout
May   Frey's Bush raid and two raids near Fort Plain
May 2   Sherwood has forty-seven scouts ranging Vermont
May 3   Raid near Mayfield; Butler's Rangers at Nanticoke
May 4   Senecas take prisoners at Canajoharie
May 9   Johnston in Indian Territory
May 10   Rogers leads large scout to Cöos country
May 31   Wehr on scout in Vermont
June 5   Caldwell defeats large force at Sandusky
June 11   St. Francis Indians patrol Hazen's Road
June 14–23   Deserontyon's raid strikes across the middle Valley
June 15   Pritchard attempts abduction of General Bayley
June 18   Nine men captured at Fort Edward
June 21   Ellice's Mills destroyed
June 30   Raiders at Fort Herkimer
Late June   Raiders strike Stoner farm; Raiders killed at Sacandaga
July 4   Raiders in Schoharie Valley
July 12   Brunswick troops scout Crown Point
July 12   Raid on Hanna's Town, Pennsylvania
July 13   Word of ceasefire reaches Ross at Fort Haldimand
July 15   Brant's raid strikes at Fort Herkimer
July 16   Raiders in the Schoharie
July 26   Raiders at Stone Arabia
July 31   Jacob Klock scouts the Palatine District
Late July   Two men captured in Mohawk Valley
August 3   Roger Stevens returns from Ticonderoga
August 4   Thomas Man returns from Hazen's Road
August 19   Caldwell defeats large force at Blue Licks
September 8   Thomas Sherwood returns from a scout
September 11   Bradt attacks Wheeling, Virginia
September 11   Roger Stevens returns from scout to Vermont
September 29   Scout to Mohawk River returns to Oswego

1

THE AFTERMATH OF THE 1781 CAMPAIGN
Shameful, Dastardly Conduct

*T*he surrender of Cornwallis's army at Yorktown, Virginia, in October 1781 marked the failure of Britain's strategic effort in the southern provinces and freed the victorious rebels and their French allies to shift their attentions northward for the 1782 campaign. Once again, Canada was seriously threatened by an Allied invasion.

When news of Cornwallis's defeat was belatedly confirmed in Canada, Governor Frederick Haldimand reacted by making improvements to his province's defences and tweaking his small army to improve its efficiency. At the same time, he was mindful of his responsibility to assist the main army at New York City by forcing the enemy to keep a body of troops on the northern frontiers.

Conventional wisdom is that, after its stunning victory at Yorktown, the United States enjoyed clear sailing on its path to independence and that the war simply fizzled out like damp priming. The contrary was the case. The rebels were unsure of how the British would react to their defeat, and terror and destruction continued to reign along the northern frontiers. The natives had been unaffected by Yorktown and, as long as the British continued to supply their war parties, the union's northern and western reaches were vulnerable to attack. As the 1782 campaign unfolded in the Mohawk region, it proved as horrific as ever, while Congress fumbled its attempts to protect those brave inhabitants who clung to their thoroughly ravaged settlements.

Nor would New York's war of words with Vermont cease. Having become fully aware of the little republic's treacherous negotiations with the British, the state belaboured Congress with the details. Vermont's sudden, bold seizure of a large area of New York, which it infuriatingly referred to as its Western Union, deeply rankled the state and, although the military posturing of the fall of 1781 between the two jurisdictions had momentarily quietened, animosity did not.

The news of Yorktown had interrupted Haldimand's plans for Vermont, but in the new year he reorganized his approach and, in the process, would keep the little republic out of the war.

In addition to Congress's worries about Canada, the Crown maintained large armies at New York City and Charlestown and, the Royal Navy, despite its failure to save Cornwallis, still dominated the Atlantic seaboard. The British also had large bases in Nova Scotia and Quebec, which were looming presences. To counteract these latter threats, the union had a tiny Continental navy and an underfed, underpaid, and undersupplied Continental Army.

Yet, all of this pertains to the future. To begin this account, it is necessary to step back in time, to immediately before the Yorktown disaster.

Although St. Leger's expedition on Lake Champlain and Ross's deep thrust into the Mohawk dominated Canada's war effort in the northeast at the end of the 1781 campaign season, of course, the province's other business continued unabated.

Of particular significance to Haldimand's army, Lieutenant-General Baron Friederich Adolphus Riedesel arrived at Quebec City on September 10. The baron was a soldier of outstanding accomplishments. Although born a Hessian in 1738, the vast majority of his service had been under the Duke of Brunswick. As an ensign, he had spent time in England and become proficient in English and fluent in French. At the outbreak of the Seven Years' War in 1756, his regiment had been recalled to Germany, where he served as an aide to the Duke of Brunswick. His actions during the momentous battle of Minden in 1759 led the duke to recommend

Lieutenant-General Baron Friederich Adolphus Riedesel, 1738–1800. Haldimand's trusted friend and confidant. After his return to Canada in September 1781, the baron became the department's de facto second-in-command until his departure in 1783.

Unknown artist. (Clipart courtesy Florida Center for Instructional Technology, http://etc.usf.edu/clipart.)

the twenty-one-year-old to his landgrave, who in turn promoted him to a captain of Hessian Hussars; however, the young baron was soon recalled to again serve the duke under whom he performed a great many important services. Two years later, he was promoted to lieutenant-colonel of Brunswick Hussars and given command of a brigade of cavalry. In 1767, his regiment was disbanded and Riedesel was appointed the adjutant general of the Brunswick army, and five years later, the colonel of a regiment of dragoons.

When the Duke of Brunswick signed a treaty in 1776 to supply a large contingent of troops to King George III, Riedesel was given command and promoted to major-general. Upon his arrival in Quebec, he was appointed to command Carleton's contingent of Brunswick and Hessian troops and, in 1777, he served in the same capacity under Burgoyne and earned widespread approbation. Unlike Burgoyne, who was recalled to England after the surrender to defend the loss of his army, the baron had remained with his men and endured four years of captivity before being exchanged to New York City.[1]

During Haldimand's first three years as commander-in-chief of Canada, he had grown very discouraged with the German troops that composed over a third of his army. Except for the Hesse-Hanau Jägers, he judged the other regiments incapable of wilderness campaigning, and he found that even the Hanau Jägers were of marginal use at the frontier posts, as they refused to perform the crucial manual labour expected of British and Provincial troops. Riedesel's unexpected appearance in September was a blessing and, with substantial relief and high expectations, the

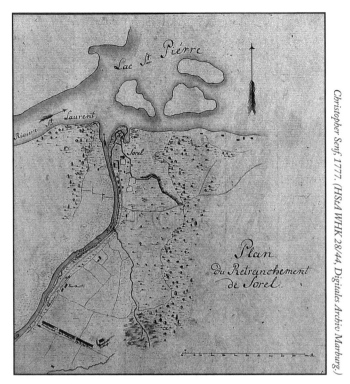

Christopher Senf, 1777. (HStA WHK 28/44, Digitales Archiv Marburg.)

A plan of the entrenchments at Sorel, 1777. From these rather humble beginnings, Haldimand developed Sorel into the third-most important military installation in lower Quebec.

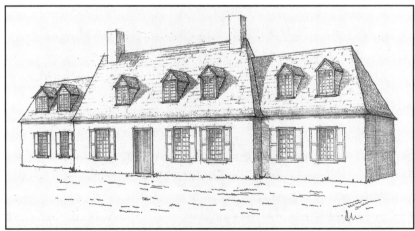

John W. Moore, 2009.

The Riedesels' house, presently the Maison des Gouverneurs. Purchased by Haldimand for the Riedesel family at Sorel, the governor had several improvements made before their occupation.

governor gave him command of the German contingent. The baron was kept very busy with his new responsibilities and a month passed before he found time to report to Lord George Germain (the British Secretary for the American Colonies) that he had brought to Quebec 970 Brunswick and Hanau troops (like himself, they had been exchanged as part of the Convention Army) and recruits from Anhalt-Zerbst. This body of men landed at the same time as a recruit transport from Hesse-Hanau arrived with men for the Jäger corps and the infantry.

In addition to commanding the German troops, Riedesel assumed responsibility for Sorel District. He was headquartered just outside of the town of Sorel, which, after Quebec City and Montreal, had become the third most important centre in the lower province. Haldimand had quickly determined that the baron was a man of keen intellect and dedicated professionalism. He had been instantly charmed upon meeting the general's wife, Baroness Frederika Riedesel, and her children and had a new spacious house prepared for them, in which the lady kept a special room for his visits. Haldimand sustained a brisk social discourse with Riedesel, as well as a detailed, often confidential, military one, until the latter returned to Europe in 1783. As a fellow foreign-born officer, the baron and family were to become Haldimand's closest friends to such a degree that the baroness later wrote, "I have hardly ever seen a man who was more amiable and friendly to those to whom he had once given friendship; and we flattered ourselves that we were included in that number."

From Haldimand's pre-war experience in Canada, he was entirely aware of Sorel's critical strategic location and, soon after his arrival in 1778, he had informed Germain that, due to the vulnerability of Isle aux Noix, St. John's, and Montreal, he intended to move a large proportion of his stores there. In preparation, he improved the fortifications and had fifty barracks and warehouses constructed. Over the next several years, Sorel became headquarters for several British and German regiments and the remnants of Burgoyne's loyalist corps and, in the fall of 1781, came under Riedesel's command.[2]

Scouting Marks, to be observed by the Scouts from Sorel, Yamaska, St. John, Isle-aux-Noix, Point-au-Fer, St François & Loyal Blockhouse.

	Dec.	Jan.	Feb.	Mar.	Apr.	May.
From the 1st to the 7th both days inclusive	(	⊠	△	⊕	†	‖‖
From the 8th to the 14th both days inclusive	‖‖	⊥	Ⓓ	△	□	D
From the 16th to the 22d both days inclusive	∈	⊟	∧	⊘	+	‖
From the 23d to the end of the Month			○	∟	□	∃

Explanation.

Sorel Scouts will put an S above the Mark, & last of all the day of the Month on which The mark is made there.	S (	On 7th of December and from Sorel
Yamaska Scouts, a Y thus	⊠ Y	on 5th of January and from Yamaska
St Johns Scouts, an I before thus	I Ⓓ	on 8th of February and from St. John's
Isle aux Noix Scouts, an N under thus	⊘ N	on 15th of March and from Isle aux Noix
Point-au-Fêr Scouts, an F before thus	F □	on 23rd of April and from Point-au-Fêr
St Francois Scouts, an St above & F under thus	St ∃ F	on 31st of May & from St Francois
Loyal Block house Scouts, an Ll before and BH, after thus	Ll ⊠ BH	on 1st of January & from Loyal Block House

Nota Bene

Scouting Parties must furnish themselves with pens and Ink or Pencils withPaper, and affix these Marks, at such distances, and in such places as their own discretion will point out to them, as the most proper, and the most likely to be seen by their Friends.

The greatest accuracy is recommended in making the geometrical figures, and in the due observation of the dates Paroles and Countersigns; and the use of each.

Commanding officers of Posts; from whence Parties go, will do well to see that their Scouting Officers and Non Commission'd Officers, are perfectly instructed in forming the figures and placing the dates of their own, as well as in the knowledge of those of other Posts whose Tracks and Marks they may fall into or intersect.

Commanding Officers will furnish their parties with Marks and Countersigns only for the time allotted for the Scout.

In the meeting of Scouts; to the Party Challenging, the Countersign is to be given; that being satisfactory, the Parole to be given by the party challenged.

Christopher Armstrong, 2008, after Library and Archives Canada, Haldimand Papers, AddMss21796, f.273.

Undoubtedly, similar instructions and codes were issued to scouts from Lachine, Kanehsatake, Oswegatchie, Carleton Island, and Fort Niagara. No doubt, these cryptic messages caused unrest when discovered by rebel patrols.

On October 19, Riedesel reported to the governor regarding arrangements he had made for the employment of two detachments over the winter. Three officers and twenty-four men from the King's Rangers and Fraser's Independent Company had been chosen for the duty. Two of the officers and sixteen men would be posted at the Upper Yamaska Blockhouse on the river of the same name and a third officer and eight men would operate from the Loyal Blockhouse at Dutchman's Point at Longe Isle on Lake Champlain. An officer and eight men would patrol south from Yamaska to the Bayley-Hazen Road, and another party would cover ground from the Loyal Blockhouse eastward along the Missisquoi River. They were "to observe very carefully all Tracks as well as those which go out of the Province as those which come in to it, and when they find any fresh to follow them; they are not always to take the same route, but they must strike some part of Hazen's Road, and they are to make particular marks at certain distances for which the Officers commanding at each Post have rec'd instructions."[3]

John Stuart, the Anglican priest who had been the missionary to the Fort Hunter Mohawk castle and its nearby European community, had been one of Haldimand's most useful spies. When the priest realized he was in imminent danger of exposure, he obtained permission from New York's governor, George Clinton, to remove his family to Canada and, after enduring an arduous journey, the Stuarts arrived in Montreal on October 13. The priest wrote of his experiences to his superiors at the Society for the Propagation of the Gospel, reporting that the rebels had first set up a tavern in his church and dispensed liquor from its reading desk. Next, they converted the building into a stable and, in 1781, into a fort, "to protect a Set of as great Villains as ever disgraced Humanity." As Stuart had been forced to come away without the protection of a flag of truce, he had left behind the mission's books and its silver plate with a trusted friend in Schenectady.

After Burgoyne's defeat, his Mohawk congregation relocated at Lachine, seven miles from Montreal, and, when Stuart arrived in the city, they enthusiastically greeted him and requested that he reside with them at their new settlement. But, Stuart had a family to support and his personal property had been so thoroughly looted that he was without resources and was therefore compelled to take employment as chaplain of the second battalion, King's Royal Regiment of New York (2KRR).[4]

The same day that Stuart wrote to the SPG, Montreal district's commander, Brigadier Ernst de Speth, former commander of Riedesel's Musketeer regiment, reported a revolt of the rebel prisoners at Coteau-du-Lac where an offshore island prison held the most intransigent captives. He had immediately reinforced the garrison with a detachment of Sir John's first battalion (1KRR). Complicating this affair was a collection of forty-seven new prisoners that was to be sent to the island from Fort St. John's in the next few days.[5]

A week later, Royal Yorker major, James Gray, wrote that the report of a revolt had been groundless and described his battalion's garrison at the post; on the island he had a subaltern and thirty men and, on the mainland, a captain, subaltern, and fifty men.

Another week passed and the post's commandant, Captain Joseph Anderson, apprised Gray about a fire in the Prison Island's joiner's shop and the prisoners' barracks. He did not say if the prisoners had had a hand in the incident, but to judge from earlier strife, the blaze was likely set as cover for another escape attempt. It seems that Gray had been indulging in another cover-up to protect the reputation of his captain and battalion. Earlier in the year, a similar "game" had infuriated the district's previous brigadier, Allan Maclean, RHE.[6]

Captain Georg Pausch of the Hesse-Hanau artillery, who had seen praiseworthy service under Burgoyne in 1777, had returned to Quebec with Riedesel. He wrote to his Crown Prince on October 16 reporting that the Hanau Jägers were on an expedition under St. Leger, "which supposedly is to cross Lakes Champlain and Ontario, in the region of Niagara and Detroit." For someone who had earlier been in Canada for well over a year, Pausch had as little understanding of the country's geography as his fellow Hessian, Lieutenant-Colonel von Kreutzbourg, revealed in his personal journals.

The captain described the material state of his artillery company, noting that, in obedience to the prince's orders, the men were without firelocks. They had bayonets with sheaths mounted on their cartridge pouch straps, but why they had either item of equipment without the requisite long arms is a matter of conjecture. With some difficulty, he had purchased a small wooden drum similar to that used by the English on which his newly recruited black drummers could practice. He praised the new powder flasks and slings supplied by the prince as being beautifully decorated, but again, of what use were these without muskets? He had unsuccessfully requested hangers from Lieutenant-Colonel Macbean, the British artillery commander. The few he had were without sheaths or scabbards, so he had the latter made locally and employed surplus flask slings for carriages, assuring the prince that they would be kept whole so they might be returned to their original purpose. He had brought new, plain uniforms from New York and had gold lace mounted. Further, he had purchased new stockings and shoes and had short, black woollen gaiters made.[7]

On October 20, Haldimand sent dispatch No. 94 to Lord George Germain to advise that Major-General Alured Clarke had arrived with his family. Clarke had been sent to Canada in response to the governor's request for a Briton to outrank his German senior officers in whom he had so little confidence, but Riedesel's surprising arrival had altered the situation. The governor enclosed a copy of a letter, in which the baron wrote of his disappointment at finding himself ranked junior to Clarke, noting that the Briton had been serving as a colonel long after his own appointment to major-general. Haldimand was concerned for Riedesel, as his claim was valid and his military talents unquestioned. To avoid giving offence, he had posted the two generals "as distant from one another as possible;" Riedesel at Sorel, where he had particular knowledge of the town and the adjacent frontiers, and Clarke at headquarters in Quebec City.[8]

Unknown artist. (John Watts DePeyster. Miscellanies of an Officer. New York: C.H. Ludwig, 1838.)

Arent Schuyler DePeyster, 1736–1832. Born in New York, DePeyster joined the 8th Regiment in 1755. In 1779, he was appointed major-commandant at Michilimackinac and took command at Detroit that October.

As to affairs at Niagara, sometime during the fall, a dissatisfied clerk employed by the trading company of Forsyth and Taylor reported that the government was being robbed of vast sums. The company had been Colonel Guy Johnson's major supplier for the Six Nations' Indian Department (6NID), particularly when supplies from Britain ran short. The trading partners were arrested and ordered down to Montreal and Guy was instructed to follow with his account books.

All of Haldimand's suspicions about the superintendent's lack of acumen and managerial skill were confirmed during the interminable investigation. In the meantime, the sick and grieving father, John Butler, who was the department's deputy agent at Niagara and the commander of Butler's Rangers, once again assumed Johnson's responsibilities.[9]

On October 20, Brigadier Henry Watson Powell, Niagara District's commandant, reported news from Major Arent DePeyster, 8th Regiment, the senior military officer at Detroit. Butler's Ranger captain, Andrew Thompson, had fallen overboard and drowned in Lake Erie en route to Niagara. Not mentioned was the fact that Thompson had quarreled with the vessel's master and, in a furious attack, was fended off and tumbled overboard to his death. It was an ignominious end to a gallant loyalist officer who had performed such good service in the 1780 October expedition and on detachment in the west in 1781.

Powell reported that Lieutenant Richard Wilkinson, 6NID, was desirous of succeeding Thompson and, "with the greatest pleasure," forwarded his pretensions "knowing him to be an active, good Officer that Colonel Butler is desirous to have in his Corps." The brigadier was unaware that Wilkinson had displeased the governor when he earlier quit the Royal Yorkers on what — in Haldimand's view — was the slim pretense of family affairs.

The report ended with the advice that Butler had sent Captain Caldwell and twenty-five men to Detroit to relieve Thompson's company. This was all that could be spared, as the commitment to Ross's expedition was so great.[10]

In a similar fashion, ordinary military business had continued at the rebels' northern posts. Just days before Ross struck, Lieutenant-Colonel Marinus Willett, the officer responsible for the defence of the Mohawk region, reported to his political master, Governor George Clinton, that he had received advice about the pay, subsistence, and clothing for his regiment of Levies and a handful of three-years' men, but there was no word about how they would be mustered. He noted that regulations required that every brigade have a Commissary of Muster, but, as his regiment was not brigaded, he had no one to turn to and earnestly requested the appointment of a major of Levies. The governor complied by appointing a major to muster and inspect the Levies in the valley and arranged for a New Hampshire captain at Saratoga to muster those Levies stationed there.

On October 23, the governor attended the state legislature at Poughkeepsie to remind the assembly that the terms of their regiments of Levies were about to expire and that a new arrangement would be required for the upcoming year. He suggested revising the law for raising three-years' men on land bounties, as the officers of the current Levies believed that, if further time was allowed and a small additional bounty granted, a number of recruits might be obtained from amongst their men.[11]

Only a few weeks remained of open navigation when Haldimand made the facile observation in a letter to Germain dated October 22 that Quebec was no longer in danger of invasion for the present campaign. He also agreed with the secretary's observations that, while offensive operations in the south occupied the Allies' attention and, as long as Vermont could be prevented from taking an active part, no serious attempt would be made against Quebec, which made his earlier concerns about an attack even less understandable. As to the offensives he was expected to mount, he wrote:

> I have always Sent Detachments upon the Frontiers of the Rebel Provinces to alarm the Country and destroy Supplies — These Continued Excursions have so desolated the Settlements and driven in the Inhabitants, that it now becomes necessary for Parties to penetrate so far into the Country, to have any Effect, as to endanger their Safety, every Peasant being now a soldier, and prepared to assemble on the Shortest notice which was Experienced upon Sir John Johnson's last Excursion to the Mohawk River, from whence his Retreat became difficult & hazardous, & if vigorously opposed would have been very fatal.

The governor then addressed the subject of Colonel Guy Johnson, which had "occasioned to me more uneasiness than I have words to Express." He had concluded from the tone of Germain's correspondence that the secretary and the King believed his removal of Johnson was the result of a personal vendetta:

> I should be the most unhappy man living, could I suppose His Majesty, or Your Lordship thought my Conduct in that Affair actuated by an unhandsome motive, or any other than that alone which intirely occupies my thoughts & directs my actions, the Good of the Kings Service & the Welfare and happiness

of his Subjects entrusted to my Direction — Your
Lordship may Depend I shall on all future occasions
most punctually Observe His Majestys Commands
Conveyed to me in Your Lordship's Letter, and I firmly
Rely on His Majesty's Justice so strongly Expressed by
Your Lordship that he will never Condemn any man
unheard, or act upon any Information he may Receive
relative to the Province in which I Command, without
giving me an Opportunity of Submitting my Sentiments
to the Royal Consideration.

As to the great difficulties of controlling Indian Department expenses,
he intended "to reduce them more to Method and render them less obscure."

The next day, the governor wrote a secret dispatch to Germain to
advise that he had just received the secretary's information of May 4,
to wit — that the French Court intended to dissuade Congress from
any attempt on Canada until all the king's troops were driven from the
thirteen colonies. Germain had recommended that Haldimand co-
operate with Sir Henry Clinton by sending a large force to Vermont
to encourage their declaration for his majesty and he was able to
report that this measure was
already in train.

In a second dispatch, he
duplicated his private letter of
July 8 and added up-to-date
information about his Vermont
negotiations, including an
explanation of the rationale
behind the proclamation he had
sent with St. Leger:

Guy Johnson habitually put the
wrong foot forward in his dealings
with Governor Haldimand, which
ultimately led to his removal as the
senior Indian superintendent.

Unknown artist, 1775. (Fenimore Art Museum, Cooperstown, New York.)

The very Strong assurances of Sincerity Made, by the agents of Vermont in this Business in Behalf of the Governor, part of the Council, and the obvious difficulties they represent in the Way of a Sudden Revolution Where the Prejudice of a People is So Violent, demand some Credit and Attention, and in a great Measure have removed my Suspicions of the Sincerity of Allen's Party.... The Prejudice of a great Majority of the Populace, and the Prevailing Influence of Congress are too powerful to admit of a Sudden Change by negotiation. The Leading Men who profess themselves in the King's Interest advised as a last Resource, My Issuing a Proclamation Confirming to Vermont the late assumed Territory, and Other Privileges ... thinking that from a Late Refusal of these by Congress, the Populace May be inclined to accept of Terms from Government.

The Crisis is arrived when Some Serious Measures must be taken with Vermont, their Strength & Influence is growing Rapidly, and the Congress are upon the Point of according to their Demands — In So Critical a Juncture I most Sensibly Feel the Want of Particular Instructions, fearing on one Side to Let an opportunity escape, which May never be recalled, and on the Other, taking upon My Self a Decision of Such Importance as is proposed in my Proclamation.... How far Incroachments by Vermont on New York and New Hampshire May Affect Future Politicks, I know not — at present, I conceive them indiscriminately engaged in Rebellion, and if a Reunion of the Most Valuable of them with the Mother Country Cannot be effected by any other means than by Sacrifising the Interest of one to another, I consider it My Duty to Make the Attempt ... But if nothing Decisive should happen this Season, and that Vermont remains in her present State, I See no other means to gain her, than by the Same Measure in the Spring when, favored by the Season and the Supply of Provisions I have now got, it May be undertaken with more Vigour.

From his description of Vermonters, it becomes clear that Haldimand's attempt to bring them into the British fold was as much from a desire to remove a potent enemy, as it was to discomfit the United States. He continued:

[They have a] Knowledge of the Country and the facility with Which Bodies, now used to Arms & to Danger can on the Shortest Notice present themselves — In Such a State are at present the Inhabitants of Vermont & its neighbourhood, the Former Much Superior, the Latter very little Inferior to the Continental Troops. — Too Much Cannot be Said upon the advantages that would Result from a Reunion of Vermont and the Evil Consequences Which Must attend Her uniting With the Other States against us. [I]n this Conviction, I have Spared no pains to bring about the former.

In yet another dispatch, he revisited the subject of the Indian Department:

I have been Reflecting upon Means to controle the Expense … and cannot devise any other than by appointing Some Person of Rank, Influence, Knowledge, Activity and Perfect Honor to Superintend the Northern Confederacy, and Make an Annual Visit to the Several Posts, to Examine into the Transactions of them, and Make Such Reformations from time to Time as he Shall find necessary, first having laid down a Regular System calculated for the local Circumstances of Each. Such a Salary to be annexed to this Employment as would be adequate to the

Laborious Duties of it, and every Consideration from Contracts, or Connections with Supplying Presents, to be positively prohibited, these to rest entirely to the Crown, but Subject to Inspection With Regard to the Qualities, Shipping &c of the Goods, by Such persons as the Superintendent shall appoint. Sir John Johnson being the only Person here, or any where Else within my knowledge, Whose Qualities in every Respect Come within the above Description, I would humbly Propose for Your Lordship's Consideration, the Expediency of this measure. Knowing that Sir John Johnson from other Views, formerly declined this Office, it was necessary for me, before I could Mention it to Your Lordship, to ask him if it would be agreeable to him to accept of it, provided Such a Measure Should take Place, which I have Just done and Find that in Consideration of the ruinous State of his Private Affairs, the great uncertainty of their being Repaired, and having a growing Family, it would not be unacceptable to him, and if he does undertake it, I have that Confidence in his Virtuous Zeal for the King's Service that I have not a doubt he would be indefatigable in forming a Reformation of infinite moment to the State. Sir John Johnson would be better Received, and assisted than any other Person by Colonel Johnson & Mr. Claus from his Family Connection With them. I have long Wished to give him the Rank of Brigadier General, but my aversion from Multiplying appointments and Expense has hitherto prevented it. This would be a favorable opportunity for me to promote him to that Rank, and it would have this good Effect, by being Joined to the appointment, it would give him the entire Command of the Lieutenant Governor & Superintendents who, in the latter Capacity, appear too apt to considere Themselves independently with Regard to the Expense they incur. The Appointment of a Brigadier General While it existed, Might in Some Measure diminish the Salary of the other — Should this Plan take Place, an interior arrangement must be naturally Considered of as every Circumstance relating to the Department should Come thro' the Superintendent. All Bills before they appear for acceptance Should be Certified by Him, as from the Separate directions. He would give, He would be enabled to judge of the Propriety, and to cheque Expenses Which appeared unnecessary — It is not in nature that a Person residing at the distance I do from these Posts, Can have any Personal Knowledge of the Variety of Contingencies, Which put together, amount to amazing Sums — when, after writing Volumes upon the Subject of Economy, I am told Such and Such Expences are Absolutely Necessary to the Service, I must Submit, or Stand by the Consequences — These Centering in one Person, whose Duty It becomes Personnally, to investigate every Circumstance, and be responsable for the Propriety of the Charges, Cannot fail to controle, and keep within Bound, the Expences.

In another dispatch, the governor addressed the topic of his problematical Provincials, duplicating an earlier report that had gone missing. He mentioned the new footing on which the king had placed the Provincial Corps appeared to have "removed a Jealousy and Langour which promised but little Success in New Levies." He had given a beating order to Sir John for a second battalion, which was currently "in great forwardness." He had "likewise directed Messrs Jessup and Peters to Compleat their Battalions ... with all possible Dispatch, and Recruiting Parties have been Some time in the Colonies for that Purpose;" however, he worried that:

[M]ore Should be expected from those Gentlemen than they can perform, [as] that they are by no means possessed of the Influence and Abilities represented by their Friends at Home.…Many of the Officers proposed for their Corps (by whom assistance alone they Can expect to raise them) have Expressed a disinclination of Serving under them, and they wished to be allowed to raise independent Companies. This I have discouraged, in order to Support Messrs Jessup and Peters who certainly are not without Some Merit.

The small corps had "Suffered Much by the Death of Major McAlpin, an Old and Valuable Officer, Who had been Settled Some Years in the Neighbourhood of Albany, and being generally beloved, had great Influence with the People." He had hopes that the new recruiting parties would "favor the Escape of a great Number of Loyal Subjects said to be in those Parts in waiting for opportunity and by that means compleat Sir John Johnson's and the two other Battalions."

On a related topic, he advised that farming at the upper posts was in a forward state and families of loyalists were established for that purpose. New settlements had been carefully selected in the Niagara region for the Six Nations' Indians; however, "these People are So averse from Labour that Little Progress can be expected …While the King's Stores remain open to their demands." (By this, he revealed a typical white prejudice against native men, as native women, in their own fashion, worked as hard and as productively as any white farmer. It was a societal division of labour that was ill-understood or accepted by Europeans.) The governor closed by commenting that rations were being issued to both natives and loyalists according to age; children under twelve received a half ration, as did the natives when they were not on campaign.[12]

―――――――――――――――――――――

―――――――――――――――――――――

Shifting the scene to the Mohawk region — while St. Leger's Provincials were setting fires along Lake George and Willett was pursuing Ross's troops through the woods north of Fort Dayton, four Tryon militiamen went to New Dorlach to harvest peas and pen in some hogs. The day was cold and raw with rain and snow falling alternately. They searched the nearby woods for the swine without realizing that a war party was hidden nearby in a barn. After looking for some time, the four were thoroughly wet and cold and retired to the house to get warm. After propping their guns against a wall, they gathered around the fireplace to enjoy a fire. The Indians crept into the house and had the men surrounded before one fellow recognized the danger and lunged for his firelock. He was easily thwarted. A chair was stripped from the grasp of another and the men bowed to the inevitable. After plundering the house, the natives led the prisoners away in falling snow. The captives experienced the usual ordeal — horrid depravation on the trip to Niagara and the mandatory running of the gauntlet at several native villages. One man was singled out for very heavy beatings and gave up and died. Another was sent to Coteau-du-Lac from where he successfully escaped with several others.[13]

In late September, Lieutenant Adam Crysler, 6NID, had been instructed by Colonel Guy Johnson to raid the Schoharie Valley. Crysler's frequent appearances there prompted militiaman John Bellinger to recall that the country was in a continual state of alarm. Over a span of six months, Bellinger had only farmed for a total of six weeks, and, even while doing so, he "was never without his gun near him & within a moment's reach."

Over a month after leaving Niagara, Crysler's band emerged in the Schoharie. Where they had been during October and what mischief they had committed is a mystery. Early on the chilly morning of November 9, the twenty-eight-man party of Oquagas and Schoharies broke cover in Vroomansland at the home of Colonel Peter Vrooman, the commander of the 15th Albany County Militia (15ACM). Their goal was abduction, as a high-ranking, dedicated rebel such as the colonel would yield a handsome reward.

As the campaign season had been judged over, Peter's relative, former committeeman Isaac Vrooman, had returned to the Valley to make preparations for bringing his family back from the Hellebergh for the winter. Peter himself had spent the summer and early fall in a hut in

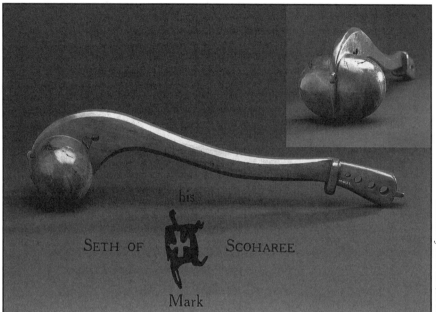

Mohawk ball-headed club or casse-tête and "Seth of Scoharee's" hieroglyph. A very effective hand-to-hand combat weapon. Note the large mass of the ball, which could readily crack a skull or break a limb. At least two of Seth's sons, Henry and Joseph, were British partisans. Seth's Henry was a particularly active, bold, and vicious warrior.

the Upper Fort and, just a few days before, had come home to organize his winter quarters.

Isaac rose before dawn to work on some horseshoes in a little blacksmithing shop near the house and took a shovel of coals to start a fire. At first light, he left the shop to call for Peter's help. Suddenly, two shots were fired, one by Crysler, the other by a native standing at his side. On hearing the gunfire, Peter burst from the house and sprinted for the fort, which lay some four hundred yards off. He had a solid lead before several warriors set off in pursuit.

The colonel's wife, Engeltie, rushed upstairs when she heard firing. Peering out a window, she witnessed Isaac bellowing in agony while the Schoharie warrior, Seth's Henry, tore off his scalp. The deed done, Henry gave Isaac a crack with his war club, slashed his throat and, using the bloody knife, cut a notch into the club's handle beside many others. In one of his bizarre and macabre acts of bravado for which he was so well known, he laid the club on Isaac's corpse as a sign to his enemies of his prowess.

When the Indians entered the house to plunder, Engeltie bravely descended the stairs and spoke to them in their dialect. Women were often spared from death and this occasion was no exception, particularly as the lady was recognized for her many kindnesses before the war. Coolly, she shook Henry's hand, which was slathered in Isaac's blood. With such a sign of friendship and show of sheer sang-froid, her children were spared from abduction.

With one child on her back and another in her arms, Engeltie was about to leave for the fort when a ten-year-old black boy clutched her petticoat and pled to be taken with her, but she knew that the natives' generosity and patience would not extend that far and told him to go with them. The shots fired at Peter had increased her anxiety, so she was relieved to find him safe and sound in the fort.

After setting Vrooman's house and outbuildings alight, the raiders marched past the Upper Fort, torched another house, and drove off fifty head of cattle and some horses. In the meantime, forty mixed rifle and musketmen of Captain Jacob Hager's militia company were assembled at the Upper Fort. The men were led by Hager and guided by a Virginia rifleman, Timothy Murphy, who had gained much notoriety with his claim to have sniped the British general, Simon Fraser, in 1777 with his double-barreled rifle. The pursuit travelled the eastern shore of the Schoharie Kill and, despite Murphy's fabled skill, he led them into an ambush opposite Bouck's Island. The militia returned fire, but one of their men fell mortally wounded and the natives' musketry grew too hot to be borne. As they turned to retreat, the wounded man pled not to be left and Murphy rallied a few men to carry him off.

Upon returning to the Upper Fort, no one in the company was able to estimate Crysler's strength, so Vrooman decided to reinforce Hager with Captain Aaron Hale's Levies' company. Hale took overall command and, after collecting three days' provisions, the two companies set off. Because of their local knowledge, Hager and his men were in the van. When darkness fell, the pursuers camped in a pine grove and, although it was bitterly cold, no fires were lit. About three hours before daybreak, Hale assigned two youngsters to guard a depot of provisions and a keg of rum, and resumed the pursuit. The lads later admitted to securing most of the liquor in their bellies.

The early morning was dark and cloudy and the rebels advanced cautiously. As daylight broke, they came to a fork in the road; one track led to Harpersfield, the other to Lake Utsayantha. Hale called a halt. Fires were lit for breakfast while scouts were sent down both tracks to determine the enemy's route. When it was confirmed that the raiders had gone toward the lake, Hale held an orders group to discuss options. He was in favour of taking the Harpersfield route to get ahead of the raiders and cut them off; however, other officers were afraid of losing them and opted for a direct pursuit down the lake fork. The latter opinion prevailed and, when the meal was finished, the detachment marched on.

The rebels had gone but a short distance when they were spotted by Crysler's piquets, one of whom ran to tell the lieutenant. After abandoning some of their plunder, the raiders marched swiftly along the road searching for a good ambush site.

The pursuers were about a mile from the pine grove when they found two of Hager's horses hobbled together. Hale was at the column's head with Murphy, who stepped up and deftly cut the animals' bonds. Continuing on, they heard a whoop and assumed that some of the Indians were searching for the missing horses, but, more likely, the shout warned of the rebels' approach. The pursuit pushed on rapidly and came across seven large fires still burning and several abandoned horses loaded with plunder and a number of beeves. When they arrived at the lake, they kept to the track as it paralleled the shore and approached a ridge that extended almost down to the lake. Suddenly, the Indians opened fire from the high ground.

In the vanguard, Hager signalled Hale to flank right and catch the raiders in a vice against the shore, but the Levies' officer judged the opposition too strong and retreated. Seeing the rebels were in confusion, the Indians burst from cover, whereupon the vanguard sprang away from their tree cover and took off down the road. A Levy who had fallen behind was cut down, as was a militiaman, and Hager's brother Joseph was hit in the head, but kept running. The natives immediately scalped the two fallen men.

After running five hundred yards, Hager's men caught up with Hale's company and the two captains exchanged hot words. As the natives had seen they were outnumbered, they decided not to run down the retreating troops. While the two companies were resting, Colonel Vrooman arrived with a forty-man reinforcement. When the chase resumed, it was discovered that raiders had escaped, although the rest of the cattle were recovered.

Crysler reported that 150 men had pursued him, but that number seems high. Everyone exaggerated their opposition; for example, one rebel rifleman reported Crysler's band was two hundred strong. With so much plunder lost, there was little to show for such an arduous and dangerous venture, other than two successful ambushes, three dead rebels, a young captive, and some scalps. Probably that was enough.

A few days later, a stranger's corpse was found propped against a tree about a mile from Bouck's Island. He had been shot through the body and his firelock and gear lay near. He was reckoned as one of Crysler's men, although the lieutenant reported no losses. Perhaps the fellow was one of those much-hated, secretive local Tories who came and went from war parties.[14]

At his Quebec City headquarters, General Haldimand had entirely lost patience with the recruiting efforts of the small loyalist units. The following document, entitled "Proposals for forming the several Corps of Loyalists," summarized the situation:

> As Lieutenant-Colonel [Robert] Rogers Corps of Rangers is raising by the Authority of General Sir Henry Clinton, and the Men belonging to it in this Province are subject to be called from it upon the shortest notice, it woud be improper to incorporate them with any Corps belonging to the Province. It will therefore remain distinct, and be formed into three Companies

under the Command of Major [James] Rogers, who
will have one of the Companies, two Captains, three
Lieutenants, & three Ensigns to be appointed to these
Companies…. All other Officers belonging or attached
to that Corps to be sent to New York or Halifax by the
first Opportunity in order to join their Corps.

Haldimand's initial displeasure over the uninvited arrival of Robert
Rogers and his King's Rangers in Canada had dissipated; no doubt, due
to the excellent service of Major James Rogers, Robert's brother, during
Carleton's raid of 1780 and St. Leger's expedition of 1781, as well as the
Rangers' performance on Secret Service, garrison, and marine duties. As
it was now unlikely that James's small battalion would be recalled to New
York City or sent to Nova Scotia, the governor had decided to make the
best of the situation and officially recognize them. He continued:

The Impossibility of Messrs Jessup and Peters
compleating separate Corps is evident from their
unsuccessful Endeavours during four years, in which
time, the former has got together no more than 127
Men, and the latter only 82 — These two Corps will
therefore be formed into one, including Lieut. Fraser's
Men, which will compose a Body of about 260 Men
these to be formed into Six Companies consisting
of one Major, five Captains, six Lieutenants and Six
Ensigns — to be completed to 3 Serjeants, 3 Corporals,
2 Drummers and 50 Private Men each — The Officers
to be chosen from each Corps, and to Rank according
to the number of Men they have raised, provided there
are no other material Objections to their Appointment,
and they will receive full Pay from the dates of their
Commissions. This Corps will be augmented by as
many Companies as can be raised, and the Officers will
be appointed from the Supernumerary, or Pension, List
according as they shall raise Men.

Putative officers' button of the King's and Loyal Rangers.

Courtesy of Horst Dresler after an example in the collections of the Canadian War Museum.

The Invalid States of Messrs Ebinezer Jessup and Peters Healths render them incapable of active Service, they will be removed to the Company of Pensioners, upon their present subsistence the Command of which to be given to one of these Gentlemen — and to insure to them His Majesty's gracious Bounty of Half Pay, they will be mustered as belonging to the Corps formed, should it be completed only to nine Companies, in confirmation of which, Letters will be given to them from His Excellency the Commander-in-Chief. Mr. Edward Jessup's robust Constitution, his Personal Activity, Merit and Experience having served last war, are Circumstances which render Him a fit Person to command the above mentioned Corps, with the Rank and Pay of Major.[15]

Peters was devastated by this decision and later wrote:

> The cruel degrading change was worked while I was at Skenesborough, where I had been sent by Gen. Haldimand with a flag and rebel prisoners, with a view to gain intelligence from the Southern Army, which I performed and reported to him. On my return to Quebec I complained to the General of the hard measures he had dealt out to me by degrading me below those who had been under my command in 1777; nor did I understand why I was invalided. Mr. Mathews, a secretary to Gen. Haldimand, gave me for answer I had

a wife and eight children and I might starve if refused captain's pay; besides I should not be allowed rations if I refused. My subsistence money being stopped, I was obliged to accept the pay of a captain … or perish with my family. My son John, the oldest ensign in the Queen's Loyal Rangers, was neglected by Gen. Haldimand when he drafted the Provincial corps in Canada, and a son of Major Jessup's[,] quite a boy, who had never done any service, was appointed lieutenant over my son and all the ensigns who had served during the war.

Peters's cause had in no way been helped by his former major, Zadock Wright, refusing to accept an exchange and rejoin his corps after three years' absence. Whether Eben Jessup shared Peters's outrage has not been determined; however, he had virtually retired from active duty and the governor's decision in his regard was more understandable. Besides, it was his elder brother who was favoured with command of the new regiment.

The summary continued:

Captain [Robert] Leake's Corps will be incorporated with Sir John Johnson's second Battalion, together with about 24 Men who will probably attach themselves to Mr. [James] McAlpin, having belonged to the late Major McAlpin's Corps. The Remainder of which, are claimed by Mr. [Peter] Drummond and others, and may be thrown into Sir John Johnson's second Battalion or Major Jessup's Corps.

There are 21 Men of Captn Leake's Corps who were raised by a Lieutenant [Henry] Ruyter now serving in it — as he is not nominated for Sir John's second Battalion, he will expect that his men continue with Him to whatever Corps he shall be placed — On the other Hand, there are about the same number mustered in Mr. Peters's Corps, claimed by Mr. [Jeremiah] French who will accompany Him to Sir John's second Battalion, in which he is nominated a Lieutenant.

The Supernumerary Officers, and all those Subsisted in the Company of Pensioners who are able to carry Arms, are to serve as Volunteers upon all occasions where their Service may be required, until such Time as they shall be entitled to Commissions by raising their Proportions of Men for the Augmentation of Major Jessup's Corps.

A company of artificers was later formed from Jessup's new corps to work with the Engineers, but its men continued to be mustered and subsisted in the companies they were drawn from.[16]

On October 28, a Brunswick surgeon named Julius Wasmus noted that the fall fleet, composed of two hundred transports and an escort of six frigates, lay in the basin at Quebec City ready to sail for Britain.[17]

───────────

Still angered by the revelations of fraudulent misspending in the Six Nations' Indian Department, Haldimand wrote to Major Arent DePeyster at Detroit on November 1 to express his annoyance that the pursuit of

Joseph F.W. Des Barres, 1777. (Library of Congress, LC-USZ62-46047.)

Southeast view of the basin of Quebec. Surgeon Wasmus observed two hundred transports and an escort of six warships assembled on this body of water ready to sail to Britain.

the Virginia rebel, George Rogers Clark (who had enjoyed so much success in prior years on the far western frontier), had been abandoned "owing to the caprice of the Indians in dispersing at the time their assistance was most wanted to give an ultimate blow to the enterprise and hopes of Mr. Clark in that country." He continued in full torrent:

> But this conduct has been uniformly their system, and notwithstanding the treasure which has been, I must say from their conduct, thrown away upon them this year, it appears that no more than one hundred could be brought to action, and those from the influence and under the direction of Joseph, a Six Nations Chief. If even as many more and the Company of Rangers had joined that party, Mr. Clarke's fate would have been decided … and in the meantime, you will have perpetual demands for assistance, equipment, &c, to oppose incursions upon the Indian villages…. [T]hose Indians who distinguish themselves with Brant should be well rewarded from the donations intended for those who have not so well deserved them.[18]

The governor was clearly already primed for the complaints he would soon receive from Major Ross when he returned from his arduous expedition.

The same day that Haldimand wrote his angry letter to DePeyster about the Lakes' and Ohio Indians, he had Mathews deliver a tough message to John Butler:

> I am directed … to acquaint you that however sensible His Excellency is of and desirous to reward Captain [Walter] Butler's merits, he cannot, in justice to the Army, promote him to the rank of Major over the heads of so many elder and more experienced officers, and to the Service commit to his care and direction the economy and discipline of a young Corps, a task so arduous that

Officers possessed of approved military knowledge and long experience without entering into a detail of the many requisites, find it difficult and are very fortunate when they accomplish it. Could His Excellency get over the first difficulty, he appeals to yourself ... whether a young Corps now complete to ten companies, and to be recommended to His Majesty, should be delivered up to the direction of (allowing him every possible merit to be derived from his experience) a very young Officer. Or whether it would be more for the advantage of the Service (which is His Excellency's chief care), and of the Corps (which is yours), to find out some officer of experience in every respect, or as nearly as can be found, qualified to take upon him that very serious charge. Such a person, His Excellency is now looking out for. He thinks it still more necessary as there are so few of your Officers who have been brought up in the Army and consequently require themselves instruction.

Mathews's letter arrived at Niagara about the same time as the news of Walter's death and must have added to the father's distress. In any event, the issue of Walter's rank was now put to bed.

There was more unpleasant news for John. Haldimand said that Carleton's promises to the two Butlers must "be considered conditional and entirely depend[ent] upon contingencies." How this news must have disappointed Butler, a man who had sacrificed so much to ensure the friendship of the Six Nations while his wife, daughter, and two sons were held hostage in the Mohawk Valley and his second-eldest son was imprisoned in New England. Guy Carleton had fully appreciated John Butler's selfless contributions, but it was Haldimand who sat in Quebec City now.

Mathews gently chided Butler that his regimental return had not been signed by General Powell, as it should have been before being sent to the king with the request for his Royal Bounty. He concluded this painful letter with a tiny bit of positive news. The governor agreed that the 10th company should be the lieutenant-colonel's and commanded by a captain-lieutenant, which would allow John to draw pay as the company's nominal captain.[19]

Mathews then wrote to Brigadier Powell about Lieutenant-Colonel Butler's memorial on behalf of his officer corps requesting that the phrase "To serve with the Indians" be expunged from their commissions, as it was considered a liability should they fall into enemy hands. The governor acceded to this appeal and promised to send out new commissions accordingly.

Further, he advised that the complaint of the Rangers' captains concerning the rank of John McKinnon (who had been thrust upon the corps as a patronage appointment) would be answered by the adjutant general and that commissions were coming for a captain-lieutenant and two lieutenants of the 10th company.

On November 2, Mathews wrote to advise Lieutenant-Colonel Butler that his warrants for pay, arms, and medicines had been approved, although the meticulous governor was upset that the indent did not specify the corps involved, nor was it signed by the regimental or post surgeon, and Brigadier Powell.[20]

As soon as Willett returned to Fort Rensselaer on November 2 from his pursuit of Ross, he celebrated the news of Cornwallis's capitulation with the firing of a 12-pdr gun and small arms' volleys by his Levies and local militia, followed by the roasting of an ox.

As the term of Willett's Massachusetts companies was now expired, their officers were ordered to have their men deliver their ammunition to the Conductor of Ordnance before marching for home.[21]

Reverend Stuart had received the governor's permission to establish a scholastic academy in Montreal and on November 3, the priest's

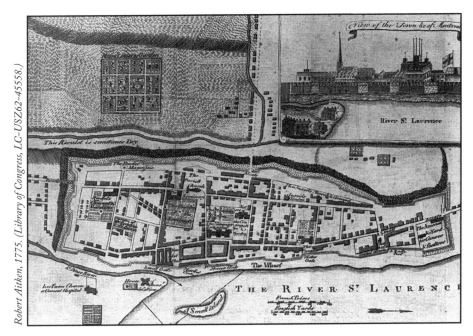

Plan of the town and fortifications of Montreal.

advertisement to attract students came to the governor's attention. Ever sensitive about Canadien Roman Catholics, Haldimand severely chastised Stuart, noting that, "Principally Intended for the Children of Protestants Could not fail to Create Jealousies, [and was] at all times improper, but more particularly so at present." Stuart was most apologetic, advising that boys of all faiths were already in attendance at his school.[22]

On November 4, Major Gray wrote to the adjutant general, Major Richard Lernoult, 8th, with a grim account of the state of the arms in 1KRR:

> Sir John Johnson has applied for arms to his Regiment sometime ago, I beg here to mention it again we have not 100 stand of good arms in the Regiment —, its true we goat 150 stand of good arms two winters ago, betwixt Prisoners taken & Arms Brock upon service & great many of them are Lost, what arms we goat before that,

were old Repaired Arms not worth sixpence for Service, nor were we ever at any time Completed with Arms, good and Bad arms we have not above 250, now I should be glad to know whether we are to have Arms this winter.[23]

The next day, 1KRR's surgeon, Charles Austin, reported that Volunteer John Thompson of the Major's Company was lying "dangerously ill at his Quarters, in consequence of the ill Treatment he met with from some Canadians last Thursday at Pt Clair." An examination into the incident was held by James McGill, the commissioner of the peace for Montreal and district. John Helmer, a fellow Royal Yorker, testified that, on the afternoon of November 1, near the church in Pointe Clair, he witnessed an argument between a 1KRR drummer boy and a Canadien lad. When Thompson stepped in to separate the boys and make peace between them, Pierre Charlebois, the local lieutenant of militia, assaulted him with a stick, striking and cutting him in the face and knocking him down. Whereupon, Charlebois's son, Etiat (who may have been the boy involved in the fight), jumped on Thompson. Helmer noted that the Volunteer's eye was "greatly swelled." Why Helmer had stood aside watching this outrage was unstated.

Canadiens were jaded with having "foreign" troops quartered in their villages who often indulged in thoughtless, and frequently drunken, pranks. Due to their declining fortunes, the loyalists were equally distressed, and, being unable to make the rebels pay sufficiently for their grief, there was a danger that the Canadiens could become a target of their resentment. An ugly incident such as this beating was precisely what Haldimand feared — a potential spark to tinder.[24]

On November 5, Riedesel reported to the governor that the Yamaska Blockhouse, a key installation in the defence of lower Quebec province, was strong enough for temporary defence, but represented very "dull and dreary" duty.[25]

That same day, Haldimand wrote to Powell about more unrest in Butler's Rangers' officer corps, which had begun during the 1777 siege

The map traces the Mohawk River from its junction with the Hudson River to Fort Stanwix, then over the Oneida Carry and along the waterways to Oswego on Lake Ontario.

of Stanwix when three Indian Department officers — captains Walter Butler and Peter Ten Broeck and Lieutenant William Ryer Bowen — were captured in German Flatts in the Mohawk Valley. The following year, Butler and Bowen seized the opportunity to escape, but Ten Broeck chose not to join them. Meantime, a company in the newly founded Butler's Rangers was being held in Ten Broeck's name at Niagara. When he failed to appear for another two years, suspicions were raised that he either lacked the courage to rejoin, or was lukewarm in his attitude toward the king's cause. That his rebel brother Abraham was a rebel militia brigadier complicated the issue. So, Peter Ten Broeck was discontinued on the regiment's pay list and his company was given to another officer. When he suddenly reappeared in Niagara, he requested full reinstatement. Haldimand consulted Sir John Johnson and the baronet thought that Ten Broeck had suffered a great deal, so the governor instructed Powell to set up an inquiry to investigate the issue.[26]

On November 6, Ross sent Haldimand a detailed report of his expedition, including a chronological return of the men killed, wounded, and missing. He assured the C-in-C that the provisions cached at Ganaghsaraga would be brought back to Oswego, indicating that he was, as yet, unaware that Captain Gilbert Tice, 6NID, had found them either consumed or carried off, probably by Captain David Hill's party of Mohawks that had been sent to destroy the boats. Ross deplored the loss of Captain Butler and Lieutenant Docksteder and commended Rangers' serjeant Solomon Secord, who had performed some unspecified exceptional service.

A major thrust of the report was a condemnation of the support he had received from the natives and Colonel Guy Johnson. "The promised succour of Indians was a mere Illusion," those that joined were the dregs of the tribes and there were no important leaders amongst them. To Haldimand, who was already stressed over 6NID's expenses and incensed about the natives' inadequate support in the far west, the criticisms struck deep and resulted in an uncharacteristically angry outburst.[27]

———

Counterespionage was an important function of Canada's Secret Service. Dr. George Smyth, the service's second-in-command, had been warned that a Canadian named Mrs. Cheshire was providing a safe haven for enemy spies. He set a trap, selecting "three cunning fellows with Old Clothes, Yankee Firelocks, a number of Vermont and Connecticut Bills & a Forged Letter which contains Instruction from, & is signed by Bailey [Vermont General Jacob Bayley] &, I hope they will soon find out Madam Cheshire & her connections." His ruse must have succeeded, as there was no more mention of the lady in the records.[28]

———

Major Balthasar von Lücke arrived from New York City with a further 231 exchanged Brunswick soldiers, which allowed Riedesel to re-establish the original regiments of 1777, except for von Breymann's Grenadier battalion, which had its few remaining companies distributed to the other regiments. One company went to the very badly depleted Regiment von Rhetz, as did another from Prinz Friedrich's. Captain of Cavalry Carl von Schlagenteuffel took command of Prinz Ludwig's Dragoon regiment; Lieutenant-Colonel Christian Prätorius retained command of Prinz Friedrich, as did Lieutenant-Colonel Ferdinand

Albrecht von Barner of the Light Infantry battalion. Lieutenant-Colonel Johann Gustavus von Ehrenkrook commanded von Rhetz; Lieutenant-Colonel Friedrich von Hille took the Regiment von Riedesel, and Major von Lücke headed up the Regiment von Specht.

Riedesel noted that the regiments' companies were about half their 1777 strength and that there was an inadequate number of non-commissioned officers — only seventy-four across all of the regiments. Consequently, only one serjeant, a quartermaster, a captain at arms, and three corporals could be allotted per company and a number of "vice-corporals" had to be appointed to offset the deficiency. As well, a great many companies lacked sufficient subalterns and those available were equally distributed.[29]

At Saratoga, the New Hampshire Continental general, John Stark, resumed the routine of commanding the district now that St. Leger's expedition had retired to Canada. He notified General William Heath (Washington's surrogate while the C-in-C was in Virginia) that he had ordered local teams to draw timber for the two blockhouses he had been ordered to construct, which he expected would be complete in a fortnight. To promote the work, he had promised the Massachusetts Levies an early discharge if they cut and drew the timber and they had fallen to work with "unremitted vigor."

Stark asked Heath to remember the poor half-naked New Hampshire Continentals at Saratoga, many of whom were unfit for duty for want of proper clothing, noting that the surgeon had attributed their nakedness to the "inflammatory disorders epidemical in camp."[30]

Governor Clinton wrote to Colonel Willett on November 8 to offer effusive praise for his "successes over the Enemy.... I am sensible of the Dangers & Difficulties you had to encounter on this Occasion & I am persuaded much is due to your Personal Exertions & that nothing was wanting on your part to have Conceived a complete Victory & I trust the vigor with which the Enemy was attacked, routed & pursued will be attended with the most salutary Consequences to the Frontier Settlements."

Willett had earlier taken advantage of his success to criticize Stark's removal of two companies of Weissenfel's New York Levies from Johnstown just a few days before Ross appeared, so it was undoubtedly music to his ears when the governor commented in his letter that, from the beginning of the alarms, he had believed the enemy's true object lay west of Saratoga, and that "being the case I leave you to judge of my sentiments respecting the Removal of Major Logan & his detachment." Clinton had recommended that the legislature adopt "seasonable & proper Measures for the future Defence of the Frontiers," but candidly feared these would be inadequate. He closed by asking Willett to accept reappointment as the commander of New York's northwestern frontiers.[31]

On November 9, General Heath posted General Orders at his Continental Village headquarters, reporting the enemy's failures "on the northern frontiers of this State." He attributed the prevention of an enemy landing "on this side" of the lakes to Lord Stirling, Stark, and "the officers and soldiers of both the regular troops and militia, who, with great zeal and alertness, pressed forward to meet the enemy." Of course, Heath was unaware of either the limitations placed on St. Leger, or of Jessup's free reign up and down Lake George, in the face of which his report seems much exaggerated, which is not to suggest that his army's response had not been superb.

As to Ross, Heath noted that he had been "defeated and pursued into the wilderness." He repeated the then-common fantasy that "many of them probably will perish." Willett was publicly acknowledged for his "address, gallantry, and persevering activity" and "the conduct of the officers and soldiers ... deserves high commendation," in particular, "Major Rowley, and the brave levies and militia under his immediate command, who, at a critical moment, not only did themselves honor, but rendered essential service to their country" — fulsome, public, well-deserved praise.[32]

On November 11, Mathews sent the deputy quartermaster general, Lieutenant Jacob Maurer, 2KRR, a list of the long-awaited farming utensils wanted for the settlement on the Canadian side opposite Fort Niagara. The tools were to be forwarded from Montreal.[33]

That same day, Lieutenant William Morison, 1KRR, wrote to Major Gray about Volunteer Thomson's beating. Fully aware that the governor might be extremely upset over the incident, Morison was concerned that the local militia colonel's report would reflect badly on his personal conduct. To justify his actions, he asked Gray to forward the doctor's certificate and Helmer's testimony to the governor through District Commander de Speth. There were four additional witnesses available to testify in court, which again begged the question of why no one had taken action to protect their fellow soldier. Were they really that concerned about earning the governor's wrath if a Canadien was hurt?

Morison knew that the Canadien militia colonel had complained that Charlebois had been detained without a warrant; however, he reported that, although there had been no magistrate nearby, the perpetrator had been correctly apprehended. Even the local captain of militia had acquiesced in the proceeding; Charlebois had not been arrested by soldiers, nor was he confined in a guardroom. "It is notorious that Mr. Charlebois['s] conduct has always been, overbearing & refractory to the Troops, & that those who are best acquainted with him, & who stand up for him now, were they put to the test, coud not but own, his being of a very indifferent Character, and from his being almost always Drunk, very unfit for his present employ."[34]

At Niagara, Captain Gilbert Tice received a shock when he returned to the fort on November 12 from Ross's expedition and, following his usual practice, promptly went to Colonel Guy Johnson's office to make a verbal report and found it empty. He wrote Johnson, "My surprise on my arrival is not in my Power to express" and assured Guy that his recall to Montreal was the result of some report from "some one that knows nothing, or little of the matter." Enclosed with his letter was his journal of the raid. He had brought sixteen prisoners and six scalps, all male, and at one point had twice that number of captives, but they were allowed to escape from the main guard and, he thought, had compromised the expedition. He made an observation about native participation that was remarkably at odds with Ross's vitriolic rhetoric:

> [T]he Indians did not attempt to meddle with any Women, Children, old men, or men not in arms, neither was any man or person killed by them, or striped of what they had on, only in the engagement, except one man who fired his piece at an Indian that Broke open the Door of his House, they took him out, and shot him, but did not as much as scalp him, which I think is remarkable.[35]

After bearing months of delays and participating in a major expedition, officers were at last appointed to the Royal Yorkers' second battalion on November 12. Of the seven captains, the senior was Robert Leake, whose independent company (which had operated with 2KRR since its inception) was to be absorbed. Deservedly, Thomas Gumersall, who had managed the second battalion's troops in lower Canada while upholding his responsibilities as captain-lieutenant of the first battalion's Colonel's Company, became second senior captain. Jacob Maurer was third senior, but would continue as the province's DQMG. William Redford Crawford, who had served with distinction in the Quebec Indian Department and earlier in the year had been active in patrolling and raiding, was seventh. Four lieutenants entered from Leake's. Five 1KRR ensigns, who had performed special duties in the Indian Department and Secret Service, were promoted to lieutenant and transferred. Two others came from the smaller loyalist corps and one was a patronage appointment. These promotions resulted in changes in the first battalion in which the senior lieutenant was promoted to captain-lieutenant, five ensigns to lieutenant, and seven Volunteers to ensign.

Officers were also appointed to the yet-unnamed "Corps of Loyalists to be Commanded by Major Edward Jessup." As major-commandant, Edward would continue to nominally command a company. As noted above, two companies — one of invalids, the other of pensioners — were ostensibly captained by the two ex-lieutenant-colonels, Eben Jessup and John Peters. Of the five captains named, Justus Sherwood (who was to continue in the Secret Service) was senior; two others were from the KLA. William Fraser and Peter Drummond, who had recently commanded independent companies, had previously served in McAlpin's American Volunteers.[36]

The same day, Major Gray forwarded to headquarters all the records relating to the unfortunate John Thomson and added a postscript, "The Soldier is still in danger of His Life from the Beating he has got from the Lt of Militia."[37]

The fact that General Cornwallis's southern army had been forced to submit at Yorktown had still not been confirmed by reliable sources in Quebec. On November 12, Riedesel wrote to the governor to offer a perceptive appreciation of the situation:

> I think as you do, my dear General, about the state of our affairs in the South, and the paper I send you persuades me that we touch on the most interesting period of this unfortunate war. Although I believe that news that the Rebels publish so much, is exaggerated to sway the people, it appears however, that Lord Cornwallis is in a very critical situation, lacking, probably, provisions and the means of getting them. In this case his destiny will depend on the ship, if ours could be reinforced, and arrive in time enough at the mouth of the Chesapeake to properly give battle to the combined fleet, before Lord Cornwallis is reduced to the extremity, chance could be

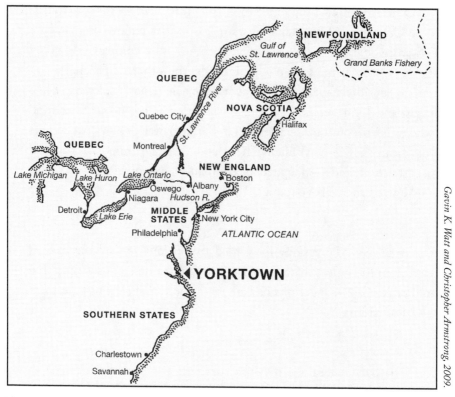

Gavin K. Watt and Christopher Armstrong, 2009.

The disastrous defeat at Yorktown led to the collapse of the British ministry that had hitherto prosecuted the war.

turned to our favor; and we, given a superiority by sea, can re-establish our affairs and end this war. But if the opposite happens, I can easily forsee unpleasantness to follow. I await news from New York with impatience. The Chiefs of Vermont appear very well disposed toward us, but the populace is always in agreement with Congress.[38]

On November 13, the prisoners that Ross had taken on his raid (a captain, subaltern, and twelve men) arrived in the lower province. The officers were to be held at Montreal and the men sent to Prison Island at Coteau-du-Lac. Coincidently, fifteen rebel officers had just been retaken after escaping from Île Perrot, an isolated island northeast of Montreal that had previously been considered entirely secure.[39]

Powell wrote to the governor from Niagara on November 13 with contradictory reports about the bateaux left by Ross at Ganaghsaraga. He had initially heard that both the sloop *Caldwell* and Ross's boats had fallen into rebel hands; however, Tice calmed those fears by reporting that he had removed eleven boats from Ganaghsaraga to Oswego and destroyed the rest for want of hands to bring them off. This report was at odds with Tice's earlier report to Guy Johnson that he and some Butler's Rangers had been forced to repair one miserable old bateau in order to get away from Ganaghsaraga. Both of Tice's accounts disagreed with David Hill's account that he had destroyed all the boats. Perhaps there been a second depot that Hill had not found and Tice had gone back to retrieve those boats? Whatever the case, the *Caldwell* was still in British hands and the original rumour was quashed.

Thirteen Butler's Rangers reported missing after the Canada Creek skirmish had joined the Indians at Oswego and Powell thought that more would do so.

This same day, Surgeon John Kerr, 2KRR, submitted his account for medical services rendered to the Oswegatchie and Mississauga Indians on Ross's expedition.[40]

In a private letter dated November 15, Haldimand confessed to Riedesel his deep concern over the fate of Cornwallis:

> By the latest intelligence, and on which I can rely, I am assured that Lord Cornwallis had been taken prisoner with his whole army, the news of which was received by express at Forts Johnsto[w]n and Arabia, the 19th of last month. The person who reports this [Lieutenant Walter Sutherland] ... was on the 30th two miles from Fort Johnsto[w]n, and from that neighborhood at noon of that day heard rifle salutes of joy. He sent trusted persons into the two forts who reported ... that

the salutes were in celebration for the capture of Lord
Cornwallis. If the news is true, how much misery can
we expect in the coming days, in the long uncertainty
— days seeming like years.... In that case I will fear that
the Vermonters will but join [the rebels.][41]

In a November 16 letter to Brigadier Powell, Haldimand praised
Ross and expanded on the themes of poor native support and the
overwhelming number of rebels encountered. "His conduct ... gives
me much satisfaction, as it seemed to be directed with prudence and
enterprise. And notwithstanding the very superior force which were at
all times opposed to him, had he been well supported, even by the few
Indians Colonel Johnson sent with him, there is every reason to believe
that the rebels would have severely felt the incursion and Major Ross's loss
would have been in a great measure prevented." He reported that Ross
would personally inform Powell of "the shameful, dastardly conduct of a
people who cost Government so many thousands yearly." The governor
wrote he was unable to think "of the subject with any degree of patience"
and expected Powell and Butler to paint his displeasure in the highest
colours. "I desire you will do it fully, and what is [of] more consequence,
let them feel it in the distribution of presents."

He offered condolences for Butler's loss of his eldest offspring,
adding the conventional expression of sympathy that John must be
proud of "the honourable cause in which his son fell."

In the second letter to Powell that day, the governor dismissed any
thought of Richard Wilkinson being commissioned in the Rangers. First,
Wilkinson had "left and returned to the Service to suit the convenience
of his private circumstances," and second, the Rangers' officers, who were
having difficulty reconciling a few experienced Regular officers being put
over them as captains, would "think it hard that an Officer of the Indian
Dept, inferior to them in every respect to rank, should be so promoted."
Contrary to the governor's expressions, it is entirely possible that the
Rangers' officers would have welcomed Wilkinson into the corps, as he
was well-regarded and scarcely a stranger, unlike the other candidates
who were being thrust upon the regiment.[42]

That same day, Powell wrote the governor to report that he had sent an express to Detroit to recall Captain Brant and been advised that there was some doubt that the Mohawk would recover the full use of his leg, which had been infected from a wound said to have been inflicted by the famous Indian Department lieutenant, Simon Girty. Whatever the cause, Brant would have to spend the winter in the west.[43]

This same busy day, the governor sent Ross his "perfect approbation of your proceedings throughout your late expedition." His losses were "inconsiderable, which must justly be greatly attributed to your Prudence and Activity, as well as to the Spirited Behaviour of the Troops under your Command, whose efforts, I am sorry to find were so ill seconded by the Indians. A circumstance, I shall not fail minutely to enquire into." Even Butler's death was laid at the feet of the natives. "Had the Indians done their duty, it is probable this misfortune … would have been prevented."

As Carleton Island's garrison had been depleted, the governor would send one hundred men with officers and non-commissioned officers in proportion. Although unstated, these were Ross's men of 2KRR who

John W. Moore, photographer, 2009.

An Indian Department fusil and land (Infantry) Pattern muskets. Long and short Pattern muskets (forty-six- and forty-two-inch barrels, respectively) were on issue to the British infantry of the Canadian Army. Both Patterns were robustly made and mounted a socket bayonet with a fifteen-to-seventeen-inch triangular blade, which was the primary assault weapon. In contrast, the Indian Trade fusil was a lightweight, smaller-calibre firearm unable to mount a bayonet.

had been training in the lower province. A letter from Mathews reported that three hundred stand of arms had been already sent upriver, although he warned there would be a delay in shipping the requested medicines. As it transpired, severe weather prevented the concentration of the battalion. While the promised issue of arms raised hopes that 2KRR would finally be properly equipped as infantry, Ross's complaint the following March revealed that more Indian Trade fusils had been sent, rather than military pattern muskets.

Surgeon Wasmus of the Brunswick Dragoons returned to his regiment on November 12 after being exchanged in Boston and making a remarkably hazardous voyage from Halifax. He had lost all of his baggage and expensive medicines in a shipwreck on the St. Lawrence River and was fortunate to have escaped with his life. Having arrived at Sorel a virtual pauper, he was pleased to recover pieces of his luggage he had left there in 1777 before embarking on the Burgoyne expedition, but, upon opening them, he discovered that his colleagues had thoroughly looted his coffer and portmanteau and replaced his clothing with dirty, worn-out stockings, shirts, and trousers. Obviously, he had not been expected to return.[44]

On November 22, Ross reported new information about the boats left at Lake Oneida:

> The parties and provisions left at Canasagara and Oswego are safely arrived by the precautions I had taken…. Seven bateaux were obliged to be left behind at Canasagara, which I ordered to be destroyed as they were old and rotten. I had them merely patched up for the expedition, being unwilling to take good bateaux which were then so much wanted for the transport of provisions. All the best have been brought to this place and Niagara, there are still five left at Oswego which, owing to the season being so far advanced, I have declined sending for them until spring. They are also very old and crazy.

Two of the Royal Yorkers "sent out as Spies just before the Action at Johnstown" had returned to Fort Haldimand with a loyalist who reported the rebels had forty-two killed and wounded at Canada Creek, including a colonel and several officers from Schenectady. Such utter poppycock! The fellow must have thought Ross's ego needed a great deal of stroking. He claimed that, after the Johnstown action, Willett had been "so sensible of his defeat that he acknowledged he was much beholden to night coming," then added that the rebels were said to have been reinforced overnight and by next morning had assembled 1,400 men. While there may have been that number of troops moving about in the Mohawk Valley, they were certainly not all concentrated at Johnstown.

The fellow also provided details of the number of men who had "delivered themselves up as Prisoners of War." Ross noted that they amounted to the greater part of the men missing from the expedition and noted that none had been taken during the Johnstown action. He added: "There is great reason to believe that the rebels exercised the greatest cruelty on many occasions which I will endeavour to know the truth of. On our part the greatest humanity was shewn nor did the Indians hurt a Woman or Child." (Perhaps he had not heard of the murder of the prisoner William Scarborough by one of his officers. On the other hand, perhaps the murder was a rebel invention.) He closed, "I every day expect a prisoner from the Mohawk, [i.e., the Mohawk River] having sent out two scouts for that purpose, by which means further particulars may be learned."[45]

General Heath wrote another plaintive letter to Governor Clinton on November 13 regarding the extreme distress in the Highlands Department over a lack of bread. When Clinton answered two days later, he offered little encouragement other than to say that he had referred the matter to the state legislature.

On November 14, Heath wrote to Stark to approve the early release of the New Hampshire militia after they returned all public stores that had been temporarily issued, such as ammunition and camp utensils. He enthusiastically mentioned a new supply of clothing for the army, part of which was already in finished inventory and the balance in materials that were on hand for the regimental tailors. He recommended that the paymasters of the New Hampshire Continental regiments at Saratoga be sent to headquarters with their complete, signed returns to be present for the clothing distribution. While it had been his intention to have these two regiments winter in the northern district, there was now some doubt, but Stark was to make preparations as if they would stay and Heath would reserve their last year's huts for them at the Continental Village until the matter was determined. The regiments' artificers and small detachments were ordered to rejoin, as soon as it was set where they would winter.[46]

On November 16, Willett reported to the governor that the inhabitants' losses during the Ross raid had been slight. "Many of the Horses as well as the Horned Cattle &c were shot and left lying dead without the enemies receiving any advantage from them." Such a fatuous observation! The rebels had no advantage of them, either, which was precisely the point of the killings. The colonel sought Clinton's advice about what troops would winter in the Mohawk, noting, "[A] state of security can never be justified as long as the war lasts and this County continues to be a Frontier." Further, whatever troops were assigned, a quantity of snowshoes should be provided to ensure mobility.[47]

Political squabbling between New York and Vermont boiled over in the Western Union. On November 20, Vermont's governor, Thomas Chittenden, accused a Yorker bureaucrat of "warning the People in Vicinity of the New City to pay a Certain Provision Tax to the State of New York." He reminded the fellow that Vermont had made proposals to New York State to desist in imposing such "coercive Measures" while boundary disputes were unresolved. The official had better comply, or suffer the consequences. As the New City (formerly Lansinghburgh)

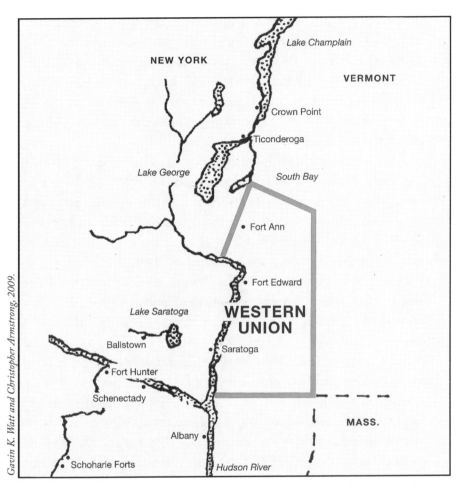

Gavin K. Watt and Christopher Armstrong, 2009.

was firmly in "old" New York, this was a contentious order to say the least. Obviously, such posturing and threats distracted New York from its war effort.

Coincidently, three days later, Governor Clinton forwarded the resolutions of the state legislature relative to the "New Hampshire Grants" for the guidance of the Congressional delegates — note his very deliberate use of the name "Grants" instead of Vermont.[48]

On November 20, Haldimand applied to the home administration for half pay for the officers of Butler's Rangers in consideration of the regiment's continued hard service and its completion to ten companies.

This same day, he confided to Riedesel that, "the misfortune of Lord Cornwallis is nearly certain." His only remaining doubt was not having received confirmation from Sir Henry Clinton, the C-in-C America who was headquartered in New York City.

On November 23, the governor reported to Lord George Germain the details of the two fall expeditions. Both had "fully answered the Several Purposes for which they were Sent — The Former [St. Leger's] by Judicious Manoeuvres, gave the Enemy Reason to think they were to penetrate into the Country, and Obliged them to Assemble all the Force they Could Collect at Saratoga & in the neighbourhood of Albany, not Venturing to Detach a Man for the Protection of the Mohawk River." This was followed by a very complete description of Ross's endeavour, painting the raid as a major achievement, which, in the sense of endurance and courage, it was. "Major Ross Marched with about 320 Men, without the least Opposition, within twelve miles of Schenectady where he Compleatly destroyed the only remaining Settlement of any Consequence between fort Hunter, Schohary & Schenectady." He emphasized the troops' physical accomplishment during their undetected infiltration across enemy territory, noting "The Fatigue the Men had endured in a March of fifteen Days from Oswego, entirely Exposed to very inclement Weather & Short of Provisions." He played upon Ross's theme of native misbehaviour in failing to run down Willett's fleeing Levies, claiming that the troops had been "Shamefully abandoned by the Indians [which] prevented the advantage to be derived from a Rapid Pursuit." Yet, "the Victory however was decisive," which the repulse of Willett's Levies early in the Johnstown action had been.

To explain how Willett managed to overtake Ross at West Canada Creek, he referred to the "unavoidable Delays occasioned by Excessive Fatigue & Hunger, the Party now living Entirely upon Horses they had taken." Ross was given credit for anticipating Willett's interception and the rearguard was excused for not repulsing Willett's van as, "The Enemy had much the Advantage of Ground & their Favorite Object of firing at a

Distance, both which precluded a Charge from our Party, which However kept up a heavy fire that did Execution." Yet, despite this rhetoric, we know from Willett's reports that he took no casualties at the ford.

Reporting Walter Butler's death, he described him as "a very Zealous enterprising & promising officer." The governor concluded:

> I have been very Prolix in my account of this little Enterprise to make Your Lordship acquainted with the difficulties attending Incursions in Small Parties into the Enemies Country, & the Many advantages they have Over Troops worn out by Hunger & Fatigue before they reach their object & who have a Retreat to make equally tedious — Major Ross's Party consisted of picked men enured to Marching & Fatigue. They nevertheless owe their Retreat to the judicious & Spiritted Conduct of their Leader, & to his Prudence in concealing from all with him the Route by Which he determined to effect it.

Very clearly, it was good to be a favourite of the governor.[49]

———————————

On the night of November 22, the Richelieu River at Sorel froze over. Just the evening before, the ferry had been operating, but wagons and carts were crossing on the ice by the next day. Two weeks later, the St. Lawrence froze over and shortly after, Surgeon Julius Wasmus recorded that snowdrifts were fifteen to eighteen feet high and on the flat, it was four feet deep, which was the precursor of one of the worst winters in Canadian memory. With wry humour, the doctor referred to Canada as the American Siberia.

With the rivers frozen, access for friend and foe alike to the posts in Riedesel's district was easy, although arduous, and to keep his troops alert, the baron made regular sleighing tours with his adjutant, a servant, and a very competent Canadien driver who travelled so swiftly that they were able to cover great distances each day.[50]

2

INVASION FEARS AROUSED
Oh God! It is All Over

*I*n another "Most Secret" dispatch of November 23 to Germain, Haldimand opened with reminders of his previous warnings of the Canadiens' reaction to the rebels' alliance with France, in particular the clergy, which before the pact had been staunch supporters of the Crown:

> The Successes, tho' fluctuating, which we have had, joined to the vigilant Attention which I have had to their Conduct, have hitherto kept them, if not within the limits of their Duty, at least within those of Decency, but the News of the Superiority of the French Fleets & a report which is whispered of Lord Cornwallis's Surrender, it is with great grief that I see their Attachment to France concealed under a Zeal for the Preservation of their Religion & will on the first favourable Occasion engage them in the interest of the Rebels, and it is with still greater Regret that I see many of His Majesty's antient [British] Subjects declaring their Attachment to the Cause of the Rebéls as openly as their own Safety will permit and their Expectation that the Independence of America must soon be acknowledged. — Your Lordship may be assured that if ever the Rebels shall invade the Frontiers of this Province, accompanied by a few hundred French

Soldiers, a great number of Canadians will take up arms in their Favor, and that by far the greatest part of them will serve them as Guides & furnish them with Provisions and every other assistance in their Power. My observations have so confirmed me in this Belief that so far from wishing to Arm them in defence of the Province, I am apprehensive that the Attempt might in my weak state be attended with dangerous Consequences, but I must Act in this when necessary, as Circumstances shall require. Their backwardness to serve is manifested in their Seamen, some of whom from Necessity I am obliged to employ on the Upper Lakes, where notwithstanding they Receive very high Wages, they serve with utmost Reluctance and will on no account remain above two years. On the other the Rebels have been lately supplied with some Money and a great Quantity of Ammunition & other Warlike Stores. They have already established Magazines in different Places on the Frontiers, inconsiderable as yet, but which from being contiguous to Districts or Townships may be easily augmented. The Inhabitants on the Frontiers of Canada have from their Infancy been accustomed to Live in the Woods, & if the Situation of Affairs to the Southward is as bad as it is represented, it will not be difficult for the Congress to engage them, partly from Enthusiasm, Resentment of Recent Injuries, and Love of Plunder to join a Kind of a Crusade in order to subdue this Country.

The people of Vermont, notwithstanding the inclinations which many amongst them have to Shake off the Tyranny of the Congress, may find themselves under the necessity to make great and Zealous exertions against us in order to wipe off the Suspicions which from many circumstances cannot but be entertained against them. The Rebels have every intelligence which they can

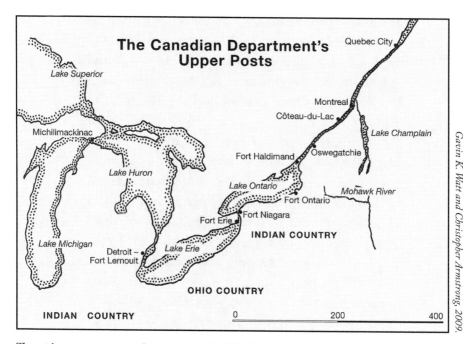

The mid upper posts were: Oswegatchie, Fort Haldimand on Carleton Island, Fort Ontario at Oswego, and Fort Niagara. The far upper posts were Detroit and Michilimackinac.

wish for, and have received assurances that the Canada Indians will at least remain neuter, if not join them. Every method will be put in Force to shake the approved Fidelity of the Five Nations, by convincing them that, as we are not able to give them protection, the only means to save themselves is to lose no time in embracing the Party of the Americans ... This Province is very extensive & is accessible in many Places. The best of the Troops under my Command are necessarily and indispensably employed in guarding the upper posts. The greater number of those I have here are Germans and consist mostly of Invalids whom General Burgoyne left behind him or of Recruits Totally Ignorant of Military Discipline. In case of an Invasion[,] after leaving the necessary Garrisons in the Posts which I cannot abandon, I cannot assemble more the 2,500 men capable of keeping the field two months, and I have every reason to fear that many of them would take that Opportunity to desert to the Rebels. This state of things is in no Respect exaggerated, it points out the necessity of a large Reinforcement early in the Spring & of our having the Command of the Gulph of St. Lawrence, as otherwise a French Squadron may deprive this country of every Resource.

The Provisions arrived too late this year to render it possible for me to take possession of Oswego, it would have required more time and workmen that I had to employ to Build a Fort at that Place capable to resist the Force which an enterprising Enemy sensible of Incursions and Devastations which their Country would suffer from it, would not have failed to Employ against it. From many Observations which I have made and many steps which the Enemy have taken during this Summer there is Reason to apprehend that the Plan of Attack found amongst Laurence's [Lauren's] Papers will be renewed and prosecuted early next Spring. The great Distance and Difficulty of communication between our different Posts will create obstacles to our resisting the Attack in every Point and as the Posts are, notwithstanding all my Efforts[,] only victualled until Spring, in case a Supply of Provisions cannot be forwarded before any Invasion of the Lower Country takes place, it will be almost impossible to do it.

I have for many Months observed in the Canadian Gentlemen an Expectation of a Revolution which was to take place in the Country, and am the more confirmed in this from a letter, dated Paris the 6th of last March (which has fallen into my hands from a Mr Lotbinière, who after having Received the King's Bounty, in London went over to the Rebels in Philadelphia) where He tells his son that He expects to see him in 14 or 15 Months from the date of the Letter and in a situation to

> settle His Affairs to their mutual satisfaction…. Many
> Letters are in the same stile and are plain indications
> of some design against this Province in which France
> cannot, now that the Provinces of Virginia & Carolina
> are recovered, refuse to give assistance to Congress.[1]

Two days later, the governor officially accepted the three companies of
the 2nd battalion, King's Rangers (KR) into the Canadian Department,
placing them on full support. Whether Sir Henry Clinton had given
his blessing is unclear; however, the governor's need was great and he
may simply have chosen to gamble that the small battalion would not
be "recalled" south.[2]

On November 26, Haldimand sent a "most Private" dispatch
to Germain enclosing duplicates of his recent messages about
"the Critical Turn Affairs may take here in Consequence of Lord
Cornwallis's Misfortune." Captain Justus Sherwood of the Secret
Service had reported there was "not a Shadow of Hope remaining
that any terms from Government will be Received by the [Vermont]
People, who are now rioting in the Excesses of Licentious exultation."
Even more alarming, "He Says that a Diversion from this Province
has been long Expected, and that Measures had been taken under the
Veil of Being Alarmed by its approach, to have Cutt off the Retreat
of our Detachment had it ventured to penetrate any Length into the
Country." This implied that the Allen faction was not in control and
their opponents had sufficient sway to put a major force into action.
Further, the rebels were "to make an Early [movement] against Canada
next Spring — that in the course of the Winter every Preparation
would be made for a General attack & that they would endeavour to
get Possession of our advanced Posts upon Lake Champlain & the
other Frontiers to facilitate their operations in the Spring, which are to
keep Pace with a Fleet by the River St. Lawrence."[3]

On November 27, Major Ross wrote from Fort Haldimand with details
of his examination into the behaviour of Lieutenant Jacob Adams of the

Quebec Indian Department. Before the war, Adams had been a trader with the Mississaugas and he had been lured into the service by the promise of a commission. When Fort Haldimand was built, Adams was assigned to manage the Mississaugas' war effort. After several years, he succumbed to the lure of his commercial interests and organized his charges to gather ginseng, a medicinal plant with a lucrative world market. Ross noted that the Mississaugas were so often gathering the plant, it was difficult to bring thirty together for military purposes. Adams was dismissed.[4]

A day later, the ex-officers serving as Volunteers in Eben Jessup's Pensioners' company were ordered to submit an exact list of the men they had recruited so that they could be given preferment accordingly when additional companies were formed.[5]

On November 29, Lieutenant-Colonel Daniel Claus, a deputy superintendent of the Six Nations' Department, reported to headquarters that he had equipped and sent off a party of six rangers with two trusty Mohawks under the command of Lieutenant Walter Sutherland, 2KRR, "an officer, I flatter myself His Excellency the General will approve of, as being particularly well acquainted with the business and route he is to undertake, and as capable of executing the orders and instructions he carries than any person I know employed in that service." As the rebels had ordered away everyone suspected of being friendly to government, he predicted Sutherland would have a difficult time finding a safe harbour; however, Reverend Stuart had provided the names of trusty people who might venture to assist. Claus noted that a foot of snow had fallen since the previous night, which would prove tiring for the party.

He reported that the rebels were selling their wheat for four shillings, six pence, New York currency, and the loyalists were compelled to sell theirs for only two shillings. The quality of the wheat was very good, but army worms had damaged the grass and summer grains — the same pest that had done so much damage to Quebec's crops.

Watercolour by James Eights, circa 1850. (Albany Institute of History and Art, Bequest of Ledyard Cogswell, Jr., 1954.59.85.)

Fort Frederick at Albany (head of State Street) 1765. A notorious jail for housing Tories throughout the Revolution.

On behalf of Stuart, Claus informed headquarters that, as the rebels had received no word about the priest's exchange, they confined his surety with the common criminals in the Albany jail, which was a most unwholesome, nauseous place. The fellow was in ill health, which gave Stuart much unrest. Obviously, Stuart hoped this news would speed up the exchange process.[6]

On November 25, two reports of the disastrous news of Cornwallis's capitulation arrived at Lord George Germain's London office within hours of each other. Prime Minister Lord North received the news "as he would have taken a ball in the breast … and paced up and down the room exclaiming 'Oh God! It is all over.'"[7]

On November 27, the various levels of the rebel command initiated a brisk round of correspondence about the defence of New York's frontiers.

Governor Clinton wrote to General Heath from Poughkeepsie about the imminent expiration of the New York Levies' terms of service. As it was usual for Continental regiments to replace the Levies over the winter, he asked what arrangements were in train, in case some strategic plan should prevent adequate coverage along the frontiers and make it necessary for him to keep the Levies in service:

> For although we have not to apprehend any formidable body of the enemy on our frontiers in the course of the winter, yet they have seldom failed visiting us with small parties, sufficient to annoy these posts, should they find them abandoned or possessed only by the neighbouring inhabitants & desolate the country. The raising of Levies at this season will be attended with a great expence & difficulty and an additional consumption of our provisions & stores. I, therefore, sincerely wish it might be avoided & I would fain hope that such a disposition may be made of the army as to render it unnecessary.

The following day, Washington wrote to Heath from Philadelphia on this same topic and confirmed that the New Hampshire Continentals would remain in the north and, he believed, would be adequate for the purpose. Hazen's regiment, which had been in the Mohawk region the previous winter, had undergone "a long Tour of March and Duty" during the 1781 campaign and would not join them. He closed with, "The Success of Colo Willett at the Northward, does him great Honor; and I hope will be attended with very good Consequences."

Stark reported to Heath on November 29 that he had dismissed all the militia and Levies at Saratoga. The two blockhouses were nearing completion and repairs were underway to the barracks, although resources were very limited. He pled for improved clothing for the New Hampshire Continentals and an adequate fuel supply, refuting Heath's supposition that fuel was "at command," for none could be had within a mile and half of the post. As to Heath's advice that materials were being sent for the regimental tailors to make up clothing, he wrote that there was only one tailor in the New Hampshire Line and he was "a drunken rascal, that could be hardly compelled to make three coats in a winter." He agreed with Heath's observation that only a few horses should be kept with the troops and the remainder sent where forage could be had; however, there was not a man in the district who knew where that place was. Naughtily, he added, "But I suppose it is romantic to issue any more complaints, when experience has taught me that they are of so little value."

Next, he displayed a nice turn of phrase:

> I can not sufficiently admire the magnanimous conduct of our soldiers. They certainly put knight errantry out of countenance; and all those whimsical tales which are generally supposed to have existed no where but in the brains of chimerical authors, seem realized in them. But I fear that this virtue will not last forever; and, indeed, it is my opinion that nothing but their too wretched situation prevents an insurrection. However, I have not heard a syllable of the kind yet, and shall take every imaginable precaution to hinder it; and I hope that their firmness and my endeavors will prove efficacious.

He reported that Willett had eighty to one hundred three-years' men and believed that two hundred men should be kept on the Mohawk River for its protection as less than that would be dangerous, but he cautioned that until the men were clothed, they should not be sent. Currently, the three-years' men at Saratoga could scarce leave their barracks for lack of clothing. Their distress was so great, it was found difficult to form a guard.

There were few troops left in the district, so Stark intended to retire to Albany when the barracks and blockhouses were finished. As he anticipated little business for a general officer, he requested leave to visit home.

On November 30, General Heath responded to Governor Clinton's request by advising that the two New Hampshire regiments, of some three hundred to four hundred men each, would winter in the north. Reflecting Washington's opinion, he suggested they would be sufficient to man the

Mohawk Valley posts when the Levies' terms expired. He was unable to spare any other Regular troops for the other western frontiers, such as the Catskills, and pronounced that the state must provide them, if necessary. Obviously, if Willett's recommendations were accepted, the governor would have to take the Mohawk into consideration as well. Heath also requested information about what places would "most probably [be] exposed to the incursion of the enemy during the winter, and when and in what numbers the troops will be most advantageously cantoned".

On receiving Heath's advice that only two New Hampshire regiments were available, Clinton wrote to Albany County's brigadiers Peter Gansevoort and Robert Van Rensselaer reminding them that the state legislature had lately empowered him to bring into service militia levies from any of the districts any time he deemed it necessary.

Considering that the United States and their French ally had just achieved a monumental victory in Virginia and their army in the north had successfully warded off two expeditions from Canada, the governor's message betrayed amazing anxiety. He spoke of New York's "present distressed situation" and his earnest desire to avoid burdening the inhabitants with unnecessary expenses and trouble. He reported Heath's plan to leave the New Hampshire brigade in the north to garrison posts on the Hudson and Mohawk Rivers and requested the opinions of each brigade's field officers and principal gentlemen whether it was necessary to make a levy before spring and, if so, what number of men would be required to protect the frontiers of Albany, Charlotte, and Tryon counties for the winter. The governor clearly recognized the enemy was not yet defeated in the north.

Clinton gave Heath his agreement on December 4 that the two New Hampshire regiments, if as strong as reported, should answer the purpose, particularly if the season was not milder than usual; however, the addition of Hazen's regiment would ease the burden of the duty, which might otherwise be severe, and give greater security and confidence to the exposed settlements. He listed the posts that were usually occupied over the winter: Saratoga (from where detachments could be made to White Creek and Ballstown); Fort Herkimer, Fort Rensselaer, and Johnstown (from where small detachments were occasionally made to small posts in their vicinities), and Schoharie. He was unable to comment on the relative troop strength required at each place, but thought it best to distribute the largest regiment to the western posts, without making detachments from it to Albany or Schenectady to secure public stores. He thought the Saratoga frontier was neither as extensive, nor as exposed, to the enemy and it was able to "derive more speedy & effectual succor from the militia. The western frontier of Ulster & Orange being more remote from the enemy's posts & of course less liable to their incursions, expecially in the winter season, may with greater ease be defended by the militia of those counties who are remarkably well affected & favorably situated for the purpose."[8]

Well affected, perhaps, but not very motivated or capable, to judge from the raid of the previous August.

There was some upset in the Royal Yorkers' two battalions. Robert Leake had been appointed 2KRR's paymaster and requested a list of commission seniorities from Quebec City headquarters, while at the same time he indicated to Captain Mathews the likelihood of a protest from Thomas Gumersall about his seniority relative to Leake's. He also argued for the seniority of his independent company's second lieutenant, William Fraser, relative to the ensigns who had been promoted from 1KRR.

Major Gray reported there was some quibbling over the men to be brought to the Royal Yorkers from the Queen's Loyal Rangers by Lieutenant Jeremiah French and the men of McAlpin's to be brought by Ensign James McAlpin. Such issues were minor inconveniences in the army's administration, but very important to those involved.[9]

On December 1, Butler reported to Mathews that he had taken an inventory of Indian stores and found several critical articles missing. He had asked Powell for permission to purchase them from the merchants, but was told the governor prohibited it; however, the brigadier agreed to allow the exchange of some coarse cloth of little utility to the Indians for some vital items; however, this scarcely met the greater need. Accordingly, Butler enclosed "a list of articles we are principally in want of." Powell had also supplied a quantity of powder and had promised more, on the understanding that it would be replaced from Indian stores in the spring.

The natives had come earlier than usual to request provisions and gave as their reason the "trifling quantity of Indian corn I issued … for planting." They claimed that, if they had received plenty of seed last spring, they would have been able to maintain themselves over the winter. "The chief part of the Onondagas are already come in, and I fear many of the different nations will follow their example." He had recommended hunting to all the natives as an alternative to war, but they were not pleased, so as a compromise, he counselled them "to keep out small parties that the enemy might not think them asleep."

Surgeon Kerr had earlier reported that refugees were draining the garrison's provisions, but Butler refuted this charge, saying they were not allowed any, nor were the farmers on the Canadian side, nor the families of the Rangers, except each company's customary two women.

As the cold season had been moderate, the farmers had been able to clear and till ground for planting and sowing early in the spring. If they waited until summer, the growing season was too short and they would fail to subsist themselves. He believed the farmers would soon be of great use to the post, as they had maintained themselves since September and had only been allowed a half ration from the outset of the project.

He then made a surprising request. As his Rangers had not been given ammunition to practice marksmanship, the corps' many new recruits made this an essential.[10]

––––––––––

At Montreal on December 3, Major Gray reported to Brigadier de Speth that the 2KRR detachment ordered for Carleton Island had been unable to leave Lachine until January 22, as they could not be provided for earlier. They had been detained at Point Clair by severe weather and left three days later and went to The Cedars that night. Gray had not heard from them since and was concerned that severe frost and snow had prevented further travel.

Four days after Gray's report, Ross wrote to advise that the detachment had arrived at Coteau-du-Lac after an inexplicable delay and could go no farther. Haldimand's reinforcement had come to naught and Ross hoped the battalion would be united at Carleton Island in the spring. He reported that the neck of land below Fort Haldimand had been fortified to protect both the shipping that would winter in the bay and the storehouses on the point.

Mathews notified Gray that the men enlisted by French would be ordered to accompany him to 2KRR; however, a handful had been "made over" to French by Sherwood and were presently employed in the Secret Service and would continue in that role, but be credited to the second battalion. McAlpin's claim was quickly dismissed, "His Excellency appointed the Young Gentleman in Consideration of His Fathers Services, as a provision for him, but that He does not consider that He has the least inherent Right to the Men who Entered in that Corps while Mr McAlpin was a Child."[11]

Captain William Twiss, Canada's chief engineer, made a tour of lower Quebec's various fortifications. Of his visit to the troublesome Prison

Island off Coteau-du-Lac, he wrote, "We found the Côteau Island extremely well arranged for the accommodation, and security of Prisoners of War, and I think your Excellency will not hear of any making their Escape from thence: the buildings as they now stand have Births for

William Twiss, 1745–1827. Canada's very accomplished chief engineer. Twiss had worked at the Tower of London, the fortifications at Gibraltar, and the defences of the Portsmouth Dockyard before coming to Canada with Burgoyne in 1776.

Sir Thomas Lawrence. (The Royal Engineers Library, Chatham, no.351–77.)

216 Men, with a separate Room for an Hospital, and another for the Surgeon's Mate, each room has a Fire Place, and contains only 12 Men ... these Buildings are commanded by a Blockhouse, and Guard House.... I judge the distance ... to the Island to be about 500 yards." (How wrong his predictions about no more escapes would prove to be.)[12]

Brigadier Gansevoort of Albany County's first militia brigade received an alarming letter written at Sancoick on December 4 by Lieutenant-Colonel John Van Rensselaer, OC 14ACM. He, Colonel Daniel Bratt, and some other gentlemen had been taken prisoner a few days before by "tyrannical ruffians who have disavowed allegiance to the State of New York [and] say they are subjects of the State of Vermount." The officers were "treated scandalously and abused and carried to Bennington," where the rioters expected aid, and no doubt praise, but were received with contempt from the authorities who allowed the Yorkers to return home.

Then, Casper Rouse of Tomhannock was taken by another armed band, but was rescued by a "number of faithfull true subjects to the State of New York." Lieutenant-Colonel Van Rensselaer had collected a small, armed force by dramatically stating his intention to uphold the state's supporters at the expense of his life. He entreated Gansevoort to send help with the greatest possible dispatch lest a superior force try his resolve. The next day, Gansevoort ordered Colonels Henry K. Van Rensselaer and Peter Yates to march their regiments to John Van Rensselaer's house and quell the unrest. He urged them to be "exceedingly cautious how you conduct yourself in this matter — the utmost circumspection is to be observed." If they took any insurgents, they were to send them to Albany with the evidence against them. The possibility of serious armed conflict loomed again.[13]

On December 6, Heath offered Stark his sympathies for the general's many complaints and assured him that the Highlands Department

An insurrection in the recruiting district of the 14th (Hoosic and Schaghticoke) Albany County Militia Regiment led to an armed confrontation between New York and Vermont near Sancoick.

Gavin K. Watt and Christopher Armstrong, 2009.

experienced the same problems and many more that the north did not. "In October the troops were ten days without bread — the last month more. We are equally naked and destitute of pay." Although materials were being collected to make clothing for the whole army, it would be late before it could be ready and the 1st and 2nd New Hampshire's paymasters would have to stay below to receive the materials. Also, the army would receive three months' pay over the winter and, again Heath asked Stark to assure the New Hampshire regiments that they would receive equal justice to the main army.

The C-in-C reminded Stark that the engagement term of Willett's Levies would expire at month's end and that the distribution of the Continentals should be done immediately, in particular, the 2NH should be sent to the Mohawk River in good time to relieve Willett. Contrary to Clinton's recommendation, he suggested that part of the regiment might be left at Schenectady and the rest sent to the principal posts above, in particular, to Fort Herkimer where there were stores and ordnance. Stark's dispositions should be "modelled" to preserve public property, curb the enemy, and protect the country. As soon as these arrangements were made, he was to forward a sufficient supply of provisions to subsist the troops until transportation reopened in the spring. Finally, he ordered that all public arms that had been issued to the militia during the late alarm be recalled. Although concern was shown about Stark's ill health, nothing was said about granting him leave to go home.[14]

Also this day, Governor Clinton wrote to Willett's major, John McKinstry, to commiserate with him over the unsuccessful attempts to complete his regiment through the vehicle of unappropriated land bounties. As less than two-thirds of the full complement had been raised and legal recruiting had ceased on August 1, he had organized the men into an independent corps.[15]

Gansevoort wrote to advise the governor about the Sancoick insurrection and report that he had activated two of his regiments to curb the affair. The brigadier understood that the legislature had recently discussed the problems of Vermont's meddling in this area of the state [the Western

Union] and requested advice, as he did not want to commit any more of his brigade without the governor's assent.

On December 7, Solomon Pendleton, a man with a checkered career as a 2ACM first lieutenant, sent the governor a great deal of information about Vermont. He had just returned from a trip to her "frontiers" and had found everything in great confusion. He observed that much was said and done that tended toward anything but peace. Folk living west of the twenty-mile line were now known as "Cattermounters" and those in "old" Vermont, "Vermounters." The two were at odds and their enmity increased daily:

> The Cattermounters compose a sort of an outrageous mob; and are supported only by the Gouvernor, Council, and a few hot-headed people in Vermont; but their supporters daily decrease in number and strength. I likewise find, that many of the people in, and about Bennington, and other parts of Vermount, are daily falling off from their new State; and would desert yet faster, if they were sure they should meet with pardon for their former conduct, from the State of New York. This change is owing to the three following reasons: first, the inconsistent and troublesome conduct of the Cattermounters; who, so far overrun the bounds of political reason, that it makes them sick of their power. Secondly, the late secret negotiations with the enemy by the Governor, council, and a few more designing men, has disgusted those who have ever had a sincear regard for the freedom of the United States in general. And thirdly, their paper currency ... has answer'd them no better purpose, than to drain all the hard money out of their Treasury, and in the roome of it, they have their paper currency of no credit. The hard money thus set on float, has gone to different States for Merchandize: so that they have now, as little hard cash, in proportion to their wants, as the State of New York. To remedy this false step, they have laid a heavy tax in specie; not only

upon all the inhabitants of Vermont, but likewise upon the Cattermounters, which three forths of the People of Vermont reject, as belonging to their State ... I am of oppinnion, that these people [Cattermounters] will, of themselves do the business for the State of New York. It only remains, for the State to act with spirit upon the one hand; and humanity and good policy upon the other. I understand there is an application gone to your Excellency, for a military force, to quell some disturbances that are now existing, between those people that are true to New York and the Cattermounters..., but I am of oppinnion that this method may better be postponed to a futer day.[16]

On an issue far from insurrection, Captain Job Wright wrote from Ballstown to the governor regarding the troublesome three-years' service. Several senior officers thought that an issue of good clothing would have done more to raise men, but the State lacked the financial capability to purchase uniforms. Wright noted the governor's advice that there was to be no further recruiting and asked that he and Lieutenants Pliny Moore and Jesse Hubbell receive some compensation for their time and trouble in attempting to further this service. He requested a commission and reminded Clinton that he had been formerly given command of what men were raised for both regiments (Willett's and McKinstry's?) and, as there were sufficient men to constitute a company, he asked whether they would be grouped together for this purpose.

This information was in such contrast to Clinton's letter to Major McKinstry wherein he had intimated that recruiting had raised almost two-thirds of a regiment — not just a single company as Wright mentioned. Was Clinton putting off McKinstry for some reason?[17]

On December 9, Governor Clinton wrote a detailed letter to Colonel Willett in response to his report of November 16:

The legislature having at their late meeting authorized the drawing out from the militia into actual service a number not to exceed 1500 men for the further defence of the State, I shall be happy in the continuation of your services in the command of one of the corps to be formed from such levies and the more especially as it will probably be stationed in the district of your present command, where I have the pleasure to observe your past conduct has afforded the most perfect satisfaction.

He informed Willett that the New Hampshire Continental regiments would continue in the north and thought it may not be necessary to raise new troops before the opening of the spring, but it would be essential to "make every preparatory arrangement so that the Levies could be embodied and ready to take the field the moment the frontier settlements become accessible to the enemy and the more expecially as that period it is probable the regular regiments may be withdrawn."

Clinton asked Willett to prepare a list of officers who would be willing to serve in the new regiment. He foresaw that some crisis might arise during the winter that would require a body of militia to repel the enemy and, as it was of importance that an experienced officer acquainted with the frontier country should be available to take charge of any detachments called into service, he asked Willett to accept this responsibility in Tryon County. The colonel was to collect regimental returns from Tryon's commanders and forward them with recommendations how they might be made more effective. Clinton agreed with the earlier suggestion about acquiring snowshoes, trusting that a small quantity would cost little.

He reported that a small company of three-years' men under the command of Captain Job Wright should be assigned to a Mohawk Valley post most conducive to the public service. Willett was to appoint one, or two if necessary, of the subalterns to Wright's company who had enlisted the greatest number of men.[18]

Stark replied to Colonel Yates's letter about the Sancoick unrest: "the insurrection you mention must be the result of folly & madness[. Y]ou will be very cautious not to begin hostilities ... but stand your ground and act defensively till reinforced." He reported that both Albany County brigades were being called out and that he was "ready to march the whole garrison when occasion may require of which you will please give me the earliest intelligence."[19]

In an express letter to a State justice, the governor reported the insurrection in Albany County's first brigade (Sancoick), advising that "conformable to the law," Brigadier Gansevoort had called out militia units to quell the insurgents. Although he approved of this action, it was his earnest wish, "consistent with my duty & the immediate safety of the State, that offences of this kind, should be referred to the cognizance of the civil authority." In consequence, he had sent an individual, who had been captured by the insurgents and had personal "knowledge of their proceedings, to wait on you, that you may take his examination on the subject.... Should you conceive it proper to issue warrants against them ... I will chearfuly afford the officers to whom they shall be directed, every assistance in the execution of them which may be required and consistent with my duty to grant."

Clinton then warned Brigadier Robert Van Rensselaer, commander of Albany County's second brigade, about the Sancoick affair and instructed him to give such aid to Gansevoort "as shall be necessary." Then, he wrote to the latter advising that none of the recent resolutions of the legislature related to the Grants pertained to problems such as the insurrection. He approved of his actions and added that, if the force already in motion was insufficient, he should call on the second brigade for assistance.[20]

———————————————

———————————————

A reader's letter to a Quebec newspaper of December 6 revealed much about local attitudes regarding smallpox by reacting to the intention of "a Surgeon of Eminence in this City" to inoculate two children with imported pox as an experiment. The writer agreed that, while the procedure had proven effective in Europe, "Here the malady prevaileth not naturally and thousands of grown Persons have never had the infection. It [the doctor's sample] is now arrived from 3,000 miles

James Hunter, 1778. (Library and Archives Canada, C-001506.)

Quebec City's lower town.

distance; it is taken from we know not what Subject, and is sent by, we know not whom." A most contentious issue indeed![21]

———————

On December 10, Mathews informed Robert Leake that Haldimand was unable to give him seniority in the (Provincial) Line over Thomas Gumersall, as the latter's commission as captain-lieutenant was dated March 9, 1778. Although Leake had served as a captain under Burgoyne in 1777, his rank had not been confirmed until he took command of an independent company on May 23, 1779. This disappointment was offset by the news that the governor held the power to decide about seniority within a regiment, "and without intending the least Injury to Captain Gumersal His Excellency thought your Services and your Losses entitled You to the Preference — in all matters relating to the corps, you will of course command as senior captain — in the Line, Capt Gumersal must take Rank from his former Commission."

Due to the amalgamation of so many different corps, seniority of rank in Jessup's new battalion was a far more complex issue than within the Royal Yorkers. No doubt, the final outcomes brought many disappointments. Ignoring the two reduced lieutenant-colonels who were listed as captains on a December 10 return, the other captains were listed in order of seniority and had seen service in the following corps: 1. Justus Sherwood, Secret Service and Peters's Queen's Loyal Rangers; 2. Jonathon Jones, Jessup's King's Loyal Americans; 3. William Fraser, Fraser's Independent Company and McAlpin's; 4. John Jones, a deputy barrackmaster under Burgoyne and at Sorel; and 5. Peter Drummond, Drummond's Independent Company and McAlpin's.

Of the lieutenants, there were: 1. Henry Simmons, Peters's; 2. Thomas Fraser, Fraser's Independent Company and McAlpin's; 3. David Jones, Secret Service and Jessup's; 4. James Parrot, Secret Service and Peters's; 5. Alexander Campbell, McAlpin's; 6. David McFall, Peters's; 7. John Dulmage, Secret Service and the Loyal Volunteers; and 8. Gideon Adams, Drummond's Independent Company and McAlpin's. Variegated indeed![22]

Another patronage appointment in Butler's Rangers was announced in General Orders at Quebec City on December 11 when Charles Godefroy de Tonnancoeur, Gentleman, was appointed a second lieutenant. The name Godefroy de Tonnancoeur ranked high amongst the provincial noblesse. Charles's father was a committed supporter of the king's government and the son had seen service in the defence of Fort St. John's in 1775 and as an ensign under Captain David Monin with Burgoyne in 1777. With his connections, his native tongue, and his military experience, he would have proven most useful to the Rangers, but there is no evidence that he ever served on the frontiers.[23]

In a letter of December 12 to General Heath, Stark revealed new information about the Sancoick riot. He had sent a request to Bennington for particulars and was informed that it was Captain John Abbot, a former 14ACM company commander, and a number of his followers who had seized Colonel Van Rensselaer and others in a public house. As earlier reported, the insurgents had roughly used their captives, took them to Bennington, and called upon the magistrates to arrest them in "a legal manner." The rest of the story was as previously reported.

When the insurgents discovered Gansevoort's troops on the march, they collected their force within half a mile of the Yorkers. The two bodies, each some two hundred strong, glared at each other for a week without incident.

Stark believed that none of the insurgents were "old" Vermonters. Using Pendleton's term, they were "Cattermounters." He hoped the upstarts would seek compromise and avoid bloodshed. "Congress would do well to pass some severe and decisive edicts, and see that they are put in execution before spring; otherwise, the consequences may be exceedingly serious, and perhaps dangerous."

He then reverted to issues he had raised in earlier letters. He was sorry to hear that other troops suffered more than his, "but, since some are more wretched, we must submit to our fate like good soldiers." It was not practicable for the 2NH to be sent to the Mohawk River until they were clothed. Indeed, only thirty-six "three years" and "during the war" men, including serjeants, were fit for duty in both regiments; the remainder were so bereft of clothing they could not even obtain fuel for their own use and he had found it necessary to retain a number of Levies to perform camp duties. He hoped there was a possibility of sending some blankets, shirts, overalls, stockings, and shoes, which would provide temporary relief. Buried deep in his report was some shocking news:

> My predictions in my last were realized on the evening of the 10th instant. The troops mutinied; but, by the seasonable interposition of the officers, it was quelled very easily. But, sir, this may be but a prelude to an insurrection of a more serious nature.
>
> Some of the most forward of the mutineers are in custody, and are to be tried by court-martial. Mutiny is certainly a crime that deserves the severest punishment, but to punish one soldier for it, is unjust and cruel to the last degree.

Whenever possible, he would send the second regiment to the Mohawk River posts, but he cautioned Heath that he "must not expect impossibilities." He reported that Willett had between eighty and one hundred three-years' men to garrison the posts until the Continentals were clothed. Presumably, these were men over and above Wright's little company. After some comments about being unaware of any Continental arms being issued to the militia, he added a telling postscript that emphasized that the war was far from over.

> I never saw a thanksgiving before that was so melancholy. I may, I believe with safety, affirm that there will not be a thankful heart in this garrison, nor one that has cause to be satisfied with his circumstances. It may be argued that it is a blessing to have trials; but life without enjoyments, and replete with misery, is rather … a curse than a blessing.

In his turn, Heath wrote to Stark again, promising that there would be ample supplies of clothing sent north, but he re-emphasized that it would be late in coming. The two New Hampshire paymasters were confident that clothing could soon be made up for the men, which suggested it would be prepared before being sent. They had drawn hose, shoes, some overalls, and shirts "for the most necessitous men," and these would be sent to Albany in a few days when the various detachments set out to join their regiments.

A supply of forage had at last been settled upon and a quantity of writing paper was on the road from Philadelphia. As he had no knowledge that a mutiny had occurred, he wrote, "The good temper and patience of the troops, exhibited on all occasions, does them honor. I am happy in having the evidence of a prospect of their being well fed and well clothed; and I hope they will receive some pay."

Heath reported he was investigating whether or not Willett's three-years' men would remain in the Mohawk region over the winter and, almost word for word, reiterated Clinton's opinions on the posts to be occupied over the winter.

As to Stark's request for leave, "I wish to gratify your inclination in visiting your family, but wish you to remain a few days, as I hourly expect General Hazen in this quarter. As it may be equally agreeable to him to spend the winter at Albany, and as I should prefer having a general officer in the northern district, I will request him to repair there; if he declines it, Colonel Reid must exercise the command."

Colonel Peter Yates wrote to Brigadier Gansevoort on December 12 from Sancoick. The general's last instruction had given Yates permission to enter into any agreement he thought best to bring an end to the insurrection, but he thought a resolution was unlikely and enclosed an affidavit to support his contention. The affidavit had been sworn that same day by Bezalial Phelps before Justice John Younglove at Cambridge. To wit — Phelps had at times been taken into the confidence of General Safford and others from Bennington who vowed they would disperse Yates's party either by killing or taking prisoner Yates, John Van Rensselaer, Bratt, etc. … and holding them until Vermont's laws were in force. The agitators made several other violent expressions. From this, Yates concluded that talks were fruitless and begged for more troops, as he only had eighty on the ground and the insurgents had 146 in a blockhouse. He requested a fieldpiece and some artillerymen to resolve the issue. As to the "old" Vermonters, he thought they would do nothing more than make a great show. Stark had promised to "march his whole camp," but he preferred that Gansevoort would come at the head of his brigade. Clearly, Yates was in over his head. Worse, the season was very troublesome and his men were restless and wanted to either fight or go home.

The governor wrote to answer Heath's queries about three-years' men, advising that Willett had recruited a number out of the nine months' Levies, but their clothing was worn out and they would be of little service until supplies arrived. He had instructed Willett to appoint officers to take charge of them and to place their companies to the best advantage along the Mohawk. Although he had received no regular return, he understood there were too few to form a regiment, but it would be a loss to the public to discharge those engaged, which must be done if they were not supplied with clothing. Clinton reminded Heath that Congress had agreed to pay, clothe, and subsist these men for whom the state had made no provisions.[24]

Continental artillery captain, Andrew Moodie, who had served in the Mohawk Valley throughout the 1781 campaign, wrote to Governor Clinton from West Point to advise that he had enlisted nine men from the state Levies into his company for the war's duration and to apply for the same bounty that was paid by the militia classes when a Levy volunteered for the duration in a regular infantry regiment. He had promised the men that he would discharge them if they did not get the payment before January 1782.

Moodie reported that when Lieutenant-Colonel Abraham Van Alstyne of Kinderhook had recently visited the Point, he said that all of his regiment's classes were delinquent and it may be that those classes would be willing to hire the nine men. He opined that it would be injurious to the service if the men had to be discharged and it would incur a great cost to him personally, as he had clothed them when they joined. Three days later, Clinton's secretary wrote to Van Alstyne with this proposal, but the outcome had not been determined yet.

Stark wrote to Meshech Weare, one of New Hampshire's most notable politicians of the time. With considerable bitterness, the prickly general said that, although his letters were "treated with silent contempt," his mind always turned to Weare when affairs seemed out of order, such as Vermont's "late riotous conduct" in claiming jurisdiction of southeastern New York and eastward to the Connecticut River. He blamed Vermont for the Sancoick uprising, an act "in open defiance and violation of the rules of Congress." He had seen the proceedings of Vermont's legislature on the subject of admission into the union and found:

[T]hey have not only rejected the resolutions of Congress, but in reality have disavowed their authority; and I farther perceive that, in their great wisdom, they have thought proper to appoint a committee to determine whether New Hampshire shall exercise jurisdiction to the Connecticut River or not. This proceeding appears too weak and frivolous. For men of sense to suppose that New Hampshire would ever consent to an indignity so flagrant, and an abuse so pointed as this seems to be, is what I own surprises me. However, I hope, and indeed have no doubt, that New Hampshire will be more politic than to take notice of this daring insolence. What I mean by notice, is to think of treating with them upon this or any other subject until Congress shall come to a final determination with respect to these people.

The very next day, Vermont's governor, Thomas Chittenden, sent a letter to Stark requesting him to intercede with New York's officers and order them to suspend any operations in the Western Union and, more important, that if they should refuse to comply, he asked the general not interfere by sending his Continentals. The governor made a quite astounding offer: "If they comply ... and liberate the prisoners they have taken, I will suspend the exercise of jurisdiction or law over any person or persons who profess themselves subjects of New York, during that time." Had Vermont's council realized their eyes had grown larger than their stomachs?

On December 16, former New York militia captain John Abott, the architect of the Sancoick insurrection, who now styled himself a Vermont colonel, wrote a petulant message to Colonel Henry Van Rensselaer claiming he had orders preventing him from holding any further negotiations. He would not meet at the time or place previously decided upon, nor would he allow Van Rensselaer to send men into his camp with messages. Little wonder that Yates was disenchanted with negotiating.[25]

On December 16, Marinus Willett graciously accepted Governor Clinton's request to remain in command on the northwest frontier over the winter and for the 1782 campaign, but not without some misgivings. He took the opportunity to broach the question of his rank:

> But whilst I reflect on my former and present situation, I become the subject of sensations of a very unpleasing nature. Having very early received an appointment in the Continental Army and by proper and regular gradation arrived to command of a regiment, I felt myself rather unhappy when the army became new modeled at the close of the Campaign in the year 1780 to find that it became my lott to retire. The cause, however, of that arrangement being urged by arguments of ecconomical import, and the finances of my Country requiring particular attention to this article, to find fault or to repine at a measure calculated to promote the common cause would be inconsistent with those principals of patriotism which have always bore sway in my breast. However, therefore, contrary to my secret wishes of continuing in the line Millitary (as long as there was a Brittain or a British ally to fight against in the American States) it might be, I determined chearfully to put on the habiliments of a private Citizen and was Industriously employed in arranging my affairs for doing business as such, when I was previous to the opening of the last Campaign called upon to receive the command which I at present possess, and which agreeable to your excellencie's desire I am quite willing to continue in, if it can be done without Injustice to my former appointments and rank in the Continental army.
>
> Your Excellency is well acquainted with the manner in which the reformed officers were obliged to retire from actual service, and must know that when they retired their former rank ceased. It is not my intention to enter

into arguments concerning the propriety, conveniency or illconveniency of this mode. I remember well that one argument which was made use of at the time of its taking place, was, that if reformed officers were to have their rank retained, and be entitled to promotion agreeable to their rank, it might happen that an officer who had spend several Campaigns at home entirely devoted to his private concerns, would step into a vacancy over the head of an officer who had encountered a large portion of fatigue and danger during the whole time in the field. This had the appearance of bearing hard upon the officers who were continued in Service, but this objection can by no means lay against me. Your Excellency well knows that four months had not elapsed from the time of my being obliged to retire from service until I was again called upon, and engaged to accept of military command on the frontiers of our State; a service that has been accompanied with a proportion of Toil and Hazard equal perhaps to any in the United States, and that the short time in which I had a recess from service was when the army was in winter quarters so that the argument which I have before mentioned can no way opperate against me.

Willett went on to provide a précis of his service, starting on June 28, 1775, when he had been appointed the second senior captain, 1NY, and finishing on January 1781 as lieutenant-colonel commandant of the 5NY. He repeated, "Four months had not elapsed before I was again called upon and have served a Campaign accompanied with difficulties superiour to any that has fell to my share in any one Campaign during the war." Then, he delivered a one-two punch:

I am happy in meeting with your Excellencie's approbation of my conduct during the Campaign, and am not only willing, but desirous if my country requires my service, to continue in my present Command, if this, as I have before observed, can be done consistent with my former appointments, and rank in the American Army.

Your Excellency cannot be unacquainted, that by the rules for the Government of the American Army, all officers of the same Denomination receiving Commissions from any particular State, are to take rank after officers who have Commissions from Congress, even tho' the commissions from the State should be of elder date than those from Congress. This being the case, your Excellency must at once see how disagreeable my situation is while I continue to serve under my present appointment, liable every day to be commanded by officer who I have always been accustomed to command and who by no just rule ought on any account to Command me, and a submission to which in the Ordinary course of things would be degrading to the Millitary character. That this cannot be either just or right is I humbly conceive exceeding clear. And for this reason beg leave, to request your excellency's assistance in endeavouring to procure, for me from Congress, a Power to rank agreeable to my former appointment in the American Army.

Just a day later, Willett wrote to the governor displaying considerable anger over his pay.

[T]o serve another campaign under such disadvantages as I did the last, and to come home in the winter and sit down with empty pockets is what I cannot find a Dissposition to Comply with Unless ... some better prospect should open.... The Restoring to me, however, if it can be done my former Rank as the Army appears to be new Established with the prospect of receiving such pay as would free me from present difficulties would

make the Command your Excellency desires to keep me
in very pleasing to me. But without this I dont see how
I can continue. All these things, I think it not amiss to
make known in Confidence to your Excellency.[26]

Adding to the Sancoick uproar, on December 15, several "friends to
New York" in the Western Union held a meeting at Schaghticoke and
were confronted by a handbill posted by two pro-Vermont Justices of
the Peace, commanding all inhabitants of the town "to leave off their
advising the people and trying to Disafect them."

After several futile attempts at negotiation at Sancoick, Colonel
Henry Van Rensselaer had scooped up some prisoners and left. Two
days later, Vermont's veteran colonel, Eben Walbridge, sent Henry Van
Rensselaer two testy notes about the dangerous unrest in the Western
Union. His first letter was critical of Van Rensselaer's preemptive
action and the second referred to the Yorker's statement that he was
not authorized to treat with anyone who was not a subject of his home
state. Walbridge demanded the release of the prisoners, the payment of
property damages by Yorker troops, and a guarantee that all inhabitants in
the Western Union, whether owing allegiance to New York or Vermont,
would be allowed to "rest Quiet and Unmolested" until Congress resolved
the jurisdictional issues.

From his temporary headquarters at Schaghticoke, Brigadier
Gansevoort countered the next day with a tough-worded letter of his
own addressed to "the officer commanding Vermont troops":

> [I]n pursuance of a law of this State a part of my brigade
> has been detached to suppress an insurrection of some
> of the subjects of this State residing in the district of
> Schachtikoke and Hoseck. For this purpose I arrived here
> this day … to aid the Sheriff of this county to apprehend
> the insurgents by virtue of legal process. On my arrival
> here I am informed that a large body of troops from the
> Grants are marching in force with artillery…. Before I
> proceed any farther, I thought it expedient to write to

you requesting you to inform me … what is the object
of your present movement into the interior parts of this
State with a military force and by what authority?[27]

After Willett had been visited in Albany by a number of Oneidas, he
approached Governor Clinton with a new concept for the management
of the rebel natives. He noted that the few Indians who continued to
support the union were primarily Oneidas and Tuscaroras and that they
had been, and must continue to be, sustained by the United States. "[I]t
is without doubt our wisdom to have as much service from them as
we can," yet whenever they were wanted for some duty, they were not
satisfied if they were unpaid, even for the most petty of scouts. To avoid
this constant expense, he suggested that they should be assigned to the
officer commanding on the frontiers who would be given the charge of
supplying them with provisions and clothing. "This will put the officer in
such a situation that he can call upon the Indians for their services and
pay them for those services with such things as otherways they receive
without having the benefit of their services." He noted that it was true
that they were, when inclined, very useful and, in his opinion, the way
to create and preserve this inclination was to keep them in a state of
dependence upon the person who needs their services. Of course, the
officer commanding the frontiers was Marinus Willett.[28]

December 15 marked the first official appearance of the name "Loyal
Rangers" to designate Major Edward Jessup's new battalion when it
was announced in Haldimand's General Orders that Serjeant-Major
Mathew Thompson, 31st Regiment, was appointed as adjutant.

Reverend John Stuart apologized in writing to the governor for his
faux pas in naming his new school a "Protestant Seminary." He had not
recognized that this term might be construed to mean that pupils of
different religions would not be admitted and he assured Haldimand
that "every Person that has offered, Protestants, Catholics, Jews &c" had

*Millicent Mary Chaplin, circa 1838–43.
(Library and Archives Canada, C-000835.)*

Although painted in a later era, the equipment and clothing is similar to the Revolutionary War and reminiscent of native scouts on patrol.

been accepted. "No Distinction shall be made on the Score of Religious Sentiments. — No Partiality shewn, either on that, or any other Pretence."

On December 18, Quebec headquarters reported that Lonas Lovelace, the widow of Lieutenant Thomas Lovelace, who had been executed as a spy by the rebels, would have her husband's pension continued until the end of the muster and afterwards would be subsisted at £20 per annum and her seven children would continue on the ration list. How she and her offspring would fare on such an allowance was an open question.

The need for reliable intelligence was unending and, on December 19, the accomplished agent, Lieutenant Walter Sutherland, 2KRR, left Ticonderoga with eight first battalion men to scout Johnstown.[29]

As the State's agent had still not made adequate deliveries of flour, Heath wrote to Governor Clinton on December 19 with another plea.

"The distress of this army for the want of bread has become almost insupportable — they are nearly half their time without — this obliges them to eat a larger quantity of meat than is good for their health — their naked condition for want of clothing obliges many of the soldiers to lay in the barracks nearly the whole of the time; these complicated wants are destroying their health — numbers are falling sick."[30]

On December 20, two state judges wrote to Governor Clinton with news about Vermont's leadership, referring to the republic with the usual dogged Yorker persistence as the "northeast Quarter of this State." The evidence that Vermont was negotiating with the British to return to the empire kept building up. Two former prisoners from Canada provided specific information about these secret activities. One fellow named the key negotiators on both sides of the question and described some elements of a potential settlement that would see Vermont raising two to three thousand troops to be fed, paid, and clothed by the British, and the Crown supplying and maintaining a twenty-gun ship crewed by Vermont for service on Lake Champlain. The second man confirmed much of this information and gave as his source Han Jost Herkimer, the loyalist captain of the bateaux company at Coteau-du-Lac. As well, the man had personally seen Ira Allen at Isle aux Noix with Sherwood and Smyth and knew that Major Jonas Fay had brought thirty of Burgoyne's Germans in for an exchange.[31]

In a personal letter of December 21, Stark wrote to General Washington and, after congratulating the chief on his success at Yorktown, he gave a brief review of events in the north, thoroughly dismissing St. Leger's expedition with the comment, "they returned, with shame and disgrace." This made it appear as if he had never suffered a moment's concern about St. Leger, which was far from the case. As to Ross's raid in the Mohawk, the Valley had felt "some of the effects of their inveterate malice"; however, the raiders were "driven from that country with indignity." So much for Canada's trifling efforts!

He went on to explain that, after St. Leger's men had killed a Vermont serjeant, the Briton sent an inexplicable letter of apology to Chittenden. In consequence, he had written to Chittenden for an explanation of why the enemy would apologize for a military action and had been told that the subject letter had been forwarded directly to Washington. Stark theorized that a doctored copy had been sent, as the governor would hardly show the original. He continued:

> The proceedings of the Vermonters have been very mysterious, until about ten days ago, when they in a manner threw off the mask, and publicly avowed their determination to continue their claim of jurisdiction to the North [Hudson] R. on the part of New York, and to Mason's patent on the part of New Hampshire, and did actually send an armed force, with a piece of artillery, to protect and defend their adherents on the west side of the 20 mile line; and indeed have done little less than to wage war with the United States ...
>
> I believe, sir, that I may venture to predict that unless something decisive is done in the course of this winter, with respect to these people, we may have every thing to fear from them that they are capable of, in case we are under the disagreeable necessity of making another campaign.
>
> This may be considered as strange language from me, who have ever been considered as a friend of Vermont; and, indeed, I ever was their friend, until their conduct convinced me that they were not friendly to the United States. Were I to judge by their professions, they are more mine and the State's friend now than ever; but their actions and their words appear to carry a very different meaning. During my command, I have been promised everything from their government and their leading men that I could wish for; but they have taken particular care to perform nothing, while, on

the other hand, the militia of New York, and those of Berkshire, attended to my requisitions with alacrity and uncommon spirit; and I believe the northern and western frontiers are in a great measure indebted to them for the protection of their houses.[32]

Brigadier Gansevoort sent two dispatches to Governor Clinton on December 21. The first included several documents detailing the clash with Vermont and a recommendation that the legislature hold a session at Albany where persons from the northeast sections of the state could more readily be examined.

One of the documents was a challenging letter from Vermont Colonel Eben Walbridge. In a convoluted manner, it essentially repeated Vermont's claim to the Western Union and refuted New York's right to intercede. "Should these proposals be rejected, and the people who profess to be citizens of Vermont, be imprisoned, and their property destroyed, I cannot be answerable for the consequences."

To this was added two affidavits given by men who had been with Colonels Yates and Van Rensselaer at Sancoick. They had volunteered to go to Bennington for intelligence and when there discovered that Vermont troops had been ordered out to oppose the Yorkers' attempts to quell the insurrection. They saw one hundred men under arms and heard a major in conversation with General Ethan Allen declare "that he would with his life and fortune protect the new union, and … that a General should not let his enemy know when he intended to strike, but give the blow and think afterwards." Allen answered, "Now you begin to talk something like and declared himself to be of the same sentiments." Further, a doctor "had been on the east side of the mountain where the people told [him] that they were jealous that the people of the west side were in alliance with the enemy in Canada; that the said doctor returned to Bennington on making enquiry, found that it was absolutely true." On the men's return to Sancoick, they came across a number of armed men and a fieldpiece drawn by four oxen inside the twenty-mile line and a few miles further on, saw armed men going to join the insurrectionists.

Gansevoort's second report told of the actions he had taken since receiving the governor's directions. He had gone to Saratoga to ask General Stark for a fieldpiece and a detachment of Continentals to assist his men at Schaghticoke and Hoosic. With these additions, he thought he could dislodge the insurgents from their blockhouse; however, Stark did not think a detachment was justifiable unless ordered by General Heath and, in any event, his men were almost naked and in no condition to march. Gansevoort doubted the validity of these reasons and suspected that Stark was adhering to Chittenden's demand that he not interfere in the affair.

Gansevoort had gone to Schaghticoke to take command of his militiamen and, shortly after his arrival, the Albany sheriff came with a warrant to apprehend the insurgents. Half an hour later, his troops from Sancoick appeared, having been ordered to retire by Lieutenant-Colonel Yates in compliance with Gansevoort's instructions not to risk an action unless their prospects of success were good. Colonel Henry Van Rensselaer arrived to report that reinforcements from Vermont had been in sight when he left. In case the reinforced rioters attempted to cut him off, Gansevoort decided to retire an additional five miles to Schaghticoke town where he could house his men from the inclement weather and secure his route of retreat. Papers were served on four captured rioters and they were jailed. He wrote a letter to the Vermont commander asking under what authority he brought a military force in "the interior parts of this State." He was sure he knew the answer, but thought that having it in writing might prove useful to the legislature and Congress.

By sunset on December 19, no answer had been received, nor had his messengers returned. He only had eighty men on hand from four different regiments and they had been "out" for a considerable time without provisions. He was convinced there was not the least prospect of success if he engaged the insurgents and he could not expect to be reinforced "in due season." He suspected that even if his and Van Rensselaer's whole brigades were turned out, they would not have been sufficient to suppress the insurrection, as "the people from the Grants" had intervened. He had been misled into thinking that Vermont would not interfere, but Chittenden's letters and the appearance of her troops "undeceived" him and he dismissed his men. Gansevoort was concerned for the people who had taken an active role in attempting to put down the uprising. They daily expected to be confronted by Vermonters and forced to swear allegiance to the republic or abandon their holdings. Indeed, several had already been faced with that dilemma. New York's attempts to enforce her jurisdiction through military intervention had clearly failed.[33]

Also on December 21, Brigadiers Gansevoort and Van Rensselaer reported to the governor that "a great majority" of the five field officers and twenty-two principal gentlemen surveyed about the defence of the western frontier had decided "that 200 men would be needed before spring."[34]

Stark wrote to Heath on December 22 hoping that General Hazen was on his way north to assume command and presenting a request by the New Hampshire colonel, George Reid, for leave to go home to address pressing family affairs. Reid and Stark had a long history of serving together, beginning with the militia concentration outside Boston in 1775, and both had fought at Breed's Hill. In January 1776, Reid had been appointed a captain in Stark's 5th Continental Regiment and, in 1780, had taken command of the 2NH as lieutenant-colonel commandant. His letter to Stark, requesting leave, gave a depressing image of duty on the Mohawk River. "A dismal gloom overspreads this quarter at present. However, two damned Indians favored me [with] a piece of venison, on which I intend to dine to-morrow ... I am invited to keep Christmas with Mr. Ensign. I think that man must be a Christian.... If you have not already wrote to General Heath, I pray you to write as soon as possible, representing my situation, and the pressing necessity of my being at home."[35]

Gavin A. Watt after E. Wyatt Kimball. (http://www.visitnh.gov/)

Lieutenant-Colonel George Reid of New Hampshire. During the first half of 1782, Reid's battle with Willett over senior command of the Mohawk region made the task of raiding much easier for British Indians and troops.

An Indian council was held at Niagara on December 20. A Detroit Wyandot, two Onondagas, and some other Confederacy representatives delivered speeches recommending that a message be sent to General Haldimand for his assistance to mount a strike against Fort Pitt in the spring. How little the natives understood the paucity would of the governor's resources.[36]

Captain Mathews wrote to Colonel John Campbell of the Quebec Indian Department on December 21 to inform him that Haldimand had rejected Dr. Kerr's claims as the surgeon to the natives on the Ross expedition. Whether this was because of the odd nature of his submission or for some other technicality was not stated.[37]

The next day, chief engineer Twiss reported to Haldimand on the state of the Yamaska blockhouses. Other than some improvements to the officers' apartments, there was nothing remarkable at the lower post; however, he had much to say about the upper blockhouse near Missisquoi Bay, which the governor had ordered built the previous winter to hinder invasion attempts from that quarter. Twiss had located the new blockhouse on a hilltop near the bottom of a cataract

P.F. Tardieu, 1801. (New York Public Library, Digital Gallery, Record 806960.)

Késkètomah, an Onondaga Sachem. Although probably too young to have held this role during the Revolution, this sachem exhibits the dignity reported to have been common to native politicians.

located twenty-one miles from the lower post. Work had begun early
in the year and by the time of his inspection, the forest was cleared 250
yards around the fortification and a nearby island was being cleared for a
garden. He wrote, "the Work is exceedingly well finished, and by having
a bomb-proof cellar, and being surrounded with a picketing and glacis,
may be considered a Post of considerable defense."[38]

Sometime in December, Powell addressed the governor's suspicions that
had been aroused by Ross's complaints. Haldimand had noted that only
150 Rangers had been sent to Ross from Niagara, despite Butler having
returned nine complete companies for a total of 450 all ranks. Powell
wrote that the report had been a mistake:

> [H]e must have meant that the 10th Company was
> complete, for I suppose the others might want forty of
> their complement to which[,] if 110 sick and convalescent
> with fifty recruits who were on duty in this Garrison
> are added[,] it appears only 100 remained for cutting
> timber and firewood, servants, guards, &c.... When the
> detachment went off, I think Colonel Butler informed
> me he had only eight men left for that [garrison] service,
> and some time after it was with difficulty that twenty-
> five men could be mustered to go to Detroit.

He referred Haldimand to the monthly return now on its way to
the adjutant general "in which every man is accounted [for]" and risked
being preachy:

> You must be sensible, Sir, that when a regiment is called
> upon it is never able to furnish the number of men
> returned in the column "fit for duty", and allowance
> should always be made for servants, convalecents, &c.
> I think [it] is right to observe that whenever demands
> are made upon the post for troops to be employed in the

enemy's country, very large allowances must be made as there are very few of the King's Regiment [8th Foot] equal to the fatigue they necessarily undergo upon that service. In the summer there are frequently 100 of the Rangers upon the sick list owing to the ague which generally rages here at that season, which with cutting timber and firewood, providing hay, guards, servants, &c, will prevent furnishing that number of men for active service, which from returns might be expected.

He noted that a lack of clothing for the Rangers at Detroit had prevented them from "acting against the enemy" and then shifted ground to advise that Second Lieutenant Andrew Wemple had been selected for a first lieutenantcy and that Butler recommended Serjeant Silas Secord, "who distinguished himself on the last expedition, to succeed second lieutenant Frederick Docksteder, who died upon the march to the Mohawk R."[39]

On Christmas Day, Captain William Fraser, LR, sent returns for the two blockhouses on the Yamaska River to General Riedesel and reported seventy-three men had been ordered for the upper blockhouse and thirty-

three for the lower one where he was personally posted. Fraser kept two scouts of six men each operating in rotation on the St. Francis River. The overall strength in both posts had shrunk, presumably due to illness, and Fraser had been unable to increase it and requested that Riedesel do so. Riedesel replied, questioning Fraser's dispositions and the captain wrote to explain why he had assigned twelve men

Although painted long after the Revolutionary War, the clothing and equipment are suggestive of a senior warrior on a winter scout.

Unknown artist, circa 1835. (Library and Archives Canada, Peter Winkworth Collection, C-150345.)

to scout the "river St. Francois," exclusive of those selected for the "Grand Scout" to Hazen's Road which numbered only twenty-eight as opposed to fifty-six of the year before.[40]

Remarkably, Haldimand was still without reliable information about Cornwallis's fate when, on December 27, he ordered Sherwood to go to the Loyal Blockhouse and dispatch scouting parties to get confirmation or denial of the capitulation.

That same day, the governor wrote to Brigadier de Speth about claims that certain rebel officers being held on Île Perrot, northwest of Montreal, were reported to have committed atrocities on prisoners taken from Butler's Rangers, cutting hands and arms off some before tomahawking and scalping them. Presumably, de Speth was to keep a weather eye on these fellows while an investigation was underway. As nothing came of the story, it was presumably apocryphal.[41]

On Christmas Eve, Governor Clinton wrote to the state's Congressional delegates, enclosing the letters, reports, and affidavits relating to "The Grants" and the Sancoick affair. He found it incredible that:

> [P]ersons against whom there are such unquestionable proof of a traitorous correspondence, should be permitted to go at large with impunity and even at times be attending our public councils ... you must be sensible of the disagreeable impression which this has made on the minds of many of our most zealous friends, who have not hesitated to attribute to this cause in a great measure our misfortunes on the Frontiers during this and the last year.

On Christmas Day, General Heath wrote to John Stark from headquarters in the Highlands commiserating over the Vermonters' conduct. "I fear that there will, sooner or later, be serious consequences produced by their disputes."

Heath went on to advise that the many promises of fair treatment for the Continentals in the north had finally been honoured. "The paymasters of the New Hampshire regiments have drawn clothing of every kind, and will convey it up as soon as possible. The naked condition of those regiments led me to direct that they should be first served." This would be very welcome news for the soldiers huddling for warmth in the freezing reaches of the frontiers.[42]

3

TO TAKE POST AT OSWEGO
An Object of Great Importance

*A*s winter gripped the Mohawk Valley, supplies of provisions grew so short that Captain Garret Putman's company of Willett's Levies had to be discharged two months early, on New Year's Day. As most of the men were from Tryon County, they did not have far to travel.

Militiaman William Feeter of Tryon's Palatine District, who was serving in Captain Seferinus Klock's 2TCM company, recalled being sent out several times to fend off the enemy. Natives attacked a settlement in Fairfield and several people were killed or taken prisoner and their property destroyed. Another raid struck in northeastern German Flatts. In both instances, Klock's company pursued the raiders without success.

Captain Job Wright's company of three-years' men had been posted at Fort Rensselaer. A sixteen-man platoon guarding Walradt's ferry was alarmed when a large scouting party of whites and natives hove into sight; however, nothing came of it and the raiders went elsewhere to commit their depredations.[1]

While these minor events were disturbing the Mohawk Valley, George Washington unofficially wrote a reasoned, powerful letter to Thomas Chittenden, which later was claimed to have greatly influenced Vermont's future course. He recommended that the republic's claims to the two unions be relinquished and gave hopes that, if the original boundary claims were returned to, Congress would view her request to join the union favourably. On the other hand, maintaining these two claims could lead to general antipathy and a likely intervention by the United States.

> There is no calamity within the Compass of my foresight which is more to be dreaded than a necessity of coercion on the part of Congress and consequently every endeavour should be used to prevent the execution of so disagreeable a measure. It must involve the Ruin of that State against which the resentment of the others is pointed.

He ostensibly accepted Chittenden's assertion that the negotiations with the British "were so far innocent, that there never was any serious intention of joining Great Britain"; however, he stressed that the talks gave the enemy great advantages and, by creating "internal disputes and feuds," encouraged all enemies of the United States, at home and abroad, and sowed "seeds of distrust and jealousy … among ourselves."

One Vermont historian later claimed this letter precipitated a grave political crisis, as some citizens who discovered the contents proposed to act immediately on Washington's advice, but "[t]he Allens, who were no longer sincerely attached to the American cause, were opposed to dissolving the unions."[2]

Sometime in January, the double agent, Lieutenant-Colonel Thomas Johnson, was visited at his home in Cöos, in eastern Vermont, by Levi Sylvester, one of his Tory captors from the previous March. Levi brought a letter from Captain Azariah Pritchard, KR, pressing for information about the movements of Johnson's friend, General Jacob Bayley, and other prominent rebels. Such visits and requests became a regular feature of the tortured Johnson's existence and, when he later revealed his secret life to Washington, he noted that several other persons in the vicinity were similarly "favoured."[3]

The January return of the two New Hampshire Continental regiments on duty in the Albany area listed eight staff, sixteen commissioned, and eighty-one non-commissioned officers and 459 rank and file, 175 of which were "Sick Present," sixty-two were "Sick Absent," 236 were on command or extra service, and thirty-two on furlough for a total of 561 all ranks.[4]

On January 2, Secretary Germain wrote to Governor Haldimand predicting that "Cornwallis's misfortune will deter Vermont from declaring for His Majesty but I trust you will find means to encourage them." It was as if the surrender at Yorktown was a mere hiccup in a very long, tiring, and indigestible meal. He encouraged Haldimand to employ his troops in the spring to recover that wayward republic. Of course, it would be weeks and weeks before this "encouraging" note reached the governor.[5]

At Niagara, a court reviewed the case of Captain Peter Ten Broeck. Two years after Ten Broeck had chosen not to escape with Walter Butler and William Ryer Bowen, Lieutenant Joseph Ferris had been sent to help him "come off" and again he had declined. The court heard Peter's account of his confinement and concluded that "his conduct ... appears irreproachable and that he took the earliest opportunity of joining the Corps." His rank was restored and he was ordered to resume duty with his regiment.[6]

On January 2, Major Jessup wrote to Captain Mathews to request green clothing for the Loyal Rangers. As his officers preferred the pattern of Captain Sherwood's green jacket with its green facings, he requested additional green cloth from stores, perhaps "Rat eaten or Damaged Coats," so that the red facings supplied with the kits in QMG stores could be replaced.[7]

During the French regime, a great many prisoners had been taken in New England by the Canada Indians. Many had been adopted and thoroughly acculturated and, as a result, large numbers of the Catholic Indians were of mixed blood. Many of them rose to prominent positions, which gave their villages a pronounced leaning toward the rebels and caused the governor's office much anxiety throughout the war. One of the most accomplished rebel spies of the period was an Oneida named Oratoskon, who skulked about Kahnawake and, according to Lieutenant-Colonel Campbell, "circulated all the poison he was charged with, and debauched ... [the] young men." Claus sent the Fort Hunter's senior war captain, John Desertonyon, to visit an acquaintance at Kahnawake and investigate the rumours of Oratoskon. Although Assharegown, a village headman, assured Deserontyon that, if the rebel was discovered, he would be secured, nothing happened.[8]

If the troops in the Mohawk Valley thought they were in the grip of winter, they would have been astounded to see the conditions in Quebec. Surgeon Wasmus wrote in his diary on January 6 that he was again snowed into his barracks at Sorel by terrible storms and no one had been able to go in or out for twelve hours. Finally, the men dug a tunnel to gain access. If the snow was deep at Sorel, one might be assured that it would be equally deep at Montreal, and worse at Quebec City. Wasmus wrote, "The Canadians cannot remember such a hard winter or one in which so much snow has fallen."

At mid-month, the day after the garrison celebrated Queen Charlotte's birthday, Surgeon Wasmus wrote in his journal that Serjeant-Major Reinemund, Colonel Baum's brother-in-law, had drowned in the hole in the St. Lawrence where the garrison drew its water. A day or two later, he dryly noted, "One does not receive any news here. In winter time, Canada has no communication with the rest of the world; it is as if this was the end of the world." This was a common complaint of German diarists, who seemed to feel the isolation worse than their British allies.[9]

Correspondence between Brigadier Johann August von Loos and his superior and close friend, Major-General Riedesel, reveals details of the

Baroness Friederike von Riedesel (née von Massow), aged sixteen, 1746–1808. A very courageous and enchanting lady, beloved by all who knew her.

Johann Heinrich Wilhelm Tischbein, circa 1762.

relations between the governor and the German officers and much about winter garrison life in Quebec City. Von Loos, who, it would seem, was one of the German brigadiers that Haldimand had little faith in, habitually employed nicknames when referring to the governor such as "the premier" or "the growler" and, considering he was quite senior himself, "the old fellow." Of the baroness, von Loos wrote, "Your wife, whom every one loves, will be a thousand times welcome here. I would strew her road with flowers, if there were any." There was to be a ball on Wednesday and the next evening, a concert and on the Saturday, a "conversation," one supposes to play cards, which were followed by "cold, fried meat, ham and cake." He added, "The people here kill themselves with eating." The venues for such entertainments were the homes of wealthy members of both Franco and Anglo society. Loos expected a ball to be held at "the premier's" in time for Riedesel's visit and mentioned that Major-General Alured Clarke intended to visit Riedesel in February. Rather cryptically, he added, "Whether he will travel as one who knows the country, and return a learned man, time must show."[10]

On January 7, Lieutenant Walter Sutherland's scouting party was at Mill Bay on Lake Champlain, having dragged a small boat from Dutchman's Point to the upper end of Tory Island and from there across open water to the bay. The next day, the party was joined by Ensign Roger Stevens and his men and Jonathon Miller with a third group. Stevens had seen tracks in the snow at Crown Point, so at midnight, the three leaders and their men set off across the ice to Chimney Point and arrived at "St. Leger's house" about 7:00 a.m. where they found a sled and horses tethered outside and a rifle, two muskets, and provisions inside.

Sutherland spotted seven men at work digging across the lake at Crown Point. Earlier, the lake had been open water and these fellows, thinking they were secure, had left their arms at Chimney Point; however, the ice now proved strong enough for the loyalists to cross and the workers were easily taken. They reported that two sleds loaded with scrap iron had already been sent into Vermont and that about thirty gun carriages had been dug up and were ready to be taken across the lake when the ice firmed up. They claimed that parties as large as twenty-one men had been digging ever since St. Leger retired from the lake, but, more important, they confidently reported that Cornwallis had been taken.

Stevens recognized a "friend to government" named Ailsworth amongst the captives and persuaded Sutherland to allow him to join his party, saying he could get all the intelligence needed, as well as supplies of provisions. Accordingly, Sutherland swore the man and sent him off with Stevens.

At Schroon Lake, Sutherland's party shot a moose and a bear, which provided a large supply of meat. Walter sent four men back to Fort St. John's with the six remaining prisoners and an interim report. As to completing the rest of his mission, he anticipated "a troublesome and tedious journey as there is no possibility as yet of leaving the lake, the snow being as soft as when it fell."

Sutherland had just left Stevens when Ailsworth announced that a party would arrive at Crown Point that very night. A large group had been earlier spotted at Chimney Point attempting to set fire to a hut (perhaps St. Leger's so-called "house"), so Stevens had hopes of a large haul. After re-crossing the lake, he and his men hid about twenty yards from the hut. At 5:00 p.m. a rebel appeared; however, when one of the loyalists ran to secure him, the fellow took off, shedding his hat, coat, pack, and blanket to make better speed, and ran to a convoy of five sleighs that was just arriving to collect the iron. In a flurry of shouts, the sleighs hurriedly turned about and escaped.

True to his word, over the ensuing days, Ailsworth visited contacts in the country and secured information and food. Stevens returned to St. John's on January 31.[11]

While these scouts and agents were on the frontiers, there was much end-of-campaign tidying up in the Canadian Department. On January 7, the deputy adjutant general issued a General Order that the British regiments and loyalist corps were to send in a state of their arms, noting all deficiencies and when each occurred.

Loyalist Christian Wehr wrote to Captain Mathews to complain that, despite Major Jessup's promise of a captaincy, he now found himself on the pensioners' list without rank and wished to be transferred to 2KRR with the men he had recruited at such effort and expense. Wehr had an interesting history. He had been a KLA captain in 1777, but rather than command a company, had served as a blacksmith during Burgoyne's expedition, yet he was listed as a captain on the KLA's 1778 roll. By June 1779, he held the same rank in the "Loyal Volunteers," but when Leake's Independent Company was formed, Wehr was not one of the chosen officers and, when the Loyal Rangers was created, he was again not selected for command. Wehr got his wish and was ranked as a 2KRR second lieutenant backdated to December 11, 1781. Obviously, this lower rank was preferred to being on the pensioners' list.[12]

Captain Robert Leake wrote to Mathews on January 10 in his role as paymaster to advise that 2KRR's non-commissioned officers had only been paid as privates since the battalion first formed in 1780 and requested permission to make up the difference.[13]

The Loyal Rangers' Regimental Orders of January 12 directed the officers commanding companies to immediately submit an exact return of their non-commissioned officers, drummers, and private men to the acting adjutant so that clothing could be issued. Men employed at work or absent from the corps, or who had received clothing since last June, were not to be included. This same day, Mathews wrote to Jessup to confirm that the uniform kits had been ordered for the corps, but there was no mention of a supply of additional green cloth to change the facings.[14]

Riedesel noted that the issuing of rum at Sorel district's advance posts was unevenly applied, and provided a set of regulations that exempted the Secret Service scouts who performed hazardous duty. A few days later, Deputy Adjutant General Lernoult withdrew the rum allowance for artificers and workmen of all branches in the lower province, replacing it with a three-pence allowance per diem.

On January 13, Captain William Fraser reported to Major-General Riedesel from Yamaska Blockhouse that Colonel St. Leger was supplying snowshoes and a guide to lead the "Grand Scout." The Rangers at the post had made all their clothes and were ready for service, and Lieutenant Israel Ferguson, KR, who was well acquainted with Hazen's Road, was to command the scout and was waiting for Riedesel's final orders and the arrival of the native guide. The "Grand Scout" departed on January 19 for the Loyal Blockhouse. A native sent to guide a second scout leaving from the lower blockhouse to the St. Francis River arrived on January 24, and this second party set out with sixteen days' provisions.[15]

Lieutenant-Colonel Claus reported from Montreal on January 14 that four of his men who had been with Sutherland had brought in six Vermont prisoners. Under careful interrogation, the captives confirmed Cornwallis's defeat, although it was said that the local loyalists considered it a "framed story." They told about Chittenden sending a body of five hundred troops into New York three weeks previously "to drive off a parcell of tax Collectors and others from New York State." Families from the White Creek area (in the Western Union) and New Hampshire were daily arriving in Vermont,

Unknown artist, circa 1770. (Library and Archives Canada, C-083514.)

Lieutenant-Colonel Daniel Claus, 1727–1787. Claus served in lower Quebec as the senior deputy agent of the Six Nations' Indian Department.

which might "occasion a dispute & rupture between those respective States."

Three days later, Mathews informed Claus that the governor wished him to send the prisoners to Sherwood for additional interrogation, as, with his New Hampshire Grants' background, he might be able to uncover more information. In addition, Haldimand wished to dispatch an "Extraordinary Scout" to gather intelligence, and Claus was to send Sherwood a native guide and two of his rangers. Did the governor still doubt Cornwallis's defeat or simply its extent?[16]

The trial of the lieutenant of militia, Pierre Charlebois, who had been charged with assaulting John Thompson, 1KRR, sentenced him to pay a fine of twenty shillings and the costs of the prosecution. All of the Crown's witnesses were allowed forty shillings for their expenses. Considering the unprovoked brutality of the beating and Charlebois's reputation as a vicious bully, this was a mild penalty indeed and reflected the administration's sensitivity over the general temper of the Canadiens. For Thompson, who had earlier suffered fourteen months of malignant imprisonment by the rebels, the finding was hardly just.[17]

Major Gray wrote to Mathews with a melancholy summation of Charlebois's bad behaviour.

> I have transmitted some time ago a Charge Against the Lieutenant of Militia of Point Clair, for Beating a Soldier in Our Regiment, which he has done some others of the Soldiers before, but rather than Encourage any disputes betwixt the men and the Inhabitants, I over looked it[. A]t this time I could not[,] so I entered a process against him[. T]he determination of the Court, I here enclose[.] I am sorry to inform you, that the men meet with many Insults from the Inhabitants, which they are obliged to Bear with, from the strick orders Given to keep clear of any Dispute.

Gray had no redress against such abuses except through civil law, which he avoided like the plague. In his words, "It must be great provocation [that] will drive me to have anything to do with the Country People.... If the Commander in Chief knows the Character of the Lieutenant of Malitia he would give orders to turn him out of His Office, in short hes every thing that's bad nor no advantage to the Service, as I knew these three years."[18]

As General Moses Hazen had either not arrived in the north, or declined to accept the command, Washington's military secretary advised Heath on January 8 that command in the north should be left in the hands of Colonel George Reid, or the eldest officer in the New Hampshire brigade, an instruction that unwittingly sowed the seeds of a future command struggle.[19]

Chittenden's response to Washington's sentiments scarcely read true in view of his council's position on boundary issues:

> I am exceeding unhappy when I view the critical Situation of the Interest of the United States and the great Evils which attend the people in this Quarter by the unhappy internal Broils and Contentions caused by the Disputes between them and the several adjacent States.

He then attempted to convince Washington of the republic's dedication to "the grand Cause of Liberty" and assured him of Vermont's devotion to his disinterested leadership. As Vermont no longer had any regiments in the Continental service, this must have been a bitter pill for Washington to swallow. The governor closed by reporting that there were many Vermonters still held prisoner in Canada, a comment likely intended to disguise the continuation of the negotiations.[20]

At Schenectady, 2NH's Regimental Orders of January 19 instructed the company commanders to immediately make out returns of the men's clothing, arms, and ammunition, and "confine and bring to tryal every man they may find that has Sold or Squanderd any article they may have Drawn." In the future, the men were to be inspected weekly. A warning was issued that any NCO or soldier who was detected destroying or plundering the barracks or the property of the inhabitants would be severely punished without benefit of a court martial. Further, any NCO or soldier found more than a half-mile from the barracks without a pass from his company commander would be punished. The adjutant was to select a police serjeant of the day, who would be answerable for the cleanliness of the barracks, the men, and their arms. Such warnings were usually indicative of problems that had already occurred.

The next day, orders were given to distribute the 2NH as follows:

	Captain	Subaltern	Serjeant	Rank and File
At Johnstown	1	2	1	8
Fort Hous[e]	1	2	1	8
Fort Harkeman	1	2	4	50
Bells House			Cpl	6
Fort Ranceler	1	2	With the remainder of the regiment.	

All soldiers who had not had smallpox were to remain at Schenectady under the care of a captain and subaltern. After their vaccinations, they would be posted to their companies. The captain at Fort Herkimer was to mount a guard in the blockhouse at Fort Dayton and a non-commissioned officer and squad at the Little Falls' mills. As well, he was to send "Continental Scouts" toward Stanwix. The detachment at Fort House was to send out scouts to range north as far as the Jerseyfield patent. Both garrisons were to furnish men to any small posts contiguous to their own to prevent enemy scouts from taking possession. As Willett had done before him, Reid set his headquarters at Fort Rensselaer, which was the most central location to assemble forces when necessary.

———————

On January 23, Captain Moody Dustin, apparently in the role of regimental adjutant, wrote to fellow New Hampshire captain, David McGregor, reporting that, as ordered by Lieutenant-Colonel Reid, he had dispatched Lieutenant Joshua Merrow to Fort Rensselaer where he was in command of a party composed of an ensign, twelve serjeants, six drummers, and fifty-six rank and file. Merrow, two serjeants, and eighteen rankers would garrison Fort House, while Lieutenant George Frost, three serjeants, a drummer, and eighteen men, would do the same for Fort Johnstown. Frost received a specific order from Reid to keep out scouts beyond Ticonderoga, which would be no mean feat in the dead of winter.

As soon as Forts "Harkiman" and "Ransler" were manned, McGregor was to prepare returns of the men in each garrison so that the colonel could order the contractors to supply provisions. Dustin set a system of rotation for the various posts and reported that Captain Caleb Robinson would be at Fort Rensselaer on February 1 to muster the troops. The soldiers were to have forty rounds of ammunition each and any deficiencies were to be made up by the artillery officer. McGregor was urged to send down all men who had not had smallpox, as the 2NH surgeon, Dr. Henry, had made "every nessary preparation for their reception." Merrow marched from Schenectady on January 24.[21]

———————
———————

On January 24, Captain Daniel Robertson, 84th Royal Highland Emigrants (84RHE) signed a return for the garrison of Oswegatchie which listed: one captain, two subalterns, one surgeon, one Indian interpreter, one gunner, three serjeants, two drummers, and fifty-two rank and file.[22]

On the first day of February, Major Ross signed a "State of the Garrison of Carleton Island":

Royal Artillery	One serjeant, one bombardier, one gunner, nine privates.
Chasseurs (Hanau Jägers)	Three serjeants, three corporals, fourteen privates.
34th Regiment	One captain, one lieutenant, five serjeants, one artificer, six corporals, two drummers, fifty-three rank and file doing duty, twelve sick in quarters, twenty-three as artificers, twenty-nine prisoners with the enemy.
2KRR	One major, three captains, seven lieutenants, one ensign, one adjutant, one surgeon, nine serjeants doing duty, three sick, three as artificers, thirteen corporals and one as artificer, nineteen drummers, and two "sick present," one hundred and twenty-six privates doing duty, forty-six present, fifty-five as artificers, sixteen prisoners with the enemy.
Naval Department	One hundred and seventy-nine.
Engineers Department	Twenty.
Loyalists	Sixteen.

Those men on command who were absent with leave and absent sick were not noted.

Brigadier Powell submitted a return for the far upper posts this same day. The numbers for Niagara were:

King's (8th) Regiment	Three captains, five lieutenants, one

	quartermaster, one surgeon, thirteen serjeants, six drummers, two hundred rank and file on duty, thirty-five sick in quarters.
Rangers	One lieutenant-colonel, six captains, twelve lieutenants, one adjutant, one quartermaster, one surgeon, twenty-seven serjeants, eighteen drummers, three hundred and seventy-two rank and file on duty, and thirty-one sick in quarters.
Navy	Twenty-four.
Royal Artillery	Seventeen.
53rd Regiment	Five.
Brant's Volunteers	Twenty-one.
Indian Department	One hundred and forty-three.
Indians	One hundred and twenty-nine.
Teamsters	Twenty-four.[23]

Watercolour by Herbert Knötel, circa 1948. (Courtesy of the Anne S.K. Brown Military Collection, Brown University Library.)

Surgeon Wasmus recorded that Sorel's garrison practised snow-shoeing every day and that the weather continued to be very cold, with more snow falling. A deserter from von Specht's regiment with frostbitten feet was retaken and it was necessary to amputate five toes on his right foot. Wasmus wryly noted, "When he is well again, he will be hanged. Why not hang him right now? He would no longer

Non-commissioned officer, Prinz Ludwig's Dragoon Regiment, 1782. A fur cap and Indian shoes keep this dragoon warm in the harsh Quebec winter.

have to suffer all that pain." Probably, that was the very point; that is, "*pour encouragez les autres!*"[24]

───────────────

On February 6, Terence Smyth, a son of Dr. George Smyth of the Secret Service, arrived in Canada after nine months' imprisonment and reported that he had broken out of jail and escaped to Arlington, where he was helped by Governor Chittenden and Ethan and Ira Allen "in a private manner, to join a British scouting party which they knew to be in the neighbourhood." Ethan had told Terence that Vermont would return to its allegiance within two months if a sufficient British force was sent and gave him an anonymous letter that read in part: "Jealousy rages high about us in the United States. The turning point is whether Vermont confederates with Congress or not which I presume will not be done. Heaven forbid it."[25]

On February 7, Lernoult notified the army that General Alured Clarke would tour the province to inspect the arms, accoutrements, and clothing of the British troops. Von Loos wrote to Riedesel advising that Clarke had left Quebec City on February 11. Meanwhile, the concerts continued and a ball was to be held at month's end and a week later a ladies' ball "at the premiers." The old brigadier had been smitten by a young Canadienne named Cornelia who frequently visited the Riedesels, and he sent her his regards.[26]

On February 14, Jessup sent a letter to headquarters on Sherwood's behalf, asking for a supply of clothing for the Loyal Blockhouse. Jessup had heard that Fraser had drawn ranging suits for his men at the Yamaska Blockhouses and wrote that these suits or, even better, blanket coats, caps, mittens, leggings, and moccasins for twenty men would answer his needs.

That same day, Fraser reported that his St. Francis River scout had returned after being out for nineteen days. After their native guide deserted, the scouts had stumbled about in deep, soft snow, attempting to break a path to Lake St. Francis, but were forced to abort the mission when provisions ran low and a storm threatened. He would send them out again with a second party, and together they could take it in turns to compact the trail.

Lieutenant William Tyler, KR, submitted a report to Fraser about the "Grand Scout" to Hazen's Road. He had left on February 2, but after a march of four and half days, the weather turned very wet and foggy, provisions ran short, and he fell ill and was forced to abort. The next day, Fraser reported that Lieutenant David Jones, LR, had set out with a new scout for Hazen's Road with one of Tyler's men who knew the way. As well, scouts between the two blockhouses were regularly maintained along the Yamaska River.[27]

On February 16, an order from Riedesel was recorded in Jessup's Orderly Book instructing all the regiments in Sorel District to assist the inhabitants in any manner necessary to execute the governor's order to thresh out all their grain.

This same day, 1KRR Light Infantryman, Private William Parker, an accomplished Secret Agent and "scouter," wrote an amazing petition to Governor Haldimand. In an age when men of humble station rarely had the nerve or confidence to address a high official with a request, the document was as remarkable for its temerity as it was for its moral content — a plea against racial inequality.

> These troublesome lines I hope your Excellency will excuse. It is Sir from a sensible feeling I have for my fellow Creatures that urges me to pettition to you. I have for a Series of time past Scouting and reconitring in the Country, but there are Black people that has been of great Service to his Majestys Scouts has this late Summer came in Volantarily with me in hopes of gaining there freedom, but for their Loyallty they now are render'd Slaves in Montreall. I was out three times last Summer and brought in Sixteen[.] If your Excellency would be so kind as to Order the poor people there freedom as they are dayly complaining to me to pettition for them. I desire nothing for my trouble for bringing them in and the Ensuing Summer I Could have the Generall part of Scanactady in with me.[28]

Von Loos reported to Riedesel on February 17 that he had inspected the Anhalt-Zerbst regiment, found it in good order and was "particularly pleased with them." He reported having much trouble with "the drunken capers of Peusch," by whom he may have meant Georg Pausch, the Hanau Artillery commander. Loos had heard that the maiden Cordelia was visiting the baron and sent her fifteen kisses. His health was poor and he had little sleep and a poor appetite and urged Riedesel to "take pity on my poor beard and my blood-letting" and send a surgeon who understood the business, as there were none in his brigade. He closed with "Adieu, dear friend. One thousand compliments to your whole house from the roof to the cellar."[29]

––––––––––––

Alarming reports of an enemy build-up had begun with Sherwood's report of January 30 regarding Roger Stevens's gruelling thirty-day mission to deliver dispatches and collect intelligence. When Stevens visited two of his contacts, code-named "Plain Truth" and "John True Heart," they reported that Washington's principal army was in the Jerseys and intended to join with four thousand French troops and invade New York City. More pertinent, it was said that four thousand French troops were assembling at Albany and that Congress had approved their enlisting and supporting six thousand rebels for an attack on Canada; however, there were no preparations underway to establish magazines or any other evidence of a winter campaign on the frontiers. The informants agreed that Cornwallis was taken. Even so:

> Friends to Government in the country are not disheartened but still entertain hopes from the universal dislike the Americans have to the French troops on account of their religion and from the Enormous Taxes for dutys which Congress have lately put on Tea, Rum, Shugar, Salt, Bread, Meat, Wearing apparel, &c. This occasions mobs and club fighting in almost every part of America. The populace say they first took arms against Taxation and will not endure it from Congress.

Although Stevens lacked judgment and was woefully indiscreet, he was as daring and clever as a wolverine. He submitted a plan to improve the collection of intelligence by using his brother Abel as a courier. Roger

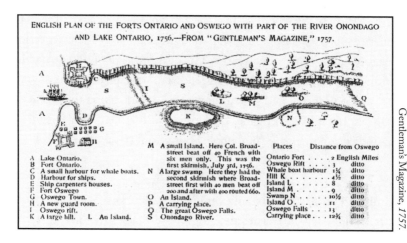

ENGLISH PLAN OF THE FORTS ONTARIO AND OSWEGO WITH PART OF THE RIVER ONONDAGO AND LAKE ONTARIO, 1756.—FROM "GENTLEMAN'S MAGAZINE," 1757.

A Lake Ontario.
B Fort Ontario.
C A small harbour for whale boats.
D Harbour for ships.
E Ship carpenters houses.
F Fort Oswego
G Oswego Town.
H A new guard room.
I Oswego rift.
K A large hill.   L. An Island.

M A small Island. Here Col. Broadstreet beat off 40 French with six men only. This was the first skirmish, July 3rd, 1756.
N A large swamp Here they had the second skirmish where Broadstreet first with 40 men beat off 200 and after with 400 routed 660.
O An Island.
P A carrying place.
Q The great Oswego Falls.
S Onondago River.

Places	Distance from Oswego	
Ontario Fort	 2	English Miles
Oswego Rift	 3	ditto
Whale boat harbour	1¼	ditto
Hill K	. . . . 4½	ditto
Island L	 8	ditto
Island M	 9	ditto
Swamp N	. . . . . 10½	ditto
Island O	 11	ditto
Oswego Falls	. . . 11	ditto
Carrying place	. . . 12¾	ditto

claimed Abel was "a Loyal Man, entirely unsuspected among the Rebels" and known as a great hunter by "the ruling men on the frontiers" and would be entirely free to roam about. A meeting place could be set and he would bring messages there from "John True Heart" and "Plain Truth" to be picked up by Roger. Sherwood harboured doubts about this proposal, but information was at a premium and desperate measures were necessary.

Stevens's intelligence about French troops at Albany alarmed the governor. Why Haldimand believed the rebels could raise six thousand fresh troops to support their ally is a mystery, but he was unaware of the great difficulty they were under trying to fill up the Continental Line and the Levies, and seemed to think the States had a bottomless pit of willing manpower. Sherwood was ordered to redouble his efforts to confirm the rebels' intentions. This fresh intelligence pushed the governor into reoccupying Oswego.[30]

The plan to occupy Oswego was a long time in gestation. Ever since the failure of St. Leger's 1777 expedition against Fort Stanwix, the Six Nations had agitated with the British to again take post there. Even before St. Leger had left Oswego to go to Ticonderoga, General Schuyler alarmed the Iroquois by stating his intention to occupy the site with a considerable force. Schuyler's claim led to a flurry of deputations to Niagara and Quebec City with complaints that, now the king's troops were gone from Oswego, Indian Territory was wide open to rebel incursions. The Indians delivered a compelling recommendation that the site be permanently occupied as a measure of Britain's commitment to the security of the Confederacy. Without that safeguard, their "Warriors could not go from Home while the Enemy were so near them, without exposing their villages, their Women and Children to Danger." True as these sentiments were, then-governor, Guy Carleton, lacked the resources to comply.

A year later, the new governor, Frederick Haldimand, answered Butler's question about occupying Oswego by saying it was not yet possible, but he thought the natives should be comforted that a fort and naval depot were being built on Carleton Island; however, the natives were quite unimpressed. In their view, Oswego was the only proper place to effectively prevent the rebels from invading their country. Shortly after receipt of this advice, the governor reported to Germain that it was "critical to take Post at Oswego or somewhere in the neighbourhood" to retain the Confederacy and that it was "impossible[,] consistent with His Majesty's Interest[,] to reject their Solicitation."

Haldimand explained to Niagara's commandant in the spring of 1779 why he had failed to occupy Oswego the year before. The governor noted that the distress that Niagara's garrison had experienced over the

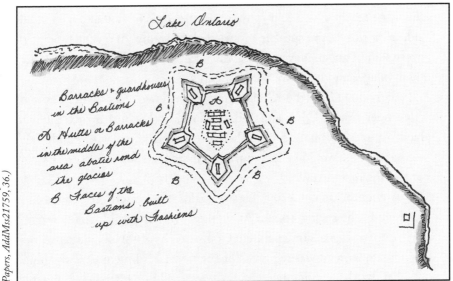

John W. Moore, 2009, after Dietrick Brehm, 1779. (Haldimand Papers, AddMss21759, 36.)

A sketch of Old Fort Ontario. Prepared by staff captain Dietrick Brehm during his tour of the upper posts, the sketch shows the foundation upon which Ross later rebuilt the fort.

winter due to the scarcity of provisions, verified the absolute necessity of making the greatest economy in their distribution, and, "if Major Butler cannot fall upon some method to diminish the consumption made by the savages, it will not be possible notwithstanding every exertion, to get up a sufficient supply. This difficulty alone prevented my taking possession of Oswego last fall. I must, however, absolutely do it this year, not only to satisfy the Indians, but for our own security."

In May 1779, in preparation for the reoccupation, Haldimand sent his staff captain, Dietrick Brehm, on a survey of the upper posts, including the site of the old works at Oswego. His report was quite discouraging, noting that substantial damage had been done to the logs facing the outworks and that the bastions were choked with earth.

Just a month later, the Iroquois were in great distress over the rebels' slow, relentless invasion of their territory with an overwhelming force. On June 19, a large deputation of chiefs came to Montreal to deliver a message to Lieutenant-Colonel John Campbell of the Quebec Indian Department (QID). They demanded to know why the governor had not kept his promise to send them assistance as soon as the ice went out and insisted that a fort be built at Oswego as a depot for their supplies. Further, that their "son," Sir John Johnson, should be sent at once to their aid. In emphasis, the speaker threw a belt of wampum on the table with every sign of anger. Nevertheless, the occupation proved impossible and their villages and fields were devastated.

Early in 1780, the Confederacy's headmen met with Captains Alexander Fraser, QID, and Gilbert Tice, 6NID, to instruct them to have Sir John, Claus, and Campbell "exert themselves" with Haldimand so that no time would be lost in the spring to take possession of Oswego, or else the rebels would.[31]

A month later, Germain gave Haldimand approval to reoccupy Oswego in the spring. In late April, the governor confidentially warned Sir John that Leake's Independent Company could not join his expedition to Johnstown, as it was required for the re-establishment of Oswego.

Yet, by that September, the post was still not established and two Onondaga and three Cayuga chiefs visited Haldimand at Chateau St. Louis in Quebec City, demanding to know why. Haldimand explained that, just after sending his message to them in early spring, he had received intelligence that the rebels were preparing boats at Saratoga and Albany to go up the Mohawk River to take possession of Oswego. He had already appointed "your Patron, the late Sr. Wm Johnson's Son, Sir John Johnson" to go there with his first battalion; however, a few weeks later, he heard this was not the rebels' true intention. Instead, they had a large army under Moses Hazen, which was said to be coming up the Connecticut River to invade the lower province, and he had put a stop to Sir John's proceeding.

So, after several years of native importuning, Haldimand was entirely aware of their opinions concerning Oswego. As well, he was equally aware that the far upper posts would be lost if the rebels gained control of Lake Ontario. Occupying Oswego would be their first ploy in that game and then the fur trade would suffer severely, as all traffic would have to be diverted along the Ottawa River route.[32]

Thus, on February 18, 1782, Haldimand ordered Ross to make all necessary preparations to be able, as soon as the lake became navigable, to take post at Oswego.

> It is unnecessary to observe to you how much depends on Keeping this Intention secret to the last instant and even on your Departure it may be Serviceable to give out your destination [as] Niagara, as the difference of a few days may Establish your Post without Loss and beyond the Efforts of the Enemy to recover. The Preparations of such Materials as do not appear to be wanted at Carleton Island will naturally create conjectures; to prevent them you would do well to intimate that Brigadier Powell had applied for all that could be spared from your Post to assist in Repairs of the Works and Barracks at Niagara and fitting up Habitations for the new Settlers.
>
> If the Enemy do intend an attempt upon this Province the Possession of Oswego is certainly an Object of great Importance to them and the first they will turn their thoughts to in the Spring. We must therefore endeavour to prevent it by a more Early

> Exertions and as the first Object to be Considered is
> to secure yourself from Insult you will pay your whole
> attention to it, taking Advantage of what remains of the
> old Bastions and afterwards proceed to Building.

Captain Twiss would take with him a plan for Ross's guidance and
Adjutant General Lernoult would advise what troops and artillery were
to be taken.

> You will nevertheless Consider that from the Confidence
> I have in your Zeal and Experience and from your Local
> Knowledge I allow every Latitude that your Circumstances
> shall appear to you to require. I leave my Dispatch to
> Brigadier Genl. Powell open for your Perusal, that you
> may be acquainted with my wishes & thence confer more
> fully with him and form your plans accordingly. It being
> impossible at this Distance and unacquainted with Local
> Circumstances to enter into Detail with the Brigadier
> and to your Prudence I trust for a Judicious Arrangement
> and Rapid Execution of my views.

Ross was to take 370 men from Carleton Island and Powell would
send another two hundred from Niagara. When Haldimand had executed
a similar task in 1759, his work parties had repelled an attack in the midst
of fortifying the place, so he was very well qualified to give advice.

Similar instructions were given to Powell, with many cautions about
concealing the plan, pointing out that, although Niagara was farther from
rebel country, there were many Indians friendly to the rebels who visited
their relatives and friends in the nearby native settlements. Even Butler
was not to be told and, as a further subterfuge, when the troops were about
to embark, he suggested they be told they were going to reinforce Detroit.

Haldimand wished to have Joseph Brant recalled, as he would be
most useful during the reoccupation of Oswego, particularly as it was
one of his fondest hopes, so Powell was instructed to advise him "that
you have something of importance to communicate" and desiring him to

return to Niagara with all possible expedition.[33]

Riedesel reported to Haldimand from Sorel on February 18 that he was about to set out to meet Major-General Clarke in Montreal to take him on a tour of the district. The baron's concerns about his seniority over Clarke had not prevented Haldimand from using his services to assist his British counterpart. Comments about Clarke in German correspondence were always guarded and it is difficult to determine their true opinion of the man as an individual or as a soldier.[34]

On a purely administrative level, Powell reported about some disturbing "transactions which have lately passed in Lieutenant-Colonel Butler's Rangers.... It was impossible for me to suppress the letter which has brought those things to light, as not only the lives and honour of several of the Officers were struck at, but a mutiny might likewise have been excited in the Corps had not Colonel Butler and his Officers an opportunity to convince the men there was no injustice done them." More on this upset later.[35]

More news came from Ross at Carleton Island on February 20. He reported that there had been no disruptions caused by enemy scouts since November and the time had been spent improving the "stockading" of the works and clearing land for cultivation. An accidental fire had consumed the naval artificers' barracks and contents, including sails and rigging and an old vessel (likely in dry dock), although a nearby storehouse had been saved. Ross noted that the vessels wintering over at the island would be ready for sailing when the lake opened. A new barrack was being sited well out of danger from flammable materials and the dangers of the excavation work. Two small pieces of ordnance had been placed as signal guns and, lastly, a party of scouts was to be dispatched soon to the Mohawk Valley.[36]

A letter from Sir Henry Clinton, C-in-C America, dated February 22, warned Haldimand that intelligence from Connecticut indicated that, despite a great deal of talk about an attack on New York City in the spring,

Brigadier-General George Rogers Clark, 1752–1818. Clark's exploits as Virginia's senior commander on the northwest frontier gave the British considerable concern throughout the war.

the real plan was to invade Canada. Apparently, Philip Schuyler had told this to one of his closest confidants and Lafayette was in France proposing the project. Furthermore, large stores of provisions were at the falls of the Ohio River and George Rogers Clark was to command two Continental Regiments and one thousand French and Spanish to take Detroit and its dependencies. The rebels had been encouraged by accounts from escaped and exchanged prisoners who revealed how weak the garrison was there.

Rebel officers claimed there would be a second expedition in the summer and that an agreement had been reached to give the country to the French if the endeavour was successful. All of this fuelled Haldimand's already high level of anxiety.[37]

Major Gray received orders from Captain Mathews on January 23:

> In Order to facilitate the Transport to the Upper Posts in the Early Part of the Season, the first and Second Battalions of the Royal Regt of new York will be Employed on that Service, for which the men will Receive a Gratuity that will be communicated to you by Captain Maurer, who has His Excellency's Commands to arrange with You, the Number of Batteaux that can be manned, and all other matter that Can relate to the Troops on that Duty — It is His Excellency's

Command that no men who are fit for this Service shall be withheld from it, Except the Officers Servants, on any Pretence Whatever."[38]

Lieutenant-Colonel von Kreutzbourg reported:

During the entire … winter my Jägers were continuously snowshoeing together with the natives of [Kahnawake] employed on patrols and scouting parties. We are the best of friends, and the natives stated that it was a good thing for the Jägers to have been sent out with them as they were men like themselves. I must confess that I have not had a single deserter during all these expeditions of scouting and small commandos. However, there is not another detachment from any of the other troops from which not one or the other has deserted, mostly of the Braunschweig troops. When requesting the General for relief of my commando at Carleton Island by other troops of Jägers, even he confessed that he could not rely upon any Braunschweig or Zerbst Jägers to the same high degree as he could mine. He is always willing to flatter and to compliment but, otherwise, nothing can be gotten out of him.

The colonel's sentiments about natives was a striking reverse from his opinions of 1777 when he referred to them as the "horrible tribes" and had them flogged out of his camp.[39]

Very specific and careful orders were issued to these Jäger scouts about methods and frequency of signaling, the uses of paroles and countersigns, precautions against surprise, the making of fires, cutting of firewood, speaking aloud at night, keeping rifles loaded, frequent inspections of priming and dealing with native parties and enemy patrols.[40]

On February 20, Major Andrew Finck, in his capacity as a Tryon County "commissioner for conspiracy," wrote to Governor Clinton about the plight of several families whose men had been carried off to Canada. In the process, he gave a picture of the hardships endured by their parents, wives, and children.

> Youll find in the List herewith inclosed you, three of the name of Shultys and Phillip Bellinger with two of his sons Christian and Andrew also Lieut John Zuiley [Zeilie] who is a Brother in Law of mine and the other very near neighbours, their Families all Suffering for the want of them and in particular that of Lieut Zuiley's who in the first place had a large Family of small children, and shortly before he was taken married into another which makes it very considerable. I therefore beg your Excellency to do every thing in your power to bring about an Exchange for the above mentioned persons (if not for the whole.)[41]

On February 22, a remarkable event occurred in Vermont's assembly when Isaac Tichenor, a former New York State Commissary at Bennington in 1777 and later a practising lawyer and influential Vermont assemblyman, engineered the dissolution of the Eastern and Western Unions. This accomplishment drove a firm wedge into the political regime so carefully constructed by the Allen faction. The next day, Governor Clinton laid documents before the New York State Legislature proving that Vermont's executive council had been in treasonable communication with Quebec's government. Ironically, in this same time frame, Ira Allen and Jonas Fay appeared in Congress and truculently refused to abandon the two unions.[42]

On February 27, after so many promises, the long-suffering 2NH finally received an issue of clothing. Pathetically, Moody Dustin's Company received only three coats and six blankets, although their receipt of fifty-seven waistcoats and twenty-nine pairs of shoes and stockings was reasonable. Yet, if Dustin's issues were representative of what the other companies received, the troops must have prayed that the rest of the winter would be mild.[43]

On February 24, Lieutenant Walter Sutherland returned from a scout and arrived at the Loyal Blockhouse where he remained in compliance with Haldimand's new instruction that all parties be detained until their reports were received at headquarters to allow them to be easily contacted to answer any questions that might arise. Sutherland's intelligence and a sheaf of newspapers were submitted to Lieutenant Patrick Langan, 6NID, and then expressed by Claus to Quebec City. Langan received a second report from Sutherland the next day advising that preparations were being made to invade Canada.[44]

In Riedesel's letter to Haldimand of February 25, he said he felt the misfortunes of the last campaign as deeply as if they had affected his own country. He was concerned that only a miracle would save Canada, which he felt sure would be attacked by Washington and the French general, Comte de Rochambeau — the same winning leadership combination that had forced Cornwallis's capitulation at Yorktown — unless orders from France changed their plans. In Riedesel's opinion, no matter how the attack was designed, Haldimand's preparations would cost the enemy dear.

In contrast, he prosaically noted that the British and Provincial troops in Montreal district had received General Clarke with all honours and hospitality.[45]

On February 26, the adjutant general instructed Riedesel to have the 34th and 44th Regiments and Jessup's Corps send detachments to Sorel to

I.F. Heerwagen, 1777, (HStAM WHK 28/40, Digitales Archiv Marburg.)

make up their small arms' shortages. The two Regular regiments were to receive "muskets" and the Loyal Rangers, carbines. The King's Rangers and Meyers's Independent Company were to be given "Black Carbines." If the first three corps had men capable of repairing arms, they were to be sent to Sorel and all arms unfit for service or not repairable were to be sent into stores.[46]

On the last day of February, Roger Stevens submitted a detailed report from the Loyal Blockhouse. As with all such reports, there were facts, speculations, and inaccuracies, all of which had to be sifted through at headquarters and compared to other intelligence sources. Stevens's brother Abel had met him at the agreed rendezvous with a variety of news: many Vermonters believed that Congress were against them and were discouraged about the possibilities of joining the union; the French army would bypass the Quebec posts, get rapidly into the country, arm the Canadiens, and cut the communications to the upper posts; tailors were busy making clothing for the Continental Army, but had not sufficient supplies to clothe every twentieth man. Lastly, forty gun carriages had been dug up at Ticonderoga. If by Vermonters, this act was in contravention of the agreement made with Commodore Chambers.[47]

Sutherland's intelligence report was received on February 28 at Quebec City headquarters. It said in part:

> Since he (Cornwallis) was taken, the Rebels are in the Greatest Spirits and think they have got the Ball at their own Feet — The friends to Government in General Still retain their Integrity, but some of them are much shaken and daily falling off.
>
> It is Reported, but does not find much Credit, that 15000 men French and Americans will be in Albany the beginning of March.... [It] is Certain that their's a french Commissary in Albany [who] buys all the Pork Flour &c he Can & has raised the price of flour ... and that Lodgings are preparing for the Reception of the Officers, Stables and forrage for their Horses — one Man in Albany has got Stables rady for 40 Horses, it is likewise Certain that a Vast deal of their Equipage is come to Windsor....
>
> Lord Sterling Commands in Albany. Colonel Willett on the Mohawk River; Number of Troops in Albany 72. — In Saratoga 150. [O]n the Mohawk River in different posts 480. — All the Militia above Albany have Received orders to get a pair of Snow Shoes each, I believe this was Occasioned by a Deserter from Niagara or some Indians who left that Place Who Reported that Col Buttler was to Make a Descent on some Part of the Country With Some Whites & Indians to the amount

of 700. The Rebels are daily Enlisting, Three Regiments are to be raised Immediately for the Defence of the Frontiers they Enlist them for three Years — The Militia are to hold themselves in Readiness — there is a great deal of artillery Sent from the Province of New York to N. England, where they are forming Large Magasines of Provisions, Especially in Hartford — It is privately Whispered that the french and Rebel Troops who are Said to Come to Albany, are to March to N. England and attack Halifax as Early as the Season will permit, and that another Army Will be sent to Niagara, and that a French Fleet Will be in the Gulph Early in the Spring.

Colonel Allan had Several Disputes with the Province of N. York about the Line Run'd between the two Provinces & Congress granted the Line Should Cross the Mohawk River three Miles above Schenectady & than go S.W. until opposite to Fort Herkimer & then W. until opposite to Oneda Lake, and N. to Lake Ontario, then to take an East Course and Come in at Split Rock — but Col. Allan took in more than granted to the East and burned 9 Houses and drove off the Inhabitants[.] Col. Van Schuyk was sent to oppose him — he took 14 Prisoners who made their Escape from Albany Goal Some time after, Colonel Hazen is gone to New England to endeavour to Settle the Matter....

The friends to Government Who used to send Intelligence is under great apprehensions and Some already Ruined on account of the Liberty given to Prisoners in Canada, particularly Captain Vroman Who sent a Letter to Shenecady by one hanson with the Names of all the friends in Albany and Schenectady.... I was likewise informed that Letters is frequently Sent to Schenectady from Montreal. Phillips & one Markham are particularly mentioned. Philips Was the first Man who Scaled the walls of Montreal to join the Rebels in the year 1775 & Remained with them until the year 1776 — Markham was a noted Rebel While in Schenectady and Came to Canada With the Rebels, it is said he was left in Montreal in order to send Intelligence down the Country.... There is two french men in Albany Who Comes very often to Canada, I was informed that they were at Albany & was making ready to Come off, when I left the Country, they Come to Chateauguary and Keep the Woods on the West Side Lake Champlain until Opposite Crown Point.

As I was not able to get a Certain Account of the french and Rebel armies Said to be Making Ready to Come to Canada (notwithstanding I remained 11 Days in the Country until our Tracks was discovered.) I left Parker and Brown the Trustiest of my party, with orders to Remain untill they Could find the Certainty of it. The Most Intelligence Persons in Albany and Schenectady are doing all they Can to get at the Bottom of the Affair, they are likewise to get all the news papers and all other Intelligence that they Can Collect — I left the Scotsh bush near Johnstown the 11 Instn.[48]

The same day, a report arrived at headquarters from Sherwood about the Secret Service activities of two Royal Yorkers, Corporal Mathias Snetsinger and Private John Helmer. A man they had sent into Albany discovered that eight thousand stand of arms and as many suits of clothes had been deposited at Claverack in late January and a number of Cornwallis's cannon destined for Claverack were at Hartford in Connecticut.

Helmer's brother had gone to Boston and discovered there were arms, clothing, artillery, et cetera ... said to be accumulated to equip an army to take Canada next spring. Part of that army would ascend the Mohawk River. After taking Niagara, they would come down the St. Lawrence. The other part, composed of seven thousand French with some rebel troops, would invade via the Connecticut River route. They were to "Embody & Arm" the Canadiens. He was also told that a vessel from Quebec had been taken in the fall with dispatches indicating that Allen had sold Vermont to Haldimand. A brigade of French troops had arrived at Norwich, Connecticut, and would be reinforced by a body of militia to subdue Vermont.

Sherwood closed by asking if Snetsinger should be sent to sink the dug-up gun carriages at Ticonderoga, where the rebels had been retrieving ironwork.[49]

Haldimand informed Ross on March 2 that, in addition to the latitude he had given him in his instructions about Oswego, should he find any unexpected difficulties in any part of the work, he had the governor's full authority to make changes and remove all obstacles whether in the engineering or any other department. He brought Ross up to date with the most recent intelligence and added that if an attempt was made against lower Quebec, he could also expect a strike against Oswego and "Diligence and Activity must Supply the Place of Resources … transport could languish or cease altogether and provisions might become scarce." The governor added a warning of likely difficulties with the Indians if the flow of foodstuffs was interrupted.[51]

Riedesel reported to the governor on March 4 that he had returned to Sorel with Clarke. Somewhat skeptically, he commented, "General Clarke has seen all that he came to see; and if he has a military memory, may have acquired a general knowledge of the country," which suggested that the two men had already exchanged some confidential thoughts about Clarke's capabilities.

The baron noted that Sherwood had made the best dispositions possible at the Loyal Blockhouse, which, although well situated, was not strong and would not hold out for long. Even with the reinforcements that had been sent, there were insufficient men for all the various duties and he recommended that Sherwood be instructed to fall back on the stronger post at Pointe-au-Fer if a superior force should appear. He added that Sherwood told him that Vermont was building three blockhouses at Castleton, Pittstown, and Rutland and that new scouts would be sent to Hazen's Road.

During his tour, Riedesel had visited Pointe-au-Fer. He was asleep in a barrack on the night of April 26 when he was awakened by a great commotion. His first thought was that the rebels had learned of his presence and sent a party to capture him, but a British officer entered the room and, in the murk of the interior, asked if he was the general. Upon hearing the reply "yes," he urged the baron to escape, as the barrack was afire. With no time to dress, the general ran through the flames and out onto the ice. There was considerable danger, as barrels of powder were stored in the barracks and the artillery pieces were loaded with canister and might discharge if the fire reached them, but Riedesel soon saw that the soldiers were successfully fighting the fire and he returned to dress himself at one of the watch fires. When he left at 6:00 a.m., the flames had been subdued and there was no further danger.

It would seem that the governor had asked Riedesel to investigate the ages of his Brunswick troops. He reported that, except for the grenadier companies which had "a large number of old people," one-quarter of the troops were over forty; however, he had also inquired about the 34th and 44th Regiments and found that the former had about seventy men over forty and the latter, about eighty. From this, he concluded that the British were of the same age range as his Brunswickers.

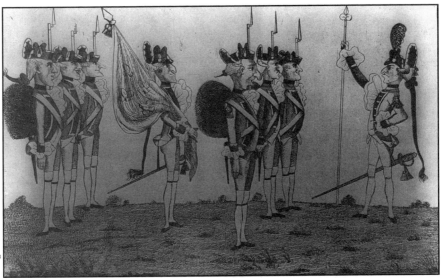

British Cartoon Prints Collection, Library of Congress, LC-USZ62-1518.

Count de Rochambeau, French general of the land forces in America, reviewing his troops, 1780. While the British enjoyed lampooning their ancient foe, the threat of a joint French and rebel attack on Canada was never taken lightly.

In another item of news, an officer and thirty Loyal Rangers had been dispatched to St. John's to cover Lieutenant Sutherland's return from Crown Point.

In the second letter that day, Riedesel evidenced that he had private sources of intelligence (most likely letters from German officers in New York City). He confirmed his earlier opinion that Washington and Rochambeau would open the campaign with an attack on Canada. It was rumoured that the Frenchman hoped he would no longer come under Washington's orders and would be able to separate his troops from the rebels and make a simple conquest assisted by Canadiens who would rise in his favour. Riedescl was of the opinion that the French court would veto the venture in favour of more advantageous expeditions. Nonetheless, preparations appeared to be underway and he would send parties down the Connecticut River to Springfield and Hartford to learn the true state of the case. He applauded Haldimand's plan to visit Sorel, as his presence would strengthen the resolve of the "good subjects" and put an end to gossip and bickering. On his part, he would attempt to smother all the news brought in by the scouts, as Haldimand had complained about the general lack of commonsense security.[52]

Perhaps fuelled by Riedesel's letter, Haldimand sent a dispatch the next day to Sir Henry Clinton, reporting the recent intelligence about preparations that indicated a renewal of the Allies' designs against Canada. He observed:

> The conduct of the Canadians obviously discovers that they are in early expectation of some revolution, from which they expect to derive advantage and tho' all my efforts have proved ineffectual in making any material discoveries there is not a doubt that an intercourse is supported between them and the French and it is from that source their Hopes are fed and their conduct influenced. A report now prevails amongst them that the Pope has issued a Bull absolving them from their oath of allegiance to the English on returning to that of France, it is likewise said that the congress have issued

a proclamation declaring pardon to all Americans who[,] having been induced to join the King's Army, will acknowledge and support the independence of the States.[53]

Loyal Ranger captain, William Fraser, asked Riedesel to request permission from the governor to allow Volunteer James McIlmoyle, formerly a serjeant in his independent company, to proceed to meet his brother, who had been left "in the country" the previous fall to enlist recruits. In a second letter, Fraser reported the return of the scout sent to Lake St. Francis. He noted that it would be of great assistance to the scouts if they were allowed to blaze a path in the same manner as St. Leger had allowed Tyler to mark the route to Hazen's Road from the Missisquoi River. Of course, such blazes were rather dangerous, as they led in two directions.[54]

Riedesel again wrote to Haldimand about St. Leger's report of a rebel flag of truce that had appeared at Pointe-au-Fer. He also enclosed Dr. Smyth's opinion about the validity of the party's passport and the newspaper that they had passed along as a "curiosity," which included a suspect speech attributed to King George. St. Leger had taken precautions to prevent communication with these fellows, as it seemed their sole purpose was to induce loyalists to desert. The governor's instructions were sought about how to deal with the party.[55]

On March 9, Riedesel notified the governor that Captain Pritchard had returned from a scout with a warning that a rebel party was heading north. As the Loyal and Yamaska blockhouses might be at risk, Sherwood and Fraser took precautions. As well, a non-commissioned officer and twelve men were sent to reinforce the woodcutters at Missisquoi Bay in case they were the target.[56]

The same day, another report sent to headquarters stated that an attempt by a Highland Emigrants' party sent via Oswego against Ellice's Mills on the Mohawk had failed because an inhabitant, who had been wounded and taken, had managed to alarm the small garrison. Of the many mills that had served the Valley prior to the war, Ellice's was the last one standing in the German Flatts district and would soon become a prime target.[57]

It was found that the rebels had reinforced their scouts below Lake George, which made the sending of dispatches and gathering of intelligence very difficult. They mounted a scout of eleven men that ranged in a circuit up the Hudson from Saratoga to Jessup's Patent and back again; another of the same strength circulated in the Fort George area; a similar one was responsible for the Kingsbury–Fort Ann district. A fourth, composed of whites and natives, patrolled back and forth from north of Ballstown to Jessup's Patent. Of course, the concern was that this increased activity was intended to mask preparations for the invasion.[58]

With all the rumours of a multi-pronged Allied attack, the Canadian Department's patrol activity was intense. On March 11, Lieutenant Luc Schmid of the Quebec Indian Department, stationed at St. Francis, sent Canadian Militia ensign, François Vassal de Monviel, one of Hertel de Rouville's company officers in 1777, and twelve Canadiens to penetrate as far as possible down Hazen's Road. As soon as they returned, he planned to send another party. Schmid reported that all of the St. Francis Abenakis were hunting and none could be found to accompany these parties, but their movements had beaten down the paths so well that patrol routes were easily covered.[59]

Fraser had sent two scouts from the upper Yamasaka Blockhouse, the first commanded by Lieutenant William Tyler of Ruiter's company, King's Rangers, and a second of Canadiens led by a serjeant.

Major Gray notified Major Lernoult, the deputy adjutant general, that an excess of 112 stand of arms had been received by 1KRR and asked what he should do with them. After six years of being inadequately armed and, ironically, well after being pulled out an active role, the battalion had received an excess of small arms and accoutrements. In contrast, the second battalion, which was still on active service, continued to be armed with Indian trade fusils.[60]

On March 15, an official dispatch was sent from Whitehall to Governor Haldimand, advising that his recommendations for overhauling the Indian Department had been acted upon. Sir John Johnson had been given a warrant as the Superintendent General and Inspector General of Indian Affairs of the Six Nations and all other Indians resident in the province of Quebec, which included the territory north of the Ohio River and east of the Mississippi. Colonel Guy Johnson was to continue in his rank, but would have no further managerial duties. Lieutenant-Colonels Claus, Butler, and Campbell were continued in their posts: Claus with the Lachine Mohawks, Butler with the Six Nations and their affiliates and Campbell, and the Canada Indians, although there was a complex overlapping of duties that remain a mystery. Captain Alexander Fraser,

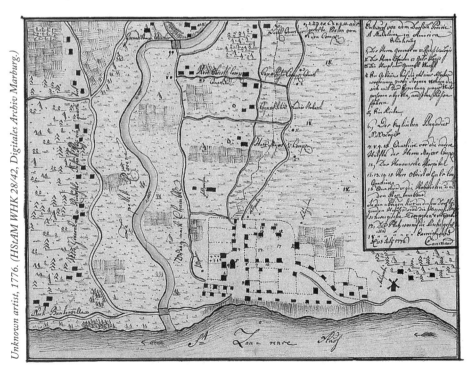

Unknown artist, 1776. (HStAM WHK 28/42, Digitales Archiv Marburg.)

La Prairie, headquarters of the Hesse-Hanau Jägers.

34th Regiment, was to continue in a key role as Campbell's deputy.[61]

On March 16, William Parker, one of Sutherland's favourite assistants, returned from the Mohawk and submitted a report requesting payment of his expenses and advising that he had brought in another two blacks who desired to join the Royal Yorkers.[62]

The same day, von Loos reported to Riedesel from La Prairie, where he was touring. He had visited von Kreutzbourg, who wished to be remembered to the baron, and together they had gone to Kahnawake. At noon, he dined well and in the afternoon listened to a duet of Bockerini, played whist, souped "*à la Bichamel*," went to bed at ten and rose at seven, drank tea, and planned to start for St. John's at nine. From there, he would go to Sorel, but realized he had missed the baroness, "Lady Fritz," and "la belle Cordelia" and the children, and asked that his respects be sent to them.[63]

On March 20, the British government that had conducted the war almost from its outset wobbled to a collapse and the king was forced to recognize that the war for America was lost. It was not the loss of Cornwallis's army that prompted the fall, but the shocking defeat of the Royal Navy, which had led to the capitulation and created a deep-set insecurity. An immense volume of treasure had been expended around the world; the Bourbon navies outnumbered Britain's and her collective will was weak. The new administration began to pursue peace talks, but all of this was unknown in Canada for many weeks.[64]

Mohawk Valley resident Elizabeth Suts recalled that, "from the early part in March … the Inhabitants [were] Continually Annoyed by the Skulking Indians" and that John Kring was taken from along the Mohawk River and William Gray from near Cobleskill. Vermonter Benjamin Sawyer was taken at Crown Point, perhaps by Sutherland when he drowned the gun carriages.[65]

On March 11, James Lovell at Boston forwarded a letter to Washington written by Jacob Bayley of Cöos. Although Lovell thought Bayley's anger over the insincerity of some of Vermont's council in its negotiations with Congress bordered on irrationality, he believed the letter's information was of substantial importance. Bayley had written:

> You may remember that I mentioned the case of Captain [Lieutenant-Colonel] Thos Johnson to you, the necessity of his being exchanged in order to prove the treasonable conduct of a member of Vermont, &c. I told you Johnson had the confidence of the enemy in Canada and knew what had been transacted between them and Vermont. I am still further convinced as Captain Johnson has lately rec'd a letter from Canada and answer demanded, which he complied with, otherwise he supposed his intent to make discovery to us would be suspected by the enemy. He showed to a friend of the United States what he rec'd from and sent to Canada, which was from the enemy an enquiry whether an expedition to Canada was intended by us, or any preparations therefore, how the people stood as to a union with them in Canada, informing they intended an exhibition early to Albany, &c. Capt Johnson's return was that he heard nothing of an expedition by us to Canada and that affairs went on well with us in Vermont. In about a month doubtless other letters from Gen Haldeman will be sent to Capt Johnson. All letters and copies will be kept. Capt Johnson wishes his exchange may soon take place. His situation is really critical, for without General Washington's particular directions he is exposed to the severest punishment. If he does not correspond the enemy will suspect him and be exposed to be recalled to Canada, by which we shall lose his evidence in matters of the greatest importance. I send you this as no private correspondence with the enemy is admissible.[66]

Early in the spring, Willett's captains, Abner French and Lawrence Gros, came to Fort Plain to complete their companies with nine-months' men. A few days later, they marched back to Fort Rensselaer and, from there, sent detachments to garrison Forts House, Timmerman, and Herkimer.[67]

To counteract the reign of terror emanating from Canada and to stiffen the backbone of its potential victims, Benjamin Franklin published a masterful propaganda piece that not only affected public opinion in America, but also reverberated throughout Britain. The item was in the form of a letter purportedly sent to Haldimand by a fictitious Captain Craufurd, describing a collection of scalps taken by the Senecas. The hair was sent to his attention for forwarding to the king as proof of the natives' ardour and prowess. The scalps were supposedly contained in eight bales, each with a horrifying description of their manner of harvesting. Bale No.1 contained "43 scalps of Congress soldiers killed in different skirmishes; these are stretched on black hoops, four inch diameter; the inside of the skin painted red with a small black spot to note their being killed with bullets." No.5 contained:

> 88 scalps of women; hair long, braided in the Indian fashion, to show they were mothers; hoops blue; skin yellow ground, with little red tadpoles, to represent, by way of triumph, the tears of grief occasioned to their relations; a black scalping-knife or hatchet at the bottom, to mark their being killed with those instruments; 17 others, very gray; black hoops; plain brown color, no mark but the short club to show they were knocked down dead, or had their brains beat out.

Bales No.6 and 7 were said to contain 410 scalps of children and, horrifyingly, No.8 included "29 little infants' scalps of various sizes."

Opponents of the war in Britain made much of this revelation of the barbarism the government had been supporting. Across America, the wavering tightened their resolve.[68]

Human scalp stretched on a wooden hoop. This trophy is similar to those described in Franklin's propaganda piece. The specific meaning of the symbols painted on this example is unknown.

During March and April, a fort was built by soldiers of White's company, WL, on a high bluff in Warrensborough on the Herrick property. A second fort in the eastern section of the patent was completed and christened Fort Guile after the property's owner. From the latter base, the intrepid youngster, Ray Guile, marched in Captain Ephraim Eaton's company of Willett's on a patrol from fort to fort — to Hunter, Rensselaer, Walradt, Herkimer, and Johnstown. The circuit was repeated throughout Guile's service; at times the patrol stopped to act as a garrison, and on other occasions it went on local scouts. On one venture along the river above Fort Walradt, the men fell short of provisions. Guile recalled stopping at a Tory sympathizer's house to buy victuals, but his memory may have skipped a beat, as demand was far more likely than purchase. In any event, the man refused, but the men had spotted an outdoor oven full of meats and bread, so while a few distracted the owner, others ran poles under the oven and carried it off.[69]

On the political front, Major Andrew Finck, who had taken such a forward role during the Ross raid, was elected to the New York Assembly as the representative for Tryon County.[70]

William Feeter was in a detachment of Captain Samuel Gray's Company, WL, that marched to Fort Rensselaer. After a few days, the detachment was sent south to Bowman's Creek to chase off a party of natives and Tories. The company served out its time assisting "the militia traversing the country in pursuit of small parties of Indians and Tories that infested the country."

Christopher P. Yates wrote to a friend on March 22: "We have already had three inroads by the enemy. The last was at Bowman's Kill from where they took three of McFee's children." He reasoned the raiders wanted to frighten the neighbourhood so they could pass through unobserved. Yates feared that the enemy would infest the south side of the river in small parties and the bush would become more dangerous than ever.

During one of these forays, Conrad Getman of Captain Abner French's Company of Willett's was captured near Fort Herkimer. The season was off to a fine start.[71]

On March 23, New York passed legislation to formalize the land bounties being offered for two- and three-years' servicemen. Any class or person who furnished an able-bodied man for three years would be entitled to six hundred acres, and, for two years, 350 acres. If the man should be delivered within twenty days from the time of notification, two hundred extra acres would be awarded.[72]

By March 24, all of the Yamaska scouting parties had returned. Ensign de Monviel had been unable to locate Hazen's Road, despite the very precise information provided to him. This failure raised quite a storm and his loyalty and competence were questioned. He would have been immediately sent out again as a test, but the snow was too deep.[73]

Von Loos had arrived at Fort St. John's by March 24, after a hazardous sleigh ride over bad roads and an ugly river crossing where he came close to drowning. Every mark of attention was given to him at the fort and he reported to the baron that he knew all the taverns between Montreal and St. John's, as he and Clarke had visited them all in the Briton's covered cariole; however, not all the Germans enjoyed a jolly winter. March 30 was marred at Sorel by the suicide of a Brunswick corporal who had succumbed to the depressingly endless ice and snow.[74]

Detail from James Peachey, 1781. (Library and Archives Canada, C-002020.)

Canadiens and Indians on the ice in winter. Inured to the worst of winter weather.

4

NOTHING BUT CURSED HYPOCRISY & DECEIT

*O*n March 17, Roger Stevens forwarded a dispatch from the falls on the Onion River, deep in Vermont. His brother Abel had brought him a great deal of information, to wit: there were twelve thousand French troops and a small part of Washington's army marching to Esopus, near Kingston, where twenty thousand stand of arms had been shipped. There was a very large depot of other stores there and, after the troops combined, they were to go up the Mohawk River and fall on the weakest British posts. Orders were expected for that same army to be met by a strong fleet from France.

He noted that paper money was dead and the common people could not pay their debts and thus had risen in Boston and Connecticut against their own laws and broken up the courts. Supposedly, Colonel Allen and Dr. Jonas Fay were confined in irons by Congress due to a complaint by a "Dutch" gentleman who had come from Canada and sworn that they had signed an agreement with Haldimand. A committee of Congress had informed Vermont that, if they abandoned their new claims, they would be recognized as one of the United States and the assembly had dropped the East and West Unions. And also that New York was jailing Vermonters found in the Western Union. Such a tangle of disparate information!

Sherwood was angry and disgusted over the failed negotiations. When he forwarded Stevens's dispatch to headquarters, he commented that Allen and Fay's imprisonment was a mere blind to cover their treachery. Nothing was to be expected from Vermont "but cursed hypocrisy & deceit … I hope speedy vengeance may overtake them before they are aware of it. I think all their Frontier Towns including Castleton, Rutland and Lower Coas may be easily burned & destroyed … by employing a number of flying parties at one time."[1]

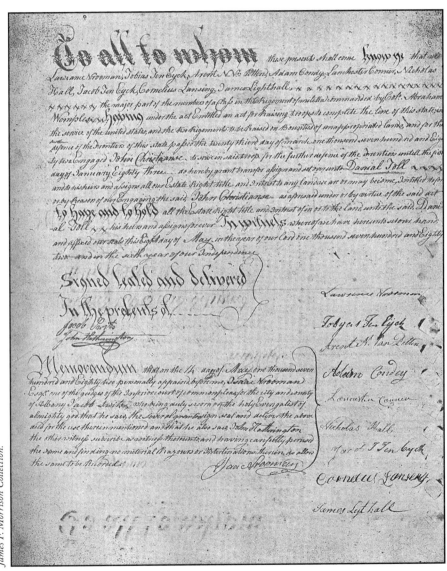

A land bounty right.

On March 23, another New York State act was passed for raising two regiments using unappropriated land bounties. As Captain Simeon Newall had received a warrant in March to raise a company, it may be that Willett's Levies had been recruiting for some time with the promise of such bounties.[2]

The spring saw the demise of John Parker, the Royal Yorker Light Infantryman who had become a particular menace to Tryon County. The English-born Parker had been brought up in Philadelphia Bush and had gone to Canada with Captain Alexander McDonell in May 1777 to join the regiment. He was a daring, active partisan whether on major raids or as a spy and recruiter. In the words of the rebel historian Simms: "He had a constitution fitted to endure all manner of hardships, and an exposure to all kinds of weather, which enabled him to traverse the wilderness at seasons most unpropitious and steal into the settlements when a foe was unexpected."

Parker had left Canada with Joe Bettys, Jonathon Miller, and a third fellow named Van Camp. Bettys carried dispatches for Sir Henry Clinton; the other three were to discover information about the French troops. Loyal Rangers' corporal, David Crowfoot, the former Green Mountain Boy who had been at the capture of Ticonderoga with Ethan Allen in 1775, left about the same time to question "Plain Truth" about Washington's plans and deliver dispatches to Ethan Allen. Soon after, Captain Meyers left Pointe-au-Fer with orders to develop a new network of informants in and about Albany to replace Smyth's, which had been betrayed. The Crown's Secret Service was hard at work.

After separating along the way, Parker ghosted into the Tory enclave of Philadelphia Bush and, in his usual bold fashion, visited a local tavern to gain news where he was seen by an erstwhile friend and betrayed.

On hearing the news, Lieutenant Amos Bennett, 3TCM, collected a party of men from south of the river and, when night had fallen, they crossed the ice on a pair of sleighs. Bennett called a halt just out of earshot of the tavern and left the men with the sleighs while he reconnoitred. Squinting through a crevice in the logs, he saw a man in a heavy fur coat standing at the fireplace. Concluding that the fellow was Parker, the lieutenant returned to the sleighs and brought his men forward, instructing them that, as soon as he entered the door, they were to take up various positions around the building.

Entering the barroom, Bennett found a number of men sitting drinking and remarked he wanted to warm himself at the fire. As latecomers often spelled trouble, the fellows nervously jerked their chairs to clear a path. Bennett stood at the fire rubbing his hands together and pretended that nothing more was on his mind than getting warm, while he guardedly eyed the man in the fur coat. When he was sure his men were in position, he stepped over, laid a hand on the man's shoulder and named Parker as his prisoner. The unarmed Tory struggled and some patrons rose to assist him, but Bennett barked that resistance was futile and, simultaneously, several armed men burst through the door.

Recognizing that Parker's friends might quickly mount a pursuit, Bennett had the captive securely bound and hustled to the sleighs. The party rushed along the snow-packed roads all the way to Albany where Parker was jailed.[3]

Just as March came to a close, there was a second victory for rebel vigilance. After separating from Parker, Joseph Bettys, Jonathon Miller, and Van Camp snowshoed to Ballstown. A misty fog was rising off the snow while the Philmore family was sugaring off in the bush. A young daughter named Lydia was collecting sap when she saw a man who was bundled in a fur coat and carrying a rifle with a knapsack and snowshoes strapped on his back. He headed toward the house of a well-known Tory widow. Ballstown had been the scene of several harrowing visits by Tories and the movement of strangers created suspicions, so Lydia ran to tell her father. Philmore simply suspected another "damned Tory" had arrived from Canada and quickly rounded up his friends Corey and Perkins. Taking up their arms, they cautiously slunk up to the widow's house.

Bettys was sitting at breakfast; his pistols lay on the table, his rifle rested on his arm and his back was to the door. One of the men went to the rear of the building to cut off an escape and the other two broke through the door. Bettys instinctively went for his rifle, but was undone, as he had failed to remove the lock cover. The men grabbed him by his collar and overpowered him. He was quickly bound and, when questioned, said his name was Smith. He was bundled over to Philmore's place and, as soon as his wife saw the captive, she exclaimed "Why, it's old Joe Bettys!"

Realizing the jig was up, Bettys coolly asked to smoke a pipe. His bonds were loosened and, when he moved nonchalantly to the fireplace to gather an ember, he was seen to drop something into the fire. Quick as a rattlesnake, one of the men snatched it out. An examination revealed a small, folded piece of lead sheeting which, when opened, held pieces of paper with writing in cipher. When Joseph offered the men the immense sum of one hundred guineas to be allowed to destroy the paper and escape, they refused, and he supposedly uttered, "Then, I am a dead man."

When the exciting news reached Second Major Andrew Mitchell, 12ACM, he urged everyone to keep it a tight secret, as he reasoned Bettys had not been alone and hoped to catch his mates. Taking a hint from Bettys's choice of a safe haven, Mitchell organized several searches of likely venues. Serjeant Kenneth Gordon led a party that included militiaman John Nash to search the home of widow Van Camp, whose son was known to have joined a Tory regiment in Canada.

After most folk were abed, Gordon's party entered the house, roused the widow, and demanded where her son was. Harried from her bed, the lady was a consummate actor and was thoroughly incensed by this unbidden and unwelcome visit. When questioned about her son, she denied any knowledge of his whereabouts and spoke in such markedly patriotic terms that she raised the serjeant's suspicions. Having noted an upstairs room, Gordon took up a brand from the fireplace and began to climb the stairs.

The ruckus below had alerted Jonathon Miller and young Van Camp. Hearing ascending footsteps and seeing a light approaching under the door, the two cocked their firelocks, which caused Gordon to bolt back down the stairs. In a stentorian voice, he threatened to set fire to the house. The Tories quickly hid some money in the rafters and surrendered. On the way to Major Mitchell's, the two prisoners were shocked to be told of Bettys's capture.

The next morning, Miller's brother Obadiah was brought to see him. As the visit was hardly voluntary, Obadiah began to shake in trepidation.

Perhaps he had been involved in Jonathon's earlier attempt to abduct the major; however, nothing came of his fears or his visit.

Bettys, Mitchell, and Van Camp were removed to Albany, where they joined John Parker in "the Black Hole." It was soon determined that Bettys's ciphered dispatch was addressed to British officers in New York City and that a second paper was an order for thirty guineas to be awarded Bettys upon delivery of the dispatch. Of course, this evidence sealed his doom.

Although an extremely large reward had been posted for Joe Bettys, for some inexplicable reason, his vigilant and enterprising captors were ignored and only received $25 from the sale of his rifle and pistols.[4]

On March 23, Powell reported to Haldimand that due to the continued cold weather, Lake Ontario would not be fully open until mid April, although Ross had said that he would be ready to move to Oswego by April 1. Powell had halted Old Smoke, the senior Seneca war captain, from going to Fort Pitt with two hundred of his best men so they would be available to provide security for the reoccupation.

As to Ross's complaints, he agreed that the natives on the raid had been "very indifferent" and said that the request for native support had arrived so late that none better could be assembled. He was anxious that the small parties of Rangers that had gone out in the fall to gather intelligence had not yet returned, nor had more recent scouts on the near frontier, or Captain David Hill, who had gone to Schoharie. He had heard that Brant might not recover from the infection in his leg wound, but would send for him and see.

Still on Niagara affairs, a nominal roll of the Six Nations' Indian Department listed three surprising names in the Loyal Foresters: Samuel Buchanan, a 2NY soldier who had been taken by Brant the previous winter at Fort Stanwix; Eben Pease, who had been a ranger under Solomon Woodworth and captured in the August ambush; and an Alexander McFee. Was this the same man whose children had just been taken on Bowman's Creek? The motivation for Buchanan and Pease working for the Crown is unclear. None of these men settled in Canada after the war.[5]

Riedesel informed Haldimand on March 26 that Twiss was at Sorel, organizing the building of more storehouses and improving the post's defences. Three days later, he wrote of arranging with the engineer to store forty to fifty thousand bushels of grain and noted that, if supplies of superfluous artillery goods and other effects were moved from Sorel to Quebec, Montreal, and Chambly, room could be found for the grain in the warehouses, instead of in barracks where there was a greater danger of spoilage.[6]

At the Loyal Blockhouse, a professed loyalist brought in by Roger Stevens had been set to work cutting firewood while Sherwood assessed his potential as an agent. Captain Mathews suggested he be allowed to escape, which would lessen suspicion amongst his friends; but, before the plan was put in motion, the fellow took off, leaving behind his fusil and ammunition. Outraged, Sherwood described him as, "A Whining designing Yankee Scoundrel like too many others."[7]

On April 1, Joseph Bettys and John Parker were hanged in Albany. As was common in those days, executions were public spectacles and this event was no exception. It is said that the people lined the streets as if "King George himself were passing by" and that the condemned men refused to reveal any information despite their sentence of death. Simms wrote, "The intrepid John Parker was tried as a spy, convicted and soon after hanged, a great loss to the loyalist cause and a relief to … Tryon

County." Miller and Van Camp were considered small fry and were shown the mercy of extended imprisonment at West Point.

When word of these several captures reached Haldimand, he immediately had Sherwood send a flag of truce demanding the surrender of Bettys and Parker as soldiers of the Loyal Blockhouse with a promise to exchange two rebel prisoners. The message was to include the threat that, if the two agents were executed, retaliation could be expected. The flag was to point out that, although many rebel spies had been caught with incriminating documents, "The war has not furnished a single instance where a prisoner has suffered death in this province." Word of the executions had still not arrived by the end of the month when Sherwood instructed Mathias Snetsinger to "take a prisoner violently opposed to Government, so that he may be held hostage for Beaty." Obviously, all these actions were in vain.[8]

A report of April 7 listed the staff and company commanders of Willett's 1782 Levies. Willett appeared as a full colonel, indicating that his request had been granted. The first major was Elias Van Benschoten, an equally experienced regular officer, who had served with Willett in the 3NY at Stanwix during the 1777 siege. Andreas Finck, his brigade major in 1781, was his second major. Lieutenant Jellis A. Fonda continued as adjutant. Lieutenant Abraham Ten Eyck was paymaster and William Petrie continued as regimental surgeon with George Faugh as his mate. Lieutenant Matthew Trotter was quartermaster; Thomas Scribner was serjeant-major; and William Sole remained as quartermaster serjeant. The list revealed a complete turnover in company commanders. Their names were: James Cannon, Abner French, Joseph Harrison, Nathaniel Henry, Abraham Livingston, Simeon Newell, Jonathon Percy, Peter B. Tearce (Light Infantry), Job Wright, and Guy Young.[9]

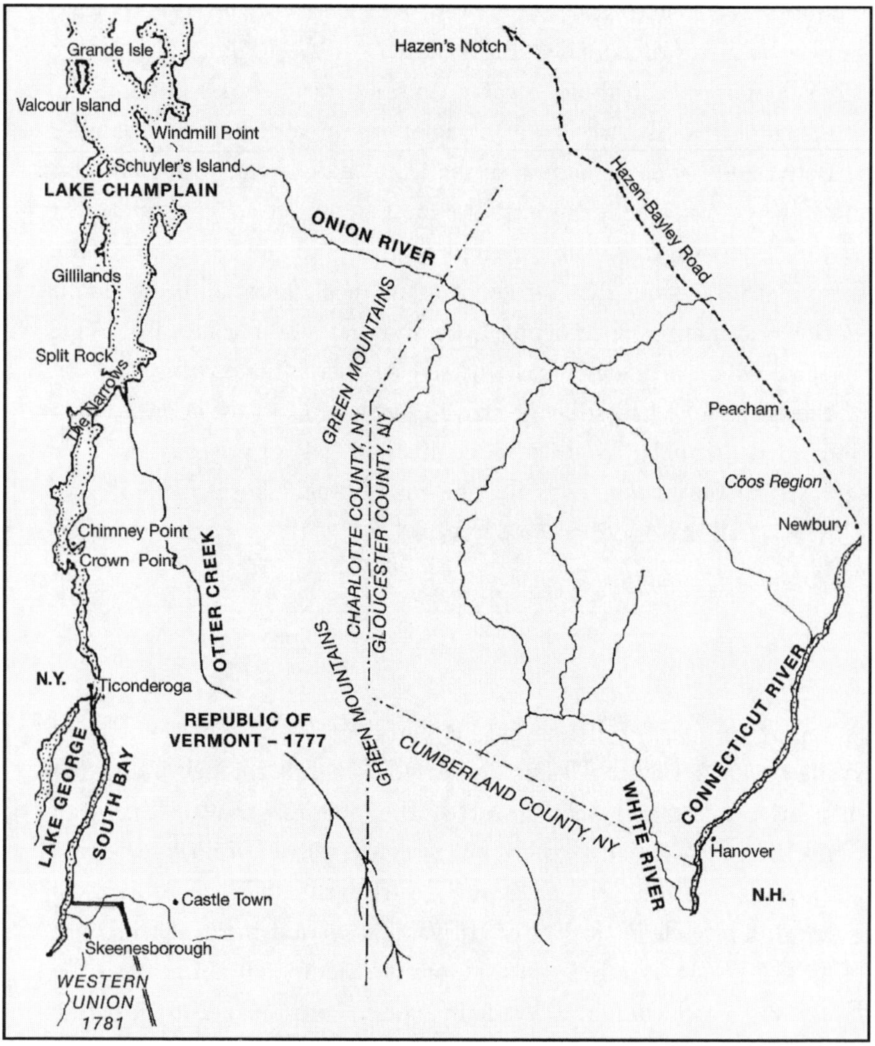

Map labels: Grande Isle, Valcour Island, Windmill Point, Schuyler's Island, LAKE CHAMPLAIN, Gillilands, Split Rock, The Narrows, Chimney Point, Crown Point, N.Y., Ticonderoga, OTTER CREEK, REPUBLIC OF VERMONT – 1777, LAKE GEORGE, SOUTH BAY, Castle Town, Skeenesborough, WESTERN UNION 1781, ONION RIVER, Hazen's Notch, Hazen-Bayley Road, GREEN MOUNTAINS, CHARLOTTE COUNTY, NY, GLOUCESTER COUNTY, NY, CUMBERLAND COUNTY, NY, WHITE RIVER, Peacham, Cöos Region, Newbury, CONNECTICUT RIVER, Hanover, N.H.

Gavin K. Watt and Christopher Armstrong, 2009.

Vermont's representatives, Isaac Tichenor and Jonas Fay (the latter secretly involved in the Haldimand negotiations), visited Congress in April and made another bid to have Vermont admitted. Not surprisingly, they found New York's representatives firmly opposed, as well as many southern delegates who feared strengthening New England's influence. There were similar contentious disagreements over land grants amongst several other states, many of whom were against sacrificing New Hampshire and New York's interests simply to gain a fourteenth state.

Three Vermonters who had assisted agents from Canada, and were openly in favour of reunion, visited Castleton and were shocked to be thrown out of town. They had expected to find the inhabitants friendly to a reunion with Britain, but instead found that the "common people" were some of the hottest rebels they had ever seen.

Abel Stevens forwarded a letter to Sherwood from "Plain Truth," which reported that one of the Allen brothers had told him that Vermont was only negotiating with Congress to prevent an army being sent to subdue them and it was generally believed that, given the chance, the republic would accept union with the United States due to the great alteration in opinion since Cornwallis's defeat. Allen had warned that far too many people knew of the negotiations and opined that the expedition reported organizing to invade Canada was actually intended for New York City.

In view of the cessation of hostilities with Vermont, Roger Stevens had an adventurous experience. His brother had told him about a small rebel outpost at Monctown, about twenty miles south of the Onion River. Roger had fallen in with a King's Ranger deserter by the name of Gibson, who promised to lead him there. True to his word, Gibson led Stevens's men to the outpost and they surrounded the camp in the dead of night. Stevens shouted a demand for their surrender and three men complied, but a sentinel, who had been lurking out of sight, escaped despite Stevens taking a shot at him. A haul of "two French pieces and one rifle and about three pounds of powder and nine pounds of lead and sixty rations" was the reward. The party lay in the camp until 1:00 a.m., then set off for Lake Champlain. At their second camp, the loyalists were so fatigued that only a single Loyal Ranger sentinel relieved the first watch, but he fell asleep and allowed the prisoners to scamper off. Nonetheless, the booty was brought back to the Loyal Blockhouse with word that the prisoners said a French fleet would invest Quebec City in the spring.[10]

On April 1, Major-General Riedesel ordered Sorel district's regiments to collect the bateaux that had been scattered about and

John W. Moore, 2009.

A pair of bateaux. These simple craft dominated the communication system across North America.

allowed to freeze into the rivers. A particular search was to be made to recover any that were in danger of ice damage or being swept away and have them raised to dry ground above the high water line. Once navigation opened, the various corps were to send those boats needing repairs to certain named posts. Boats in good repair that were not in danger were to be left in the water and, when freed by the thaw, were to be bailed out and made ready for immediate service. When all the bateaux were collected, each regiment was to submit a return to his headquarters. Lieutenant-Colonel St. Leger was ordering a similar return in his district. Requests for boats from the engineering department were to be honoured once a receipt had been received.

In a private letter to Haldimand that same day, Riedesel addressed the news from England that the two Houses of Parliament and the king enjoyed a sense of mutual confidence, which, in his opinion, would not avert the looming ruin. Only firm measures or a new, strong alliance could offset the enemy's numerical superiority and the last two years' misfortunes. He had heard hints of a reinforcement of ten thousand Hanoverians and an offensive alliance between Great Britain, Austria, Russia, and Prussia. If true, he thought the theatre of war would take another face and there might be a prospect of escaping "this labyrinth." It was said that a French operational plan had been uncovered which showed that an attack on Canada had been abandoned. And, that the new ministry hated Sir Henry Clinton and was attempting to tar him with responsibility for Cornwallis's defeat.[11]

––––––––––––

An April 2 return of 1KRR prepared at Montreal showed twenty-seven serjeants, twenty drummers, and four hundred rank and file fit for active service. Three serjeants and 104 other ranks were considered fit for garrison duties only and eight were too young to do duty. There were ten invalids unfit for service and thirty-one prisoners of the rebels. In all, 613 men were reported, exclusive of some thirty-five staff and commissioned officers.[12]

Major Gray made an odd request to Lieutenant-Colonel Claus this day, asking that Captain William Redford Crawford be replaced by Lieutenant Walter Sutherland, as he believed the other second battalion captains were "aggrieved" to be performing extra duties for Crawford while he continued in the Quebec Indian Department, where he had been since 1778. Gray wrote, Sutherland "deserves some Incouragment for his Risques and Services, and I know Colonel Campbell's Sentiments as to him which is very favourable." Although Gray was senior to Ross within the regiment, his interference in the second battalion's affairs seems inappropriate.

The exact outcome of this appeal has not been found; however, Crawford was soon at Carleton Island with his battalion and Sutherland continued in Secret Service work. Between November 25 and March 28, Walter had been 125 days on the frontier gathering intelligence under Claus's orders and performing other hazardous duties.[13]

––––––––––––

Surgeon Wasmus wrote in his diary that a Brunswick Jäger was hospitalized on April 3 after attempting to shoot himself. Four days later, the ice on the Richelieu River at Sorel broke up and a single chunk in the St. Lawrence some seven to eight feet thick came loose. The surgeon, who was clearly no devotee of North American river travel, bemoaned that the "dismal bateaux will soon be ready for action again."

In a letter dated April 3, Brigadier von Loos revealed a problem to Riedesel, whose recent warning of a possible invasion had alarmed him. He had in his possession a large cache of coin, 9,000 thalers (almost £4,000

Franz Xaver Habermann, circa 1770.
(Library of Congress, LC-USZC4-6506.)

German Troops Marching in La Rue des Récollects, Quebec City. The tinted engraving depicts a marching platoon of blue-coated German Regulars led by an officer, fife, and drum. They are observed by red- and blue-coated soldiers and civilians.

Sterling) and he asked his superior to give him early advice of an attack so he could arrange to have it hidden. He also noted his strong preference for Quebec City over Montreal, as "the people here give their bread with more grace and good will than those in Montreal. I like Quebec a thousand times better." Loos added a cryptic note about Major Samuel Holland, the Dutch-born, British muster master of the German troops who had played such a significant role in the 1759 siege of Quebec. "Holland went to Montreal this morning. He is reported to have betrayed some state secrets. He is very likely afraid of the whip, and will try to make it all right with the premier by denying it. He is — well, you know him."[14]

———

Corporal David Crowfoot, LR, filed a report on April 5 from the Loyal Blockhouse advising that, after he had separated from Bettys and company, he had been taken prisoner on his way to Arlington, but managed to destroy his dispatches "in a bag of mud and water." While being marched to Saratoga, he escaped at White Creek and snuck into

Arlington, where a friend hid him. He could have visited Ira Allen, but, with the dispatches gone, he felt he had nothing to say to the man and instead returned to Canada.[15]

On April 6, Riedesel wrote to the governor about an old road, said to have been cut before the war, which passed to the west of Pointe-au-Fer and ran from the Chateauguay River to Crown Point. Everyone who should have known about it seemed to have forgotten its existence. He sent scouts to survey the road and report. This little alarm soon fizzled out.[16]

This same day, Commodore Chambers, who was a key player in the governor's secret plan to reinforce Isle aux Noix, reported to Mathews that the *Maria*, *Carleton*, and *Trumbull* were nearly ready to sail, but Lake Champlain would not be open until about May 1. He reported that he wanted to get the *Royal George* hoved out before he left St. John's and requested guidance as to what vessels would be required and noted that, if the same as the previous campaign, he would require sixty soldiers to act as marines.[17]

Sherwood reported to Mathews on April 6 that Roger Stevens's party had returned after giving assistance to the detachments of Ensign Thomas Sherwood and Serjeant Caleb Clossen of the Loyal Rangers and Serjeant Ziba Phillips of the King's Rangers. Stevens had also brought in Dr. Smyth's son, Terrence, with two Regulars.

Lieutenant Richard Houghton, the QID resident agent at Kahnawake, reported on April 7 that tracks earlier reported by Jägers and natives had proven to be friendly. He still had two scouts out below, one had been away for thirty-three days, the other for thirty-one.[18]

Riedesel ordered that, when the various corps sent their bateaux in for repair, they were to return all snowshoes, retaining a sufficient number to mount their patrols. St. Leger issued similar instructions to his outposts.

A report was filed on April 8 from Montreal after the arrival of Serjeant William Green of the Queen's Rangers (1st Americans), who had brought dispatches from New York City. His information was similar to that gathered elsewhere, to wit — French troops were on their way to Claverack or Albany and that arms and ammunition had been conveyed over the winter to Claverack and then diverted to Philadelphia. Although it was expected that an attack on New York City would open the new campaign, on his way north, Green found the people were more inclined to believe Canada was the first object, yet he saw or heard nothing about preparations for such a movement. Here was further indication that the rebel Secret Service was sowing alarming rumours in the same fashion that its British counterpart had done so successfully the year before.[19]

As Powell had predicted, Lake Ontario's navigation did not open until April 14. Ross embarked his soldiers with a small band of Mississaugas in bateaux and they forced their way through fields of floating ice to beach at Oswego the next day. Two days later, the store ships left Carleton Island and followed the detachment.

The same day as Ross had taken to the boats, Powell informed the governor that it would be impossible to supply Rangers for Detroit once the detachment for Oswego had been sent, as there would scarcely be enough left to carry on the works and defend Fort Niagara. On the contrary, Niagara would need reinforcing, in case the threatened rebel attack was to take place.[20]

On April 15, the experienced patroller, Lieutenant Gideon Adams, LR, reported he had made an extremely trying scout to Hazen's Road through heavy, wet, soft snow. After several days, he had struck a marked trail, followed it through Hazen's Notch to the road, where he found a mark left by some Vermont rangers. A short distance along, Adams left his own scouters' mark, proceeded farther to another landmark, left a second mark, and found one from another British scout. On the return march, two of his men had fallen into the Yamaska River and were almost lost.[21]

On April 17, the ice broke up in the St. Lawrence River at Sorel with a resounding crash, but because Lac St. Pierre remained frozen, the water rose quickly and flooded some of the barracks and the bakery, brewery and a waterside redoubt had to be temporarily abandoned. Four days later, the ice went out on Lac St. Pierre and, shortly thereafter, the water level had receded to below the banks.[22]

On April 18, Powell reported to Haldimand that although the snow *Seneca* was blocked by ice, she and the sloop *Mohawk* would sail that day for Oswego. There had been no room for any natives, but another vessel was expected soon and would take fifty there.

As Powell was concerned that Ross would be unable to get all the people under cover, he was sending tents with the 8th Regiment's detachment which was composed of a serjeant, drummer, and twenty-five rank and file commanded by Lieutenant George Clowes. He had purchased new blankets for the detachment from the traders, as theirs had earlier been given to the Rangers. The troops were provisioned for five days and had one hundred rounds per man, although no decent flints, as there were none to be had. Although Ross requested entrenching tools, only seventy-two felling axes could be spared.

Captains George Dame and the controversial John McKinnon commanded Butler's Rangers' contingent with five subalterns, seven serjeants, three drummers, and 175 rank and file.[23]

On April 19, Commodore Chambers reported to headquarters that the *Carleton*, *Trumbull*, *Lee*, and *Washington* had been hove out. The first three and the *Maria* were ready for service and in better order than ever before. The *Washington*'s hull was in excellent order, but she lacked stores, which were coming from Quebec City, and that would also allow other vessels to be rigged out once blocks arrived from Montreal. The vessels would be ready for lake service once the *Royal George* and *Inflexible* were hoved down, but that could not be accomplished without more seamen.[24]

With the return of Lieutenant Adams, Riedesel reported to Haldimand on April 18 that the "Grand Scouts" were now discontinued.[25]

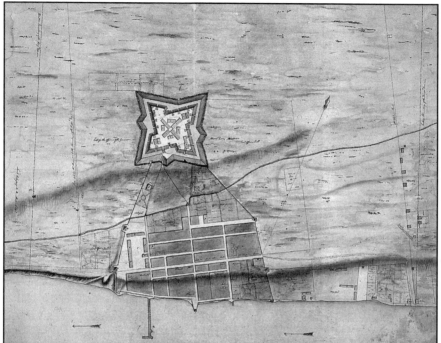

Plan of the Town of Detroit and Fort Lernoult, *circa* 1792.

In a letter to Powell dated April 20, Haldimand revealed his anxiety about how the Canadiens might react to the rumours of invasion. He noted that he could not possibly reduce his small army to reinforce the upper posts, as he might be required to make a diversion in favour of Sir Henry Clinton. As Detroit was concerned about rebel general Clark's plans, he recommended that Powell send a reinforcement of two Ranger companies and he would replace them with the balance of 2KRR. Obviously, the governor had not yet received Powell's letter explaining his inability to send troops to Detroit.

That same day, Lieutenant Robert Nelles, 6NID, wrote to Colonel Butler from Pine Creek on Pennsylvania's frontier. His party had taken possession of a blockhouse on Bald Eagle Creek, killing five of the garrison and capturing nine privates and a lieutenant who claimed that the Allies would attack Canada up the North River on May 1.

Also on April 20, an Indian Department serjeant, Ebenezer Allen, reported from the outpost at Chenussio in Indian Territory that John Abeel and his party had brought in a prisoner named Wolf, taken near

Canajoharie, who told of the French wintering at Philadelphia and of guns being brought to Albany for an expedition against Canada, but added that lately there had been no more talk of it. Wolf also claimed that Ethan Allen was an open enemy of Congress.

Serjeant Allen noted that a party of Senecas would leave for Wyoming the next day and, on April 22, he reported that a Tuscarora runner had just arrived to advise that the party sent to the Wyoming Valley had taken five prisoners; however, when hotly pursued, a chief was wounded through the body and the prisoners had to be abandoned, except those killed and scalped, but not before they revealed that six hundred rebel troops were in the Wyoming garrisons.

On April 21, Powell heard from Detroit that Brant was on his way down to Niagara.[26]

––––––––––––

A day later, Captain Joseph Anderson, 1KRR, reported to Mathews from Coteau-du-Lac that he had followed instructions and reprimanded Captain Johan Jost Herkimer of the bateaux company for gossiping with the rebel prisoner, David Abeel. Herkimer insisted he had simply inquired about his near relations, the Ten Broecks, who lived near Abeel, and denied mentioning a word about the Vermont negotiations. This disclaimer came in the face of the newspaper account of their dialogue that was in Haldimand's hands. Herkimer had been in hot water with the governor before and, in this instance, he either suffered a memory lapse or lied outright, as Abeel's affidavit to Governor Clinton had specifically named him as the source of information about Ethan Allen leading Vermont's role in the negotiations.

Anderson felt that a measure of the governor's displeasure was directed at him personally and gave assurances that he had taken the utmost care to prevent the men from discoursing with prisoners, strangers, or boat passengers.[27]

––––––––––––

––––––––––––

At Cöos on April 10, Colonel Jacob Bayley wrote another letter to Washington, again explaining the apparently treasonous conduct of his friend Thomas Johnson:

> The substance of the accounts from Canada are that if we do not go into Canada this year (which they enquire about) they shall pursue their plan early in May which was to go to Albany and then seat themselves [there], for the protection of Vermont. [T]he last of this month or first of May another packet will be brought [to Johnson.] We shall doubtless have it in our power to secure the bearer. I must think the correspondence of Vermont with the enemy is sent to deceive them, but was actually designed to destroy the United States. Their present excuses are to deceive us until the enemy can seat themselves at some convenient point on the [G]rants which I am afraid will be early this Spring. There is not the least doubt but General Arnold's plan reached to Vermont and Canada, and if he had succeeded there would nothing have been said by Vermont about discovering the enemy or if provisions had not failed in Canada last season no excuse would have been made by the Traitors. Was not the commander of Vermont troops in 1780 in council with the enemy at Crown Point? Was it not in his power to have defeated the enemy at Ft. Ann, Ft. George and Ballston that season? It was not for want of men. Vermont now says they did deceive the enemy last season, but they raised for something 1500 men and kept them in pay all last summer when, by their own confession, there was no danger. The question, who did they mean to deceive, Congress or the enemy? Now they say the Enemy are undeceived and the number of men called for this campaign is three hundred where if the enemy have been deceived, there is the utmost danger. Doubtless Vermont is an asylum for

all Continental deserters.... I wish for some orders to be given respecting Mr. Johnson; his case is critical. If he [does] not correspond[,] he is discovered, if he do[,] it is in the face of the act of congress. Your Excellency will pardon all mistakes, I doubt not, in this, also for giving so much trouble to you, as I cannot forbear until matters are settled by Congress in this quarter.[28]

In some manner, Joseph Bettys's fellow agent, Jonathon Miller, escaped the jail cell at West Point, but whether or not with Van Camp is unknown. He was soon retaken and sent to Albany from where he broke loose a few weeks later and made his way to Canada.

General Riedesel wrote a confidential letter to the governor on April 22 commiserating about the lack of detailed information coming from New York City. He commented that he had expected Sir Henry Clinton's letters to be short and laconic, revealing that the two men had shared observations about the C-in-C America's limited communications on prior occasions.

In General Orders from headquarters dated April 24, Adjutant General Lernoult ordered the British and German troops and the Royal Artillery to prepare "their Camp equipage and Every Necessary to take the field on the Shortest Notice."[29]

Concerning preparations for the new campaign on Lake Champlain, Haldimand instructed Riedesel, "I leave entirely to you to send from what corps … you should think fit, the detachment to serve as Marines — The sooner it proceeds to St. Johns the better — that part of it from the Royal Regiment of New York shall be sent immediately."

This was followed by a Most Private letter to the baron:

> I received orders from the Ministry to send a considerable detachment to the frontiers of the State of Vermont to furnish the people the occasion to declare themselves openly in favor of the government. Should it be necessary to protect them against the resentment of Congress, I think in order to cover up the real purpose that I'll decide to augment the works on Isle Aux Noix considerably and employ there (weather permitting) as many troops as possible. This idea[,] which was thought of at St. John, would appear outwardly very natural, and would furnish us the means of assembling there, troops, provisions, stores, etc., without any one suspecting the true purpose. I am writing you, Sir, a letter on this same subject while waiting till I can confer with you on these matters, I hope, in a few days.[30]

Detail from O.V., 1777. (HStAM WHK 28/34, Digitales Archiv Marburg.)

Plan and works on Isle aux Noix, 1777. The fortifications as they appeared before Riedesel was ordered to make improvements.

On April 23, Ross submitted the first, "State of the Garrison of Oswego":

Royal Artillery	One bombardier; nine matrosses.
8th Regiment	One lieutenant, one serjeant, two corporals, one drummer, and twenty-three rank and file.
34th Regiment	One lieutenant, six serjeants, five corporals, two drummers, sixty-three rank and file, three "sick present," twenty at Carleton Island, twenty-nine "prisoners with the rebels."
29th Regiment	One ensign, one private.
84th Regiment	One private.
1KRR	Two privates.
2KRR	One major, three captains, five lieutenants, one adjutant, one surgeon, thirteen serjeants (two at Carleton Island), fourteen corporals (two at Carleton Island), fifteen drummers (six at Carleton Island), 156 rank and file, four "sick present" (sixty-four at Carleton Island), sixteen prisoners with the enemy.
BR	Two captains, five lieutenants, eight serjeants, seven corporals, four drummers, 175 rank and file.
Herkimer's Bateaux Company	Nine privates.

The next day, the major reported to the governor that he had made good progress, "nearly according to the plans sent." If the weather co-operated, he expected to be in a good state of defence by the middle of May. The only accounts of the enemy's movements had come from Oswegatchie. There were rumours that Stanwix would be rebuilt and an attack made on the upper posts early in the spring. Mississauga scouts had spotted a party of

Oneidas about twelve miles up the Oswego River, which fled on being seen. Ross thought the enemy remained ignorant of his activities, as everything had been conducted in such deep secrecy at Carleton Island and Niagara.

The following day, Ross passed on Oswegatchie's information to Powell, noting that the rebels had supposedly begun their march to Niagara around April 20. In response, Powell sent him a reinforcement of twenty native scouts in a ship and promised to send a larger party in canoes.[31]

On April 25, Haldimand received a warning from Halifax concerning a report from Boston that the French would try to get a fleet up the St. Lawrence to attack Canada, although his informant thought it unlikely they could penetrate the Royal Navy's screen along the coast.[32]

Gray apprised Lernoult of the fact that 1KRR Ensign Thomas Smyth would be sent with the forty Yorkers marching to St. John's to do duty as marines aboard the shipping and, when there, he was to be examined by his father, Dr. George, for some sort of ailment. The major cryptically referred to another incident between his men and the Canadiens, noting that Captain Duncan said the account was to "not half as Bade as the Inhabitants Represents it." A day later, Gray went to Rivière du Chêne to investigate the details concerning his Grenadier second lieutenant, John Thomas Prenties, son of the Quebec City Provost, who was under arrest for several indiscretions.[33]

On April 26, Riedesel applied to Haldimand for permission to retrieve a number of Brunswick soldiers of the Convention Army who had made their escape through Virginia and Pennsylvania to Niagara and were serving in Butler's Rangers. The outcome of this request is unknown.[34]

On April 28, staff engineer Dietrick Brehm sent Commodore Chambers minute instructions as to the stores and provisions to be loaded for the Isle aux Noix venture and the duties to be performed over the summer by each ship in the Lake Champlain squadron.[35]

On April 24, the son of New Hampshire's governor, who was an aide to Washington, wrote to Governor Clinton on behalf of the C-in-C, asking that the New Hampshire's Continentals, who were "exceedingly scattered" on New York's frontiers, be collected as soon as possible for the upcoming campaign.[36]

Four days later, near Fort Plain on the Mohawk River, 1TCM militiamen John Brookman and his brother-in-law John C. Cramer, "one of the smartest men in the company," and "old Mr. Shively" were captured by Indian raiders after Frederick Witmosure was killed. Captain Adam Lype led some of the garrison in a pursuit, but the war party eluded them.

Another militiaman, George Lighthall, was driven into a swamp by three of the raiders and captured. He later recalled that John Cramer was killed and scalped at Andrustown; however, John was alive long after the war, so it may have been the oldster, Shively, who was dispatched for not being able to keep up.

After making several escape attempts, Lighthall feared retaliation and grew morose, which led Brant, the party's war captain (likely Brant Johnson, as Joseph had not arrived from Detroit), to inquire as to what was wrong. When George said he expected to be killed, Brant supposedly promised his warriors two gallons of rum when they got home if they left him alone.[37]

———————————

Haldimand wrote in cipher on April 28 to Sir Henry Clinton in reply to two of his February dispatches and one from Germain in January. The governor expressed his concerns about the new ministry's change of approach toward Vermont and his personal lack of information regarding the future military plans in America.

> To Conduct an Intercourse with the Vermonters, encouraging them to expect that their Interests will be attended to, proved a too general & ineffectual Doctrine

before Lord Cornwallis's Misfortune, now it would be a matter of Ridicule, which is sufficiently manifested by their Concessions to Congress and relinquishing their late assumed jurisdiction [Western Union,] (on which our Hopes were founded), notwithstanding the Encouragement I gave them of its being Confirmed. To attempt to Treat with them upon Conditions short of that would be adding to our lost time nor will they even be accepted if not Attended with an apparent Prospect of our Affairs on the Continent taking a prosperous turn. This Crisis is arrived when Coercion alone must decide the Part Vermont will take and that measure should be determined upon from the moment the Troops directed by Lord George Germain to appear upon their Frontier shall take Post and must be carried into Execution as far as possible (after giving them sufficient notice), by laying Waste their Country if they do not accept the Terms offered, Otherwise the bare appearance of the Troops will only Serve to Confirm them in their prevailing and Too Just Idea that we want Abilities to force them to compliance and will enhance their Merit and Influence with Congress....

The moment I can form any certain judgment that this province is not to be attacked by the river, &c ... I shall not fail appearing with as great a force as my strength and circumstances will admit of upon the frontiers for the purpose expressed in his Lordship's letter, (for which I have already made preparation) but the impossibility of penetrating far into the country with so inconsiderable a force as that will be, is too evident to require enlarging upon and our expectations of success should be proportioned to that disadvantage.

Haldimand reported that during the previous autumn, Vermont had assembled three thousand men and had another three thousand in preparation for cutting off St. Leger's retreat. He emphasized that it was not the number of Regulars that Washington could spare from his main army that was the concern, but the multitude of armed militiamen that were ready at an hour's notice to turn out when a single Continental regiment made an appearance — "The facility of which has been fatally experienced."

His move against Vermont could not be made before the middle of June, not only because of the possibility of a Franco-American invasion, but from the want of flour.

He had sent two companies of Rangers to reinforce Detroit against Clark and reported that preparations to take post at Oswego had been undertaken at Carleton Island over the winter. "[A] detachment was to proceed the moment Lake Ontario became navigable. I have more to hope from the secrecy with which this was conducted and the activity of Major Ross than from the strength of his detachment which is very inadequate to this necessary undertaking but proportionate to my force and circumstance."

As a final word on Vermont, he referred Sir Henry to a Fishkill newspaper article "wherein all that has passed in my negotiation with Vermont and as communicated to you is related. This proves that our confidence has somewhere been betrayed & God knows what bad effects it may have in that affair particularly if Allen & Fay have been sincere." He requested that Clinton not leave him solely responsible for reclaiming Vermont, as he simply did not have enough resources to succeed. He planned to send a provincial field officer to Haverhill on the Connecticut River to hear a proposal from a Vermont colonel that might shed new light.[38]

On the last day of the month, Powell reported to Haldimand that a Serjeant Secord and a "party of picked Rangers" were at Oswego. Further, that a runner had come from Lieutenant Servos, 6NID, advising that a scout had taken two scalps and a prisoner at Bowman's Creek in the Mohawk Valley on April 18. Servos had heard that a great number of boards had been sawed in the valley and sent to Schenectady to build a provisions warehouse for the army going to Canada in the summer.[39]

Gavin A. Watt, photographer, 2009. (Courtesy of the Niagara Historical Society & Museum.)

The Servos brothers, Daniel and Jacob, joined the Six Nations' Indian Department in 1779 and served as lieutenants. Reputedly, Daniel wore this rather odd coat during the Revolutionary War, perhaps for formal occasions rather than on campaign.

Captain Azariah Pritchard returned from a mission to the Vermont frontier with some prisoners and recommendations to build a new outpost on the Onion River and to mount a raid to burn the barracks at Corinth. Neither idea was approved, even though Dr. Smyth thought a raid on Vermont's frontiers might prove fruitful.[40]

In an idyllic early May farming scene, George Cough was plowing peas in his field in the Mohawk Valley while his sons, aged fourteen and twelve, cleared out a fallen maple. Near the pea field, Andrew Bowman was in a deep hole, gathering potatoes that had been stored since the previous fall. The two boys spotted a party of thirteen painted and clouted Akwesasne youths just as they broke out of the woods. George Jr. took flight, but the athletic natives easily vaulted the field's fence, looking to him like flying angels. All were armed with knives, hatchets, and firelocks, except one who carried a spear. The party quickly divided and ran down the two brothers.

Upon hearing the fence topple, Bowman peered out over the edge of the hole and was snatched, as was George Sr., who was probably quite uneasy, as he had already been a prisoner of the Indians in 1778. Some of the natives took the captives into the woods and recovered their packs while the others ran to loot the buildings.

Bowman's wife and children were visiting the Coughs' place when their home was rifled through and set afire. As the two houses were close together, everyone had warning of what was to come. The Bowmans and two Cough girls took to the woods, but Mrs. Cough and her eldest daughter stayed, hoping to save their home. The natives did them no harm, but thoroughly ransacked the place, even stripping a length of partially woven linen out of a loom. Perhaps out of pity, the house was not set afire. When the war party was gone, flames from the Bowman's place were discovered crawling along an adjoining fence and the two women beat them out.

The eldest daughter left to warn the neighbours and her mother went in search of George and the boys. She found one of the plow horses standing in its traces and recognized that the natives had taken the other. She searched until dark, without success and, exhausted, she collapsed onto George's seed bag and fell asleep. In the morning, the second horse was found, but not the men.

The war party had immediately set off for Canada, climbing the mountain north of Mayfield and fording the Sacandaga River. The stories later told by their captives of native skill and stamina were similar to those related by all folk who had been carried off. When George Sr. was suspected of planning to escape, great care was taken to secure him, but while his captors' attention was diverted, he got free and, although hotly pursued, made it back to the settlement with news of the others.

After a particularly difficult patch of travel, the two boys began to fade, but when the Indians sternly told them they would have to be killed, they quickly revived.[41]

––––––––––

Also that month, a rare lighthearted incident occurred when a detachment of French's Company, WL, went to Frey's Bush where Indians were marauding. Daybold Meyer was bringing up the rear of the detachment when he spotted a native with a pair of horses. Assuming him friendly, Meyer good-naturedly hailed him and asked for a ride. Startled, the Indian abandoned the horses and ran off. Of no surprise, the animals were later found to belong to a local farmer.

The area around Fort Plain was the scene of two raids in May. In the first, two men were killed and scalped and, in the second, a woman was killed and a militiaman was captured. Captain Adam Lype pursued the second party to Young's Lake and recovered a large drove of cattle. In yet another foray, Johnson's gristmill, the last in the Palatine District, was destroyed, a customer killed and the miller carried off. On May 10, Private Henry Stoner, 2TCM, was killed.[42]

––––––––––
––––––––––

A letter of April 24 from Riedesel to Haldimand confirmed that, even under the stress of the times, the governor's recognition of the importance of horticulture had not abated when the baron gave thanks for the governor's gift of two hundred apple trees and a few days later for a gift of vegetable seeds.[43]

––––––––––

On May 1 at Carleton Island, Captain William Ancrum, 34th Regiment, signed a "State of the Garrison," which plainly illustrated the tremendous gamble that Haldimand had taken in sending Ross to Oswego. The

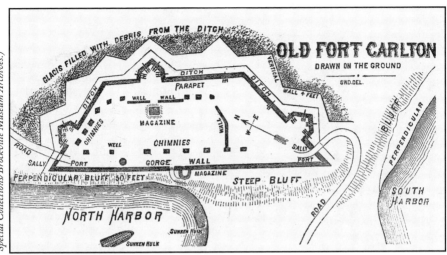

F.W. Curry, 1947. (Courtesy Colonel Curry Collection, Special Collections/Brockville Museum Archives.)

Plan of Fort Haldimand, Carleton Island. Although Curry incorrectly named the fort and drew the northern bastion off centre, he has nicely recreated the installation's interior.

only British Regulars on duty were two Artillery gunners and a captain, corporal, and nine privates of the 34th, with another eleven men sick. The Hanau Jägers had a platoon of two serjeants, two corporals, and sixteen riflemen. Of Provincials, there was only a small company of 2KRR comprised of four subalterns, four NCOs, two drummers, twenty-eight privates, and a number of sick men. The Naval Department had fifty-five men; the Engineers had nineteen, and there were sixteen loyalists employed in various tasks. If Haldimand had gauged the moment incorrectly and the rebels had made a thrust for Carleton Island, the works must have fallen.[44]

___

At Sorel, the weather continued cold and overcast, with a great deal of snow still lying about. Surgeon Wasmus dryly observed, "There is not much evidence of spring and fall in Canada, nothing but summer and winter."[45]

___

On May 2, Sherwood shared his concerns with Mathews. He now had no doubts that Vermont would rejoin Britain if the decision was left to Chittenden, the Allens, and the Fays, but he feared the "Benningtonites,"

Governor Thomas Chittenden of Vermont, 1730–1797.

especially the "two Mob Colonels: Warner and Herick" and wished "those two Rascals could be put nicely out of the way." He also announced that he had an astonishing forty-seven scouts in enemy territory.[46]

Butler's Rangers' corporal, Cornelius Winney, reported from Nanticoke on May 3 that, when he left the lower settlements in late April, the rebels were raising militia (by which, he meant Levies); 150 were to range the Blue Mountains, another 150 would go to the Mombackers region, and 300 would be sent to the Mohawk Valley. He had heard that the rebels were concerned that a British army was coming south by way of Lake George.[47]

Also on this day, Captain Robert Leake signed a return of 2KRR's men still in lower Quebec, who were at long last on their way to Carleton Island: three captains, one lieutenant, four ensigns, the quartermaster, three serjeants, a drummer, and fifty-nine rankers. Two lieutenants, the chaplain, and forty-seven privates would remain behind, as well as Captain Maurer as DQMG and Lieutenants Sutherland in the Secret Service and Langan in the QID.[48]

5

A MAJOR STRIKE IN THE MOHAWK
A Rare Day Affords Us No Alarm

*O*n May 7, Haldimand informed Ross that a prisoner taken at Ellice's Mills by the 84th Regiment's scout from Oswegatchie had betrayed the fact that the facility was poorly guarded. As this was the only operational mill left on the upper river, the governor viewed its destruction as "an Object Worthy of Attention not only inasmuch as it will distress them but by increasing their difficulties in the Movement of any Considerable Body of Troops up that River." The building was described as a two-storey stone house lightly prepared for defence. At the time of the Emigrants' attack, there had been only a six-man guard, but recent intelligence revealed that the garrison had been increased to an officer, twenty men, and a piece of ordnance.

Captain John Deserontyon proposed to attempt a surprise with an eighteen-man war party, but the governor thought his chances were slim, so, if Ross could spare twenty to thirty active men to join his party, the mill might be taken in a coup or by lodging some kegs of powder under a wall to make a breach, which would allow an assault. As a fort lay just six miles off, the mill must first be surrounded to prevent anyone from escaping to give an alarm, and the mill's destruction would have to be completed in quick time.

Haldimand was aware that Ross could ill afford to spare men; however, he persuasively added that "if the Stroke can be effected your Post will be amply repaid for the lost time." He stated that Deserontyon would leave the day after to scout the Mohawk area and would return through Oswego.

In another letter, the governor praised Ross's progress with the refortification. Joseph Brant would be sent to join him when he arrived from Detroit and would be "extremely useful in many respects." On a different matter, he enclosed Captain Alexander Fraser's (QID) sketch map of the different scouting trails of the backcountry from Lake St. Francis upwards for Ross to add corrections in order to make it more useful for the scouts and parties from Oswegatchie and Carleton Island and to assist in interrupting enemy scouts coming into Quebec. He also warned Ross that he might lose one or two companies of Butler's if George Rogers Clark moved against Detroit.[1]

———————————

Grim events continued at Sorel. The German deserter whose toes had been amputated and three other soldiers from various Brunswick regiments were all given a death sentence. A week later, the body of the serjeant-major who had fallen into a hole in the ice washed ashore on an island in Lac Saint-Pierre. Wasmus believed the fellow had committed suicide.[2]

———————————

Lieutenant William Johnston, 6NID, sent a dispatch to Niagara from Indian Territory enclosing a newspaper and letter collected by Butler's Rangers' serjeant, Adam Vrooman. Because of terrible weather, Vrooman had taken forty days to reach a point near Albany and Schenectady from where he sent spies into both towns. They found no evidence of preparations being made to invade Canada, but heard the usual half-truths about Ethan Allen. Vrooman had met up with the four Rangers who had been sent out the previous fall and they told him about the capture of Bettys, Miller, and Van Camp.[3]

Sir Guy Carleton arrived in New York City on May 9 to relieve Sir Henry Clinton and take command of all the British forces in America. He promptly informed Washington of his appointment as a commissioner to conclude a peace and provided him with copies of the recent Commons' resolutions and a draft bill introduced by the new ministry to authorize the king to conclude peace with "the revolted colonies of America."

Unknown painter. (Courtesy of the Niagara Historical Society and Museum.)

Serjeant Adam Vrooman of Butler's Rangers, d. 1810. The only known image of a Butler's Ranger serjeant. The original work is now lost. To judge from Vrooman's bushy sideburns, he is wearing a postwar militia uniform.

Washington was cautious. To his knowledge, the bill had not yet been passed and he and his advisors were highly skeptical. Although there was much unrest throughout the Continental Army, Washington retained his composure and held tight to the reins. He believed Carleton's documents were meant "to amuse this country with a false idea of peace, to draw us from our connexion with France and to lull us into a state of security and inactivity." He intelligently reasoned, "No nation yet suffered in treaty by preparing, even in the moment of negotiation, most vigorously for the field."[4]

On May 10, Major James Gray reported to adjutant general Richard Lernoult that he had men searching for several deserters who were hiding at "River De Chine," two of whom had worked at lumbering for the inhabitants. One of his Canadien employees had heard that the fugitives intended to go into the upper country to work and he proposed to lay a trap.[5]

On May 14, a packet of Sir Henry Clinton's dispatches, some of which had been written up to five months earlier, arrived in Quebec from New York City. These included the long-awaited response to Haldimand's request for intelligence from General Benedict Arnold about Quebeckers who had assisted the rebels during their 1775 invasion. Arnold named a Jesuit priest and a Canadien as inveterate enemies of the Crown and five Franco- and Anglo-Canadians who were friends of the rebels. On a positive note, none of the noblesse had given the rebels any friendly aid.[6]

Joseph Brant had arrived at Niagara by May 13. When he heard of Ross's criticisms of the natives and their general disinclination to offer assistance, he was apathetic about going to Oswego and preferred the Fort Pitt venture that Powell had delayed. Four days later, Guy Johnson wrote to the governor from his exile in Montreal to say that he had

A postwar study of a contemplative Joseph Brant, 1743–1807.

William Berczy, 1794–97. (Château Ramezay Museum, Montreal. Winkworth Collection, C-150345.)

heard from the department's officers that the natives were displeased with Ross and refused to go to Oswego.

Captain Ancrum had complained long and often that his tiny garrison at Carleton Island was made up of old men and invalids unable to perform their duties. In the middle of the month, the remainder of 2KRR was sent from Montreal, although that small number of men would scarcely be sufficient to meet his needs. Therefore, two companies of Highland Emigrants soon followed with orders to proceed to Oswego if necessary.[7]

Major James Rogers arrived at Cöos with a large force and boldly camped in the hills. He had Haldimand's instructions to assess local attitudes and, according to one Vermont historian, he conversed with a number of "men of doubtful loyalty to the American cause." When the major sent for the double agent, Thomas Johnson, he at first evaded the summons and later purposely missed a rendezvous. When Jacob Bayley heard of Rogers's arrival, he had a strong guard mounted at his house for fear of an abduction attempt.

On May 13, Johnson wrote to Washington to tell him of Rogers's arrival and how he had evaded the Tory's summons. Rogers's messenger had claimed that the British had come over the lake with six hundred troops and were fortifying. He added that the British were going to evacuate New York and Charlestown and take the whole army to Canada, which would certainly constitute a major threat to Vermont. Eight days later, King's Ranger Levi Sylvester visited Johnson and again invited him to visit Rogers, but Johnson used Sylvester's inability to produce the proper Secret Service identifying token as a convenient excuse not to comply.[8]

On May 13, Mathews informed Butler that a supply of native presents would be sent by the earliest transport along with seed corn for the loyalist farmers across the river. He also forwarded the puzzling and disappointing news that John Docksteder's petition for assistance on behalf of his brother Frederick's widow had been denied without explanation.

Haldimand wrote to Powell about Butler's recommendation of Serjeant Solomon Secord for a commission. "I do not wish Promotions of the Kind to take place, for altho' they may give emulation[,] yet mankind are so blind to their own imperfections that they will seldom acknowledge a superiority in those of their new rank, and the rewards of merit are construed into partiality, which, of course, creates discontent and it often happens that a good serjeant is lost for a bad officer." Nonetheless, if Butler wished to proceed, the governor would waive his objections.[9]

On May 18, Ross reported to Haldimand the details of the plan to destroy Ellice's Mill. A detachment of sixty soldiers and one hundred natives would set out from Oswegatchie on May 30 and a second party from Oswego would co-operate. The combined force would be at the mill about June 10.[10]

Corporal David Crowfoot arrived at the Loyal Blockhouse after a visit with the Allens. Sherwood reported that their treatment of him was noteworthy:

Genl. and Col. Allen treated Crowfoot with every mark of sincere friendship. Genl. Allen told him for God's sake, for his own and their safety, to take care of himself, for the mob were watching every night before he came away, and offer'd him any assistance he should require in money, provisions, or anything else in his power, caution'd him to take care of himself while on his way to keep his Secrets after he arriv'd here. Sent his best compliments to the Doctor & me … God Bless'd him and wish'd him a safe passage."

Then, Lieutenant Mathew Howard appeared at the Loyal Blockhouse. His August 1781 attempt to abduct Squire Bleecker had ended in farce when his written instructions that he had foolishly hidden on his person had been found and endangered the other kidnapping missions that were simultaneously underway. Howard was sent packing in disgrace to resume regimental duties with the Loyal Rangers.[11]

Major Gray reported to Mathews that he had successfully apprehended two Royal Yorker deserters; however, there were complications. The pair had written a memorial to Colonel St. Leger, claiming they had received no provisions, clothing, or pay from the regiment and complaining they had been forced into the bateaux service. Gray said that several of his soldiers had been made bateauxmen in the Artillery in May 1777 and were on the regiment's books until that November when they deserted. In exasperation, he noted that every man in the Royal Yorkers might say he was his own master and, if these two were allowed to escape punishment, a terrible precedent would be set. Walter Sutherland had been adjutant at the time of their desertion and could give evidence against them, although, at present he was laid up with a badly inflamed eye. A few days later, Gray sent a second letter enclosing information from one of his captains, which proved what scoundrels the two deserters were. He pointed out how damaging it was to general morale that the miscreants were wandering about doing as they wished, while others, who had joined at the same time or even before, continued to do duty as soldiers. Worse, the villains had been hard at work over the ensuing years, dissuading other men from joining the regiment.[12]

Surgeon Wasmus wrote in his journal about one of the other joys of Canadian life. "Last night I received many mosquito bites. These can rightfully be called a natural scourge, in which, in contrast to other good qualities, Canada surpasses all other countries in the whole world. These pests always breed prolifically after a winter of heavy snows as there is so much standing water from the melt." He added a gruesome note — the luckless Jäger who had attempted to shoot himself was sentenced to run a gauntlet of two hundred men eight times.[13]

In a most private letter to Haldimand on May 24, Riedesel stated his belief that the change in ministry would lead to peace, which he strongly desired, both for the public's sake and for the king, but he deplored seeing the government in the hands of men whom he believed were the real cause of the war and the king's greatest opponents. Strong sentiments!

Two days later, news arrived that the king had made peace with the colonies and that the Brunswickers and Hessians in Canada were to be relieved by a corps of Hannoverians and a further twelve thousand of them were being sent to relieve the Hessians in New York City. All the British troops would be sent to the West Indies where the French had already taken two islands. It was said the king had dissolved Parliament and appointed a new one. Sir Henry Clinton and Benedict Arnold were on their way to England and Guy Carleton was sent to take command. These misleading reports had been carried on a vessel from England, which was wrecked on a cliff twenty leagues below Quebec City with the loss of all hands and passengers except four.[14]

Major Ross reported to Major Lernoult from Oswego on May 25, reporting the arrival of Captain Leake and his detachment and expressing his pleasure that Haldimand had ordered two companies of the 84th to Oswego in view of Powell's announcement that he would withdraw the Rangers. He continued on a happy note concerning his second battalion:

The musquets &c Sent for the use of this Post were

Received & I had the Honor to acknowledge them[,] as the men of the Battalion under my Command have never untill now had proper arms[.] [I]t will be necessary to practice firing Powder wherefore I could wish to have Some Cartridge Paper which shall be used with Oeconomy... The Indian fusils Shall be Sent to General Powell as Ordered.

The 71 musquets in the Store at Carleton Island I had put in good firing order before I left that place[.] they were almost the only arms I had to depend on for the 2n Batt. on my landing here & on my Receiving new arms have been returned into that Store therefore I have not ordered them to be sent to montreal.

Ross noted that the Onondaga chief, Teaquanda, who was visiting Fort Ontario, had voiced his pleasure that Oswego had been reoccupied, as he had recommended this be done some time ago, but he was not pleased that his nation was not permitted to join him and asked that the Oswegatchie Indians, who were predominantly Onondagas, be moved there. The major warned that Haldimand might not approve. Ross thought Teaquanda was a great man and very devoted to the king's service and wrote that, as long as Brant was not permitted to come to Oswego, the Onondaga's presence "would be exceeding satisfactory."

The major ended his letter by joking that he would answer the governor's letters of June 7 and 10 as soon as he heard from Robertson, as co-operating with the captain was always a pleasure, because they differed in their opinions.[15]

In late May, Dr. George Smyth was shocked to discover that he was vulnerable to attack at his house, which stood only a mile from Fort St. John's. He was sitting at his door one evening when a passing King's Ranger spotted a man lurking behind the outhouse. From that day forward, Major Rogers posted a guard at the doctor's home.[16]

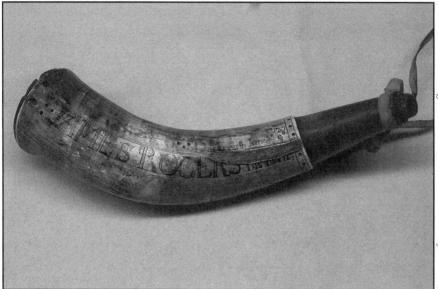

John W. Moore, photograph, 2009. (Courtesy, The Queen's York Rangers' Regimental Museum, Fort York Armoury, Toronto.)

Powder horn of Major James Rogers, 2nd Battalion, King's Rangers. This horn was engraved during Rogers's Seven Years' War service and was likely carried by him throughout the Revolutionary War.

Gray registered an old soldier's complaint to headquarters on May 26, noting that his regiment was scattered about in so many cantonments and in the king's works that it was "not in My Power ever to make soldiers of them." He feared they would appear very awkward and reflect badly on himself that they were unable to "Rest their Firelock." He had stated earlier that it would be much better for the men to be put up in barns rather than to go directly from Canadiens' houses into tents. He asked that General Haldimand be sounded out about the possibility of having those of his men who were in quarters brought together in one place and lodged in barns, which would be no hardship on the inhabitants, as the men would cook for themselves in their camp kettles and he would be answerable for any damages they might cause. Moreover, in this manner, they would be kept healthy and seasoned for the field.[17]

Commodore Chambers reported to Mathews on May 30 that a number of loyalist families had been conveyed to Fort St. John's under two flags of truce — one from New York, the other from Vermont. An additional two hundred loyalists had assembled at Skenesborough and more were expected every day and he requested instructions about how to deal with them.[18]

In General Orders this same day, Captain John W. Meyer's Independent Company was absorbed into the Loyal Rangers as the ninth company and Lieutenant Thomas Fraser was promoted to captain of a newly formed tenth company. Both companies had a lieutenant, an ensign, and some men appointed from the pensioners.[19]

New Hampshire colonel George Reid was thrown from his horse and broke four ribs and the New Hampshire brigade's senior colonel, Benjamin Tupper of Massachusetts, had come north to Albany to assume command during Reid's recovery. On May 23, Tupper reported to Washington that Shem Kentfield, who had been sentenced to death for desertion and serving the enemy, had disclosed that Haldimand had sent two men to Portsmouth, New Hampshire, to burn a sixty-two-gun ship being built for Captain John Paul Jones. Although he incorrectly identified the two agents, the governor's scheme was very much a reality. A ciphered warning was sent to Portsmouth and, upon receipt, a guard was mounted every night, which prevented the deed from being accomplished.[20]

On May 27, Willett reported to Washington that the 2NH would be concentrated at Fort Rensselaer and mused that erecting a small blockhouse at Fort Plain would prove a strong barrier against incursions. If some money were sent to buy materials, his Levies would complete the work.[21]

On May 28, Ross reported to Lernoult that a flagstaff had been erected at Fort Ontario and he wished to have flags sent to him. In the interim, he had received one from Fort Niagara.[22]

The month was coming to a close and the summer campaign season was rapidly approaching when Haldimand wrote to Powell about the difficulty of obtaining sufficient Six Nations men to work with Ross. He was surprised that they cited the major's reports of their poor performance as a pretext for not co-operating, as their behaviour, with few exceptions, deserved censure, which could be "readily proven beyond dispute were it a time to enter into such details."

Haldimand viewed the matter as too serious to be ignored and Powell was to acquaint Lieutenant-Colonel Butler that he had the governor's positive commands to not only use every possible avenue to discover the causes of their discontent, but to determine who had been agitating them. Butler was to report "the least tendency to incendiary." Powell should not hesitate to send down "on a pretence of business any and all persons concerned therein."

The governor had worked himself into a froth. He referred to Powell's earlier letter in which he had said, "[T]he Indians sent out last fall were certainly very indifferent," and noted that Major Ross and all the other officers (surely not Tice!) confirmed that, except for David Hill and a very few more, "They were never seen in action and abandoned him when they could have been most useful and were most wanted. The Six Nations, instead of being offended at a reproof on the occasion, should themselves have reproved those of their people who were deficient and not have made a national matter of it, and they would have done so if the necessity had been properly urged." This last rebuke was pointed squarely at the 6NID officers.

He observed that over the last four years, the Six Nations had petitioned for a post at Oswego, saying the safety of their wives and children depended on it, and promising they would have one thousand men ready "at all times" to co-operate with the troops. Self-righteously, he claimed, "I seized on the first moment I could accomplish it, more to gratify their wishes and protect Niagara than for any essential use it can be of to the King, and what is their return? Instead of meeting the troops there in force to welcome them and share any little hazard or glory that might be obtained in establishing a post for their own security with much persuasion twenty of them set off to join Major Ross fifteen days after he had taken post, and thirty or forty promise to follow." His diatribe continued, undoubtedly intended to buck up Powell and Butler and give them ammunition with which to shame the allies.[23]

On May 31, Haldimand wrote to DePeyster at Detroit about the report of a frightful slaughter by vengeful rebels of Moravian Christian Delawares at Muskengum in the Ohio country. This ugly affair proved to be far more successful in thoroughly reviving the enmity of all British-allied Indians toward the rebels' cause than all of the governor's diatribes.[24]

On May 31, Lieutenant Christian Wehr, the former Loyal Volunteers' subaltern who was trying to work his way off the Loyal Rangers' pensioners' list, had returned from a Secret Service mission to Vermont and reported that Congress was raising seven thousand troops for Washington. Vermont had been asked to provide 1,500, but Allen and Fay refused, which raised a ruckus in the republic's assembly.[25]

Colonel Tupper received notification on May 29 that he should remain in command at Albany until Reid was recovered, or until the New Hampshire troops were removed. Tupper had embraced Willett's idea for a new blockhouse at Fort Plain, but was told that there was no money available. Headquarters approved sending the New York Levies to the Mohawk region's posts as soon as possible and his bringing together of the NH Continentals so they "may be reinstated in their proper Discipline, and be ready for any compact Service."[26]

At month's end, Colonel Jacob Bayley informed Washington that, "Rodgers has been in here and has gone back satisfied that most of the leading men in Vermont will not oppose British Government." Bayley believed otherwise, but had to admit that many had been swayed and, although the region's towns stood fast in the cause, he anticipated trouble if the negotiations with Canada reopened.[27]

A May Inspection Return for the 2nd New Hampshire was completed at Fort Rensselaer by the assistant inspector of the Northern Army. The regiment was woefully under strength with only 262 privates compared to an establishment of 612 and twenty-three serjeants compared to the required forty-five. As to its arms, there were no espontoons for the subalterns or hangers for the non-commissioned officers. Of the men he was able to inspect, 96 were without muskets, 124 without bayonets, 90 without cartridge pouches, 131 without worms, and 94 without screwdrivers, and there were only 37 cartridges per private. Almost all had coats, but many were without vests, breeches, or overalls.

The inspector added some damning remarks:

> The mens cloating[,] altho it has originally been of a good kind, is nearly worn out, which has doubtless been occasioned (in some measure) by the severity of their service ..., but this can by no means be an excuse for the filthy condition their cloathing is kept in — the men want shoes, shirts & blankets — their arms are greatly out of repair and in very bad order — many bayonets have been carelessly lost.... The soldiers are generally stout able bodied men and they have been long in the service, but they appear to have lost their discipline, and their officers their spirit of emulation.

If this was the state of the Continental infantry in the Mohawk Valley, what might have been said of the Levies?[28]

On June 4, a regimental court martial sat at Montreal to review a number of charges laid against Second Lieutenant John Thomas Prenties of the Grenadier Company, 1KRR. In part, these read:

1. His "constant practice of fighting and abusing inhabitants, which brought much censure upon the Regiment." Perhaps John Thomas's upbringing in Quebec City, where his father held a position of prestige and influence, had given him a false sense of superiority over the so-called "conquered people."

2. [His] conduct at the Riviere Du Chaine where he stabbed a Canadian in his own house which was like to bring on a Rupture between the Regiment and the Inhabitants when a number of the Canadians assembled to defend the wounded man, till Captain Duncan then Commanding Officer interfered by geting his men under arms, sent a Guard to the house of the wounded man and was obliged to apply to the Priest, to assure the Inhabitants who were then ready with Arms and Bludgeons to begin the Fray; that he would secure Mr Prenties and give the injur'd man all the Justice that could be expected at the same time order'd Mr Prenties to deliver his Sword and go imme-diately to his room Both which Mr Prenties refus'd to do.

This charge told a part of the story and only from the viewpoint of keeping the peace between the inhabitants and the soldiery. The event had unfolded as follows — Lieutenant Prenties, Ensign James McAlpin, and Adjutant John Valentine (later reported to be Ensign Jacob Glen) had been on the town one night. They arrived late at the door of Valentine's (Glen's?) billet "disguised in liquor" and pounded on the door to rouse the owner. Said owner, one M. Lavallée, was the local captain of militia, a man of means and influence who was not happy to be pulled from his bed in such a fashion, and he went to the door and told them to "sod off." When the pounding and shouting continued, Lavallée discharged his firelock through the door and slightly wounded Valentine (Glen?), whereupon an enraged Prenties broke down the door and took his sword to the man, but whether he employed the blade or the hilt went unstated. The rest was as written in the charge. While one might have sympathy with Prenties's reaction to the shooting, his refusal to submit to Captain Duncan understandably roused the ire of the regiment's officers.

3. "Braking his Arrest at Several times" and "Disobedience of Orders." Obviously, John Thomas was a proverbial "loose cannon."

4. "His drinking and keeping Company with the soldiers, going to their Quarters at unseasonable hours in the night, Challenging them to fight," and "Boxing with his Servant in his own Quarters." The officer corps viewed this type of behaviour as most inappropriate, as it was believed essential to maintain a social distance from the rankers in order to foster respect and obedience. Brawling with the men was utterly beyond the pall. To challenge Grenadiers, the regiment's tallest, most muscular and athletic young men, required considerable nerve and showed Prenties to be one tough fellow.

Clearly, John Thomas was quite the lad. It would be many months before these problems played out.[29]

———————

At Niagara, Lieutenant-Colonel Butler proposed to headquarters that Captain John McDonell (Aberchalder) be ranked senior to Peter Ten Broeck, as he was "the most capable officer in the Corps to command in my absence, which will often be the case if I am to have the care of the Indian Department, he is also the best liked by the Indians, who soon after the death of my son desired in a very pressing manner that he should step in my son's place." On a second issue, Butler reported that several essential articles of native clothing were missing from the department's stores and that Powell had allowed him to exchange a few items of marginal utility with the traders to get what was needed, but that stopgap was insufficient.

Detail from James Peachey, circa 1784. (With permission from the Royal Ontario Museum © ROM, 956.129.)

Fort Niagara from the American shore. This view features the French Castle, the eastern redoubt, and several shoreline outbuildings utilized by the Indian Department and traders.

To "keep [the Indians] in temper," he had been compelled to purchase some articles. Mindful of the uproar over Guy Johnson's mismanagement, he added, "I hope His Excellency will not think me extravagant."

In a second letter, Butler sought the appointment of Richard Wilkinson as departmental deputy secretary, noting he had been of great assistance as acting adjutant and secretary and in the handling of the presents. Clearly, Powell had not warned the colonel about Haldimand's displeasure with Wilkinson.

Haldimand's harsh letter about the Six Nations' failure to support Ross's efforts at Oswego had not yet been received, when Butler reported that Old Smoke and 250 warriors had set out the day before to destroy a town near Fort Pitt. Because of the large size of the war party, he had supported it with 6NID captains Powell and Lottridge, two lieutenants, three Volunteers, and some Foresters.

He concluded by writing that Captain Brant was going to Oswego with about seventy warriors, which was hardly sufficient to assuage Haldimand's anger. Unwittingly, Butler made the situation a bit worse by stating that Brant's decision was "seemingly against his will," as he thought he could be of more use by joining the Shawnees at Sandusky; however, as Ross was pressing for natives, he had decided to comply.

Haldimand's blistering letter must have arrived by June 12 and set a fire under Powell and Butler, as the situation had altered remarkably when they reported that day that Brant would leave for Oswego on the morrow with 290 warriors. Eighty Senecas would follow shortly. In addition, several small parties were expected to return daily from the frontiers and would be sent there.

The next day, Lieutenant Jacob Servos, 6NID, wrote to Butler from the Seneca settlement of Canawagara (Kanawagoras), one of the few towns that had escaped Sullivan's depredations in 1779. He advised that Great Tree, the prominent Genesee region chief, and his party had arrived with five prisoners and ten horses taken at Canajoharie on May 4. One prisoner spoke of an Albany newspaper that mentioned a six months' cessation of arms. It was said that, in anticipation of a British army coming from Ticonderoga, the guns at Albany had been moved to Fort Edward. Two hundred troops were stationed at Fort Herkimer and more at the neighbouring posts so that one thousand men could be marshalled in a day to answer an alarm. Further, it appeared that the rebels remained ignorant of the reoccupation of Oswego.

Joseph Brant, three hundred warriors, and ten white volunteers left Niagara bound for Oswego on June 14, although Brant's 6NID company of Mohawks and Oneidas stayed behind to raise corn and vegetables at Buffalo Creek, as did most of his white volunteers.[30]

Captain John Deserontyon reported to Claus that he had sent nine warriors to scout Ellice's Mills for current intelligence before the main party of 170 natives and eighty Highland Emigrants left Oswegatchie on June 5. He had heard that the rebels were prepared to receive them, which animated the Indians rather than intimidating them.[31]

The same day as the raiders departed, Riedesel wrote to Haldimand from Sorel to advise that the recently reported exchange of more German

Resplendent in white coats with red facings reminiscent of French Regulars, the Anhalt Zerbst regiment spent its time in Canada garrisoning Quebec City and labouring in the works.

officers at New York City would allow him to restore von Breymann's Grenadier regiment. Four days later, the baron informed the governor that he was about to leave Montreal after reviewing the German troops there. He was greatly satisfied with their condition, which he felt did great honour to the small number of officers with them. When instructed, he would leave for Quebec City and inspect the Anhalt-Zerbst battalions and the von Rhetz Regiment en route.[32]

204 | *I am heartily ashamed*

On June 9, Commodore Chambers reported that he had loaded the requisite victuals and stores on his vessels at St. John's and, due to abnormally low water in the Richelieu River, had moved them to Isle aux Noix. He was concerned that leaving the ships anchored offshore would betray the governor's intentions and suggested sailing them farther south to the bay behind Valcour Island where they would be out of sight of prying eyes.[33]

An electrifying article appeared in a special issue of the *Quebec Gazette* on June 10 with the news that British Admiral Rodney had fought a major action of "unabating fury" with a stronger French fleet between the Caribbean islands of Dominica and Guadeloupe. Although the French had deployed the greater number of guns, their losses were crippling and their admiral, de Grasse, had been taken. This news caused great joy amongst the British and Germans. At Sorel that evening, "the houses of the English ... were lit, but the French acted as if they did not notice anything, although some of their windows had been smashed." This same act of vandalism occurred in Quebec City, where sailors threw stones at the windows of any Canadien house that was not illuminated.

On a gloomy note, detachments from the outlying Brunswick regiments marched that same day to Sorel to witness the execution of the four deserters. Next morning, they were under arms at 3:00 a.m. and the court began its final deliberations. Two hours later, the offenders were taken to the gibbets. Dramatically, Lieutenant-Colonel von Barner opened a sealed order and read aloud that Major-General Riedesel ordered that none were to be hanged; however, all four were to cast dice on a drumhead and the two losers would be shot. The fellow who had lost all of the toes on his right foot and a fellow with a crooked arm escaped execution, but were condemned to serve "as slaves on a frigate."[34]

On June 11, Major Ross reported to headquarters that a party commanded by Captain William Redford Crawford with a subaltern, serjeant, and twenty-five Royal Yorkers supported by nearly one hundred Indians had left Carleton Island to join Captain Robertson on Deserontyon's raid into the Mohawk Valley.[35]

At mid-month, Chambers received a letter from Skenesborough, written by a Vermont colonel, appealing to him for vessels to be sent to pick up the distressed loyalist families accumulated there, as his own craft were shattered. Then followed a spate of letters between Chambers and headquarters about the use of gunboats to retrieve these folk and the lack of suitable boats aboard his vessels at Crown Point. In some manner, the refugees were brought north and accounted for on June 16.[36]

On June 17, Brigadier de Speth reported to headquarters that, of five rebels who had escaped from Prison Island, three had been retaken near Fort St. John's. As a result of this breakout, Major Gray and four of his captains went to Coteau-du-Lac to examine the escapees' complaints about the conduct of Ensign James McAlpin. A week later, the major reported the details of the youth's crimes to Adjutant General Lernoult. The soldiers who had been in the guard under McAlpin's command testified that he had been drunk for the better part of a week in mid February during which time he had somehow discovered that some of the prisoners had been involved in the plundering of his family home near Albany and the abuse of his mother and sisters, and therefore had them strung up. When he sobered, he pled with the prisoners not to complain, as it would be the ruin of his career. To excuse this abuse, Gray noted that the prisoners had been very insolent and refused to assist in unloading provisions sent to the island for their own consumption. They complained of a lack of soap, shoes, and tobacco pipes, but they had plenty of provisions and clothing. More would be revealed at McAlpin's court martial.[37]

Brant and his men arrived at Oswego on June 18. He bitterly complained that Butler had inadequately outfitted his party. After some investigation, it was found that Butler had supplied a long list of demands, including five hundred pair of moccasins, an item which Brant had specifically complained was lacking. Ultimately, it emerged that the uproar was over an old jealousy between the two men.[38]

———————

Early in June, a party of St. Francis Indians was sent to scout Hazen's Road in Cöos country. On their way out, they came across three of the rebel officers who had escaped from Montreal and sent them back under guard. By June 11, the warriors were on Hazen's Road and found that the most northern of the blockhouses had been burned out. Advancing south to the next one, they found it unoccupied. At the first dwelling they came to, they took a prisoner as proof that they had followed orders and, on their return march, set fire to the second blockhouse. (Vermont had just received a tiny taste of what constantly occurred in the Mohawk region.)

The Vermonter had a great deal of news. He said that Carleton had arrived at New York with ten thousand men and that the city's garrison was very badly off and threatened not to bear arms and that "the army of cowboys [presumably rebels in this case] had made headway toward Albany and 4000 French troops." The scouts were given a handsome reward of "four Portuguese" coins for their efforts.[39]

———————
———————

On June 13, Washington's secretary informed Brigadier-General Bayley that the C-in-C agreed that Thomas Johnson's intelligence was of a very serious nature. "The insidious Designs of the Enemy, I believe, are not to be doubted; but the Evil he mentions has not, I hope, reached the Minds of the people at large, however it may have influenced the Conduct of some Individuals." Washington could offer no further assistance. The New Hampshire Brigade and a regiment of Levies were on the western and northern frontiers and their duty extended to keeping a watchful eye on the enemy's activities on Lakes Champlain and George. Washington advised Bayley to watch for enemy movements and the "internal Machinations of evil Men and Emissaries who may be sent among you, or be contained in your own Bosoms." He should "counteract them by every Means in your power; And at the same time to keep the Exertions of the people active and alert, and always prepared for speedy Action, in Case of an Appearance of the Enemy on your frontiers." The C-in-C doubted the news that the British were in force at Crown Point, as he had heard nothing from Albany about it.

A day after this letter was written to Bayley, Cöos country became the focus of another raid. Thomas Johnson's first inkling was when he received a visit from an acquaintance, a colonel of local militia, who said that a party from Canada had arrived to carry off some of his neighbours. Johnson was unsure whether to trust his visitor and made the non-committal answer that the Tories would have to fend for themselves.

Captains Azariah Pritchard and James Breakenridge, with Corporal Abner Barlow, Levi Sylvester, and five other King's Rangers, had been sent by Sherwood to abduct General Jacob Bayley. When they arrived "in country," they were joined by Joseph White Sr., who was said to be Bayley's "implacable enemy," and his son, Joe Jr., with several other locals.

On Saturday, June 15, Sylvester visited Thomas Johnson and told him that Pritchard's party was encamped about two miles back from the oxbow in the river. Johnson followed Sylvester to the camp, where he had a long talk about the negotiations. He was told that Bayley was a key man thwarting reunion and the raiders had come to abduct him.

While riding home, Johnson mulled over what he had heard. He had taken Bayley entirely into his confidence and the general had been representing his delicate case to Washington, so Thomas was duty-bound to give him warning. Yet, how might he accomplish that without compromising himself with the Tories? He decided to have his brother-in-law secretly deliver a small note.

Near sunset, Bayley was plowing not far from home on the oxbow with two of his sons when a man rode across the field and dropped a note into a furrow. The general saw it fall and surreptitiously retrieved it as he passed. It read, "Samson, the Philistines are upon Thee." Bayley coolly plowed two more circuits, then told his boys to turn in the team.

This was Bayley's second warning; the first was a gallows' confession by the New Hampshire deserter, Shem Kentfield, which had arrived by express just hours before. Bayley had many enemies who might wish him harm. Obviously, there were the British and Tories; however, his opposition to the Allen faction was so strong, so open, and so resented, a blow from that quarter was entirely possible, and "Philistines" could describe either.

Pritchard's party struck Bayley's house at early candlelight. They rushed across the road from a meadow and were not seen or heard until a few feet from the house. A single guard stood at the door; the others had propped their firelocks against the hallway wall. Corporal Barlow and Sylvester were the first through the door and snagged the guard. A few others were rounded up, but most escaped through doors and windows, and one fellow was wounded as he ran from the house; however, "to their inescapable sorrow, the Villain was not at home." (It is said that this was the only hostile shot fired and the only blood shed in Newbury during the Revolution.) Pritchard immediately had men search for Bayley's correspondence, but a brave, foolhardy young girl who was babysitting in the house repeatedly blew out the candles.

Ironically, it was Thomas Johnson's wife who sounded the alarm by loading and firing several times. Hearing the shots, Pritchard realized he dare not dally and he immediately retreated with two prisoners. Johnson had given him a packet of intelligence for Haldimand and the captain had left it in a safe place in case something went awry during the abduction, so when they were clear of the house, he instructed Barlow to retrieve the packet and make his own way back to Canada.

Outside of the community's cemetery, one of Bayley's sons was captured as he walked home barefoot from his father's sawmill. Next, the raiders captured an old soldier, who cunningly feigned terror and was released. At one house, the Tories consumed all of a woman's milk and bread and, in the hamlet of Corinth, they mischievously rounded up the inhabitants and forced them to swear allegiance to the king before pressing on.

A half-hour after the attack, thirty to forty men were in pursuit of the abductors, but they soon gave up and, in frustration, rounded up two Tory suspects and took them to Newbury. At 5:00 a.m. on Monday morning, Thomas Johnson was arrested and taken before the Haverhill Council of Safety to answer the charge that he had planned the attempt to abduct the general. Bayley appeared, and, without revealing Johnson's assistance, managed to get him released. The two suspects were sent home after interrogation.

Two days into the march, a young captive composed a mysterious letter to Sherwood dated, "Woods, 18 June 1782." It said that their treatment was "indearing to some and Exasperates others to see us so well us'd. In acknowledgement of the favours, I have taken cair to get Information how it happened the Party was in part Defeated at Newbury: was Informed that they would have taken Gen'l B....y had not he had Notis of Thair Coming a little before night by which means he got out of the way … Treachery is so much in fashion it is Dangerous Trusting friends [as] Captain Pritchard knows." It was signed, "Vermont Boy."

An influential Haverhill farmer reported the Bayley attempt to New Hampshire's Meshech Weare saying that Pritchard had told Thomas Johnson that Chittenden knew that all but three or four Newbury inhabitants had applied to New Hampshire for protection and that Bayley was very active in promoting this matter. Chittenden had informed Haldimand and urged him to have Bayley abducted, as he kept the area in tumult and confusion and would prevent the governor from carrying out his plans. Supposedly, Johnson had pled with Pritchard that he would be uncovered as a British agent if Bayley was taken, but the captain said he would immediately come to his rescue if something went awry, as he had 150 men available at a moment's notice and would lay waste to the country. The correspondent confided that Johnson had given Bayley warning and urged the strictest secrecy on that account.

He had more news. Two enemy deserters from Montreal had told him that the British were fortifying Oswego and strengthening Quebec City. They claimed that all Vermont prisoners would be sent home immediately; in fact, a number had already arrived. Some had been paroled, others exchanged, but all generally had little to say.

When Pritchard made his report on June 21, he blamed Joseph White Sr. for the failure, probably suspecting him of betrayal. Undaunted, he proposed a full-scale raid on the Cöos district.[40]

General Washington wrote to Lieutenant-Colonel George Reid on June 15, sending best wishes for a recovery from his fall and informing him that the QM Department had been directed to supply his district with cartridges.

> [B]e very active and vigorous in your Command, and give particular Instructions to your Scouts to be watchful and Alert in their Duty; not only to prevent Surprises from the Enemy, but to gain every Intelligence possible of any Movements or Approach of the Enemy ... I have been lately informed ... that the Enemy are coming in force ... to take post at Crown point; you don't make mention of any Discoveries from that Quarter: have any Scouts lately been on the Rout?

Perhaps Washington had read the recent inspector's return, as he instructed, "you will, as far as it is practicable ... attend closely to the disciplining and training of the Men of the New Hampshire Regiment, make the rules and regulations for the government of the Army your guide."[41]

At Ballstown, Lieutenant Pliny Moore, WL, posted Garrison Orders on June 18, lauding his men's "alertness & spirit" during alarms; however, he stressed that they should take their posts in utter silence to avoid distressing the inhabitants and that they were not to pick the strawberries in the meadows. Such orders suggest a relatively quiet existence compared to the agonies of the Mohawk Valley, yet the war was not all that far away, for just a few miles to the east at Fort Edward on the Hudson, nine men were captured the day Moore issued his quaint orders.[42]

On June 16, Ethan Allen penned a remarkable letter to Haldimand:

> The last refusal of Congress to admit this State into the Union has done more to awaken the Common People to

a sense of their Interest and Resentment of their Conduct than all which they had done before. By their own act they declare that Vermont does not belong either to the Confederacy or to the Controversy but are a Neutral Republic. All the Frontier Towns are Firm with those Gentlemen in the present administration.... [T]hey have a clear Majority of the rank and file in their favour.

Allen added a postscript saying he would meet Haldimand on Lake Champlain, but he feared for his life, as a majority in Congress and many senior Continental officers constantly plotted against him. He vowed, "I shall do everything in my power to render this State a British province."

Sherwood and Smyth were unimpressed. They believed this letter and many others like it were ploys to forestall an invasion from Canada until the war came to a close.[43]

In the Mohawk Valley, Deserontyon's big raid struck the German Flatts about June 14. An anonymous officer doing duty at Fort Rensselaer reported that the raiders killed and scalped 2 men, took 50, destroyed 15 horses and killed 13 horned cattle, and that 180 beeves had been driven off, but not before 12 houses and 5 barns had been set alight. He noted that the raid consisted of 500 natives, Tories, and British Regulars. According to Deserontyon's report, by June 16, his men had collected 300 head of cattle from in and about German Flatts and Canajoharie.

On the third day, the raid split into two elements. The first was composed entirely of natives. Their "shotgun" goal was to create major distractions along the river while the raid's second element, composed of troops with native support, had the pinpoint goal of destroying Ellice's Mill at Little Falls.[44]

Captain John assigned a party of fifty warriors to drive off the cattle, while he and eight men roamed the area below old Fort Hendrick at the Mohawks' Canajoharie Castle. After the failure of the 1777 Stanwix siege, Molly Brant's house had been occupied and picketed by the Oneida war captain, Honyery Doxtator Tewahangaraghkan, whose home village

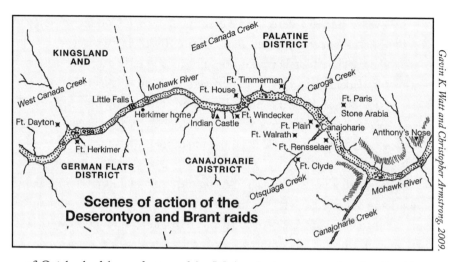

Scenes of action of the Deserontyon and Brant raids

Gavin K. Watt and Christopher Armstrong, 2009.

of Oriska had been destroyed by Mohawks in revenge for the Oneidas opposing them in the Oriskany battle. Deserontyon's party laid up nearby to await developments. Soon, two riders came out and, as they passed, the warriors jumped them. Honyery's son was immediately seized, but the other fellow struggled to get away and was shot by a young Delaware. As the ball had lodged in his lower belly, it was realized that he would soon die and he was abandoned. It is unknown when the victim's identity was realized, but he proved to be the son of Philip Sanorese, an influential half-blood Kahnawake interpreter. His parentage later caused considerable unrest.[45]

The party moved on and captured George Nellus of Lype's 1TCM company and two women who were driving cattle downriver. Nellus told the war captain that an express had come down from Fort Dayton the evening before and reported there were only three or four cattle left alive at the Flatts and "it was thought that [the] Settlement must break up." At the same time, another fifty natives broke into the old Mohawk castle, wounded a man, took two prisoners, and drove off more cattle.

Matthew Calkins, a light infantry private in Tierce's company of Willett's, recalled that, when word of the raiders' attack on the German Flatts was received at Fort Rensselaer, his company's lieutenant, John Thornton, roused the men before daylight and warned them for a special mission. It transpired that a rebel native had told the thirty-man garrison at Fort Plain that the raiders would attack them the next day and they had requested reinforcements and the Lights were being sent.[46]

Thornton's Light Infantry left Fort Rensselaer and marched four miles through the darkened woods to Fort Plain and arrived just as dawn was breaking, bringing the number of troops there to sixty. The senior officer gambled that the attackers would have no idea of the size of his garrison and risked ordering virtually all of the troops to sally "forth to look about and make such discoveries as they could." The soldiers were marching out the fort's gate when two young fellows who had ventured out in the early morning to hunt for horses were seen riding for the fort "upon a full jump." The lads were quite close when, in a remarkable display of marksmanship, two shots rang out and the youngsters tumbled from their mounts. In the blink of an eye, a pair of warriors sprang from the woods, sprinted to their victims, struck their hatchets deep into their heads, ripped off their scalps, then bounded back into the bush. Moments later, a mass of Indians appeared along the margin of the woods and the fort's guns drove them back into cover with charges of cut-up chains that whirled through the air with a frightful noise. The sentinels manning the palisade spotted figures flitting through other sections of the woods and the guns dispersed them with more chain shot.

It was thought that the natives had been driven off to the west, so the commander decided to take another risk and recover about sixty head of beef and dairy cattle that locals had hidden in a bush pasture south of the fort. Wishing to deceive any Indian scouts still lurking nearby into thinking that the fort was heavily garrisoned, he had the troops boldly march off with drum beating and fife shrilling. After crossing the cleared land around the fort, the column halted at the pathway into the woods that led to the pasture, where the commander now decided that it would be better if only a couple of men travelled the mile through the dense woods to retrieve the animals. Calkins and another fellow were chosen for this dangerous task and set off at a run. Arriving at the pasture, they opened the bar gate and the cattle rushed through the opening, it was thought in fear, because they could smell natives. The two men had little difficulty driving the cattle down the path toward the fort and, when they arrived at the cleared ground, the troops formed a funnel on each side of the opening, then closed behind the beasts to drive them to the fort.

About halfway there, the men were startled by a cannon firing over their heads and they looked behind to see that the path to the pasture and the forest's edge was crowded with Indians who had been attracted to, rather than deceived by, the fifing and drumming. The soldiers and cattle were soon safe in the fort and, after the disappointed natives vanished, the soldiers settled down for a well-earned breakfast.

Willett reported to Governor Clinton that he had arrived at Fort Rensselaer on the night of July 15 to discover that, "All the inhabited Places from the foot of Fall Hill to Fort Herkeimer are burnt; and that District gleaned of its Stock, one hundred & fifty Cattle & fifty Horses are reported to be carried off." Fort Rensselaer's anonymous officer reported that the 2NH's first major, Amos Morrill, assigned his second major, Jason Wait, and Major Finck of Willett's to take 220 men to pursue the raiders. However, Calkins recollected that Willett himself was in command and noted that the Light Company was added to the pursuit when it returned from Fort Plain in the afternoon.

Meanwhile, Deserontyon's eight-man party was busy rounding up more cattle when a woman was spotted riding up from downriver and they lay in wait to take her. Upon being questioned, she said that Colonel Willett was close by with three hundred troops, so the natives quickly herded their prisoners and cattle into the woods. Deserontyon lay near the road and watched an officer and troops march past, then rejoined his men. After a couple of hours, he released the woman and the party set off through the woods to catch up with the main party. On catching up with the cattle drove's tracks, he saw that the rebel force was ahead, so he dogged along behind.

Calkins recalled marching through the night and closing in on the cattle and raiders around daylight. The natives were discovered cooking their breakfast, but before an attack could be mounted, they took up their arms and fled. When the troops came up to their fires, Willett would not permit a stop and many soldiers stripped the spits of half-cooked meat and stuck it in their haversacks. Not long after, the colonel called a halt. He selected one hundred white troops (including Calkins's company) and a similar number of rebel Oneidas and Stockbridges under Colonel Louis Atayataghronghta to continue the chase while he and the rest of the force headed back.

Calkins doubted the wisdom of this decision. In his opinion, their original force greatly outnumbered the Indians and he was sure that victory was certain if all the troops caught up with the enemy.

The two hundred men followed the raiders' tracks and recovered a considerable number of horses laden with plunder from the settlements, as well as some wayward cattle. They found one horse with a side of leather wrapped around its barrel under which a split hog was stretched with its hooves tied above the horse's back.

The chase continued into the afternoon. The pursuers had just passed over the high ground east of Cherry Valley and were ascending into "a well-known gloomy range of hemlock wilderness" when, in fear of an ambush, Colonel Louis refused to take his men any farther, and the whole party turned about for Fort Rensselaer.

Deserontyon reported that he camped nearby the rebels, but as they did not report camping at any time, it is difficult to interpret his assertion. Next morning, the war captain saw that the rebels had turned about, so his party rejoined the drovers. After another day's march, he and nine of his warriors and one of Claus's rangers diverted toward Oswego to join Joseph Brant "and make the Campaign with him."[47]

In the Valley, the other native raiders were far from finished. On July 19, a party scalped two youngsters, took an old woman prisoner, and wounded a lad, who escaped and ran to Fort Clyde to give the alarm. Ensign Lemuel Mason, 2NH, and twenty men turned out to intercept the raiders and were followed by Second Lieutenant Neal McGaffey and an additional twenty Continentals. Mason closed on the raiders, but was almost cut off when a previously unseen large group suddenly ran between his detachment and the fort. Despite the raiders' smart fire, Mason had his men retire firing by files and regained the fort, even though they passed as close as forty yards from the foe, again proving the difficulty of hitting a moving target.

When the enemy detached men across the river to sweep up cattle on that side, Mason and thirty men were sent to prevent them and, with the assistance of some militiamen, saved the beeves.

Captain David McGregor, 2NH, who commanded at the Flatts, reported he had done everything in his power to protect the inhabitants' effects, but as the enemy was so superior in numbers, he chose not to sally out. Obviously, McGregor was not as fearless or foolhardy as Fort Plain's unnamed commander.[48]

Not to be forgotten, a major target of the raid was Ellice's gristmill, which had been built for £600 in 1775 at great financial risk by Scottish brothers named Ellice. Like so many New York families, the brothers divided their loyalties and brother James was managing the mill for the partnership of Phyn and Ellice right up until its destruction.

The structure had a stone foundation fifty feet long and forty-five feet wide and was topped by a large room housing the machinery. The building contractor had been a local man named Ebenezer Cox, who became the first miller. When the Johnson clan was deposed from their militia commands in 1775, Cox took command of the 1st Tryon Regiment and he was the first officer to lose his life at Oriskany in 1777. Thereafter, Gershom Skinner and another fellow named Cox took over as millers.[49]

At the time of the attack, the mill was garrisoned by a serjeant and six men from Dustin's Company, 2NH, which suggests that the rumoured reinforcement had not taken place. They had been joined on June 20 by a small convoy of German Flatts folk bringing grain for milling, guarded by a few 4th Tryon militiamen.

On the same day the convoy arrived at Ellice's, one of the soldiers in the tiny garrison at Fort Herkimer, who was watching over scores of women and children, got married. That evening, a noisy celebration was held with squawking tin horns, banging tinware, and a sawing fiddle. The merrymakers later believed that, when the raiders heard the noise, they thought that reinforcements had just arrived and diverted their attention to the mill. However, as we have seen, Ellice's was the primary target from the very outset.[50]

Captain Daniel Robertson, 84th, described the attack. The assault went in at "half past One in the morning" on June 21. The mill's doors were forced with a crowbar while native archers "amused" the garrison by firing burning arrows into the roof's oak shingles. "We destroyed everything about the Place of the least necessity or Value." This included five hundred bushels of wheat, one hundred barrels of flour, quantities of Indian corn, and a great store of salted beef and pork that was being held for the forts. "The mill had been capable of grinding 200 bushels in 24 hours. A second mill and a small dwelling nearby were burned along with four good houses

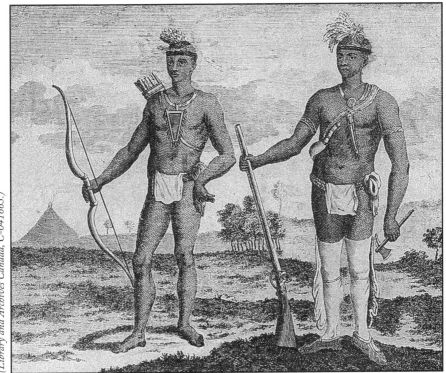

Detail: Thomas Morris, engraver, circa 1775; Christopher Armstrong, 2009. (Library and Archives Canada, C-041663.)

Although continued use of bows and arrows at this time has been thought highly unlikely by many historians, it is evident here that one warrior is armed with a bow, while the other carries a firelock. Fire arrows were used to set fire to the roof of Ellice's Mills.

and excellent barns about one mile either side of Ellice's."[51]

Robertson's pragmatic account did little to describe the sheer terror of the night. According to rebel accounts, only a few shots were fired. Two Continentals managed to escape, but five others were captured. Two men took refuge in the raceway, but were soon forced out by flames and rounded up with eight to ten others, including a captain, ensign, serjeant, and a few militia privates.

An elderly militiaman named Daniel Petri chose to resist, probably recognizing that he could not survive a march through the wilderness. He was recognized by some Royal Yorkers who urged him to surrender, but he refused, fired his musket, and turned its butt on his attackers. He was overwhelmed and, in the fracas, must have killed or wounded a native, as he was dragged outside, thrown to the ground, and mutilated with knife, hatchet, and arrows. After his head and body were slashed, his heart was torn out. Petri's wife, Elizabeth, and Mrs. Skinner, the miller's wife, witnessed this horrific scene. That Robertson did not report the act demonstrates how hardened British officers had become to such ferocity.[52]

During the melée in the darkened building, Gershom Skinner received several wounds, yet he and his fellow miller Cox managed to hide under the water wheel and escaped the flames.[53]

Once the mill and outbuildings were thoroughly destroyed, Fort Hunter war captain, Isaac Hill Onoghsokete, and four of his Mohawks left the troops and headed east to take an "intelligent" prisoner and return to Canada via Crown Point.[54]

That same day, another band of raiders surrounded Fort Herkimer. Local families were still streaming into the fort and a man was shot dead at the gate. Another fellow was captured and tortured within the garrison's hearing; it was supposed the natives thought his cries would lure the garrison out and weaken the fort so it could be stormed. Despite his horrendous screams, the troops held firm and the fellow died. A brisk fire was exchanged, during which two soldiers of the garrison and two inhabitants were killed. The rebels took comfort that the invaders had probably suffered more. Many nearby farms had been burned and a number of animals were killed or driven off.[55]

Although Ross later reported that Skinner was dead, the miller was able to make his way to Fort Dayton the next day. After what his wife had seen, she was no doubt overjoyed to find him alive. His arrival prompted the dispatch of a burial party.

Another independent war party carried off nine people, mostly boys, from Canajoharie district near the ruins of Frey's Mills. Parties of troops pursued, but they were without rations and unable to keep up with the Indians and their prisoners, although they managed to recover some horses.[56]

Six days after the mill's destruction, the same unidentified officer stationed at Fort Rensselaer penned a poignant comment about the state of affairs in the Mohawk Valley. "It is a rare day that affords us no alarm. Murder is become so common that it is hardly taken account of."[57]

On July 13, Commodore Chambers reported to Mathews from aboard the *Royal George* off Pointe-au-Fer that Isaac Hill had arrived with four warriors. His party had made excellent time; they brought three prisoners, a man and two boys from Fort Hunter and two scalps and a "small paper" for the governor.[58]

Captain Robertson's son James served as a Volunteer on the raid and was later appointed an ensign in his father's company in recognition of the elder's accomplishment and the lad's performance of his duty.[59]

Perhaps this raid has received sparse notice because it was led by the native, Deserontyon, and a relatively obscure Regular officer, Robertson. In the eyes of history, their names lacked the notoriety of Old Smoke, Brant, Butler, and Johnson, yet their efforts were more than noteworthy, particularly for the span of time that their parties raided at will throughout the central Mohawk Valley — nine days, from July 14 to 23. Equally noteworthy was the ineffectual rebel opposition, especially after the example of the 1781 campaign, when reaction had been so prompt and often successful.[60]

On June 29, Major Ross reported from Fort Haldimand that Captain Crawford had returned with his detachment, as had Captain Robertson's party to Oswegatchie.[61]

Norman J. Agnew, 1984, after J.H. Durham, 1889.

An interpretation of Fort Haldimand's interior.

6

AN END TO ACTIVE OPERATIONS
Scarce a Day Passes Without Experiencing Their Ravages

*S*ir Guy Carleton wrote to Governor Haldimand from New York City on June 20 to formerly declare that he had taken command in America. When he left England, it had been "the determination of the Ministers and the sense of the nation to pursue all possible means consistent with Honor to bring about an accommodation with America, in consequence of which he purposes to confine his operations entirely to defence."[1]

Haldimand must have received similar information from another trustworthy source, as he wrote to his upper posts' commanders the next day, long before he could possibly have received Carleton's letter. "You will ... give such orders in the district of your Command as will prevent any offensive operation being undertaken untill you shall hear further from me but in such a measure as not to occasion a Belief of a Report prevailing in the Colonies that there is a Cessation of Arms which is by no means the Case."[2]

Two days later, a "Most Secret" dispatch arrived at Quebec City from Lord George Germain's replacement, William Petty-Fitzmaurice, the Earl of Shelburne (Lord Shelburne), the new Whig government's secretary of Home and Colonial Affairs. This document had been written on April 22 and had encountered excessive delays in crossing the ocean.

Shelburne was no novice to government. After a stellar career as a colonel in the Seven Years' War, when he distinguished himself in two ma-

William Petty-Fitzmaurice, the Earl of Shelburne (Lord Shelburne). The new Whig ministry's secretary of Home and Colonial Affairs.

Unknown artist, The London Magazine, 1780. (Library of Congress, LC-USZ62-45272.)

...jor European battles, he entered Parliament in 1763 and served under William Pitt as southern secretary in 1766, but he was dismissed two years later due to his opposition to the government's American policies. He agreed to re-enter government after receiving the king's agreement to recognize the United States and became a key player in the Rockingham ministry, which was devoted to ending the American war and making peace.

The new administration gutted the old one and many men of great knowledge, talent, and experience were tossed aside in a rush of housecleaning. While Shelburne is remembered as one of the most intelligent ministers of the century, he was a strangely hesitant decision-maker and was often unable to act on critical planning issues; however, there was no hint of this failing in his dispatch.

He warned Haldimand of "undoubted Intelligence ... that an Armament is now preparing at Brest for America. It is said to be destined against Quebec, and is to consist of Six Thousand Troops convoyed by a considerable Naval Force" (although he thought their real object might rather be New York or Halifax).

A Royal Naval squadron was cruising off Brest to prevent the enemy sailing; however, if that measure failed, Shelburne had "such Confidence in [Haldimand's] Zeal and Military Abilities, in the large Body of Troops under your Command, and in the Strength of the Works you have constructed for the Defence of Quebec at so vast an Expence that I cannot entertain a doubt of your repelling any Force that can be brought against you." Haldimand's gut must have wrenched. Had the new ministry even read his previous dispatches about the likelihood of a Canadien revolt if the French appeared and of the marginal utility of his German troops? "Large body of troops" indeed! His whole army, British, German, and Provincial, numbered only 10,500 and was spread in penny packets across his vast responsibility. If the Canadiens rose up and the rebels made simultaneous attacks, it was plain to see how his troops would be occupied. As well, Shelburne advised that, if necessary, Carleton had the king's direction to go to Quebec "with such part of the Forces under his Command."

Haldimand was "to take every precaution, and use the utmost Vigilance, to be prepared against an Attack." He was to send out "some light and swift Sailing Vessels to watch the Entrance of the River." If an enemy fleet appeared, two of the ships were to sail for New York City, the others return to Quebec. He was directed to set up a system of signals along the river linking the various posts.

Shelburne commented, "Our great Naval Force upon the lakes will be a good Guard against an Attack on that side." While this comment was valid for Champlain, the few skimpy ships on Ontario and Erie hardly warranted the descriptive adjective, "great." (Perhaps Shelburne thought the lakes were interconnected?)

His Lordship thoroughly approved of Haldimand's earlier decision not to employ natives against Vermont and strongly recommended "the same Policy ... throughout, and on no account to order, or permit, any predatory Excursions to be made upon the Frontiers of the Revolted Provinces." Here was a tall order. The very thought suggested that the natives were serfs or vassals without minds or political goals of their own.

Copies of the address of the commons to the king and his reply were enclosed. "You will see by these that the King's Servants are bound ... not only to avoid all Measures of Offensive War, but in truth, every Act that carries the Appearance of attempting to reduce the Revolted Colonies to obedience by Force." There it was, in black and white — an end to active operations.

As if he should have been clairvoyant, Haldimand was scolded that his 1781 proclamation to Vermont was "totally repugnant to these

Resolutions." He was told that a review of his dispatches failed to reveal "sufficient ground or Confidence in these People to justify the hazarding Steps" taken. (So, his dispatches were read!) If Canada were attacked, Haldimand was to bring Vermont to his assistance by assuring her of the "King's Disposition" to recognize the land grants.

So, the little republic, which worried about tempting Congress into taking overt action, was expected to hazard its existence to gain the king's approval of land grants! And, of significance, the king clearly favoured the grants made by New Hampshire over those made by New York.

"All the American Prisoners of War ... confined in Great Britain and Ireland" were to be exchanged straight away. Haldimand was to send his to Boston.

Carleton would come to Quebec only if Canada became "the Seat of War." As Haldimand would be again faced with the possibility of being commanded by his junior in rank, the same reasons that he had been given for his recall to England in 1775 would have "equal Force at present." Should this situation be impossible for Haldimand, the King had been "graciously pleased to grant you Leave of Absence from the Province retaining at the same time your Commissions, and all their Emoluments."

After digesting this momentous news, Haldimand turned to Shelburne's dispatch No. 1 of the same date. His Lordship noted that Haldimand had already been apprised of the government's adoption of his proposal for a superintendent general for the Indian Department and that a warrant had been issued to Sir John Johnson for this purpose. Under Haldimand's direction, Johnson was to implement a "thorough reform ... in this vast Branch of Expence."

Shelburne ordered that the post commanders and their officers must attend all native councils to witness the distribution of presents by the deputy superintendents. Further, Haldimand was to be responsible for settling Johnson's pay, travelling expenses, and other contingencies.

As Sir John's "Merit and Services, and his early exertions in the Royal Cause entitle him as an Officer to particular attention," the king had approved his appointment to brigadier-general in Canada and, as his first battalion was complete, the king accepted the governor's recommendation to allow the officers permanent rank in America and half-pay on reduction. (Was this what Sir John had understood to be an elevation to the American Establishment?)

The letter went on to severely chastise the governor for his great expenditures and demands for large amounts of cash. In future, he was not to undertake any large, costly works without first providing estimates and waiting for approval, except "in cases of the last necessity."

There was more difficult news. The special hospital he had established at Quebec City was too expensive and had to be shut down. Then, another slap — a number of dangerous Anglo- and Franco-Canadian malcontents had petitioned the home government against his treatment of them. Germain had viewed these people as being of no account, but Shelburne was not of that mind and expected the governor to send an explanation for each complaint. He cautioned the governor to ensure "the Affections of the People ... by shewing the tenderest regards to their Rights and Liberties."

For a dedicated man, so thoroughly exhausted by overwork and sickened by the agony of bladder gravel, these chastisements must have rained like blows.[3]

On June 25, the other ranks of the two companies and detachment of the 47th Regiment, which had been serving at the upper posts alongside the 8th (King's), were drafted into the latter and the officers were returned to Britain to rebuild the regiment. This allowed the 8th to establish an eleventh and twelfth company, making it the largest British regiment in Canada. Nominal command of the eleventh company was given to Captain Stephen Watts, Sir John Johnson's brother-in-law, who had lost his leg at Oriskany while commanding the Royal Yorkers' Light Company.

Dr. Smyth informed headquarters that Ensign Thomas Sherwood, LR, had brought in three previously trusted men who admitted to frequently warning the rebel garrison at Saratoga about British Secret Service scouts and had even guided patrols to hunt them. How these traitors were dealt with has not been found.

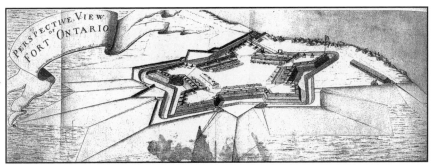

Ross wrote from Oswego on June 26 to report that, although Joseph Brant had been greatly affected by the change of ministry in Britain (in which he had had many personal allies), he had conducted himself "with the greatest propriety." Joseph thought that the natives could expect no friendship from the new men (how prescient!) and asked Ross many difficult questions that the major was at a loss to answer. The next day, Ross reported to Mathews, again commenting on Brant:

> I cannot say too much in his favor, his conduct is surprising. He rules his Indians as he pleases and they are all rejoiced at seeing this place occupied. I can assure your Excellency that we are much indebted to the Indians for assisting us to work, a Circumstance which I believe never before happened. Joseph shewed them the Example. I never saw men work so hard and it greatly encouraged the Troops.… The Works … are about Thirty feet Perpendicular which exceeds the plan by one-third. I hope in a few days to begin the outworks, every part will be easily repaired except the Glacis which is deficient in the most necessary and exposed parts of the Fortifications.

In less than two weeks, Ross expected to have completed two magazines and four storehouses, each sixty feet long, capable of containing provisions for one thousand men for a year, and bombproof quarters excavated under the platforms of two bastions.[4]

On June 27, Powell reported that the Six Nations had taken Haldimand's criticism very seriously and, in evidence, noted that two of their chiefs had been severely reproved "for their misconduct last fall." As to the governor's comment that the natives had promised one thousand men to assist in reoccupying Oswego, he opined that whoever said this "probably did it to raise his own consequence," as Butler had commented to Powell that he had never seen more than six hundred Six Nations' warriors on expedition until now. The brigadier postulated that this unprecedented turnout proved their attachment to the war. He believed Ross's "affair of last fall" was reconciled, "and they are properly fixed in their former confidence" and hoped it would not be "necessary to bring it on the carpet again."

With such a show of support for the British cause, it is not difficult to imagine how the news of a cessation of active operations was going to be received, especially after all the nations had been scourged by Haldimand's anger over their supposed wavering resolve.

Powell reported that while the natives were still at Niagara, he had been invited to visit and christen their main settlement about eight miles from the fort, where a large number of Mohawks and Oneidas (Brant's 6NID company) lived with smaller bodies of Onondagas, Tuscaroras, Cayugas, and Delawares. He reported that he had done so with great pleasure and named the place "Loyal Confederate Valley."

That same day, Butler wrote to Lernoult, giving his approval of Lieutenant Charles Tonnancoeur's appointment. Considering the several lectures he had received about appointments by headquarters, he could hardly do less. He continued saying that, if he was to properly take care of the Indian Department, he hoped that a major would be appointed to the Rangers, as it would be "necessary for me to stay on the other side of the river, for crossing the river twice a day does not agree with the rheumatism, my constant companion." Butler's health was in decline, no doubt spurred on by Walter's untimely death. Two days later, he answered Brant's criticisms of the supplying of the Indians that went to Oswego.

> I have enclosed you a return of the Indian presents sent
> to Oswego, also what were given that party before their
> embarkation, and [Brant] himself were present and saw

the clothing, &c, &c, given them with every appearance of satisfaction. In short, I made it my business to give everything he asked for. … [T]hey have been more extravagantly loaded with presents than any party that every left this post in my time.

In his typically circumspect manner, he politely chastised Ross's overreaction. "I am exceedingly sorry that Major Ross has troubled His Excellency with Indian complaints without first knowing whether they were just or not. Had he wrote General Powell or myself, he would have then immediately been acquainted with every particular."[5]

In the face of a Franco-American invasion, Haldimand's preparations in lower Quebec included pressing the loyalist pensioners into service who had not been incorporated into the Loyal Rangers. On June 28, Mathews instructed that all persons receiving subsistence on the pension list who were able to carry arms and were fit for the scouting service were to hold themselves in readiness whenever called upon. Sherwood would make application for men as required.[6]

General Washington arrived in Albany on June 26 to examine "the Situation of Affairs on the Frontiers" and was awarded the freedom of the city. Next day, he penned a letter of thanks to the mayor, aldermen, and "Commonalty" for the honour they had bestowed upon him.

Colonel Willett met with the C-in-C and broached the subject of his seniority over Lieutenant-Colonel Reid of New Hampshire. He was distressed that Reid had been conducting himself as if he were senior. Willett was very likely unaware that Washington had given orders to General Heath in January that the senior New Hampshire colonel was to take command in the north until General Hazen arrived. If that order had not been rescinded, it would explain Reid's stance. In addition, Reid

An Albany street.

seems to have genuinely believed his commission pre-dated Willett's and, he either chose to ignore Willett's recent promotion to full colonel, or believed it related to the command of Levies only. Disappointingly for Willett, Washington chose not to adjudicate the question, but suggested that both officers' claims would be reviewed.

Escorted by forty mounted men, the C-in-C rode in a carriage with General Schuyler to tour the 1777 Saratoga battlefields and view the barracks and new fortifications.

Simultaneously, the men of Wright's company upset Lieutenant Pliny Moore's happy little Ballstown garrison by accusing the commissary of making profits off the bakers. While Moore dealt with this disturbance on June 30, Washington and Schuyler drove to Schenectady. Outside the town, one hundred Oneida warriors were drawn up to greet the "Great Father," who presented them with a belt and urged them to raid Oswego and Oswegatchie and seize as many prisoners as possible.

That evening, Washington attended a dinner with several officers and prominent citizens at a tavern owned by General Braddock's former drum major. He knew that Colonel Frederick Visscher of Tryon's third regiment was in town convalescing from wounds he had received in the spring of 1780 and was upset to find that the veteran had not been invited to the dinner. In a typical, thoughtful, Washington-style gesture, he had the meal delayed until Visscher could be fetched and, when he arrived, the C-in-C seated him on his right hand. A very warm address was delivered to the general, to which he replied:

> Gentlemen, I request you to accept my warmest thanks for your affectionate address.
>
> In a cause so just and righteous as ours, we have every reason to hope the Divine Providence will still continue to crown our arms with success, and finally compel our enemies to grant us that peace upon equitable terms, which we so ardently desire.
>
> May you, and the good people of this town, in the mean time, be protected from every insidious and open foe, and may the complicated blessings of peace soon reward your arduous struggles for the establishment of the freedom and independence of our common country.

Washington wrote a letter of thanks to Schenectady's "Minister, Elders and Deacons of the reformed Protestant Dutch Church," which included the sentiment, "May the same Providence that has hitherto, in so remarkable a manner evinced the justice of our cause, lead us to a speedy and honourable peace."

Washington reported about Deserontyon's raid to Congress, "A party of 300 or 400 of the enemy, consisting of British refugees and savages … attacked and captured (after a gallant defence) a small guard of Continental troops, who were stationed at the only remaining mill in the upper settlements, which they also destroyed." ("A gallant defence"— such an odd description. Someone was gilding the lily; succumbed in mortal terror, more like.) The C-in-C advised that a Tory deserter had revealed that the British had "extend[ed] themselves on the frontier" and reoccupied Oswego.

Brigadier Peter Gansevoort's brother, Leonard, demonstrated the high regard so many Americans felt for Washington when he wrote to a friend:

> I expected to have seen you in Town on the Occasion of General Washington's arrival. It was well worth your

while to come this far to see the greatest character in the world, who has no equal in History. I am surprised that numbers have not come from the Country to see the Deliverer of their Country.[7]

On the evening of June 30, Corporal John Pettit and about twenty Stockbridge Indians of Newall's Company of Willett's were led into Fort Rensselaer where they joined Major Jason Wait, 2NH, and the regiment's light infantry company under Captain Cherry. That same night, the combined detachment marched for Fort Herkimer, arriving early the next morning. Their timely appearance drove off yet another large force of enemy troops and natives, which retired across the river into the woods.

Newall's Company was a departure from the norm in the NY Levies. When Newall was given his warrant as captain, he was authorized to recruit from Stockbridge, a Massachusetts River Indians' community that had supported the rebellion from its earliest days. Its warriors had faithfully served in the northern and southern campaigns and suffered grievous casualties. In view of the Oneidas's and Tuscaroras's effectiveness, it had been decided to reinforce them.

Newall had been immediately successful, recruiting a dozen warriors. The men enlisted for pay, rather than land grants, which they probably were not entitled to in any event. His early success

Captain Johann Ewald Diary, circa 1781. (Joseph P. Tustin Papers, Special Collections, Harvey A. Andruss Library, Bloomsburg University of Pennsylvania.)

A Stockbridge warrior. He wears loose linen garments and a straw hat and resembles a European farmer except for the rings in his nose and ears, his firelock, quiver of arrows, and bow.

Captain Hendrick Aupaumut, *circa* 1757–1829. Aupaumut supported the rebellion from its earliest days. He took command of the Stockbridge contingent after Captain Daniel Ninham was killed in August 1778. As senior Stockbridge war captain, he likely served in the Mohawk Valley in 1782.

Gavin A. Watt, 2009, after an unknown artist.

continued and more men were added in June. The Stockbridges served together under Newall's lieutenant, Ryal Bingham, and were denominated rangers. Records are available for two. David Nawnawnikan, twenty-six, and Jacob Nawnomtim, eighteen, enlisted on June 20. Both were a strapping six feet tall, with olive complexions and black hair, and they listed their occupation as hunters.[8]

Sometime in late June, a small British Indian war party appeared in the Valley. There were seven warriors and, to judge from what transpired, they may have been some of the same Akwesasne youngsters who had raided in May. It was said their original goal was to capture or kill state representative William Harper, or 3rd Tryon's captain, John Littel. The party stopped at Andrew Bowman's place just east of Johnstown. As Bowman had "escaped" from the Akwesasne raiders back in May, he would have felt the party's menace if he recognized any of the warriors. In a ploy to save his scalp, or perhaps to settle old scores, he identified his neighbour Henry Stoner as a prominent local Whig who had two sons in the Continental army and even led the raiders to Henry's house. On the way there, a man named Palmatier fell in the party's way and was taken. At Stoner's, the warriors were pleased to observe that the place stood away from its neighbours and was ideal for attack.

Stoner and his nephew were hoeing corn when Mrs. Stoner blew a horn to signal breakfast. When the nephew turned to leave, he was startled to see two tomahawk-wielding natives sneaking through the woods and shouted a warning. Both men had foolishly left their firelocks at the house and Henry ran to fetch his, but a warrior easily intercepted him and sunk a hatchet into his head and stripped off his scalp. Simultaneously, other natives ran to the house and Mrs. Stoner scarcely had time to throw a gown out a back window. After looting the building, the warriors set it alight, then waited long enough to be sure the fire had caught. All that Stoner's wife had left to her name was the gown she had managed to save.

Either from a sense of guilt, or to allay any suspicions of complicity, Bowman helped Palmatier and the nephew carry the plunder to the Indians' food cache near the Sacandaga River. Palmatier escaped that night and Bowman was released in the morning before the party set off with Stoner's nephew.

Mrs. Stoner had gone to a neighbour who, with some friends, went to the burning ruins of the house and found her husband alive, his head a welter of blood. He made a sign for water, but expired upon taking a swallow.

When Palmatier returned, he speculated that Bowman had a role in the attack, but the culprit swore his innocence. Nonetheless, he was put into the Johnstown jail, whereupon Godfrey Shew, his son, and two other vigilantes, probably "disguised in liquor," decided to force a confession. Somehow, they got into the cell, threw a noose around Bowman's neck, and stood him on a barrel. After questions and threats, the barrel was kicked from under his feet and he strangled for a few moments before being cut free. Sometime later, he was released with a severe warning.

On another occasion, the ubiquitous Ray Guile of Warrensborough and five other Levies were scouting toward the dry marsh on the Sacandaga River when they discovered eight natives cooking in two small camp kettles. They crept very near under the cover of some trees and signed to each other to select targets. In their first discharge, they felled five. The other three fled and were pursued and two were cut down. Gathering up the natives' arms, ammunition, and kettles, the patrol returned to Fort Rensselaer where Willett "called them good fellows" and rewarded them with rum.[9]

On July 1, a return of the New Hampshire Continentals showed the 1st regiment stationed at Saratoga with 270 rank and file fit for duty. The 2nd was widely dispersed with three companies at Forts Herkimer and Dayton and eighty rank and file fit for duty. A thirty-man company was posted at the Herkimer home and the Canajoharie Indian Castle and the remaining companies of almost 150 men at Fort Rensselaer from where guards were detached weekly to various outposts such as Fort Willett and Walradt's Ferry. In a postscript, Lieutenant-Colonel Reid wrote that the return might not be entirely accurate, as it was based on last May's musters.

On the same day, "A Return of the number of State troops and Levies Commanded by Colonel Marinus Willett" was prepared at Albany. It showed a total of 609 non-commissioned officers and privates; 307 of the men had enlisted to serve for two- and three-year terms and Willett believed there was "a prospect of a Considerable increase of the men for the three years service, [and] the men who now engage for that service are to serve two years from the first day of next January."

The captains and their company strengths were: James Cannon, 61; Abner French, 75; Joseph Harrison, 60; Nathaniel Henry, 75; Abraham Livingston, 71; Simeon Newell, 51; Jonathon Pearsee (Pierce), 72; Peter B. Tearce (Tierce), 75; and Job Wright, 61.

Their postings were: Livingston at Saratoga and Ballstown; Wright at Ballstown; French, Henry, Newell, Pierce, and Tearce in Tryon County; Harrison and Cannon at Schoharie with a guard at Catskill.

It was noted that, "Arms and Accoutrements are wanted for the three-years' men — which with Clothing as well as pay and Subsistance is to be furnished by the public."

Willett signed this return as a full colonel, which was no accident, as two days later, he again signed a document as a colonel of "States Troops and Levies." Clearly, he had received the promotion he had sought.[10]

Although there was a battalion of Continentals and a battalion of State Troops and Levies spread across the Mohawk Valley, the pace of raiding was too great for them to handle and Captain Gerrit S. Veeder and his forty-man 2ACM company were called out to reinforce Forts Rensselaer and Plain and guard the area's harvesters. The works and magazine at Rensselaer had deteriorated and Washington advised Lieutenant-Colonel Reid that he had instructed the quartermaster at Albany to furnish all the materials in his power "to put the installation in a proper state of defence."[11]

The Schoharie Valley did not escape the raiders' attention. On Independence Day, Peter Feeck and Adam Vrooman, the son of Isaac, who had been brutally killed in late 1781, left the Upper Fort to drive some cattle to pasture. Ironically, Feeck had been engaged in this same activity when he was the first man to spot Sir John's column in October 1780. Feeck was herding the beasts when Adam went to throw open the gate and was killed by several balls fired by ambushing Tories and Indians. Feeck ran a mile to the safety of the fort. A body of rangers was immediately sent in pursuit, but was unable to overtake the raiders, who were mounted on stolen horses. During their retreat, the raiders captured another fellow who was also herding cattle. Due to the number of signs and sightings, the locals concluded that a large body of Indians had taken up temporary residence in the area. When scouts discovered indications of a native encampment on a ridge near Cobus Kill Creek, Colonel Vrooman ordered Serjeant David Freemoyer of Harrison's Company, WL, to take a few of his best men to determine the natives' strength.

The five-man party set off at dark, but after a couple of miles became lost and lay over until dawn to get their bearings. Just as they crested a rise at about 9:00 the next morning, they were startled to find the enemy camp only a few steps way. A great deal of meat was hung from spears and sticks as it slowly cooked over low fires, but no Indians were in sight. Freemoyer decided that the natives were berry-picking in a nearby field, but when he turned to comment, he found that his handpicked "band of brothers" had deserted him. Thinking to get an accurate count of the natives, he hid in

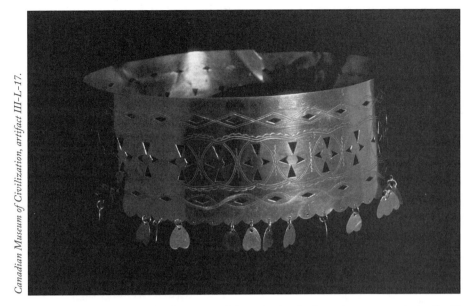

Canadian Museum of Civilization, artifact III-L-17.

A silver headband similar to that stripped from the head of a native war captain by David Freemoyer of Willett's Levies.

the brush near to what he thought would be their return route.

He had been squatting there for quite some time when he was surprised by noises coming from an unexpected direction. As the sounds drew nearer, Freemoyer realized he was about to be discovered, so he popped up and shot a warrior with a ball to the torso. The native was carrying a fine English fusil, like those supplied to war captains and principal warriors, and was wearing a great deal of trade silver. There was a cylindrical piece bound in his topknot and Freemoyer slashed it away, taking a bit of flesh in the process. Then he ran for the fort at top speed.

He had gone about three hundred yards when he heard the natives' dogs. Although he forded a stream, the barking came ever closer. At another stream, he ran along the bed to throw off the scent. After a piece, he left the stream bed and "ran up a bottom about two miles, then took to a ridge," but from the experiences of an earlier escape, he knew the dogs would be persistent. He threw off all his clothes other than his trousers and moccasins and kept on at such a rate that he arrived back at the fort before his men. Telling everyone to keep mum, he hid himself to hear what kind of report they would make. They soon arrived and told of finding the native camp, but said that Freemoyer refused to come away and, on their retreat, they heard a rifle shot, which undoubtedly signalled his demise. "Much to their astonishment and chagrin," their serjeant suddenly appeared.[12]

On July 1, fifty-two-year-old Prime Minister Rockingham suffered an early death, marking the end of a very short, ineffectual term in office. He was succeeded by Shelburne, and Thomas Townshend assumed the role of Domestic, Irish, and Colonial Affairs secretary.[13]

Haldimand wrote to Powell on July 1 about the furor Brant had stirred up over Butler's supposed neglect. Ross had reported that the "chiefs and warriors" who came with Joseph from Niagara grumbled of "their wants, particularly … shoes and ammunition, notwithstanding repeated applications." The governor gave recognition to the previous lack of stores at Niagara, but said that, now that they had been built up, Butler should have been able to meet their needs. Obviously, Butler's detailed explanation had not yet been received.

Unknown engraver. (www.fotosearch.com/clip-art/sydney.)

Powell reported to Haldimand about the ritual killing of the Virginia militia colonel, William Crawford, in the Ohio country by Delaware Indians in retaliation for the massacre of their close relatives, the Moravian Christians. The

Thomas Townshend, 1732–1800. The Domestic, Irish, and Colonial Affairs secretary in Shelburne's administration.

coming months would show that all the loyal natives were inflamed by this slaughter. Although the Moravians' German missionaries had supplied intelligence to the rebels, the natives themselves had been quite passive during the war and their horrific murder was recognized as racially motivated rather than an act of war.

The brigadier closed with the advice that he would send a company of Rangers to Sandusky. If Caldwell did not need them, they would go to Detroit to assist in repairing the works, which the late heavy rains had badly damaged. The second company taken from Oswego would be held at Niagara as a strategic reserve. He confirmed that he would go to Detroit on about July 10 and would stay there to observe the outcome of George Roger Clark's expedition.[14]

On July 1, Ross submitted a return of the Oswego garrison, which made note of the addition of Captain Lauchlin Maclean's Grenadier Company, 84RHE, composed of the captain, two ensigns, two serjeants, two corporals, two drummers, and forty rank and file. The other detachments of Regulars and Provincials were little altered. Total strength, including a number of "sick present," was 628 all ranks, a respectable garrison of well-equipped, seasoned troops.[15]

Sometime during July, Ensign John Magrath of the 84th was dismissed from the service. Whether his crime was a first offence is a matter of conjecture; however, the severity of the penalty suggests otherwise. Magrath was found guilty of confining a serjeant without orders, refusing to submit to arrest, and behaving in an improper, challenging manner to a superior officer.[16]

Word arrived on July 1 confirming that many German officers, who had been held under the Saratoga Convention, had been exchanged to New York City and that they would come to Canada with the first fleet. At Sorel, Surgeon Wasmus was distressed that the Dragoons were ordered to encamp. Now all their flourishing gardens would have to be abandoned. Six days later, he read in a Quebec City paper that the

Royal Navy had seized ten French transports with 130 guns and 1,012 men aboard. There was news from St. Lucia that a French warship of fifty guns had been captured and another of seventy-four guns had been taken off Antigua and yet another sunk. If all these reports were true, the war in the Caribbean was going well.[17]

On July 5, Ross reported the departure of a raid led by Joseph Brant composed of a truly amazing 460 warriors supported by 2KRR's Light Infantry Company under Captain George Singleton, a Canadian from Montreal. It was fitting that Singleton assisted Brant, as both men had fought at Oriskany, the first major action of the Valley's long war. Singleton had forty-three Light Bobs, including officers and three Volunteers. Their target was the Mohawk Valley. This raid would prove to be the final expedition mounted by the allies against that war-drenched region. For a man who had decried native support only months before, Ross displayed great sympathy:

> [Brant] is much to be pitied and if I mistake not feels it exceedingly, he wishes to make a great Stroke, which

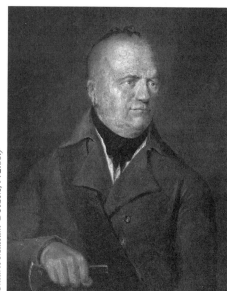

William Berczy, 1797–1808. (With permission from the Royal Ontario Museum © ROM, 972.80.)

he thinks from his numbers is expected, but is doubtful of the Indians, the different Tribes are much divided, Jealous and unsteady, his management of matters is much to be applauded, he used often to come to me at nights and get what

Joseph Brant, leader of the last major strike into the Mohawk Valley. "He wishes to make a great Stroke."

little things I had to give them, and distribute them privately among the needy & no man could study more the oeconomy of Provisions and Rum than he did. There has been not less than five hundred of the Six Nations here in one Group, many of whom came immediately from their Villages and expected to find everything they wanted. I have put them off as well as I could and given them some Indian Fusils and powder. I have brought them a little Paint and even strip[p]ed many of the Mississagoes of their half worn Mocasins to prevent numbers from returning discontented to their Villages.[18]

On July 7, Lieutenant Walter Sutherland wrote a detailed report from Montreal. In addition to suffering with an infected eye, he had accidentally cut himself with an axe and was down with a fever. The doctor said he might lose two toes, but his marching would be unaffected. He pursued payment of the funds owed to the loyalists who had so selflessly supplied Ross's troops in Johnstown the previous October; in particular McDonell and McNaughton, who had sacrificed all they owned and then sheltered Sutherland's scouting party in the winter. Now, the pair had been driven from Johnstown and stripped of what few items they had managed to reassemble. Sutherland thought that no payment was a very poor reward for such dedication, so he had sent them some cash from his own scant resources.

He had been employing a Highlander named Robert McGlashen and an unnamed "Dutchman" to collect intelligence in the Valley. In the past, both had supplied Snetsinger's party with provisions and sent information to Sherwood. When Sutherland had spent time "in country," these two had given him some provisions and he had paid them "a trifle" for their trouble. McGlashen had gone to Albany to visit John McDonell for information and found him in a most distressed state.

McDonell was convinced that the money owed by Ross had been sent by Haldimand and filched by the courier. Sutherland asked Dr. Smyth about this claim and was told that £5 had been sent to Albany and given to a man named Kineer. Sutherland was unable to vouch for Kineer, but stressed that all the intelligence Sherwood had received last winter from the Albany area had come through McDonell. Smyth assured the lieutenant that any additional money would be given directly to him to deliver.

Sutherland had spoken to the wife of Captain John Johnston, 6NID. She had come to Canada through Vermont, which was a safe route now favoured by loyalists who were forced to flee New York. As her husband had served with the Iroquois, particularly the Senecas, long before and during the war, she may have been considered a friend by some Oneidas who told her that scouts "frequently came to Canady." She heard from some Canadien refugees in Albany that they knew when these scouts came and went and that two Kahnawakes were their pilots. And, while in Vermont, she heard of two expresses that had come down from Canada to Albany. Sutherland wrote that as soon as his foot wound was healed he would be ready for any service and, in particular, to take these rebel scouts and pilots.

The next day, he prepared an account of the cash he had expended while on Secret Service. His accounting proved that he had been a very busy man and indicated that he was running his own little department of spies. There were the expenses for his twenty-one-man party that went from Montreal to the Mohawk River; expenses incurred sending Angus Cameron to New England in March 1782 for intelligence; payments to McGlashan for going to Schenectady for intelligence; funds to John Helmer for going from Johnstown to Stone Arabia on three occasions; money paid for provisions for his own scouting party and for necessaries for eight 1KRR soldiers sent on a Secret Service mission from Ticonderoga to Johnstown by Sherwood; however, the wheels of the army's finances ground ever so slowly and Sutherland would face a long, long wait for compensation.[19]

In the absence of the Hesse-Hanau infantry commander, Lieutenant-Colonel Carl von Kreutzbourg was temporarily in command of all Hanau troops, including his Jäger regiment. He arrived at Point Levis on July 8 to put into execution his prince's orders to organize the infantry into the first battalion of "Erbprinz von Hessen" by forming six equal companies. As the second senior Hesse-Hanau officer in Canada, Major

Georg Pausch of the artillery company was placed in titular command of the battalion, although Pausch voluntarily deferred to Captain Friedrich von Schoell, who had so very professionally led the Hanau infantry detachment since 1777.

Kreutzbourg had brought the colours of the old Hesse-Hanau Grenadier Regiment to Pointe Levis, which had been saved at the time of Burgoyne's capitulation and recently carried back to Canada by General Riedesel. Pausch had the battalion's name embroidered along the colours' top edge. Kreutzbourg advised the prince that the new staffs had been painted yellow and that brass finials had been crafted for their tips, but their cords lacked the proper ornamental tassels.

About this time, von Kreutzbourg had a revelation. Since Haldimand's arrival in 1778, the colonel had resisted all of the governor's demands to have his Jägers share in the burden of labouring in the works by arguing that the terms of the Crown's treaty with Hesse-Hanau prohibited it. In discussion with his fellow Hanau officers, Pausch and von Schoell, he discovered that their men regularly performed such tasks and that, over and above their normal pay, received additional funds and allowances of flour. Moreover, the work was not very difficult, was beneficial to the men's health and they received a daily ration of rum, and enjoyed making some money for themselves. Even more persuasive, if he continued to refuse, Haldimand threatened to return his men to England, which would have been a disgrace. The problem was resolved.[20]

———————

On July 8, Haldimand wrote to Ross recommending that the outworks of Fort Ontario be raised as high as possible and asked for a plan of the works as presently constructed so that he could give instructions concerning two redoubts that had been of great utility when the place was attacked during "the last war."[21]

———————

Brant's expedition was at Fish Creek between Lake Oneida and Fort Stanwix's ruins on July 9 when he sent a scout of thirteen Indians into the Valley to take prisoners for interrogation. When the expedition advanced the next day, a great many tracks were discovered that had been made by the rebels' native scouts.

The composition of Brant's native contingent is a mystery. Earlier, hundreds of Six Nations warriors had arrived at Oswego and Ross reported that he had politely dismissed them without being able to offer much in the way of campaigning supplies. If they returned to their villages, they were little better equipped for service than when they left Oswego. If they went to Niagara, they may have been supplied by Powell and Butler and gone off to Sandusky to work with Caldwell and the Lakes' Nations. Or, did some return to join Brant? No answer has been found.

When Brant had arrived at Oswego, it was reported that his Indian Department company of Oneidas and Mohawks were not with him and only ten of his white Volunteers were present. Had his company and Volunteers now joined his expedition? And, as many of the Mississaugas had been stripped of their worn moccasins to supply Brant's warriors, can we assume that few of them joined the raid? Answers to these questions have not been found, but it is known that Deserontyon was present and it may be assumed that some his fellow Fort Hunter Mohawks attended, but beyond that, nothing more is known.

As for the septuagenarian Sayenqueraghta (Old Smoke), on July 10 Powell reported to Haldimand that he expected the Seneca war chief's party to co-operate with Captain Caldwell, as they understood each other's intentions. This meant that the Confederacy's primary leader was elsewhere and not with Brant, and begs the question whether his co-chief, Captain Abeel Cornplanter, was with him or with Brant?[22]

A series of letters from Washington to Lieutenant-Colonel George Reid revealed much about service on the New York frontiers in the summer of 1782. On July 10, he wrote:

> For my own part, I am more apprehensive for the safety of the Country on the Mowhawk River than for any other part of the frontier; because I think from circumstances, the principal effort (should there be any invasion) would

be made against it, and therefore it seems to me, that withdrawing the Companies of State Troops from Saratoga and that Quarter (where they cannot be very necessary) and extending them together with the other Levies on the frontier of the Mowhawk, and at the same time concentrating your Regiment to the neighbourhood of the place you mention, would be a judicious plan.

The general recommended that Reid confer with Willett and suggested that any dispute over rank should be laid aside for the good of the service. Washington chided, "These disputes, as I before observed, may be determined whenever the claims and documents of both parties are handed in."

The C-in-C next addressed a nuts-and-bolts issue that pointed to Reid having, in some measure, assumed control over Willett's troops. "As to Cartridge Boxes for the Levies, it will be impossible to supply them from the public Store; because we have not more than are absolutely necessary for our troops; the best substitute that can be devised, must therefore be made use of; and I have a confidence, that you and the other Officers commanding on the frontiers will Oeconomize ... to the best advantage."

What a remarkable revelation! While the United States lacked the industry to produce the large quantities of muskets, bayonets, and uniforms required by the army, surely leather, wood, and labour for cartridge pouches were within indigenous means.

The next day, he wrote Reid to introduce Captain Montour, who would deliver his first letter. Montour had been employed in the rebel Indian Service along the Pennsylvania frontiers and was travelling to Schenectady to visit his Oneida and Tuscarora friends. Reid was to arrange subsistence for him during his stay. This request provides more circumstantial evidence that Willett and Reid continued to clash, as the former usually managed Indian affairs in the Valley. The following day, a third letter was penned to Reid. Washington had "learned from the Commandant of Artillery, that there are a number of damaged Cartridge Boxes in the Store at Fishkill; an Order is given to deliver 400 of them for the use of Col. Willets command; they will be forwarded by the D.Q.M.

as soon as may be." One has to wonder what the State Troops and Levies had been using to hold their cartridges — haversacks, hunting bags?[23]

Returning to July 10, General Washington wrote to Lieutenant-Colonel John Laurens, the son of Henry, whose capture the year before had revealed the Allies' plan to invade Canada to the British. The C-in-C was responding to the colonel's report:

> I must confess that I am not at all astonished at the failure of your Plan. That spirit of Freedom, which at the commencement of this contest would have gladly sacrificed every thing to the attainment of its object, has long since subsided and every selfish passion has taken its place. It is not the public but the private Interest, which influences the generality of Mankind, nor can the Americans any longer boast an exception. Under these circumstances, it would rather have been surprising if you had succeeded …
>
> Sir Guy Carleton is using every art to sooth and lull our people into a State of security. Admiral Digby is capturing all our Vessels, and suffocating all our Seamen who will not inlist into the service of His Britanic Majesty, as fast as possible, in Prison Ships and Haldimand (with his Savage Allies) is Scalping and burning … the Frontiers. Such is the Line of conduct pursued by the different Commanders, and such their Politics.[24]

Although Haldimand had received orders to cease operations, the instruction seemed to enhance his pleasure in the defeat of a large body of rebel militia in the Ohio country by Butler's Ranger's captain, William Caldwell. He wrote to Powell, "Since the enemy have invaded the Indian Country and forced our troops and Indians into action, it affords me infinite satisfaction that they have rec'd so signal a check with so immaterial a loss on our part." As to the ritual execution of the rebels' commanding officer, Colonel Crawford, he wrote, "I fear it will give occasion to objections and difficulties in whatever may be transacting with the Congress, who will not have the liberality to attribute the misfortunes to the real cause, the massacre of the Moravian Indians, nor to make allowance for that innate fixed principle of retaliation by which Indians alone conceive their existence is in any way secure."

The governor had ordered the 84th's Light Company to immediately proceed to Carleton Island and to continue on to Niagara if necessary. His letter continued:

> Yours and a letter from Colonel Butler enclosing a return of articles given and sent to Joseph are very explanatory of his unreasonable complaints, but the same motives that operate against renewing Major Ross's affair engage us to conciliate and keep Joseph and his brethren in temper if possible.

Such phraseology points to how deeply the native allies had been affected by Ross's criticisms and Haldimand's angry reactions.[25]

According to Surgeon Wasmus, a thirty-three-man scout of Brunswick Dragoons and Light Infantry supplied with thirty cartridges apiece left Sorel on July 12 with orders to travel to Crown Point and "wreck havoc there." Just how this adventurous mission was to be accomplished at an abandoned post is a mystery.

As Haldimand had repeatedly denied British medical supplies to Wasmus, the Brunswicker bitterly noted, "For his thriftiness, he is hated by the English. — He is Swiss by birth" — as if the governor's national origin explained everything.[26]

The Prenties' disgrace continued down its sordid path in Montreal. Captain Duncan reported to Gray from Rivière du Chêne on July 12:

The affair between Mr Lavalla and Messrs Prentice, McAlpin, & Glen [note, Glen not Valentine], I have done every thing in my power to settle it, but to no purpose — I offer'd Mr Lavalla Twenty pounds on condition that he wou'd give a Receipt in full for all damages done, & to withdraw any Suit in Law commenc'd against the aforesaid Parties – he said his accepting any Sum of Money wou'd appear mercenary in the Eyes of the General [Haldimand], but that whatever sum His Excellency wou'd name, he should cheerfully abide by and accept.

Three weeks later, Gray informed headquarters that he had instructed Duncan "to acquaint Mr Lavallu to make up his Damages done him by Prentice, McAlpin, and Glen, his Expenses going & coming to Montreal will be the most, as I have seen what he Complen'd." Seven days later, Gray wrote to Major Lernoult, "I was Presented by Mr Lavala from the River Duchine, with an Acct of £50, for his Damages, I Refused payment, as the sume was Extravegant, but offered him an Reasonable sume, for his Expenses, he would have the whole or non[e] — I suppose thyle send it to the Commander in Chief, — I sent Capt Saml Anderson to Isle Jesue to get Mr Prentice to sign a Certificate Agreeable to the form you sent me, which he has Refused to doe."[27]

On July 13, Major Ross received Haldimand's orders to cease offensive operations. That same day, Captain Singleton was at the ruins of Fort Stanwix with Brant's expedition. Brant proposed striking through the woods to arrive at the settlements undiscovered, but his warriors refused, complaining they had insufficient moccasins. Consequently, the raid risked alarming the rebels by advancing along the "high Road" and, in anticipation of later criticism, the Mohawk asked Singleton to note this fact in his report.

At Carleton Island, Ross wrote to Haldimand in response to the new instructions. He opined that Brant was likely on his return march and hoped to restrain the natives from committing depredations, although

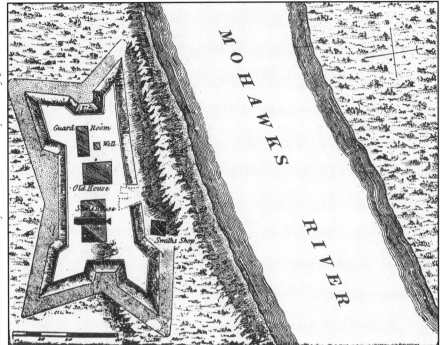

Nathaniel S. Benton. A History of Herkimer County... Albany: J. Munsell, 1856.

Plan of Fort Herkimer, 1756. A plan of the Revolutionary War fort has not been found, but the works were located on or near the 1756 site on the south side of Mohawk River in German Flatts.

Joseph had warned that the warriors needed to be "managed with caution for fear of disgust, and he doubted much if all the Young men would listen to their Chiefs." Of course, this assumed that the sachems and war captains could be persuaded to accept the order.

On Sunday July 14, at about 4:00 p.m., the scouts Brant had sent out from Fish Creek rejoined the expedition with two prisoners in tow. Rebel records show that four men were captured on July 11 along the Mohawk and, two days later, that two NH soldiers were killed and one captured.

The scouts had found many fresh tracks and the country seemed to be warned of Brant's approach. This news spurred the raiders on, and after a force march, they arrived a short distance above Fort Dayton by about 11 o'clock that night and lay over until an hour before daybreak. Singleton noted with surprise that, although there were a great many Indians present, they complied with their promise made at Oswego and none of the prisoners were in any way abused.

Next morning, the raiders bypassed Fort Dayton and marched directly to Fort Herkimer, arriving around 4:00 a.m., and "surrounded the fort in every Quarter and in such a manner as to avoid a discovery from the Garrison. In this situation we detached a small Party of about twenty men with orders to go as close to the Fort as possible thinking by this means to decoy the Garrison to sally out." This party fell upon two local men, killing one outright. The other fellow raced for the fort and several men sortied out to help him, but he was cut down and they were only able to prevent his scalping. Singleton continued:

> [A]bout forty of the Enemy having ventur'd out of the Fort under cover of their Cannon to a plain some little distance we immediately began a movement from the Main Body to cut off their Retreat which tho' done in as secret a manner as the nature of the Ground would admit of had reason to think they discovered us, as soon after they went back with the utmost precipitation before it was possible for us with the greatest exertions to prevent them. Finding this we kept up a Constant Fire on the Fort untill we had got into our possession a number of Cattle and some Horses, and we killed about 8 or 9 of the Enemy about the Fort, amongst which there was one Onida Rebel Indian. At 12 o'clock finding the Enemy would not venture out we proceeded to Fort Deaton [Dayton] which we attacked in the same manner as the former, but with no Success they having collected all their Cattle and drove them into the Fort upon hearing the firing at Fort Harkeman, both the Forts fired upwards of fifty Cannon Shots at us and luckily not a man of the party was hurt, we left that place about 4 o'clock [p.m.] and marched to German Town where we had sent our cattle.[28]

Captain Simeon Newell's company, Willett's Levies, was stationed at a fortified house with a number of families approximately three miles below Little Falls when the raiders struck. John Pettit recalled having "to

Although a postwar gift of a British nobleman, this axe is an iconic example of the better quality sidearms carried by Brant and other senior natives.

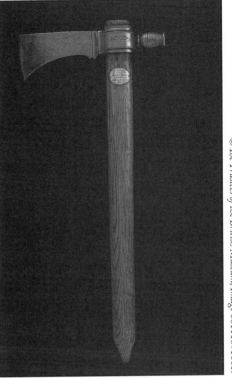

fight … to save our own Scalps, and to secure those under our protection. The enemy were beaten off after they sustained considerable loss, nor did our little band escape harmless."[29]

Some of the natives decided there were too few prisoners to satisfy the promises they had made to bereaved families hoping for adoption candidates and, after breaking into small parties, set off to seek prey.

Understandably, Brant believed that a greater result would be expected from such a large expedition and he and Deserontyon decided to continue the raid. Singleton "did not think it my duty to interfere with them nor consistent with my orders to make myself a party to such enterprises"; however, when he turned to leave, he found that some of the natives were "bent on making a property of the whole of the Cattle without paying any attention to my men and it was with great difficulty with the assistance of Captain Brant that I got twenty five head (out of two hundred and twenty four.) All the rest of the Cattle were drove of[f] to Niagara in spite of every argument to the Contrary." Yet, even this small number was too great a temptation and, as soon as Brant left, some warriors "made an alarm … to make us abandon our cattle, but we judged it to be false and disappointed them."

Singleton added, "Captain Brants conduct on every occasion for Gallantry, Generosity, and Humanity exceeds description and his management of the Indians truely conspicuous."[30]

Willett arrived at Fort Rensselaer on the night of July 15 to find that five to six hundred raiders had "made another depredating incursion at the German Flatts." Two days later, he wrote to the governor:

> All the inhabited Places from the foot of Fall Hill to Fort Herkimer are burnt; and that District gleaned of its Stock, one hundred & fifty Cattle & fifty Horses are reported to be carried off. This is the second Insult this Country has rec'd this Campaign without resenting — the third if it is possible to avoid it shall not be so. But in order to enable us to pursue the Enemy, it is essential that salt Provisions and hard Bread be furnished which at present is not the case. I wish this Matter to be represented to His Excellency the Commander in Chief. The whole of the force in this County at present appears to be truly inadequate for the Defence and the Want of Arms Accoutrements and Clothing deprives us of the Service of a considerable proportion of the Troops raised on Land Bounties.[31]

A letter written at Fort Rensselaer on July 15 and published in a Pennsylvania newspaper noted somewhat different statistics. "A large body of the enemy made an incursion at the German Flatts ... two inhabitants of that place, were killed and scalped, 50 horses were taken and 15 killed, 13 horned cattle killed and 180 drove off, 12 dwelling-houses and 5 barns burnt. The party consisted of Indians, Tories and British Regulars, to the amount of 500." (The Royal Yorkers' redcoats must have suggested a British presence to the writer.)

Several days later, another newspaper reported that two prisoners who had escaped from the British claimed that Sir John Johnson, five hundred natives, and a number of "green coats (as they call them)" had set out for the Mohawk River. Although unable to comment on their intentions, the escapees said both the British and their natives "seemed much alarmed, and quite in confusion." A second party of fifty had set out earlier, but joined Johnson en route. This information must have referred to Brant's raid, as Sir John was not even in America.[32]

Despite Willett's promise of retaliation if a third raid struck the region, just such an event was already underway in the Schoharie, as reported in a letter from Fort Rensselaer dated July 15. A diary entry written the next day by a 2NY Continental stationed in the Catskills noted, "a large party of Indians [had been] discovered at Schoharry."[33]

As the two raids had struck the Mohawk River in short order, Willett decided to withdraw Wright's Company from Ballstown. Their first duty was to march to Stone Arabia to guard farmers while harvesting.[34]

On July 22, a return indicated the new distribution of Willett's Levies. Livingston's Company was located in Charlotte County and Ballstown. It had a captain, two lieutenants, four serjeants, and fifty-five rank and file. Harrison's and Cannon's companies were at Schoharie and Catskill. Harrison's had a captain, two lieutenants, three serjeants, two drummers, forty-three rank and file. Cannon's had a captain, two lieutenants, four serjeants, two drummers, and fifty-seven rankers. In Tryon's lower district, there was Pierce's company with three subalterns, five serjeants, two drummers, and fifty-three rank and file. In the middle district there were three companies. Tearce's Light Infantry had a captain, two lieutenants, five serjeants, two drummers, and sixty-one rank and file. Young's had a captain, two subalterns, five serjeants, fifty-four rank and file, and two deserters. Wright's had a captain, two subalterns, four serjeants, one drummer, thirty-three rank and file, and fourteen deserters. Details of French's company were not provided. In Tryon's upper district, presumably at Forts Dayton and Herkimer, Newell's Company had a captain, two subalterns, five serjeants, two drummers, forty-eight rank and file, including his Stockbridge Indians. A staggering 215 men were still in need of clothing.[35]

Two days later, Willett wrote an extraordinary letter to Washington offering an opinion that was in marked contrast to the role of absolute native subservience demanded by the United States once victory was secured.

> The Indians are committing ravages in most parts of the County and hitherto [we] have not been able to do anything with them, they are everywhere doing

mischief but never to be found so as to do anything effectual — They are not deficient in art to improve the many advantages they have over us —

Your Excellency may recollect my mentioning on your way to Saratoga the value of the friendship of this people. This has uniformly been my sentiment and experience has assured me I was always right in it …, But a contrary policy appears to have been pursued by us, for I never yet could see that any price had been offered for their purchase while vast sums have been expended in vainly endeavouring to Conquer them, even the few that yet remain in our Interest appear to have very little Incouragement to continue so. Their chiefs have offered me their service to go out against our enemies, but they say they want shoes and stockings. Was it in my power I would not only furnish them with these articles but they should be the gayest and finest savages in the Wilderness, and in this way I would not only preserve their friendship but I would allure others if possible to be at peace with us. In this way and in this way only in my opinion are they to be subdued. I most humbly beg leave to recommend this subject to your Excellency's consideration, and perhaps it may be found out worth the attention of Congress. I beg likewise to remind your Excellency of their services at a time when they are very much wanting.

Governor Clinton also wrote to Washington on July 24 to note, "[T]hat since the Enemy have taken Post at Oswego, our Western Frontiers are invaded by very formidable Parties and I am apprehensive unless the Force in that Quarter is augmented the whole of the Settlements on the Mohawk River will be destroyed or abandoned." Clinton noted that he had been empowered by the state "to call into actual Service any additional number of the Militia, to reinforce the Army," and offered to do so if Washington so required. He advised that hard bread and salted meat were ready to be forwarded, but the lack of a secure storage magazine in Tryon County at any of the posts (after all those long years of warfare!) was a serious problem.[36]

———————————————

———————————————

During Colonel von Kreutzbourg's visit to Point Levis, a series of courts martial of Hesse-Hanau troops were conducted. An artillerist and a grenadier were found guilty of burgling a merchant's shop and were awarded the severe punishment of running a gauntlet of two hundred men for twenty times on the first day and twenty on the second. The first twenty passes began on July 16, the day of their trial. Whether their punishers struck them with musket ramrods or wooden cudgels went unstated.

The second crime was the desertion of three artillerists who had set off for New England. As Major Pausch had taken special precautions against just such flight, the culprits had been quickly rounded up. The instigator was sentenced to run a gauntlet of two hundred men twenty-four times in two days. His punishment also began that day. His fellow deserters were to run on the second day for twelve times.

The third crime was again desertion, but was a more complex and disturbing incident. It was determined that a bombardier was the instigator and he had been abetted by the artillery company's surgeon's mate, who had access to army funds. Two grenadiers and four

Detail from James Peachey, circa 1782.
(Library and Archives Canada, C-045561.)

Montmorency, General Haldimand's country house. Located above the falls of the Montmorency River, this large summer house was noted for its extensive vegetable, herb, and fruit tree gardens.

artillerists had been persuaded by the mate to make the attempt. The bombardier and his six adherents confessed, but the surgeon's mate denied any knowledge of the plot and the examination was stalled. A third grenadier had also been in the plot, but he deserted before the court martial sat. He was later taken by some Canadiens, delivered to Pausch, and locked-up in chains, but managed to get away again, leaving his chains behind, which implicated the corporal and two privates who had been his guard.[37]

Shortly after announcing the ceasefire to the natives, the British withdrew all supplies of war materials, effectively shutting down their capability to mount raids. Of course, small parties of warriors continued their war on a personal basis. The terror along the frontiers wound down, but not quickly enough for the exhausted inhabitants. On July 26, an aged man and his wife were killed and scalped back of Fort Paris in Stone Arabia while they were pulling flax. It was impossible to have soldiers at every farm, every moment of the day and night.[38]

Clinton wrote the Secretary of State on July 29, repeating many of the sentiments earlier expressed to the C-in-C:

> The diff't parts of our Frontiers, except Tryon County[,] have hitherto been preserved ag't. the incursions of the Enemy, but since their having taken Post at Oswego, where I presume you have heard they have collected the greater Part of their Northern Force & are fortifying, that Country has been frequently visited by Parties too large to be resisted by the force we have in it & scarce a Day passes without experiencing their Ravages of the most cruel & distressing Nature; so that it is more than probable that County will be totally desolated before

the Fall, notwithstanding any Efforts the State may be able to make to save it.[39]

Such fascinating comments — why was the rebel system of defence, which had reacted so admirably against Docksteder and Ross the year before, incapable of confronting Deserontyon and Brant in 1782? Their raids had been scarcely larger than Ross's of the year before. Willett's combination of New York State Troops and Levies gave him a full-strength regiment. In place of the Massachusetts Levies of the year before, there was the 2NH, and the Tryon Militia must have been as robust as in 1781. Contiguous regions such as the Champlain and upper Hudson were relatively quiet, and the angst with Vermont was marking time, which should have allowed greater concentration on the Mohawk region.

Perhaps the more fluid and dispersed raids led by native commanders were a more difficult challenge. As a foe, the natives were unrestrained by military convention, more subject to unpredictable whim, and certainly more terrifying.

Evidence points to a serious lack of coordination between Reid and Willett and, with the relatively unknown Reid at their head, the militia may not have been as willing to assist.

In any event, the British-directed war had ended in the Mohawk region, although raiding continued to sputter and spark due to native resentment, which meant the inhabitants saw little sign that the ceasefire was real.

7

STUMBLING TOWARD PEACE
Hostilities are Effectually Stopped Thro'out this Province

*T*he common business of war continued in Quebec, as well. On July 12, Riedesel sent Haldimand copies of the orders given to Major Jessup for the cutting of hay for the use of the garrisons on the Richelieu River and upper Lake Champlain.[1]

Three days later, Haldimand's General Orders announced the court martial of seventeen-year-old Ensign James Murray McAlpin for the "most barbarous and inhumane treatment" of rebel prisoners on Prison Island at Coteau-du-Lac. A week later, the court ruled the ensign was "Guilty of the Crime Laid to his Charge in Breach of the twenty-third article of the fifteenth Section of the articles of War and Sentenced to be Dismst his Majestyes Service."

A man who had successfully escaped from the island recalled that the prison's biscuit was "old and hard enough to almost strike fire like a flint." The prisoners were crawling with vermin and loaded with irons and were given no clothes but what they had on, nor any blankets nor straw to sleep on. In the winter, one man's feet were frozen so badly that when he tried to walk "they clattered like stones striking upon the floor; and this made him a cripple the remainder of his life." In the summer, the prisoners were denied water, although the river ran nearby; "some of the men became so dry and thirsty they were attacked with raising of the blood" and they were bled until they were in danger of circulatory collapse.

When two escapees were recaptured, their pitiful condition and their reports of brutality prompted an official investigation that soon focused

John Arthur Roebuck, circa 1823. (Library and Archives Canada, C-120321.)

Fort at Coteau-du-Lac and rapids from Prison Island. A view of the boiling rapids that separated the island's prison from the fort. The octagonal blockhouse was built in 1813.

on the island's only officer, the callow Ensign McAlpin.[2]

Even while McAlpin's examination was underway, Montreal District's commander, de Speth, notified headquarters that Captain Joseph Anderson had reported the escape of fifteen prisoners from the island; two had been quickly retaken and natives were tracking the rest.

James's dismissal was one of the many wartime tragedies heaped on the McAlpin family. Common to all loyalists who came away to Canada, the McAlpins had lost all of their New York property, but it was the details that made their case different. From the earliest days of the rebellion, the father, Daniel, an elderly, distinguished veteran of Wolfe's assault on Quebec, had been pressured to join the rebels. When he refused, he was imprisoned and fell so desperately ill that he was released, but the harassment continued and he was forced to spend the winter of 1777 hiding in the woods before he could get away to join Burgoyne. After his flight, his wife and daughter were humiliated by being paraded in a cart through the streets of Albany clad only in their shifts and the family's holdings were thoroughly looted. Daniel performed yeoman's service during the campaign. Later in Canada, he was promoted to major and given the management of the bits and pieces of Burgoyne's loyalist corps, but the rigours of his long, troublesome service soon caught up with him and he died in 1780. Young James had been permitted to enter the Royal Yorkers as a favour to his mother and his dismissal forced the family to retreat to Britain where the disgrace had a better chance of being kept quiet.

WO28/5, 102.

It is speculation whether Anderson resigned over the scandal at Coteau-du-Lac or an undisclosed health condition. Haldimand insisted that he abandon all claims to half-pay, which represented a significant loss.

The final chapter of this ugly episode came with the Christmas Eve resignation of Captain Joseph Anderson, 1KRR, whose reputation had been sullied.[3]

On July 17, Haldimand acknowledged receipt of Lord Shelburne's "Most Secret" dispatch, which had warned of the French expedition being prepared at Brest, and the secretary's thoughts that, because Admiral Rodney had so decisively defeated the French Navy in the West Indies, there was no danger to Quebec during the 1782 campaign. Haldimand gracefully accepted the minister's instructions and displayed immense gratitude to the king for his approbation of his conduct and for permitting him to return to England. As to serving under Sir Guy Carleton, he wrote, "I persuade myself that Your Lordship will feel the impossibility of my subjecting myself to an Officer who in every Rank has been my Junior during a Service on my Part of forty-three Years as an Officer, whatever Commission he may at present hold in America."[4]

That same day, John Butler directed a request to General Haldimand through Mathews that could have altered the face of North American history if action had been taken. He wrote, "I wish [my regiment] might have some other [name] than merely Butler's Rangers."[5]

Brigadier de Speth reported that a Light Bob of the 84th Regiment had been dangerously wounded by one of his drunken mates during the company's march to Lachine.

On an entirely pacific matter, a Quaker had appeared at de Speth's headquarters with a pass from Riedesel, permitting him to join his family who were living in Montreal's "St. Lawrence suburbs." The fellow requested that a man of the same sect be allowed to leave Coteau-du-Lac and join him, and that a fourteen-year-old girl being held prisoner by the natives at Niagara (presumably also a Quaker) be liberated and sent to Montreal. Further, he requested authorization for all of them to return to their home country. Four days later, the governor granted permission for the reunion and for the party to leave Canada.[6]

As the month closed at Oswego, Major Ross confessed his regret to Haldimand that the natives would not be allowed to continue raiding the frontiers. He reported that Brant had been gone eight days when the ceasefire order had arrived and, in any event, he doubted that he could have prevented the Indians from going, although he had sent a runner to recall them. He mentioned that General Washington had been in Schenectady and, equally interesting, the news that the rebels had been unaware of the occupation of Oswego until June 24, and, even then, had only found out through the evidence of an escaped prisoner. Obviously, their intelligence system had failed miserably.

On August 3, Ross reported to Haldimand that the garrison had received his praise for their performance with great marks of satisfaction. His strength had been weakened alarmingly by the removal of one hundred Rangers to Niagara and he longed for the 84th Regiment's reinforcement from Carleton Island, as so many of his men were sick. Although the body of the fort was complete, he reckoned that the building of the glacis would be a "tedious piece of work."

Again, Ross commended Joseph Brant. (Had the major undergone an epiphany regarding natives?) "He highly merits the good opinion your Excellency is pleased to entertain of him and[,] besides his abilities as a Partizan, I think I do not say too much in his favour if I presume to give him great praise in his disinterested and exemplary management of the Department."[7]

Although active operations were at an end, formal peace had not been declared and no one could predict what the rebels might do. There remained a pressing need for a continuous flow of intelligence, lest the enemy use the lull to disguise preparations for an attack. The usual flood of scouts was sent out from all the border posts, but the one dispatched by Ross from Oswego is of particular interest. A new 2nd battalion Gentleman Volunteer, Jacob James Klock, a personality of no little notoriety in the Mohawk Valley, was sent at the head of a party composed of two privates, his cousin Jacob Conrad Klock, and Bart Forbes and Serjeant Henry Deal. Their written orders were:

> You are hereby ordered to proceed to the frontiers, in order to procure intelligence on the prospect of an accommodation between Great Britain and America, and should it fortunately so happen, you will take the earliest opportunity to make me acquainted with it; in order that I may use my endeavours to avert, as much as possible, any further hostilities against the frontiers. It is a tedious prospect that I have in this remote place of knowing the event of affairs from headquarters, wherefore

much diligence is recommended to you on this occasion.

The party paddled a bark canoe from Oswego to the Oneida Carry, then set off on foot across the top of Kingsland District and arrived undetected on July 31 near Fort Nellis in the Palatine District where they laid up within sight of Jacob J.'s parental home for the remainder of the day. Volunteer Klock told the others that he would find out if a certain loyalist were at home, as he would supply them with provisions and news. About midnight, he left them and hid himself in a field of oats. Early the next morning, Deal and his men watched the Volunteer shout to a black man working in his father's field. The farmhand left and soon returned with the colonel and "Squire" Nellis. Jacob J. had thrown himself on "the mercy of his country."

Deal had earlier planned to visit his own home nearby, but, in concern that the traitor would betray them, he took off with his two men. As suspected, Jacob J. soon informed his father of the other three. After debating whether or not to return to Oswego, the remaining scouts went to Timmerman's Creek. They hid for some time on a hill within sight of Fort Walrath, but saw no soldiers. Looking northward, Forbes saw his father at work in his fields and suggested he might provide some information. Perhaps Deal should have known better; however, he allowed Forbes to hide his musket and go down to see his father and the miscreant promptly turned himself in.

In the meantime, Jacob J. was being examined by Captain Abner French of Willett's. He gave the names of the two soldiers who intended to give themselves up and led French to where his cousin, who had somehow ditched Serjeant Deal, was hiding.

When the officers of the Stone Arabia militia company heard that Jacob J. was at his father's house, they gathered a party of men together and came down to administer some rough justice; however, the colonel and other regimental officers interceded.

During their examination, both Forbes and Klock's cousin, Jacob C., claimed in their defence that they had enlisted in the Royal Yorkers simply to find an opportunity to desert. This was a common story and always had a ring of truth. Of course, Jacob J. was a very different case.

He had deserted to the enemy and, in the process, took away a number of local men. Then, he brought them back to raid the families of soldiers in his father's regiment. Worse, his band was rumoured to have planned to abduct and rape girls with whom he was well acquainted. Forgiveness for Jacob J. would be a long time in coming and he knew it. So, when he was examined at Fort Rensselaer on August 10, he sang like a bird.

He began with general news, advising that most of the natives who had not participated on Brant's expedition had gone to Niagara. He had met up with some of Brant's Indians in a bark canoe at the Three Rivers who said that the captain was on his way back with eight prisoners and a scalp. He then claimed that he had told his cousin and Forbes about his plan to deliver himself up when he left them; however, their testimony suggested otherwise. The truth of the matter was of no account, but undoubtedly the variance in their stories did little to help Jacob J. who was already under deep suspicion.

The Volunteer provided quite accurate details of Fort Ontario's garrison and artillery, information that was most significant, as it was the first eyewitness account that the rebels had received. He reported that the garrison was composed of some four hundred troops.

Royal Artillery	15
8th Regiment	20–30
34th Regiment	50–60
84th	30–40
2KRR	150–200
Butler's	60–70

There were twelve to fifteen pieces of iron ordnance ranging from 6- to 18-pdrs and one brass 18-pdr. Captain Ancrum commanded at Carleton Island and had about one hundred men of the 34th and 2KRR.

Klock told tales about Major Ross — some that rang true and others that were perhaps fanciful. All of his stories suggested that he had managed to gain the major's confidence. Supposedly, Ross had told him that he would rather have given up five hundred guineas than allow Brant to go out and perform "mischief" and that he was about to send a messenger to recall the Mohawk war captain. If Brant returned with prisoners or cattle, Ross would send them back. The major had Haldimand's orders not to send out any more raids, but these had come after Brant had left and, although Sir John was expected every day, there was no news of additional troops coming upriver.

Jacob J.'s examination was followed by that of Jacob Conrad and Bart Forbes. J.C.'s testimony varied very little from his cousin's, other than to give details of his experiences between his capture and entry into Sir John's regiment. He added that Major Ross expected peace to be declared soon and Forbes told much the same.

Jacob C.'s testimony was confirmed by a witness at Fort Willett on August 11, who had also been a prisoner in Montreal. This fellow had heard Jacob refuse Colonel Campbell's attempt to have him take an oath of allegiance to the king, saying he preferred to join Sir John's regiment "where he would have no occasion to swear." Privately, he told the witness that he would make his escape at the first opportunity. What a remarkable anecdote! Were men joining the Royal Yorkers really not required to pledge allegiance? Doubtful![8]

Returning to July 30, Washington wrote to Governor Clinton about the "repeated depredations that have been committed on your Western frontier" and enclosed a copy of Willett's dispatch. He explained that he would have preferred to have sent a larger detachment from the main army to "cover the whole Country," but could not. He left it to the governor to decide whether to call out additional levies of militia, as he was "better acquainted with the circumstances of the frontier," and asked him to report the strength of Willett's Levies along the Mohawk and any news of the enemy's strength at Oswego. He also advised that, since the date of Willett's letter, he should have received four hundred cartridge boxes, which had been his regiment's most serious deficiency and he trusted that the Levies, "in conjunction with the Continental Regiment stationed in that quarter will be able to give a better protection to the Country than has lately been the case, and to chastise the insolence of the Enemy … especially since they are now likely to be supplied with hard bread and salted Meat." Judging from their performance to date, there was little reason for such optimism.

His next suggestion revealed the United States' desperate lack of funds. He had given the quartermaster general orders to furnish proper storehouses in the Mohawk Valley, but that officer had been unable to comply for lack of cash, so he recommended, "they may be preserved from spoiling by temporary sheds, or Cellars covered with good thatch, or substantial well-wrought shade of Boughs, which may be constructed by a little care and attention of the Officers and labour of the Soldiers." Compare these scant measures to the Crown's secretive and energetic rebuilding of the post at Oswego, far from the interference of raiders and without the crippling restrictions of inadequate funds.[9]

While the dangerous armed clashes between Vermont and New York were in a lull, the British Secret Service traffic with the former continued apace. Two loyalist agents arrived at the Loyal Blockhouse with a message from Governor Chittenden and Ethan Allen saying they would welcome a secret treaty with Britain, which would be made public when four thousand British Regulars and supplies for Vermont's army arrived in the Green Mountains. Haldimand chose not to respond; undoubtedly due to the verbal whipping he had taken from Lord Shelburne as much as from his distrust of Vermonters.[10]

As July closed, Willett sequestered eleven head of cattle, a supply of flour, 1,960 hides, and tallow from the disaffected, reminding those Tories with the temerity to remain in the Mohawk that the war was certainly not done.

Ceasefire or no, terror still strode the Valley. A man and a nine-year-old boy were taken one Sabbath; then, a man and his wife were killed and scalped and later another fellow was killed. And, there was the alarming news from a fellow who had recently escaped from the Six Nations' Indians that they were "meditating a very serious blow on the Mohawk River." For valley folk of all stripes, the war was very much alive.[11]

At Montreal, the investigation into Colonel Guy Johnson's accounts ground on interminably, stoking Haldimand's anger at every stage and adding to his expectations for Sir John's performance. A clerk who worked for Taylor and Forsyth, the merchants at Niagara who had enjoyed a virtual monopoly of trade under Colonel Guy's regime, revealed that the firm had overcharged the government £13,000 — an immense sum in those times. It was shown that the firm kept a double set of books with the intention of defrauding the government and, by May, the partners had lost their licence and been denied any future right to trade at the upper posts. Worse still, the evidence was strong that Guy had colluded with the trading partners and his personal accounts were later described as "extravagant, wonderfull and fictitious." By the end of October, he had been suspended from his post and barred from returning to Niagara.[12]

At Whitehall, Thomas Townshend, the new Secretary of State for Home and Colonial Affairs, wrote to Haldimand on July 31, acknowledging receipt of the governor's "alarming accounts … of the state of Canada" which had caused "great apprehensions." He said these worries had been removed by a later letter the governor had sent aboard the *Surprise*, Letter of Marque, which told of the occupation of Oswego. Obviously, Haldimand had never meant to convey that refortifying Oswego would keep Quebec safe from invasion, but to the naive, inexperienced minds of the new administration, the action was a panacea.

Townshend continued, "His Majesty is much pleased at the account you give of the Establishment made at Oswego by the Detachment under Major Ross, of whose Conduct upon that occasion you will signify His Royal Approbation as well as that of the officers and men employed in the Exped'n and I make no doubt but the judicious measures you have taken for opposing the force intended by the enemy against Detroit will not be unsuccessful." As if a transfer of one hundred Rangers was going to secure Detroit from a determined rebel expedition! Of course, these warm words of encouragement would take weeks to cross the ocean.[13]

The monthly return for Fort Niagara, excluding the detachments at Forts Schlosser and Erie and the Landing, listed:

8th Regiment	Three captains, five first lieutenants, one surgeon, eleven serjeants, seven drummers, and 183 rank and file fit for duty, twenty-five "sick present," and nineteen at Oswego.
Butler's Rangers	One lieutenant-colonel, three captains, five first lieutenants, three second lieutenants, one adjutant, one quartermaster, one surgeon, eighteen serjeants, twelve drummers, 234 rank and file fit for duty, thirty-eight "sick present," ninety-three at Oswego, and eleven in Indian Country.
Royal Artillery	One lieutenant, one bombardier, twelve matrosses, and one conductor.
53rd Regiment	Three
Provincial Navy	Nine
Teamsters	Twenty-four
6NID Officers and Natives	2,036.[14]

Brant returned from the Mohawk Valley frustrated and angry. He found a letter from Mathews that had been delayed by being misdirected to Niagara. He opened it in the midst of several officers, perhaps in the major's office or the mess. As he read Mathews's assurances that the governor had reoccupied Oswego solely in the natives' interest, he is said to have blurted incredulously, "My Friend Captn Mathews, this wont do, it was not for the Reasons you give, it was owing to the news of last winter that the French and Rebels intended Invading Canada otherwise it would not have happened."

Early in the month, the natives at Oswego sent deputies to talk with Sir John Johnson at Montreal and then to visit Quebec to speak to Haldimand.

Having been stopped from going to war, they were most anxious about their future. Brant, Captain David Hill, and a prominent unnamed Cayuga were chosen as spokesmen. Ross saw Brant leave with great reluctance, as he had come to rely upon his support. The delegates must have been disappointed, as Sir John had not yet arrived from England and no record has been found of whether or not they visited the governor.[15]

On August 3, Dr. George Smyth reported from Fort St. John's that Roger Stevens had come in that morning from Ticonderoga and added to earlier information about rebel activities in the Saratoga area. They were keeping a forty-man scout out of Saratoga patrolling the route between the two lakes, Skenesborough, and the Scotch Patent, with the goal of intercepting parties from Quebec. They had even managed to waylay Vermont's flag boat, but to what effect was not stated. Stevens believed "The people of Vermont are altering fast and wish soon to be united with Canada. They heartily pray that His Excellency might send a party to cut off the Saratoga Scouts." If this observation were true, it probably reflected Vermonters' renewed anger over the Continental Congress continuing to refuse the republic's entry into the union.[16]

Loyal Rangers ensign Thomas Man, reported from Sorel on August 4 that six men from his patrol to Hazen's Road had deserted him. Two days later, Captain William Fraser reported that five of the six had previously deserted from the rebels and mentioned how frequently such men deserted from one side to the other in the pursuit of bounties. (Why did his appreciation of this problem not inform his choice of scouts?) He added that he suspected two other men and would keep a close eye on them.

The deserters seem to have gossiped to Man about Fraser filching his men's pay, and Riedesel concluded it would be best to relieve the garrisons of the two blockhouses. He informed Haldimand that the Fraser brothers were willing to remain in command, which indicated that he continued to have faith in them. In a return letter, the governor commented on the men's frivolous grounds for desertion and noted that, if Fraser asked for an inquiry, one would be ordered, but it was unnecessary.[17]

———————

When Deserontyon's prisoner, George Nellus, was interrogated in Canada, he said that Colonel Willett was at Fort Plain with forty men and that the troops between Schenectady and the Flatts numbered about five hundred. Further, there was "Talk of a Cessation of Hostilities in the Spring, but since the many Incursions of the Indians[,] People gave up all hopes tho very much tired of the War." Nellus had heard that the Royal Navy had defeated the French in a major battle in the West Indies, and Washington had promised to send another five hundred men to the frontier, although it was also said that every fifteenth militiaman was to be drafted for the main army below. Nellus claimed he had been forced into taking the last oath, and, as his father-in-law and brother were in the "Regt Yorkers," he wished to join them rather than go to jail.[18]

Another prisoner of a quite different stripe had been taken on the Mohawk River — one Antoine Payfer, the nephew of the lieutenant of the St. Geneviève Canadien militia. Why he had been consorting with the rebels was a question of some moment, particularly with the rampant paranoia about Canadien loyalty. His uncle made immediate application for his release and an interrogation must have concluded that he was simply on a lark, as he was released after his uncle pledged security for his good behaviour.[19]

On August 5, the governor sent the astonishing news to Riedesel that he had received a letter in cipher from Carleton reporting that preliminary peace talks had begun in Paris and that the demoralized king had granted the American provinces their independence even "before a single article of peace was proposed."

On the same day, the baron informed Haldimand that he had heard that Washington was at the Windsor cantonment with a regiment; that there were six thousand men at West Point and six hundred along the Mohawk River with another seven hundred marching to reinforce them.

On a less momentous note, the barracks at Sorel were full of bedbugs and other insects, and Riedesel requested permission to encamp the men until the pests were eradicated. He also asked for an issue of powder to practice the district's troops by firing at marks.[20]

––––––––––––––

On August 5, Lieutenant-Colonel Butler reported to Mathews that:

> Sayengaraghta [Old Smoke] and His Party are Returned from War, after burning and destroying Hannah's Town and the Country for seven or eight Miles round it. This Settlement was about 30 miles below Fort Pitt, on the Road to Philadelphia, they Kill'd between three and four Hundred head of horn'd Cattle, 70 Horses, Sheep and Hogs innumerable, and brought away to their Village 70 Horses and two Cows. Also Killed 15 of the Enemy and took 10 Prisoners.

How the Pennsylvanians must have wondered about Carleton's ceasefire![21]

Although Hanna's Town was only a small settlement of thirty houses and a palisaded fort, it was significant as the seat of Pennsylvania's recently created Westmoreland County. The site lay astride the Forbes road, which had been built in 1758 to connect the eastern state to Fort Pitt on the western edge of the Ohio country. Judge Robert Hanna's home served both as a tavern and courthouse and there was also a one-room jail and a gallows' hill. As the state's western political hub, Hanna's Town constituted an excellent target to avenge the Moravian atrocity.

Old Smoke's 250-man force of natives, 6NID officers, and Foresters had arrived in the area a few days before launching their attack. Although local legend claims that the much-feared Allegheny Seneca war captain, Kayashuta (Guyasuta), was amongst the party, his presence has not been confirmed.[22]

On July 12, Hanna's wife, two daughters, and several other townsfolk travelled two miles to Miller's Station for a wedding. At Hanna's Town the next day, the court held a morning session and, in the afternoon, many people were harvesting fields just outside the village. The first field was finished at about two o'clock, when one of the reapers saw a body of natives approaching and gave the alarm. Everyone ran for their lives, some directly to the fort, others to gather up their families and release the prisoners in the jail. For some reason, the raiders did not immediately pursue and everyone was able to gain the fort's sanctuary.

Next, a mounted officer and four riflemen on foot left the fort to scout the natives. The officer was the first to arrive at the harvested field where he discovered the whole enemy force drawn up. When he urgently reined his horse about, several warriors gave chase. As he drew up to the four riflemen, he shouted for them to run for their lives and then galloped off on a sweeping circuit to warn the outlying farms. Once the pursuing warriors saw the riflemen, they abandoned their chase of the rider and came on at top speed toward the scouts.

One fellow ran into town to confirm that his kin had escaped and, as he stood on his father's threshold, he looked back and saw warriors with their hair tufts flying and tomahawks brandished just as they began to whoop. Swinging up his rifle, he fired and saw a native bound into the air and fall; then he ran for the fort.

The Indians were disgusted to find the town abandoned. After ransacking the houses, they set them afire and slaughtered most of the livestock. Other natives kept up a brisk fusillade against the stockade, and one warrior, who was parading around in a looted uniform coat, was dropped by a rifle shot from the fort.

Meanwhile, inside the stockade, a young woman was mortally wounded when she ran to save a child who was exposed to shots coming through the gate's apertures. She was not the only courageous woman in the fort. Eve Oury's two brothers had been captured on the Ohio by Brant the year before and, in a local Indian raid that May, her father and a third brother were killed and two other brothers taken. These tragedies had forged Eve into a very determined woman.

With bullets smacking against the palisade and acrid smoke drifting into the fort from the crackling flames that were consuming the village, Judge Hanna panicked. He urged the tiny garrison to surrender before everyone was killed and it was the resolute Eve Oury who stood firm and refused his plea. Immediately after Hanna had been faced down, the garrison commander was seen galloping toward the gate through a hail of gunfire. Oury ran forward and threw the portal open and, although his clothes were perforated by several rounds and his horse shot out from under him, the major scrambled free and ran inside unscathed. Assuming command, he immediately asked about ammunition and word came back that there was very little powder left. An immediate search turned up a supply in the fort's office, but then lead ball began to run out. Oury told a soldier to start a fire while she searched the buildings for pewter and, soon after, a fresh supply had been moulded and the defence was sustained.[23]

A large element of the raiding force split off to attack Miller's Station where the wedding party was enjoying the "day after" in the big house. Workers were mowing in a meadow and several refugee families from earlier raids were in small cabins clustered about the house when a war whoop sounded like a clap of thunder. Those in the fields and cabins ran off to safety, but those in the main house were quickly surrounded. Inside was Jack Brownlee, a local partisan who was notorious to the natives. Seizing his rifle, he dashed out the door, but his wife Elizabeth's shouted plea to not abandon his family instantly halted him. Turning about, he settled himself at the door beside his lady to await his fate. While the others were being rounded up, the mounted officer from Hanna's Town, who had earlier in the day set off to warn the outlying farms, rode up and was almost taken, but he managed to rein his horse about and escaped in a swarm of lead that severed his bridle.

The plunder from the house and cabins was loaded into makeshift packs and each prisoner was ordered to hoist one before being led away. Not recognizing Brownlee's danger, a woman prisoner spoke his name and, after a few hundred yards, the warriors began to talk amongst themselves and eye him suspiciously. The partisan was carrying his three-year-old son and a heavy pack, and, when he stooped to adjust them, a native stepped up and sank a hatchet into his skull. As Brownlee collapsed, the warrior tomahawked his son and, when a woman screamed in horror, she too was dispatched. Brownlee's wife, Elizabeth, and their baby daughter were safe because she somehow managed to watch the horrific deeds in stunned silence.[24]

272 | I am heartily ashamed

The raiders reassembled in a creek bottom just outside Hanna's Town and began to sort through their spoils and make plans to renew the attack on the fort the next morning.

That evening, thirty stout local men had assembled at a farm not far from Miller's Station to reinforce the fort's little garrison. As they drew near, they sent out scouts who found the natives fully occupied in their camp along the creek, which allowed the reinforcement to quietly slip into the fort to be greeted with great joy. Their arrival raised the number of rifles to forty-five, a mere fraction of their opposition's firepower.

The garrison then employed some clever stratagems to persuade the raiders that the fort was being heavily reinforced. Those men with horses rode back and forth over the gate's plank bridge while those afoot marched in and out and a fife and drum played through the night. The ruses had the desired effect and the raiders had gone by morning. A search of the ruined town turned up two human skeletons in the burned-out shell of a house and the inhabitants assumed they belonged to the two fallen warriors. Several discarded 8th Regiment jackets were found, which were thought to be gifts to the natives and indicated that the war party had come from Detroit or Niagara.

Several militia detachments were raised in nearby communities and sent off in pursuit, but the raiders' retreat was too swift and the militiamen soon gave up. Thus ended what proved to be one of the war's final raids by natives and Europeans, which one historian characterized as "an event of the greatest historical importance in the annals of Western Pennsylvania."[25]

Washington wrote to the secretary at war in response to Willett's recommended approach to the natives: "I take the liberty to inclose you Copies of two Letters from Colo Willet. I entirely coincide in Opinion with that Gentleman with respect to the Indians; nor is it inconsistent with our strictest plans of Oeconomy, for it will be much less Expense to gain and to keep the friendship of these People than to oppose them in the field."

The same day, he wrote to Willett,

On the subject of the Indians, I am at a loss what to reply to you; the matter has often been under the Deliberation of Congress, at times much more favorable for conciliating the affections of that people, but, either the Means of carrying the Measure you mention into execution, have not been in their power, or the Measure itself has not been tho't proper to be adopted. At the present time, I am persuaded, that the finances of the united States are not competent to the Object, in the Extent in which you view it. In the mean time it may be well to make the best we can of the favorable disposition of the tribe now under our immediate protection; but it is not in my power to give you the Means; the Subject shall be mentioned to the Secretary at War; to whom your Ideas shall be communicated, with my Approbation of your Sentiments.

Of course, the many land-hungry congressmen were extremely wary of taking any action that might slow down westward expansion after the peace. Washington himself was a major land speculator, but, with a war to finish, his viewpoint in these matters was understandably more short-term than Congress's. Besides, he had faith that "the gradual extension of our Settlements will as certainly cause the Savages[,] as the Wolf[,] to retire."

The C-in-C added, "Not considering it to be within my Province to give directions for the issue of Clothing to the Three Years State Troops of the State of New York, I will transmit your Return and Letter to the Secretary at War, under whose directions all issues of Clothing are to be made."

In a third letter of that day, Washington wrote to Lieutenant-Colonel George Reid with news that Congress had ruled that rations were no longer to be issued to the rebel Canadien refugees and volunteers in and about Albany and Schenectady. The C-in-C recommended that General Schuyler would be able to provide information on this point, as the Canadiens were his responsibility, and added, "Hard as it may appear, that those poor Refugees, who have been driven from their Country for their Adherence to our Cause, should be denied the pittance of provisions for their Subsistence, yet it is not in my power to contravene direct Resolutions of Congress."[26]

As noted earlier, Haldimand had agitated with the home government for some time to have a senior British officer posted to Canada. Yet, when Major-General Alured Clarke arrived close on the heels of Frederick Riedesel, the governor had immediate regrets. This situation became even more uncomfortable when the governor found it necessary to bring Brigadier Henry Watson Powell down from Niagara to assist Clarke, who was struggling in his new role. On August 8, he sent orders to Powell "to repair to Quebec with all convenient dispatch" and announced that Lieutenant-Colonel Alexander Dundas, 8th Regiment, would take command of the upper posts until a brigadier arrived.[27]

In exasperation, Haldimand confided to Riedesel that some news had at last been received from Carleton. It appeared that the rebels were not as eager to receive peace proposals as was believed in England and, consequently, he thought it may have been premature not to reinforce New York City. Beyond that, the C-in-C had said nothing of his success or lack of with his negotiations and, significantly, reported that he had received no communications with Britain since his arrival at New York. Clearly, both commanders were starved for advice and instructions from their superiors.

Carleton had added a ciphered warning to his dispatch: "I must inform you that there are at present indications of hostilities designed, pointing equally at your province and New York; but I am disposed to think that their views are upon this place; in the case that a French fleet shall arrive here to co-operate, you will be, of course, on your guard."[28]

The frontispiece of Claus's Mohawk school primer. In addition to his duties as Deputy Agent for the Six Nations, Daniel Claus translated the Anglican Hymnal into Mohawk in 1781 and a school primer in 1787.

James Peachey, 1786. (Library and Archives Canada, C-003364.)

Joseph Brant arrived at the Mohawk village at Lachine on August 10 accompanied by Captain David Hill and Tekaeayoh, a Cayuga chief. Leaving his companions there, Brant pressed on to Montreal to deliver letters for the governor to his close personal friend, Lieutenant-Colonel Claus. The next day, he returned to his companions and participated in a council to discuss the implications of the killing of Sanorese's son by Captain John's party at Canajoharie, as the man's death had given the Kahnawakes great umbrage. Brant informed Claus that, according to custom, the Fort Hunters had decided to condole with the Kahnawakes and "take the War Ax out, wh[i]ch they [had] struck in their head." In turn, Claus told Brant to take no further action until the governor was heard from on the matter and offered the opinion that Colonel Campbell might "explain the Matter to the Caghnawageys [Kahnawakes] in its due Light, and by a good Belt of Wampum make them burry it [into] Oblivion."

After an exchange of letters between the governor, Claus, and Campbell, Claus reported that the Fort Hunters had reached an accommodation with the Kahnawakes, through a condolence ceremony and probably a gift of presents to the victim's relations. In this negotiation they had recognized their role as the raid's leaders and behaved as an elder brother of the Delawares, as it was one of their young men who had killed the fellow. Such customs over the death of an enemy were viewed as very odd and quite suspicious by the natives' European allies.[29]

The Allens and their associates had sent an emissary to Haldimand to urge upon him the concept of a secret treaty for Vermont's reunion with Britain. In a letter of August 11, the governor told Carleton that he viewed this manoeuvre as a gambit through which the Allens expected to attract a flood of British sympathizers as settlers from the neighbouring states, which would, of course, strengthen their position. That aside, he declined to accept the idea out of concern that a secret treaty, which Vermont's assembly had not approved, would expose the republic to attack by the union and force the commitment of British troops contrary to the new administration's instructions.[30]

Haldimand wrote to Governor Chittenden on August 17. The tone of his letter was reminiscent of the early war, stilted and on the edge of condescending, as if the two men had not been negotiating for the past two years, and as if the letter was directed to Shelburne, not Chittenden, which, of course it was, as the minister read copies of all of Haldimand's correspondence. Plainly, his Lordship's criticisms and directions had taken effect.

> I would permit Captain Adiel Sherwood and Lieutenant Holson /Prisoners in this Province/ to return to their Homes upon Parole — Influenced by a liberality of Conduct I have perceived in the People of Vermont towards Prisoners, which distinguished them from the Other part of His Majesty's revolted Subjects, I readily Comply With Your request in favor of those Gentlemen — Desirous of embracing every opportunity to Testify His Majesty's Gracious Inclinations to withdraw by the Mildest Means, his once happy People from the fatal Error into which they have been deluded, and to discriminate between the Most Violent, and those who altho' unhappily engaged in the same Cause, have

discovered Some Moderation, I Could not but with pleasure observe that the District of Vermont have never, as far as I have learned, connected themselves in any Respect, with the natural Enemy of their Country [i.e. France], nor, like the other Colonies, had recourse to the assistance of a People, Whose Religion and Laws are so incompatible with those of the Mother Country, and I have from that Motive, long been induced to forbear the Distresses With Which the Neighbouring frontiers have been Visited, to agree to an Exchange of Prisoners, and to promote the Exercise of Humanity in every Circumstance Where it has been possible. Still wishing to pursue the Same Conduct while induced by the Same Motives, You May rest assured that I shall give Such Orders as will Effectually prevent Hostilities of any kind being Exercised in the District of Vermont.[31]

Riedesel reported to headquarters that Major Jessup had found it necessary to go to Crown Point to harvest hay. He had been ordered to stay in that exposed position for as short a time as possible and Commodore Chambers had been requested to send an armed vessel to cover the activity. The major reported he had sent scouts to Castleton and the Scotch Patent to watch for rebel movements.

On August 17, Haldimand reacted sharply to this news, displaying his annoyance that Jessup had gone so far without his orders, and instructing that an express be sent to demand his recall and instruct him to make do with the hay that could be found in less exposed locations. Seven days later, Jessup reported to Riedesel that he was about to leave Crown Point as ordered and that all the hay would be taken off, except one small stack. Further, all the hay collected below Split Rock had been secured.[32]

Haldimand notified Shelburne "that Hostilities on our Part are now effectually stopped thro'out this Province." He wrote about the large rebel scout that ranged between Lakes George and Champlain disrupting his communications with New York City and Vermont. This patrol deprived him of useful intelligence and could readily be "cut off," but, in keeping with his instructions, he would not interfere.

The governor believed that Washington's northern visit had been prompted by a report that the British provisions' magazine, which he had organized for a venture into Vermont, had been interpreted as a preparation for an expedition against Albany. "So cautious am I at this Juncture of giving Room for the least Jealousy, that I have defered sending the number of Troops I intended to work at the Isle aux Noix, knowing the Impossibility of keeping secret from the Enemy the most trifling occurrences in this Province, but as the Report dies away I shall forward by degrees the Troops for that Service."[33]

The ship *Hero* landed at Quebec City with Sir John Johnson, the newly appointed superintendent-general of Indian Affairs, and Lady Johnson. The voyage had been distinguished by the birth of the Johnsons' seventh child, who became their second son to be christened John.[34]

Unknown artist. (© McCord Museum, M17590.)

Governor Clinton wrote a detailed letter to Colonel Willett on August 16 about the conundrum presented by the two Jacob Klocks and Forbes. "It is difficult to determine on the Measures most proper to be taken with the <u>Klocks</u> and <u>Forbes</u>. If they really came out on this Business to avail themselves of an opportunity of quitting the Enemy's Service, it

Brigadier-General Sir John Johnson, superintendent and inspector general of Indian Affairs, 1741–1830.

would be impolitic to punish them but if on the contrary their Surrender was the effect of Fraud or Necessity[,] they are undoubtedly Objects of exemplary Punishment." He asked Willett's opinion about sending Jacob J. through to Carleton in New York City with the original copy of Ross's instructions, where he would pick up British headquarters dispatches and bring them to Clinton. The governor could peruse them, have them resealed, and take them to Ross for forwarding to Haldimand. Willett may have thoroughly distrusted Klock, as the idea was not pursued.

Clinton mentioned rumours about peace talks taking place in Paris, but said he had little faith in them.[35]

On August 16, rebel efforts to gain current intelligence about Oswego at last paid dividends when two Butler's Rangers were taken prisoner. Ross reported that Stockbridge Indians had carried them off while they were woodcutting, but how he knew the natives' identity is a mystery. Three days later, the rebels enjoyed a second piece of good fortune when two Rangers deserted while woodcutting.[36]

On August 21, Sir John set out from Lachine in a canoe brigade to take the Ottawa River route to Lake Huron with Joseph Brant; James Stanley Goddard, the chief clerk of Indian Stores, and Lieutenant-Colonel Henry

First Lieutenant Ralfe Clench, Butler's Rangers, 1762–1828. Schoharie-born Clench served as a volunteer in the 53rd Regiment in 1777 and later in the 8th. In 1780, he was commissioned as a second lieutenant in Butler's and saw distinguished service in the far west.

Unknown artist, 1827. (Courtesy of the Niagara Historical Society and Museum.)

Hope, one of Haldimand's senior staff officers. Hope was to examine the post at Detroit and determine if an interior route could be developed to Michilimackinac, a route that would avoid dependence on the Great Lakes should the peace negotiations grant the Americans control of them. Johnson was instructed to visit all the nations in the west and reconcile them to the cessation of active operations — a tall order indeed.[37]

Speaking of the far west, the orders to cease operations had not yet reached a combined force of Butler's Rangers and Lakes' Nations' warriors led by the accomplished Ranger captain, William Caldwell, when they fought a major action on August 19 against a large body of militia cavalry at Blue Licks in Kentucky in which 146 rebels were killed or captured.[38]

On August 21, Riedesel reported that during an inspection of the Brunswick Regiment, von Retz revealed it to be much inferior to the other German regiments for want of a commander and good officers.

Haldimand had found a close friend and most trustworthy professional in Riedesel, who had become his de facto second-in-command, despite the fact that the British general, Alured Clarke, outranked the German for national considerations. Consequently, Riedesel was assigned the vital task of improving the defences at Isle aux Noix against a Franco-American invasion.

In preparation for his move to the island, the baron ordered sixty Hanau Jägers and their officers with eighty-five Prinz Ludwig dragoons and von Barner's Light Infantry Regiment to garrison Sorel in his absence. Chief Engineer William Twiss had requested an officer to assist him with the island's works and Riedesel designated a captain and a number of men from the Prinz Friedrich Regiment for the task. The Light Infantry of the 53rd Regiment had already marched for Isle aux Noix and the 29th Regiment was on its way.

On August 23, Riedesel reported that the routes taken by scouts from the Loyal Blockhouse had been altered since the desertion of six men from Man's patrol, presumably to avoid possible ambushes, and noted that a shorter route to the northern terminus of Hazen's Road and Cöos country had been found.[39]

Captain Pritchard's patriotic prank of forcefully administering an oath of allegiance to several Cöos inhabitants in June backfired when the rebels persecuted these hapless folk for succumbing. The harassment was so extreme that one fellow ran off to Canada. The governor declined to add the new refugee to the pension list, but did find him employment as a labourers' overseer.[40]

Riedesel returned to Sorel on the afternoon of August 24 and found that the 53rd Lights had left at noon for Fort St. John's. He issued orders for part of the garrison to be ready to march on the morrow, which distressed Surgeon Wasmus, as he had paid for the building of an excellent cabin and feared he would have to abandon it. Two nights later, he slept inside it for the first time and found it "safe from insects." To his great pleasure, the next morning he was ordered to remain in the garrison while the Dragoons and detachments of the 29th, 34th, and 53rd Regiments went to Isle aux Noix. The remaining garrison at Sorel would be composed of seventy Brunswick Light Infantrymen and Jägers, a company of Hanau Jägers, and a British artillery detachment under von Barner's command. Accordingly, at 5:00 a.m. on August 28, the "General" was beaten and the Dragoons boarded bateaux to go up the Richelieu as the balance of the Brunswick Light Infantry began to march overland. As Wasmus had unhappy memories of the "cursed island," it was with much satisfaction that he remained in garrison. Contented, he moved out of his new cabin and returned to his plush billet in a merchant's home.[41]

At Niagara, John Butler wrote a letter to Powell on August 27 to report that he had been ordered to relinquish his position as senior deputy agent in the Six Nations' Indian Department in favour of Dr. John Dease, who had recently appeared at Niagara. Dease was a nephew of Sir William Johnson and had been the baronet's personal physician. Guy Johnson had appointed him a deputy agent in April 1775, just days before the outbreak of hostilities in Massachusetts. Now, Dease had a warrant to supersede Butler, which smacked of the Johnson clan's dirty work. Likely, Guy blamed Butler for his recent misfortunes and wanted a sycophant in position at Niagara. With typical understatement, Butler wrote, "I cannot ... help feeling myself injured by Colonel Johnson in having concealed this affair from me in so unaccountable a manner."

A month passed before Haldimand became fully aware of what had happened. He acted in his usual methodical manner to correct the wrong by asking Sir John to advise under whose authority Dease had succeeded Butler and pointedly noting that Carleton had appointed Butler "when the Superintendent [Guy Johnson] and every officer of any rank [Daniel Claus and Gilbert Tice] in that Department abandoned the duties of it." He also quoted an excerpt from an earlier letter he had written to Brigadier Powell.

> Colonel Butler acted in that capacity in the absence of Colonel Johnson and since his return has always acted, and has been returned by him next in seniority to himself. From these considerations, added to my approbation of Colonel Butler's services, and his experience in the Department, I thought fit to direct that in Colonel Johnson's absence, Lieutenant-Colonel Butler should take upon him the direction of the Indian Department.

In a new letter to Powell, Haldimand displayed his anger by thoroughly vindicating Butler at Guy's expense.

> My predecessor's [Carleton's] appointment and my own orders appear to have been superseded by a warrant of Colonel Johnson's which has lain dormant [for] years, and produced at his pleasure, without any cause given, and this warrant (allowing Mr Dease every other advantage) in favour of a person unacquainted with the language of the people and of very little experience in the duties of the Department to the prejudice of a person allowed to possess these requirements, and whose influence and

good management with the military assistance and
support he experienced, the conduct of the Six Nations
entirely depended upon.

Once again, Guy had made a misstep. Butler was fully restored as
senior deputy.[42]

Although Fort Rensselaer had word that the natives had been "called
off," many senior rebel politicians seemed unaware of Haldimand's
orders to cease active operations and, even if they had heard, the action
at Blue Licks screamed deception. On August 20, one of New York's
newly elected senators wrote to Governor Clinton: "I feel most sensibly
for our fellow Citizens in Tryon County. While the Enemy remain
posted in Force at Oswego, we have nothing to expect short of total
Desolation of the scattered remains of that once flourishing district."
In fact, the behaviour of the British was a mystery to the American
administration. There was said to be a ceasefire, yet attacks continued in
New York, Pennsylvania, and Virginia and there was talk that even worse
was to come. In the face of a passionate desire to see it all end, the sheer
complexity of communications was forgotten. The senator continued:

> I anxiously wish for Intelligence from our Ministers
> which may unravel the equivocal Conduct of the
> Enemy. While they profess an Intention to withdraw
> their Troops from this Country, it is positively asserted
> that upwards of 1500 Hessians and 500 British arrived
> within Sandy Hook in a large fleet of Transports,
> under a Convoy of 6 Ships of the Line. While Sir Guy
> Carleton and Adm[iral] Digby write of Propositions
> for peace, — officiously publishg this Letter before it
> reached Congress — one of their ministers insults us
> in parliament with the offer of an *Irish* Independence.

While their General calls aloud on the Americans to soften the Rigours of War and lay aside Acts of Barbarity which are disgraceful, & even proposes to set the Example, Tryon County is made a scene of Blood, Devastation & Wanton murders. While they irritate, provoke (and we have Reason to apprehend) chicane and deceive, they have the Effrontery to charge us with a want of Moderation and a Thirst for War; and to hold us up to the world as implacable Tyrants!"[43]

On August 21, Willett wrote a rather plaintive letter to General Washington from Fort Rensselaer:

Whenever I write to your Excellency I feel a degree of reluctance in doing of it, least I should be a means of Creating unnecessary trouble to a mind so exceedingly burdened with business as yours must be. Yet I sometimes find myself in a measure compeled to do it. This happens to be the case at present.

I have thought proper to inclose your Excellency a letter which I have received from Colonel Reid…. Your Excellency may recollect my acquainting you at Albany, that as I ever have been so[,] I still am a Senior officer to Colonel Reid…. The inclosed letter[,] like every other part of Colonel Reids Correspondence with me[,] holds up an Idea of his conceiving me to be under his Command. As this has not nor can be the case so all suggestions of this kind are disagreeable I have therefore only to request that measures may be taken to have this matter placed in its proper point of light.

With respect to Colonel Reids regiment I have hitherto and still continue to study its case and give it every advantage our situation will admit to Improve in its Discipline by having those troops posted as compact as possible. Indeed I have rather carried my politness to a degree of excess not perhaps Consistant with strict military principals. For I have in ordering Detachments for Commands or other Duties as well as in fixing of … guards along this frontier not only Consulted Major Morrill (who Commands the regiment) But I have Usually left the particular tour or guard to his choice.

This letter revealed that the disagreement between Reid and Willett was protracted. It was obvious that Willett resented having to pander to the NH Continentals, giving them choice assignments to the detriment of his own regiment.[44]

The term of Willett's nine-months' Levies was about to expire and further efforts were made to raise more two- and three-years' men. Former first lieutenant James Cannon was offered a Continental captaincy if he raised a company. He and five others were successful: Joseph Harrison, Simeon Newall, Jonathon Pearce, Peter B. Tierce, and Job Wright. Major-Commandant Elias Van Benschoten commanded the six-company battalion that was known as the State Troops.[45]

General Washington wrote a puzzling letter to Governor Clinton on August 23, noting that much time had elapsed since word had been received that Brant was starting out with a new party. He thought the raid would have reached Canajoharie "long since." Concerns ran high, ceasefire or no.[46]

On August 29, Washington ordered his trusted confidant, Lord Stirling, to take command of the forces in the north at Albany, as he had done during the October 1781 crises over the Ross and St. Leger expeditions. Stirling was advised that his taking of command would allow Reid to leave Albany and join his regiment on the Mohawk River. The C-in-C added:

In case of any dispute respecting command between Lt Col Commandant Reid and Col Willet, you will, my Lord, enquire into the Matter, ascertain their claims of rank and the Commission under which they act, and settle the dispute if practicable; if it appears that Willet is now acting in the field as full Colonel, he will, I suppose, take rank according to the practice established in such cases; if otherwise, the decision may probably be made at once upon the principles already adopted; but in every case I shall confide the accommodation of this dispute, to your Lordship's discretion, as well as all the Minuter dispositions of Command and arrangements in the Department.

One thing however, I must particularly recommend, that all superfluous and unnecessary Posts (if upon a strict examination any such there should be) may forthwith be discontinued and broke up. Major General Knox has instructions to draw from the Northward all the Ordnance, Stores, &c. which are not absolutely necessary there. The Qr Mastr Genl will also have direction to transport some of the publich buildings from Albany, where they are useless, to W[est] Point, where they are much wanted.

His letter continued with instructions that might have increased Willett's discomfort, as it made it clear he occupied a relatively junior position, even if his local seniority should be confirmed.

As there is a considerable Corps of state Troops serving in the Northern Department, it is my wish that the outposts may be garrisoned and the detached duties performed by these Troops, so far as circumstances and the nature of the service will admit; in order that the Continental Regiments may be kept as compact as possible, and held in a state of readiness to remove, shuld it become expedient to order them elsewhere at a short Warning.

I have only further to request your Lordship to point your attention, to the re-establishment of discipline in the regular Corps, to the protection and security of the Department, especially in the issues of ammunition; as there have been great abuses in the consumption of this Article by the Militia and Irregular Troops at the Northward, notwithstanding all the measures which have been taken to prevent it.[47]

On September 2, Washington wrote to Major-General Benjamin Lincoln, the union's first secretary at war, from his headquarters at Verplank's Point to explain his inability to act on a request from Pennsylvania. Raiders from Niagara had ravaged her northern frontier and, in considerable alarm, the state's council had approached the C-in-C for approval to mount two expeditions to remove the threat:

In my answer to the Letters from the Council and Assembly of Pennsylvania ..., I have informed them Generally that I have no objection to the employment of the Pennsylvania Recruits and Hazens Regiment upon the service for which they are requested provided the first is agreeable to Congress, and you can be furnished with a relief for the last to guard the Prisoners at Lancaster. I have also informed them, that if Congress agree to the expeditions in contemplation, you will furnish such necessary Stores as are under your direction, and that you are at liberty to concert with Gentlemen who may be acquainted with the Country which it is proposed to penetrate ... and give directions to the Commanding officers accordingly. I have after this taken the liberty of telling them candidly that I foresee an insurmountable difficulty to putting the expedition in motion, which is, a want of Money provided it is to come out of the Continental treasury, and which I plainly perceive is their expectation, ultimately if not immediately. You are too well acquainted with our distresses on the Score of Money to enumerate them. Had it not been for this, I should have been for carrying into execution, what you call the Northern Expedition, and which, successful, would have struck at the root of the evil we are now experiencing. But alas! How was that to be done when we could barely find means of moving the Army from the Highlands to this place by Water and now we are here, with scarcely a Horse attached to us, we shall find it difficult enough to subsist. I do not imagine you will be able to get the Troops in question further than the Frontier. That alone may afford temporary relief and protection to the Inhabitants.

I cannot at present promise the cooperation, or rather diversion which you recommend upon the Mohawk River. The Troops in that quarter, consisting of two New Hampshire Regiments and one State Regiment of New York, are rather for defence than offence. Major Ross, with a Party of three or four hundred British and a numerous body of Savages and Irregulars is at Oswego, and would not fail to meet any number of Men which we might advance so far up the Mohawk as to give any jealousy. However, if the Western expeditions are prosecuted, and the Troops to the northward should be then continued in that Quarter (which they will not be should there by any occasion for them below) I will endeavour to make any practicable diversion with them....[48]

At Detroit, Major Arent DePeyster, 8th Regiment, wrote to Brigadier Powell on August 27 to confirm that he had received the instruction to cease active operations. He had immediately sent "an express to Captains Caldwell and Bradt ... ordering them not to make any incursions into the enemy's country, but to act in the defensive only." He hoped this message would reach Bradt in time, as he was just at the point of setting out for Wheeling. He also warned that Caldwell was "already over the Ohio to check on the enemy's motions and will likely strike some stroke before he returns." Further, he had heard from a deserter that 1,500 rebels had been assembled to march on Sandusky.[49]

Riedesel reported to Haldimand on August 29 that he had been joined at Sorel by Chief Engineer William Twiss and that they were on the point of leaving for Isle aux Noix. Two days later, they were on the island and had examined the existing works. A number of German troops had arrived and others were delayed for lack of transport. Twiss was concerned that the ratio of artificers to general fatigue men was off the mark and fifty men of 1KRR were requested. By September 1, a detachment of von Barner's Light Infantry had arrived and Riedesel predicted that six hundred men would be at work by the morrow. He awaited the 29th Regiment and had requested the necessary camp equipage.[50]

On August 29, the general physician at Quebec City certified that Butler's Rangers' Captain John McKinnon was "for the present incapable of doing duty due to a paralytic affection on one side of this body." So much for the fellow who had been thrust upon the Rangers by a patronage appointment and had caused so much angst to their officers' corps. McKinnon later went to Britain to recover and was never heard of again.[51]

A return from Oswego dated September 1 was entitled, "State of the Garrison of Ontario." Very little had changed from the previous month except for a note stating that Volunteer Jacob Klock had been taken prisoner at Fort Klock on August 7 and his cousin Private Jacob deserted the same day and Private Bart Forbes deserted the next day. These entries suggest that Serjeant Henry Deal was unsure of precisely what happened to Jacob J., or perhaps that Ross was protecting himself from Klock's blatant betrayal of his judgment and trust.[52]

By August 30, Captain William Fraser had become so agitated about the accusations of his mishandling of his men's pay that he requested an inquiry and named several witnesses he wished to have called. On September 9, the court cleared him of all charges.

Ensign Thomas Sherwood had returned from a scout with dispatches for Haldimand, which Riedesel forwarded from Isle aux Noix to St. John's with some newspapers. He noted that, if the account of a letter from Carleton to Washington were true, a general peace was imminent, and he was intensely humiliated that the rebels were to be granted independence before the terms of the peace were concluded and lamented that the war had lasted seven years, had cost fifty million (pounds?) and 50,000 casualties.[53]

Riedesel wrote privately to the governor on September 3, stating he was sure that efforts were being made in Europe to bring about a general peace and that they would be successful, as Rodney's spectacular victory had humbled the pride of the Bourbon monarchies. He cautioned that the enemy would make another expedition to lever their position during the negotiations and thought that New York City would be the target, especially as the ministry had chosen not to send reinforcements. He gave several reasons for forming this suspicion, including Washington's studied neglect of the city, which in his experience signalled his intention to attack.[54]

On September 9, Haldimand wrote to Ross in reaction to the news that some Rangers had been carried off, implying that loyal natives may have been the perpetrators:

> You cannot be too much on your Guard while the Indians are in their present Disposition — if the Rebels hear of it they will undoubtedly improve the Opportunity to tamper with them, and altho' they have hitherto behaved well, there is no saying what disappointment & the apprehensions of being forsaken by us may tempt them to do, so that

without discovering any Distrust, I recommend to you an unremitting Vigilance and Attention to the safety of your Post — If the Rebels should obstinately hold out against the Overtures now making — this Province must become an immediate Object of their Attention, and in order to secure the Indians it will be necessary to regain Oswego, much will be certainly in their Power should the Indians join them or even look on — November is a favourable month for that Attempt and it will be indispensably necessary that you keep out Intelligent Persons to procure you the best Information as well for your immediate safety as to give you time to communicate with Niagara.[55]

That same day, Haldimand informed Lieutenant-Colonel Alexander Dundas, 8th Regiment (who had assumed command at Niagara), that Ross was in difficulty with his native auxiliaries. All of the Indians, other than the loyal Oneidas, had left Oswego after exhibiting "much discontent on being prevented from going to war," and the Oneidas refused to give Ross any assistance with scouting and patrolling. The governor thought it most fortunate that Sir John Johnson's tour of the upper posts was underway. "I … have no doubt that his presence will have a good effect in conciliating the minds of the Indians." Mindful of the chaotic Pontiac uprising of 1763, he warned Dundas to:

[N]arrowly watch over their conduct and by the strictest vigilance and attention at all your outposts to prevent possibility of surprise…. From Col Butler's influence and zealous attention, you will always be furnished with the best intelligence from the Indian Country and have timely notice of every event of consequence. I have no apprehensions on this account, but precautions are so easily taken that it were unpardonable to risk anything neglecting them.

The worm had turned.[56]

In bizarre contrast to the early years of heavy campaigning endured by 1KRR, Major Gray notified Captain LeMaistre on September 9 that a captain, two subalterns, three serjeants, and fifty rank and file had been sent to Isle aux Noix for garrison duty. The balance of the battalion had gone to cut cordwood for Montreal's garrison, except for the Grenadier company, which continued to do duty in the town. All that remained in quarters was a sick officer and twenty lame and sick men.[57]

Colonel von Kreutzbourg wrote to his prince on September 10 to express his hopes that he had received his dispatches of October 20, 1781. His comment revealed the great difficulties he and his fellow Hesse-Hanau officers laboured under because of terrible communications. Virtually a year had passed and he had no idea of whether their actions had been approved of, nor had he any answers to his many questions.

He reported that his Jägers were still using blankets issued in 1777 in England and were wearing clothing from the 1779 shipment. As the blankets had been used to supplement the clothing on every march, scout, and expedition, only ten useable ones remained. Needless to say, the clothing was threadbare and the colonel feared what the winter would bring if shipments from home did not arrive. Requests to Haldimand for new blankets were fruitless, as the governor said that the Crown was not to supply the foreign regiments, even though his Jägers were employed on more rigorous duty than the infantry.[58]

The governor informed Riedesel that a ship from Halifax brought Carleton's warning about a French fleet of thirteen or fourteen ships of the line and three thousand troops that had been seen off the coast. The vessels were believed to be the remnants of the fleet defeated by Admiral Rodney in the Caribbean and were thought to be putting into Boston for repairs. Rather than waiting for additional news from below, Haldimand sent an Indian Department officer overland to the British post at Penobscot in northern Massachusetts to discover what news of this enemy fleet might be heard from there.[59]

On September 11, John Butler's nephew, the brash, young Ranger captain, Andrew Bradt, who had earned the governor's censure on two occasions the year before, struck the settlement of Wheeling, Virginia, the staging area for several rebel incursions into Indian Territory, most notably the infamous slaughter of the Moravian Delawares.

Bradt had set out from Sandusky just a day or two before Powell's orders to cease active operations arrived. He had with him about fifty men of his Ranger company, a few Indian Department rangers, including Simon's brother, James Girty, and 238 Lakes' and Ohio Indians. The young leader's haughty manner soon caused a rupture with his allies and co-operation faltered. As a result, the raid accomplished little. This strike marked the last coordinated offensive action of the war by British troops and natives.[60]

Secret Service agent Roger Stevens had returned from Vermont and submitted a report on September 11. Three-quarters of the inhabitants he had contacted had been willing to house and feed him; but the others were "not reconciled with government nor their own leading men." Some of the latter heard of his presence and surrounded several houses where they thought he might be hidden, clearly hoping to take or kill him. Vermont was as restless and divided as ever.[61]

Riedesel privately wrote to Haldimand that, from his reading of various rebel newspaper accounts, he had no doubts that a peace had been concluded and he would be on his way home in the spring. He was greatly pleased on his own behalf, but for professional reasons he lamented such a shameful conclusion to the war. If the outcome restored rest and tranquility to "the best of Kings," he would be satisfied, but he thought that Britain's immense debt, loss of trade, and onerous taxation must raise discontent. And, if Canada and Nova Scotia were the only provinces left to the empire, they must be made as inaccessible as possible. He noted that Haldimand's decision to fortify Isle aux Noix before the peace had been wise. Twiss was well satisfied with the work of the German troops and, if the carpenters could be kept as hard at work as the labourers, the three casemented stone redoubts would be complete by the end of October.

In a second private letter the next day, Riedesel spoke of receiving official letters from a senior German staff officer in Halifax which spoke only of peace and the return of the troops to Europe. The French fleet had come to the American coast to avoid the hurricane season in the West Indies and the three thousand troops aboard were too small to give weight to an attack on New York City. In any event, the fleet would have gone to Rhode Island, not Boston, if New York City were the object. When Haldimand replied on September 15, he registered surprise at still not having heard a word from General Carleton.[62]

On September 13, Captain William Ancrum, 34th Regiment, acknowledged receipt of the governor's eagerly awaited permission to "go down to Canada" from Carleton Island with his company; however, there would be a delay while he investigated a report by some loyal natives regarding the tracks of a suspicious, large party just south of the island. On a different issue, he reported that the snow *Haldimand* was no longer fit for lake service and that, as a surrogate, he had armed and manned two gunboats with the ship's crew. Five days later, he reported that the Indians' warning had been without foundation and his company would now set out for the lower province.[63]

Surgeon Wasmus made note of a terrible affliction that was raging through lower Quebec:

> The French disease is so common that one finds villages in which all the inhabitants, large and small, young and old, have been infected with it; thus they all have cankers in their throats. The King and Parliament had been informed about it and it is expected that a radical cure

Horatio Nelson. Britain's great naval hero endangered his career over his infatuation with a young Canadian girl.

may now be undertaken at Royal expense. This indeed is the only way."[64]

Haldimand again confided his frustration over the chronic lack of information from Carleton in a letter to Riedesel dated September 16. "I am very much astonished at not having heard from General Carleton, and am very impatient to procure some news…. It is singular that when he has such a safe opportunity of writing me he expresses neither hope nor fear, and that he leaves me, since his arrival, in so much uncertainty concerning everything. I am very sensitive about this." He then displayed his gratitude for the baron's efforts. "No one, my dear sir, could have taken more pains than yourself in perfecting our works on Isle aux Noix."[65]

On September 18, the twenty-eight-gun frigate *Albermarle* put into Quebec under the command of Captain Horatio Nelson. The ship's crew was suffering from scurvy and Nelson himself was very ill and sought a chance to recuperate. During his month-long visit, he wrote to his father, "Health, that greatest of blessings, is what I have never truly enjoyed until I saw Fair Canada. The change it has wrought, I am convinced, has been truly wonderful." It is moot whether it was the climate or romance that agreed with Nelson, as he had become infatuated with a sixteen-year-old Canadian girl named Mary Simpson. Legend says that, when he was ordered to New York City, he deserted his ship on the eve of sailing and it was only through the efforts of a friend, who bodily carried the swain back to the vessel, that saved Britain's brilliant naval hero from a disastrous end to his burgeoning career.[66]

At Point Levis on September 18, Captain-General Haldimand; the Royal Artillery commander, Lieutenant-Colonel Forbes Macbean; and Lieutenant-Colonel Barry St. Leger attended the encampment of Major-General Johann August von Loos's brigade to observe a series of manoeuvres in the fields and woods. Loos's brigade was composed of infantry from Hesse-Hanau, Hesse-Kassel, and Anhalt-Zerbst, supported by the latter's Jägers and the combined artillery company drawn from the various principalities under Major Pausch.[67]

That same day, Haldimand somehow found time to write to Carleton in New York City to apprise him of the natives' temper and his deep personal concern that injustices may be done to these loyal allies of the Crown:

> Unacquainted with the Terms that may be intended for the Six Nation Indians in the proposals of Peace ... — I think it necessary as a Commissioner to inform you that my having Restrained them from Hostilities has occasioned a general discontent amongst them. Major Ross who commands Oswego informs me that they have all left that Post in disgust and that he is in daily expectation of being insulted. They are alarmed at the appearance of an accommodation so far short of what our Language, from the beginning has taught them to expect, deprived of their Lands & driven out of their Country they reproached us with their ruin, & project of severe Retaliation from the Hands of the Rebells. Your Excellency is too well acquainted with the Situation and Interests of these People to make it necessary for me to enlarge upon their consequence with respect to the Trade and Safety of this Province, the Expectations their services entitles them to from us, or upon the fatal consequences that might attend our abandoning them to the Intrigues of the Enemy, should they persist in the war, or to their Resentment in case of a Peace, and I persuade

myself they will be amply considered by Your Excellency either in a Representation to the King's Ministers or by such arrangement as shall be agreed upon in this Country. Your Excellency will not understand from what I have said of the Six Nations that the King's attention should be confined to them only, many of the Western & Indian Nations in the neighbourhood have suffered equally by shameful encroachments of the Virginians upon their most valuable Hunting Grounds, and have been equally attached and serviceable to the Royal Cause.[68]

General Von Loos responded to some criticisms he had heard regarding the manoeuvres of his brigade on September 18. He wrote Riedesel to explain:

The platoon firings ought most certainly to have been stopped at once; but the terrain was too small, and I was obliged to give Rauschenblatt [commander of the Anhalt-Zerbst Regiment] time to retreat, and it was therefore necessary that the firing on that spot should not be interrupted. The main thing in executing such manoeuvres, are quick evolutions, rapid movements, good positions, turnings, strategy, alignments, and marching. Firing makes only noise, and amuses the unmilitary spectators. I have another manoeuvre which I intend showing to the premier, who, by the way, to the astonishment of every body, is polite, when he comes here.... The growler [Haldimand], however, will not allow us to have huts.... [T]hink of having tents which have already served three summers, no straw, a little wood, and no blankets![69]

It may not have occurred to von Loos that Haldimand might be attempting to toughen up his Germans, as he often complained that they were unable to campaign in the wilderness and, as they formed such

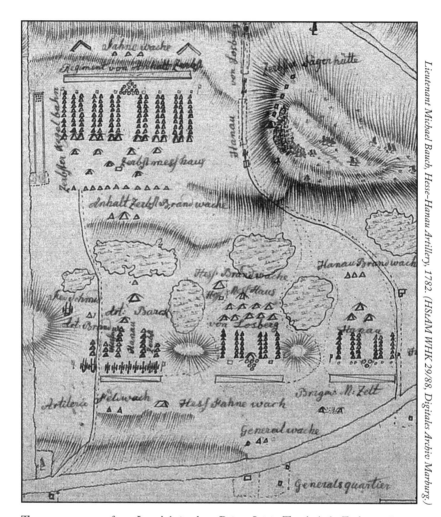

Lieutenant Michael Bauch, Hesse-Hanau Artillery, 1782. (HStAM WHK 29/88, Digitales Archiv Marburg.)

The encampment of von Loos's brigade at Pointe Lévis. The Anhalt-Zerbst regiment is camped in fields at the top left of the map and its Jägers' are located to the right in huts on a wooded hill. Below are three separate camps. On the left, Major Pausch's combined artillery with guns arrayed to the rear. In the middle, Hesse-Cassel's von Lossburg's Regiment, and, on the right, the first battalion Erbprinz von Hessen. Von Loos's headquarters is at the bottom margin.

a large proportion of his army, their incapability put severe restrictions on his strategic options.

On September 29, Ross reported that five rebels had been seen near the fort, but, as no natives were at hand, they escaped. One of his scouts from the Mohawk River reported that there was no movement of troops in that quarter and that the French troops had gone to join Washington. He conjectured that, should the overtures of peace be rejected, Oswego would become "the object of the enemy."[70]

Sir John and Lieutenant-Colonel Hope arrived at Fort Niagara via Detroit on October 1. Johnson advised the Indian Department's officers that they would have to implement stringent economies and new control procedures. He immediately called for a council to be held at the Loyal Confederate Village, although he found it necessary to proceed without John Butler, who was too ill to attend. A dispatch from Haldimand had been awaiting his arrival and set the tone for his address. His task was to soothe the natives and calm their fears, advising them to "firmly rely on a Continuance of the King's Favor and Protection in all situations." He was to "leave no means untried to persuade their Affections."

When Sir John addressed the council, amongst many other "soothing" comments, he told the natives that the king had only stopped active operations to give the rebels time to consider their madness and recover their senses and that the Indians' services would never be forgotten. In his dispatch to Haldimand, he reported the Indians had been placated and, in confirmation of this opinion, a party of thirty immediately returned to Ross at Oswego.

What must Johnson have been thinking during his oration? He was not a stupid, duplicitous, or dishonourable man; he knew of Cornwallis's defeat; he was aware of the new ministry's radically different policies; he understood that peace negotiations were underway; he knew that Hope had surveyed an alternate water route to the west in response to Haldimand's concerns that control of the Great Lakes might be surrendered. Was he simply following orders and earning his bread? How he must have shuddered over his words when the articles of peace later became known.[71]

An incident that could have embarrassed Sir John in a material sense was the French capture of two merchant vessels bearing next season's native presents, valued at £80,000 Sterling. Fortunately, they were recaptured and arrived at Quebec on October 6 in the company of nine other ships carrying a body of exchanged German troops. Amongst the officers was Colonel Johann Lentz, who had commanded the Hesse-Hanau Grenadier Regiment under Burgoyne. He assumed command of the reconstituted infantry battalion. Lentz had brought very welcome news for Carl von Kreutzbourg; his prince had promoted him to full colonel.[72]

On October 6, Sherwood reported from the Loyal Blockhouse that backcountry people on New Hampshire's east bank of the Connecticut River were enraged by their state's new taxes, as such levies had been touted as a primary reason for the rebellion. After a forced tax sale, at which livestock was bid on by affluent persons for scandalously low prices, the people went to the Liberty Pole, "and cryed aloud Liberty is gone, Cut it down … [and] Huzza'd aloud for King George and his Laws."[73]

On October 1, the day that Sir John arrived at Niagara, Lieutenant Pliny Moore noted in his journal that an agent had arrived at Fort Rensselaer from Canada with confirmation that the natives had been called away from the frontiers and that Johnson, as the new superintendent of all Indians, was on a tour of the upper posts "on some very urgent business."[74]

Gavin A. Watt, after an unknown artist, 2009.

Lieutenant Pliny Moore joined Willett's Levies in the three-years' service in July 1781, and was appointed adjutant of State Troops in November 1782. He maintained an active correspondence throughout his service.

———————

A fog lay over the intentions of the protagonists, made all the more opaque by the British having no simple method of calling off their native auxiliaries. They had spent so much diplomatic energy and such staggering amounts of money to persuade the natives to join in the war and to maintain their constant support, it was difficult to turn off the tap.

8

*L*ord Stirling arrived at Albany on September 7, and, in only eleven days, had resolved the nagging issue of Willett's seniority.

> The General having with great attention perused the claims in writing of Colonel Willett and Lieut. Coll. Commandant Reid — does find that Coll Willett was commissioned by Congress as Lieutenant Colonel of the 3d New York Regiment on the 25th of November 1776 — That at the reform of the Army on the 1st of January 1781 he was oblidg'd to retire on half pay — that on the 27th of April 1781 he took charge of a regiment of Levies raised by the State of New York — that on the 7th of April 1782 he was by the same State appointed Colonel Commandant with charge of all their State Troops and a large proportion of their Levies — On the other hand that on the 5th March 1778 a vacancy of a Colonel of the 2d New Hampshire Regiment happen'd which Lieut. Coll Reid conceives he was entitled to, as oldest Lieut. Coll in that Line — that on the 2d of June 1778 Congress Resolv'd to make no more Colonels, and instead thereof Lieutenant Colonels Commandants to Command Regiments.
>
> That sometime about May 1779 Congress among other Commissions for the New Hampshire Line, sent

one for Lieut. Coll Reid, appointing him Lieut. Colonel Commandant of the 2d New Hampshire Regiment and to take rank from the 3rd March 1778 which was previous to the before mention'd Resolve of 2d June 1778, and therefore Lieut. Coll Reid conceives he was entitled to a Commission of full Colonel from that date instead of Lieutenant Colonel Commandant.

However hard it may appear on the part of Lieutenant Coll Reid, yet the fact is that Colonel Willett has a grade in Rank above him and is now acting in the field as full Colonel and cooperating with the Continental Troops; according to the established practice in such cases, and agreable to the Resolves of Congress he must have right to Command all Lieutenant Colonels or Lieutenant Colonels Commandant cooperating with him.

Wherefore the General does determine and order that Colonel Willett is to act as full Colonel in the department, and is to be respected and obeyed as such.

So, after a spring and summer of acrimony, tacit disobedience and interference, the situation was resolved, but not before British raiders had enjoyed a free reign of the Mohawk region.

When Stirling reported this finding to Washington on September 18, he enclosed a copy of a letter from Willett:

By the inclosed resolution of Congress of the 20th of last month, your Lordship will perceive that the conditionary clause of the 2d of April 1781 respecting Cloathing two Regiments of Infantry to be rais'd in this State is taken off — In consequence of this act of Congress I am directed by His Excellency Governor Clinton to make immediate application to the commanding Officer of the department for Cloathing for said Troops; the bearer of this Lieut. Ten Eyck, waits on your Lordship with a proper return for that

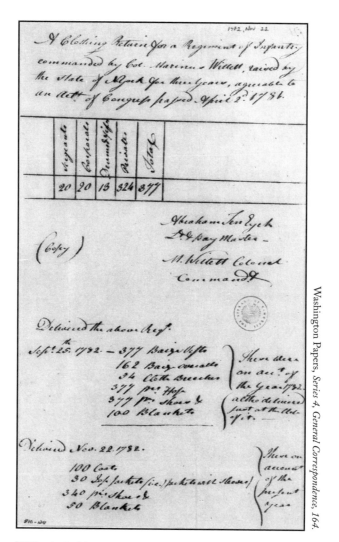

Willett's clothing return.

Washington Papers, Series 4, General Correspondence, 164.

purpose; Lieut. Ten Eyck will likewise exhibit to your
Lordship a return for a few musquets and Bayonets, and
for Cartridge Boxes, Drums & Fifes, which are much
wanted for these troops.

An accompanying return for the infantry regiment commanded by
Colonel Marinus Willett showed a strength of 20 serjeants, 20 corporals,

13 drummers, and 324 privates — a total of 377. In response to Congress's resolve to clothe these men, 100 coats, 30 sleeved jackets, 340 pairs of shoes, and 50 blankets were delivered on November 22 and, at the end of the year, 377 Baize vests, 162 Baize overalls, 34 wool breeches, 377 pairs of hose, 377 pairs of shoes, and 100 blankets. What the men had been wearing throughout the campaign season remains a mystery.[1]

On September 20, Lord Stirling issued a General Order at Albany, which set the distribution of troops in the Mohawk and Schoharie valleys.

The 2NH was to concentrate at Johnstown. On September 28, the various companies were to march at five in the morning, taking the best route to their new post. Those from Forts Herkimer and Dayton were to form one body and proceed together. Those from the other posts and in the vicinity of Fort Rensselaer were to assemble, and form at that post, and march from there. In keeping with Washington's instruction to restore discipline, Stirling issued the following order, which surely must have discomfited Reid:

> Each body is to march in compleat Order, and exactly Agreable to the establish'd rules, and not to Suffer any Straglers.
>
> The Quarter Master … is at least two days before hand with a proper number of Camp Colour men and Pioneers to proceed towards Johnstown to mend the roads and bridges, and to prepare the Quarters for the regiment —
>
> The Contractors will take care that there be a supply of Provisions at Johnstown early in the day of the first of October.
>
> Lieutenant Colonel Commandant Reid will be pleased to proceed to Johnstown and join his regiment there; he is to see that The Regiment be put in the highest state of discipline; the Men are to be habituated to appear clean and neat, their hair must be either short cropped or Reined. They must be taught to put on their Clothes and Accoutriments properly, so that the whole

may appear soldierlike and uniform, and above all — They are to keep their Arms in the most brilliant Order.

Colonel Willett will take care to Garrison such posts as are to be retain'd with the State Troops and Levies under his immediate Command, agreeable to his Instructions.

Lieut. Coll Commandant Dearborn [at Saratoga] will no doubt take The same care to have the discipline of the 1t Regiment perfect indeed[. M]ore will be expected from them as they have had an opportunity of being in a more compact situation —

The Regiments are to be exercised in detail one day [and] Manoevered in Battalion the next, and this is to be repeated every day while the Weather admits of it. The General Sincerely wishes to see the New Hampshire Brigade in as good order as the rest of the Troops of the Army, who have justly merited the approbation of the Commander in Chief and the applause of every judge who sees them; and he does not doubt (especially as he shall give oppertunities of being together not only in Regiment but in Brigade) that by the Officers assiduously exerting themselves with a spirit of excelling, they will soon overtake those, who by having greater oppertunities are exhibiting examples to the world of Military appearance and discipline.

The Cannon Ammunition and Millitary Stores at Fort Plank, Willett and Paris are to be deposited at Fort Ranselair and Then a new return of the whole at that Post is to be made to the Orderly Office — The Brass three pounder now at Fort Ranselair, with a proper quantity of ammunition and stores is to move with the Troops to Johnstown — A proper Number of Artillery men are to attend this piece, and Capt. Seward will also Order a proper officer and men from the Artillery to take charge of the Cannon, Ammunition and Millitary Stores at Fort Ranselair.

He specifically ordered Reid to maintain an outguard at Fort Hunter of a serjeant and twelve men, which was to be rotated weekly, and a second detail of a corporal and six men at Veeder's Mill, if it was felt necessary or requested by Veeder himself. A patrol was to be sent to the Sacandaga River and beyond it for a few miles. He then turned to the critical topic of discipline, which, by his words, left no doubt that Reid had been derelict in his duty and allowed affairs to slip far below an acceptable level:

> As the perfecting your regiment in discipline was a principal motive for collecting them at Johnstown I must request your very particular attention to this important object — The kind of duty the men have been upon with their detach'd situation I fear has been very destructive to their Cloathing, and hurtful to every truly military feeling, to correct these abuses and introduce such a spirit of Soldierlike pride and ambition as well make them appear with respect, will most undoubtedly require your constant and unremitted care and attention. The season for manoeuvring and field exercises will shortly be over, and I need not suggest to you the importance of establishing a steady and strict discipline previous to the Troops taking quarter — but when I reflect that you will feel yourself compell'd to this duty by the love you bear your Country, and the value you place upon your own reputation as an Officer with that of the regiment under your Command, without a doubt of your spirited exertions, I cheerfully resign the subject to the consideration of a Gentleman in whose millitary abilities I have the highest confidence.

In contrast, Willett's orders lacked any pejorative overtones:

> I have thought proper to reduce the Posts on the Mowhawks River to five — You will therefore be pleased to post the State Troops and Levies under your immediate command at No. 1, 2 & 5 as pr Margin in such

proportion as you shall find best, and at such other small Posts as you may from time to time think necessary — the Company at Balls Town and Charlotte County will remain in their present situation until farther Orders — you will please to keep your Scouts West as far as Fort Schuyler [Stanwix] and North and South as far as you may think proper, giving them such orders for communications as will in your opinion give the earliest information of the approach of an Enemy — I wish you to maintain the strictest discipline consistent with the nature of your situation, and have no doubt of your giving such orders and instructions, as will tend most effectually to protect the frontiers, and in all respects best answer the just expectations of the Country.

The marginal note listed: "1. Herkimer and Dayton; 2. Ranslair; 3. Johnstown; 4. Hunter; 5. Schoharie."[2]

Jacob Bayley's report to General Washington from Cöos gave details of Haldimand's stationing of a large number of troops at Isle aux Noix. One of Bayley's spies had been at Fort St. John's and had witnessed three thousand men embark from there and proceed up the lake. When his informant had arrived at Isle aux Noix, he found some three to four thousand men encamped. Although their destination was not public, it appeared they intended to take possession of Vermont. There was circumstantial evidence that something would occur at Crown Point on or before October 10 and, to add to this alarm, Bayley wrote, "the Allens are with a number of armed men taking up, confining, judging, and condemning those who do not adhere to them in Champlain County. They carry their Court with them and make short work."[3]

On October 19, Washington addressed the situation at Isle aux Noix with Governor Clinton:

In the present quiet state of the frontiers, and with assurances from Sir Guy Carleton, that the incursions of the savages are stopped by authority, I have it in contemplation to withdraw the Continental troops from the northward. There are many reasons, which will make that measure eligible, unless the troops, which have been raised on purpose for the defence of the frontiers of this State, should be thought incompetent to the duty, even taking into consideration the inactivity of the season and the situation of affairs; for, indeed, I confess, I do not consider the late reports of the enemy's being in force at the Isle-au-Noix to indicate any thing farther than an attention to their own security. The severity of the approaching season, and every other circumstance, appear to me to militate against an attack upon our possessions this winter, and we shall not be at so great a distance, but that succor may be afforded as early in the spring as shall be necessary. At any rate, some measures must be taken relative to the troops now there. I should be happy in rec'g your sentiments.

Clinton replied the next day:

I very candidly confess I am of opinion with your Excellency that nothing extraordinary is to be apprehended from the late accounts. We have had [news] of the collection of the enemy's force at Isle au Noix & Oswego; and this sentiment I expressed to Lord Stirling in the first communication I made to him of the intelligence I have rec'd; tho I thought it my duty … to order a part of the militia to be held in readiness. I learn, however, that the frontier inhabitants are much alarmed at those hostile appearances; and I am, therefore, very apprehensive that if any part of the troops on the northern or western frontiers were to be removed before the season is somewhat farther advanced & thereby even the possibility of the enemy's visiting them with large parties, it might create great uneasiness among them & perhaps induce the more exposed to abandon their settlements & remove into the interior parts of the State; which would be exceedingly distressing to themselves & injurious to the public.... I should conceive that the continuing of a small regular force to the northward during the winter might be attended with good consequences.[4]

On September 21, General Schuyler wrote the president of Congress, enclosing a letter he had received from a Canadian informant. It read:

Dispatches have been lately received by General Haldimand from the ministry, the following is what I have collected of their contents. That a reinforcement of between three and four thousand men might soon be expected from England and about fifteen hundred of the foreign troops from New York. That the posts in the upper Country were to be reinforced and the works strengthened. That all the fortifications in this province are to be put in the best state of defence possible. That It was in contemplation to point the whole force of the nation against the French and Spanish settlements In the west indies. That incursions into your country by Indians and small parties were no longer to be permitted. Since the arrival of these dispatches battoemen are engaging to convey a large quantity of flour and military stores to the westward. Beef and pork they have none to send at present, but a fleet from Ireland is daily expected with a large supply. About seventy Chippeways[,] 200 Otawas and as many six nations left this a few days ago[. T]hey were told by Campbell that they must not go to war as the King had compassion on his American subjects they having exposed their sorrow for what they had done[.] [Sayengaraghta] the seneca sachem replied that the Americans and French had beat the English, that the latter could no longer carry on the war, and that the Indians knew It well and must now be sacrificed, or submit to the Americans, that it was time to attend to their own concerns and listen no longer [to] his lies[.] Campbell tryed to sooth and make them believe otherwise, but in vain, I was present at this conversation which took place in presence of all the Indians, and many Inhabitants. The Indians after receiving considerable presents went home little satisfyed with their situation.[5]

Throughout the fall, a garrison of Tryon militia commanded by Lieutenant-Colonel Clyde and Major Copeman was maintained at Fort Plain, although the nine-months' Levies companies of Lawrence Gros and Abner French were discharged at Fort Herkimer. Schenectady's militia was also active, sending a detachment with a detail of Oneidas to apprehend Tories and deserters at Jessup's Patent.[6]

———————

On October 23, Stirling wrote Washington from Albany, commenting that during his visit to the Mohawk River posts, he had been delayed by a severe snowstorm, which prevented him from reporting earlier:

At Johnstown I found that by a little repair of some of the deserted houses a Regiment may be Comfortably quartered there during the Winter. If your Excellency would Chuse to have one remain there; there is plenty of wood at hand and I have directed them to cut a quantity of it for their fireing; the troops appeared to me better than I expected to have found them. [A]t fort Ranselaer I also found the levies and State troops in tolerable good order, the latter in want of Clothes and Arms; the blockhouse which is an excellent one, projected by Major VilleFranche is Just under Cover and in defenceable order against any force which I believe will come against it this Winter.

The Milatary stores are now in a Safe & dry Magazine, the weather deter'd me from going higher up the River, the Snow was deep and the roads bad. I shall enclose returns of the defeciency's of Arms &c, as there are none here fit for Service, all that are unfit, are returned into the Store and now go to West point with the other Military Stores which were here. I also now send Returns of the New Hamshire Brigade and of the levies and State Troops. Whatever of Arms and Cloathing are designed for this department I should be glad your Excellency would order to be sent up immediately least an early Winter, which we have strong appearances of, should render the River unnavigable so high as this place.[7]

General Washington wrote to Governor Clinton on October 30 to inform him of "the general arrangements of Winter Cantonments for the Army." It had been decided to send the two New Hampshire regiments to New Windsor and replace them with the strong, well-disciplined Rhode Island Regiment (RIR). He believed that the Rhode Islanders, coupled with Willett's State Troops, would be "sufficient to keep up the necessary defence of the Winter and to calm the apprehensions of the Inhabitants." Further, he reported that Stirling would retain command in the north over the winter.[8]

In 1778, Rhode Island had experienced weak enlistments for its two battalions, and enacted legislation to accept "every able-bodied negro, mulatto, or Indian man slave." Those who volunteered were "to receive all the bounties, wages and encouragements allowed by the Continental Congress to any soldiers enlisting into this service." As well, their owners were compensated for their loss. In actual practice, the number of blacks and natives who enlisted was moderate, and the blacks, both enslaved and free, were primarily concentrated into three segregated companies of the 1st Rhode Island (1RH). Black recruiting had been common in most

A Rhode Island Regiment Light infantryman. This image does not represent the uniform worn on the Oswego venture.

Jean-Baptiste-Antoine DeVerger (Courtesy of the Anne S.K. Brown Military Collection, Brown University Library.)

states, but not in such a high concentration and, when 1RI became known pejoratively as "the Black Regiment," Washington ordered the nickname abolished. Soon after, Rhode Island's assembly passed a new law excluding "Indians, Mulattoes and Negroes" from militia drafts and ordered the state's recruiting officers to accept no additional black men.

As part of the 1781 reorganization of the Continental Line, 1st and 2nd Rhode Island were combined into a single regiment (RIR) under the command of Colonel Jeremiah Olney of Providence, a veteran officer of several campaigns and actions. An October return revealed that the new regiment was one of the strongest in the Continental Army with fifteen commissioned officers, forty-four non-commissioned officers, five staff officers, 275 rank and file fit for duty, thirty-two "sick present," nineteen "sick absent," and 171 on command, a total of 565 all ranks.[9]

On the same day, Washington suggested to Lord Stirling that he locate his quarters at Albany and instructed that the New Hampshire regiments be sent south as soon as possible in time for the men to build their huts. Although he left it to Stirling to decide on the disposition of his troops, he noted the importance of keeping the RIR "in as collected a state as circumstances will admit," and suggested Saratoga.[10]

———————————————

———————————————

Von Loos complained virulently about the "growler" in a letter to Riedesel of October 19. "It is damnable that the old fellow should make a secret of the winter quarters. This causes me a loss of sixty piasters, which I have to pay to Madame Lanandiere ... for house hire per quarter. Duke Ferdinand had secrets too, but he furnished free quarters." Anticipating his superior's mirth over his predicament, he continued, "It is easy for you to laugh: you live in your manor house at Sorel, free and easy."

Four days later, Surgeon Wasmus recorded that twenty-six ships at Quebec had had bunks installed for the transportation of troops and that they were to sail for New York City. Rumours abounded that the city was to be evacuated and the troops sent to the West Indies.[11]

Two significant notices appeared in General Orders at headquarters in Quebec City on October 21. Barry St. Leger was promoted to brigadier-general of the army in Canada with a captain of the 31st Regiment as his brigade major. Sir John Johnson was promoted to brigadier of Provincial troops with Captain Thomas Scott, 53rd Regiment, (who had acted in this capacity for Johnson during the 1780 campaign) as his brigade major.

The winter quarters of the army were located in several districts and the commanders of each were noted as follows:

1. The troops at Quebec and the parishes between St. Paul's Bay and Machiche inclusive upon the north side of the river St. Lawrence under Major-General Clarke.
2. Those at Kamaraska and the several parishes as far as Bécancour on the south side of the river under Major-General de Loos.
3. Those at Bécancour as far as Pointe-au-Fer, including the Loyal Blockhouse, as well as those from thence to La Prairie down the south side of the river to Sorel, inclusive under Major-General von Riedesel.
4. Those from Machiche and all the Parishes on the north side of the river to the passage of Répentigny under Brigadier-General de Speth.
5. On the island of Montreal, Isle Jesus, and the islands as far as Lachine on the north and from there to La Prairie, excluded on the south side of the river under Brigadier St. Leger.
6. The posts from Oswegatchie to Michilimackinac and what concerns the Naval Department upon the Upper Lakes under Brigadier Maclean. Oswegatchie and Carleton Island will also (from their proximity) report to headquarters.

7. The officers commanding in each quarter or post will report to the general of the district and they will report to the commander-in-chief.

8. Captain Chambers, having the command of whatever relates to the Marine upon Lake Champlain, will directly report to the C-in-C.

9. Brigadier Powell to act as commandant of Quebec to whom all reports of guards and other matters relating to the duty of the garrison are to be made. He will report all extraordinaries to the governor. (This was an obvious sop to Powell who had been brought down to headquarters from Niagara to bolster Clarke).[12]

As noted above, Haldimand had selected Maclean to replace Powell at the upper posts. His responsibilities were outlined in a document of October 21 entitled, "Distribution of the Troops in the upper Posts under the Command of BGen Maclean, Officers Included."

Posts	Officers Commanding	Total Number
Oswegatchie	Lieutenant McDonnell	30
Carleton Island	Major Harris	442
Ontario	Major Ross	300
Niagara	Lieutenant-Colonel Dundas	665
Detroit	Major DePeyster	432
Mackinac	Captain Robertson	100
Total		**1969**
Naval Dept (Carleton Is. to Mackinac)		355[13]

The day before, Deputy Adjutant General Lernoult had instructed Maclean to take on board two Ranger deserters held prisoner at Fort Ontario and have them tried by court martial at Niagara. Further, Captain William Potts, 8th Regiment, was to act as the major of Butler's Rangers, while retaining his company of Regulars.[14]

The governor was concerned that Ross would not have been able to construct sufficient barrack space to house his garrison over the winter. Should that be the case, the brigadier was to withdraw part of the garrison to secure Carleton Island, but that draft must not leave until the last possible moment so that Oswego's construction could be advanced to the maximum; however, when Maclean arrived at Fort Ontario, he reported that the garrison numbered about four hundred rank and file and, within a week, quarters in the barracks and blockhouses would be finished for six hundred men. Maclean had been impressed by Carleton Island's vulnerability and he reminded the governor that the ships and storehouses, which lay on the point below the works, were subject to attack by raiders when the river froze over.

> There will then be no occasion to diminish the [Oswego] Garrison for want of Barracks, but as Carleton Island is a place of very great consequence for many reasons, with which Your Excellency is perfectly well acquainted, I have settled it [with] Major Ross that he is to send there by the last Ship the Detachment of Colonel Butler's Rangers, now here, they consist of 74 men including Officers. Major Ross wished to keep here the whole Detachment of the 84th, and all his own People, which in my opinion is by no means too numerous a Garrison for Oswego, at the same time as the Garrison of Carleton Island consists only of 60 men fit for duty, some of them old and infirm, I by no means can think the 74 Rangers to be sent from here reinforcement sufficient for the protection of so consequential a place during the Winter, when it will be very difficult to send them any assistance, but of this Your Excellency will be the best Judge.
>
> I cannot conclude without acquainting Your Excellency that Major Ross merits great credit for his Activity & indefatigable diligence in carrying on the Works here notwithstanding the last month has done some small damage to some Parts of the Works but nothing of any Consequence and what will very soon be put in its former state, they have not had a fair day for some weeks, in spite of which they will be in a state

beyond insult in a fortnight.[15]

Haldimand had another issue on his mind. He expressed to Secretary Townshend on October 23 his concern that the new administration would overlook the natives during negotiations with the United States:

> From an apprehension, Sir, that the Disposition of the Indians, and the indispensable necessity of preserving their affections may not be Sufficiently understood at Home, I think it my duty to assure you that an unremitting attention to a very nice management of that People is inseperable from the safety of this Province, which has been indisputably preserved hitherto in a great measure by their Attachment.

Two days later, Haldimand wrote Townshend about a second critical issue:

> In case a Peace or Truce should take place during the winter, tho' I apprehend it is unnecessary, yet my anxiety for the good of the Empire makes me observe to you that in making the one or the other, great care should be taken that Niagara & Oswego should be annexed to Canada, or comprehended in the general words, that each of the contending Parties in North America should retain what they possessed at the time. The Possession of these two Forts is essentially necessary to the security as well as the Trade of the Country.[16]

As it transpired, this second cautionary note fell on the same deaf ears as his first.

––––––––––––

Carleton wrote to Haldimand on October 26 with very belated intelligence about the two expeditions planned by the Pennsylvania

Assembly against Indian Territory. The principal thrust was to consist of four hundred Continentals, six hundred militia and volunteers. It was to assemble near the Susquehanna's West Branch on October 8 and march into Seneca Country. The second, consisting of one thousand militiamen and a handful of Continentals, was to assemble at Fort Pitt and march toward Lake Erie at the beginning of October. Further, the French, and the bulk of the Continental Army, were encamped at Verplanck's Point on the lower Hudson and the French fleet was at anchor at Boston. At least, the last warranted no reason for alarm.[17]

On October 27, Riedesel decided that the season was too advanced to continue with construction at Isle aux Noix and gave orders for the troops to march to winter quarters; however, three days later, the weather must have improved, as he decided to retain thirty-seven axe men and artificers from 1KRR's fifty-man Light Company. Captain Samuel Anderson protested and suggested a like number could be found from the Royal Yorkers' line troops working at Coteau-du-Lac; however, the Lights were kept back and were not released until November 11, albeit their replacements from the Brigadier's Company had not arrived.

The heavy work continued as October drew to a close and, although it was repeatedly interrupted by incessant rains, the efforts would not cease until stopped by frost. Over the winter, the garrison would prepare materials for the resumption of construction in the spring.[18]

In a letter to Riedesel dated October 27, the governor confessed his amazement at receiving word from Carleton that the upper posts were about to be attacked so late in the season. He was incredulous that he had been told to seek reinforcement from Halifax, "at a time when nature has closed the communication." As he dare not ignore the warning, he ordered the 34th Regiment to Niagara and von Barner's Light Infantry regiment to replace the 34th at Montreal. Poor Captain Ancrum — after finally escaping frontier duty at Carleton Island, he was on his way upriver yet again; however, it was concerns about declining Provincial

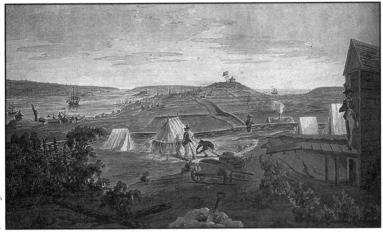

Edward Hicks, 1781.
(Library and Archives Canada, C-011213.)

North aspect of Halifax, Nova Scotia 1781. Britain's major naval base seen from a sentry post and outlying camp, showing the harbour and citadel hill rising in the background.

ardour and worries over the native allies that had prompted Haldimand to send the 34th Regiment as much as the C-in-C's warnings about rebel intentions against the upper posts.

Haldimand also sent instructions to Ross to:

> [Keep out] proper Scouts and Messengers for Intelligence, [whereby] you cannot fail to procure a knowledge of the Enemies Motions on the Susquehanna and if they do proceed on the Intended Route, it is highly probable a Diversion will be made in your Quarter to call the Indians that way, but as that cannot be effected without a Movement of Troops by the Mohawk River you will have early intimation of it by means of the correspondence you have Established at Albany and you will not fail to communicate immediately to Brigadier General Maclean as well as to me all Intelligence that you may think Interesting.

Ross was to send regular reports by express messengers every fifteen days. In a similar letter to Maclean, he instructed him to constantly keep out small parties of "intelligent, prudent men" over the winter, accompanied by a few well-chosen natives with "positive orders not to commit any acts of hostility by which they may be discovered[,] for the late instructions from home as well as the object of their pursuit would in that case be counteracted."[19]

———————

After receiving the governor's letter of October 27, Riedesel replied, "The confidence which you place in me binds me stronger to you every day. You may rest assured that whatever you intrust to me is most sacred; and your kindness may command me always." As to the rebels' movements against the upper posts and the expectation that Haldimand could draw support from Nova Scotia, the baron commented, "It is to be regretted that Sir Guy did not immediately send orders to Halifax to have troops forwarded to your excellency. Had he done so, they might have been here now, and you would have been able to increase the detachments considerably. But this is policy again, which does more harm than the enemy!"

Three days later, the baron reported that, notwithstanding the praiseworthy efforts of the troops, persistent rain and mud at Isle aux Noix had retarded the work and the casemented redoubts had fallen substantially behind schedule. All of the masons and carpenters would be kept on the island; the former to continue working until "the ice comes" and the latter to stay the winter to prepare timber for the spring. Excess provisions would be sent to St. John's and a captain, two subalterns, and fifty rankers were to be sent to relieve the light company at Pointe-au-Fer, and an officer with fifty Jägers would be posted at the Lacolle River Blockhouse to guard the woodcutters there. The regulars in the Yamaska blockhouses' garrisons were to be relieved by Loyal Rangers and the Frasers would maintain the scouting schedule of the previous winter. Major John Nairne had command at Pointe-au-Fer, Rivière Lacolle, and the Loyal Blockhouse and another Regular major at Chambly and Fort St. John's. He had left instructions with both officers and would leave for Sorel in four days.[20]

———————

M.O. Hammond, photograph, circa 1910–30. (Archives of Ontario, F 1075, I0016659.)

Erected in 1781 on the Lacolle River to guard a sawmill and lighthouse.

After a careful examination of his deputy agents' estimates for Indian presents, Sir John Johnson forwarded his final assessment to Governor Haldimand. Included was an inspection team's report, noting that the invoices for goods sent from Britain on the government's account displayed "an enormous overcharge upon almost the whole of the Cargo." Johnson recommended the appointment of a manager and clerk to guard against such abuses.[21]

Although von Kreutzbourg had altered his opinion about having his troops labour on fortifications, he still harboured an attitude about the duty as evidenced by his order to enforce discipline dated October 30:

> I solemnly assure you herewith that if I hear any complaints again from one or the other company concerning any intemperance, this company will have to send out a night picket of fifty men during the entire winter, and, as may be thought fit, it will be sent next spring as a fatigue party to work on entrenchments in the fortifications at either Quebec or Isle aux Noix.[22]

Ross reported to the governor from Oswego on November 1, announcing that Lord Stirling had retired from the north and that the Mohawk Valley inhabitants were very anxious about a possible attack. They believed that Sir John Johnson was collecting the natives for that purpose. Evidently, the ceasefire still meant very little in the Mohawk region.[23]

That same day, Baroness von Riedesel gave birth to another daughter. The Riedesels' two-year-old had been christened "Amerika," and the new baby was named "Canada." As a measure of the family's depth of friendship with the governor, Haldimand was asked to be her godfather, as he had been previously for Amerika. Against the baroness's better judgment, baby Canada was weaned too early and she soon sickened and died.[24]

Haldimand sent instructions to Riedesel on November 4 regarding the relief of the Light companies at Isle aux Noix and advised that he wanted to keep two 1KRR companies in a fit state for immediate service and that the baron must very soon release the Lights. In a second letter, the governor expressed his doubts about Captain Pritchard's intelligence concerning Vermont. He harboured suspicions that the Ranger captain was engaged in secret trading, which was a sore temptation, as there was a great demand for supplies and hard money could be made. He reminded the baron that he had always opposed such trade, as such commerce might prod Congress into action before Vermont was ready to oppose it, or the king's troops were prepared to support the republic. That oft-imprudent, daredevil Pritchard was to be stopped from going out again without the governor's express orders, and he was to be closely watched by a few well-chosen agents and apprehended if he attempted to flee.[25]

On November 4, John Ferguson, the serjeant-major of the 29th Regiment, was appointed to the Loyal Rangers as quartermaster.

Von Loos again vented his anger and frustration over Haldimand's practice of setting the locations for winter quarters so late in the season:

> To my sorrow, all my most valuable effects were covered
> with sand and mud during the last storm…. The ship
> stranded; and I have now no dry bed, clothing or
> shirts. All my winter supplies are destroyed, and I have,

therefore, nothing to eat. My sugar, tea and coffee are also entirely destroyed.

This is all on account of the premier, who, without raison de guere, sends the troops into winter quarters. Not a single year had passed that the soldiers have not lost their baggage…. Who pays the poor subaltern for his losses?[26]

On the fifth, Haldimand sent Riedesel a letter and recent newspapers from New York City, which, strangely, mentioned nothing about a peace settlement. He theorized that, if New York and Charlestown were abandoned, Quebec and the upper country would be the focus of the Allies' attention and, in such an event, he hoped that plenty of good troops would be sent. He had learned that the recruits who had arrived at Halifax were very poor and said he would rather have none at all instead of useless people. Despairingly, he ended with the expectation that no good troops would be sent unless Carleton himself came to Canada.[27]

After six days of extremely stormy weather on Lake Ontario, Maclean arrived at Fort Niagara on November 5. This was the same day that the governor wrote to him about the decision to award Captain John McDonell (Aberchalder) seniority over Captain Peter Ten Broeck, which meant that one of the brigadier's first business dealings with Butler's Rangers would be to deliver this potentially contentious news.[28]

On November 7, Brigadier St. Leger informed headquarters that two divisions of the 34th Regiment had just passed Lachine on their way up the St. Lawrence to Niagara. He noted:

The severity of the weather and the lateness of the season, as well as the shortness of the notice not admitting of the full complement of winter cloathing being made up had induced me to take the liberty to put a constructive sense

John Singleton Copley.

Captain David Forbes, 34th Regiment. Forbes entered the 34th as an ensign in 1764 and was promoted to lieutenant in 1770 and captain-lieutenant in 1777. He served as adjutant from 1775 to 1780, when he was promoted to captain and took command of a company.

upon the general order against allowing rum, I trust his Excellency, in his usual tenderness and humanity for the troops will deem this breach of it, as an affair of necessity and not likely to be quoted as a precedent; this indulgence is to cease at Carleton Island.

If his Excellency should not be pleased to see this measure in the same view that I have done, the Regiment will most willingly indemnify Government for the Expense.

Riedesel reported that the garrisons of the Yamaska blockhouses had been relieved to the satisfaction of Fraser. In a second private letter, the baron confessed his puzzlement over rumours about French troops in the neighbourhood of Lake Champlain. A few days later, there were further tales of six hundred French troops being at Castleton and that their engineers were waiting for the British fleet to withdraw from the lake so they could survey Ticonderoga and Crown Point with a view to establish a post at the more eligible of the two.[29]

The movement of the regiments into winter quarters located Prinz Ludwig's Dragoons at St. Antoine on the Richelieu River, six leagues below Sorel. Wasmus's Canadien landlord provided him with a bed, table, chairs, firewood, and kitchen utensils, and he was pleased to note that "we are receiving royal provisions as good as any soldier has ever received on earth," which doubtless made the prospect of another Canadian winter a little less daunting.[30]

_____

On November 10, Ross confirmed the need for concern about morale in the loyalist regiments in a letter to Maclean:

> I have according to my Ideas formed an opinion that the Rebels will attack this Post in March and shall prepare accordingly. We must rely on the Indians then. The Indians here are on the point of leaving us — In two days I do not think there will be an Indian on the ground — It may be of bad consequence for I assure you, Sir, the Colony [Provincial] Troops have not the relish for the War, they had when carried on offensively. They do not think the King will succeed, and from every quarter they have unpleasing tidings, their little propertys on the Mohawk River are taken possession of every day by the New Englanders; they conclude the best chance they have now is to make peace with the Rebels. Deserters they Know are received and live quiet at Home. I'll venture to say that there are many men who would have suffered Death rather than Desert some time ago, that nothing now but the fear of Death prevents them — in Short their spirits are low, and I humbly beg leave to observe that the Troops raised from the Colonies are by no means so proper for this Garrison in the present situation of affairs as British Soldiers — I have made some slight observations to the Commander in Chief on this Subject — perhaps, Sir, you may think it proper to write him more fully. I cannot now give them the same hopes of the success of Our Arms in America as formerly in that I am puzzled how to Rouse them — if New York [City] is abandoned it will be worse.[31]

The rebel command along the Mohawk River was also starved for accurate intelligence. At the end of October, Lieutenant Ryal Bingham of the State Troops, with three non-commissioned officers and a native (likely one of his company's Stockbridges), was sent on a month-long scout of the country up to Lake Ontario.[32]

On November 4, the NH brigade was relieved when part of Olney's RIR arrived at Albany. The remainder was expected later in the week. Three days later, there was a little excitement amongst the officers of the State Troops at Fort Rensselaer when Lieutenant Pliny Moore was appointed adjutant in the room of Lieutenant Jelles A. Fonda, who had replaced Abner French as a company commander. At the same time, Captain Guy Young was permitted to return home after transferring his command to Joel Gillett. On November 8, permission was granted to four prominent rebels to harvest trees for fuel, fencing, and timber from properties nearby Fort Plain, some of which were owned by known Tories.[33]

The State Troops had been ordered into winter quarters at Forts Plain and Rensselaer and were to be rotated between the two posts "for their health" and to relieve chronic boredom. Part of their time was spent improving the works, no doubt using lumber from the logging operations. Nevertheless, the men still found time to get into mischief. A court martial of November 15 saw three men tried for stealing potatoes from an inhabitant. Two were acquitted and the third was awarded sixty lashes "on his bare back by the drummer of the Regt," which was put into execution that evening at roll call. Despite the woodcutting, fuel was still in short supply and, on November 19, Garrison Orders stated that all NCOs and soldiers were "strictly forbidden to burn or destroy any of the inhabitants fences, or molest or deprive them of any of their property whatever, under penalty of 39 lashes." On their part, the inhabitants were strictly forbidden to purchase any article of clothing from soldiers on the pain of having the articles taken from them and the offending soldiers were threatened with courts martial.[34]

On November 13, Major Gray confirmed Ross's observations regarding declining loyalist morale when he wrote, "in the present apearance of the American War the Royalists may bid adieu to their property in the Colonies, Independence puts a bar against our ever living in that Country, even, should they upon any treaty, give up our Estates, We must live like Dogs amongst them." Bitterness and despair was not very far under the skin of the old loyalist.[35]

The next day, Haldimand informed Maclean that the remainder of the 84th Regiment had been ordered to Oswego. Although the Highland Emigrants had many American loyalists in its ranks, there were far more old countrymen, Quebeckers, and Newfoundlanders who would be unaffected by the terms of the peace. Consequently, the regiment was more reliable than provincial units whose ranks contained almost 100 percent Americans by residence or birth.

The governor instructed that the Butler's Rangers at Oswego should not be sent to Carleton Island. He noted that the officer commanding there, Captain James McDonell, 2KRR, whom Ross had characterized as "an active officer," had replaced Ancrum and his 34th company. McDonell had been ordered to "contrive some means of putting the provisions under cover by making sheds or employing vacant barracks and putting it on board vessels that winter there."[36]

In a dispatch of November 14 to Secretary Townshend, Haldimand reported "that an Express arrived last Night from Niagara with an account of the Enemy having, to all appearance, abandoned their Intentions, at least for this season, of Invading the Indian Country."[37]

A return of November 18, signed by the Deputy Quartermaster General, Captain Jacob Maurer, 2KRR, reported on the number of bateaux sent to Carleton Island from Lachine. In October, 1,245 had been dispatched — 229 carried troops and 1,016 bore provisions. Between November 3 and 18, fifty craft had carried troops and four carried provisions. Every brigade conductor was Canadien, indicating that elements of the population were contributing to the war effort, albeit for pay and with some reluctance.[38]

On November 21, DePeyster reported to Maclean from Detroit that the Virginians were determined to destroy the western natives. Captain Caldwell's detachment of Butler's Rangers could scarcely turn out thirty-six men fit for duty and the men of the 8th (King's) Regiment (whom he affectionately referred to as "the most excellent soldiers") were not properly equipped for a winter campaign. He would need five additional companies to repair the works and conduct the duties of the post. "Light troops are, therefore, what we want, and believe me there will be amusement for a good number of them in the ensuing campaign without acting on the offensive."

Maclean must have previously asked DePeyster for guidance about the method of sending expresses, as the major recommended that two Indians be sent with each dispatch, and often with an interpreter. The natives should be promised a gift of trade silver at the post they are sent to, providing they make a prompt delivery. When they return to their home

Montage by Christopher Armstrong, 2009.

post, they were to receive further payment, which they most frequently take in rum.[39]

On November 25, Ross informed Haldimand that most of the rebel troops had been withdrawn from the Mohawk Valley. Presumably, he meant the New Hampshire brigade. In consequence, he was more confident that an attack from that quarter was unlikely before spring. (He was clearly unaware of Olney's Rhode Islanders.)

Typical trade silver items.

Fort Ontario was in good condition and he would strengthen the outworks over the winter. There was plenty of barracks room, but he lacked bedding and the stores at Carleton Island were worn out. Although many men were sick with a lung inflammation, his garrison was 545 strong, of which his own battalion supplied 238, as well as another sixty-six at Fort Haldimand.[40]

Suspicions about Captain Pritchard's illicit activities were proven valid when a Loyal Ranger corporal from Sherwood's garrison arrived in a British vessel off the Loyal Blockhouse with two Vermonters and three tons of fresh beef. Sherwood placed all three under arrest. An investigation exonerated the corporal when it was found that he had been acting under Pritchard's orders. The captain was dismissed from the Secret Service and sent to Quebec City, as the governor thought it dangerous to leave "a man of his stamp" at St. John's; however, in recognition of his daring exploits, no further action was taken. Part of the meat belonged to the corporal's father and was purchased by the commissary, but the balance was ordered destroyed in front of the garrison as an object lesson.[41]

The tale of the Cöos double agent, Thomas Johnson, continued to unwind. As seen earlier, Bayley had reported that Johnson was no longer able to provide useful intelligence and, in early October, a loyalist sympathizer warned Sherwood that Johnson "would sell either party for money." The knife-edge that Johnson had been balancing on was proving too sharp and he wanted to be seen to stand clearly in the rebels' favour, especially with victory in sight. On November 25, the respected New Hampshire politician, Meshech Weare, wrote a letter of introduction to Washington:

> The Bearer Col. Thomas Johnson of whose Conduct with Respect to procuring Intelligence from the Enemy your Excellency has been informed, now waits on you

to comunicate some things which Appear to be of importance. From every information I have been Able to Obtain, I have no Reason to Suspect his honesty or fidelity. His Situation at this time is very Difficult As he will fully inform you, and Requests Your Assistance is such way do you may think proper. I cannot help Expressing my fears of what may be the Consequence of the Negoisations carrying on between Vermont and Canada, of which there seems now to be Scarce a Doubt.[42]

Early the next month, Johnson enjoyed "a very satisfactory interview" with Washington at his Newburgh headquarters. The C-in-C assured him of his sympathy and the value of his services, but cautioned that he was unable to offer any direct intervention to resolve his conflict.[43]

———————

In the final days of November, Willett's troops at Fort Rensselaer mutinied. The post's commandant, Major Andrew Finck, posted orders on the 26th:

It is the greatest concern that the Commandant observes the mistaken notions which it seems some mutinous villains have suggested which has been rec'd & practiced by a considerable part of the garrison, this morning[. H]e is surprised, that admitting the grounds of their complaints to be well founded, (as in some particulars they may be) that they should be so infatuated as to suppose they could march to Albany in a body as they proposed, without meeting the opposition of the Civil & Military Strength of this and the neighbouring Counties who are bound, on all occasions to Surpress mutiny to the utmost of their Power and that [should] they accomplish Their design & reach Albany[,] Maj Genl Lord Sterling would countenance a procedure of so heinous a nature. The consequences of which is death to as many as are found Guilty. He considers it as a personal ill Treatment, the officers commanding that they should at this time when the Colol[,] the only person in whose power it is to redress some of their Complaints[,] is absent — They must be sensible that their whisky had been retain'd by a Regt Order of Colol Willett ___ that unless the said order is Countermanded by him, no other officers can Legally order it ___ without making himself Liable to pay for it, and as it was Retain'd for Certain purposes therein mentioned ___ As far as it concerns the Two and Three years men, to purchase Armaments, pay Taylors, Shoemakers and other purposes for the uniformity of those Troops, for those uses they must be Sensible, that a considerable part of their retained whisky has been apply'd — Witness the nine months mens shoes which the whole of their retain'd whisky will not pay for — Their complaints respecting the Cloathing he is sorry to find it so reasonable but not with standing the reasonableness it will by no means Justify a Conduct like the present. He is very sensible of their Sufferings and is willing to show them every indulgence in his power and assure them that it is his sincere belief that they will soon receive their full Cloathing and further that he will use his influence that they shall receive their allowance of whisky. He therefore requests them to wait patiently till Colonel Willett's return which will be in a Short time when he has no doubt that their grievances will be fully Redressed & he expects the Cloathing with the Colonel — But reminds them at the same Time that if the offence is Repeated [or] the Least remains of mutiny discovered itself amongst any[,] that the utmost rigors of the Law shall be Inflicted.

In regimental orders the next day, two men of Pierce's company were acquitted of the charge of abusing a civil magistrate in the execution of his office. A more serious court martial was held on November 28, when six men were charged with absenting themselves from the guard with their arms during the mutiny. All were found guilty and awarded one hundred lashes "on their Naked Backs," but the punishment was suspended until further orders for reasons unknown. Eight days later, yet another court martial was held to try a husband and his wife for inciting mutiny. Found guilty, the soldier received fifty lashes that evening and was drummed out of the regiment (presumably with his wife) with orders not to return. Yet another court martial awarded two men of Newell's company one hundred lashes each for being absent without leave and stealing their arms. Persistently, the war ground on.[44]

On December 7, Adjutant Pliny Moore received returns from Gillett's and Harrison's companies stationed in the Schoharie. Harrison lamented the grim situation in the valley and advised, "I have had no Desarters Sence Last return[.] I have had four Disearted[,] three Two years and one Nine Mos man." The next day, returns arrived for Captains Livingston and French at Ballstown.[45]

―――――――――――
―――――――――――

Sir John informed Haldimand that Dr. Dease had reported sending out runners to warn the Niagara villages and outposts of a possible invasion of 1,500 rebels from the Wyoming Valley and that he and the post surgeon had gone to the natives' Buffalo Creek settlement to tend the sick and make a request for the return of all white prisoners. Four of the six nations had complied, although Joseph Brant was against the measure. Further, Brant had asked for two hundred pairs of snowshoes and twenty to thirty birch canoes. A few days later, Johnson explained that the snowshoes and canoes were wanted for a strike against the rebel Oneidas at Canajoharie in the spring. Haldimand approved of the venture, with the proviso that no white inhabitants be harmed, but warned that no snowshoes or canoes were available.

The governor's consent reflected his understanding that the native agenda was firmly at odds with the present administration and displayed his sympathy for their distress over the ceasefire. As well, such a raid would also answer his own long-held desire to punish the intractable Oneidas.[46]

On November 27, a return was made from Fort Ontario, entitled "Effective Strength of the Garrison of Oswego as fixed for the Winter."

Royal Artillery	One serjeant, one bombardier, nine Mattrosses.
29th Regiment	One lieutenant.
34th Regiment	One lieutenant, three serjeants, four corporals, and forty-nine privates.
84th Regiment	Three captains, three lieutenants, one ensign, one surgeon, seven serjeants, nine corporals, seven drummers, and 136 privates.
1KRR	One private.
2KRR	One major, two captains, four lieutenants, one ensign, one adjutant, one surgeon, twenty-one serjeants, twenty-four corporals, and 164 privates.
Butler's Rangers	Two lieutenants, three serjeants, three corporals, four drummers, and sixty-three privates.[47]

Haldimand must have again persuaded Riedesel to analyze the ages of his Brunswick troops as a measure of their suitability for active campaigning. The baron reported that, of 2,029 rankers in his regiments, 1,380 were young men "fit for all Sorts of Duty." As this statistic compared favourably to the Royal Yorkers' first battalion, it is difficult to see what conclusions were drawn. Yet, the fact remained that, in opposition to the Yorkers, Brunswick troops had not been sent on a major frontier operation since 1777. Clearly, there was far more to this mystery than simply age.[48]

Prime Minister Lord Shelburne had proven incapable of managing his cabinet or of explaining himself to his ministry. His administration had fumbled through the peace negotiations while juggling a world war that ranged across the Atlantic from Britain's shores to the Mediterranean, the

Caribbean, South America, and even to India. With fighting at Minorca, Gibraltar, and the West Indies, the squabble with the American colonies had shrunk in importance. In any event, Shelburne had grand visions of founding a new Atlantic trading community and expected that the United States would want concessions to bring this concept to fruition that would be at the expense of Canada's fur trade south of the Great Lakes and the natives upon whom it relied. The plight of the American loyalists was not even on his agenda.

The preliminary articles to ease the United States out of the war were signed on November 30. Every concern that Haldimand had expressed for Canada's security and trade and the plight of his native allies was ignored. Every painstaking, meticulously crafted method for the country's defence and its very existence as a British colony were put at risk.[49]

Sherwood advised Riedesel on November 29 that the rumours of French troops in Vermont and their engineers at Ticonderoga were false; however, a regiment of Rhode Island troops had relieved Saratoga, one half of them black.[50]

The strange story of a deserter named Piper emerged at month's end. He was a German recruited for service in the 29th Regiment who, upon arrival in Canada in 1776, had deserted, as he thought the terms of his recruitment had been defaulted. He took shelter with the Fort Hunter Mohawks at Lachine and, over time, was adopted and married into their society. He went to war with them and, in their opinion, served well and bravely. Accordingly, the Mohawks made representations to Colonel Claus to have the fellow returned to their village. With Claus's background experience in both modes of living, he astutely commented to the governor, "Whether from the wandering life and uncontrold life he has been usd [to] for some years, he will be brought to submit to the restraints of military discipline I think is a matter to be much doubted, whereas as a Ranger among the Indians he has avowedly provd himself an useful fellow upon many occasions."

On December 2, St. Leger cryptically informed Lernoult that Piper had been sent down to Quebec City for trial and that Colonel Claus had "managed the business with the Mohawks with little trouble." The deserter's final disposition has not been determined.[51]

———————————

On December 9, New York's Congressional representatives informed Governor Clinton of "sundry resolutions" to allow him, "To judge the present temper of that body respecting the affairs of the grants."

> We cannot, however, absolutely rely upon the execution of the coercive part of them if the matter should require an exertion of force. Many[,] who at a distance adopt very decisive ideas, might shrink from a measure replete with consequences at least delicate, if not dangerous.... It is to be recollected in particular that a considerable part of the army is interested in grants of land to a large extent under the usurped government of Vermont. Much will depend upon their disposition in the progress of the business, and it is, therefore, of primary importance that they should be secured at all events. We apprehend there should be a confirmation of their titles unfettered by any condition whatsoever.[52]

———————————

Although the Richelieu had not yet frozen over, Wasmus noted that there was already two feet of snow accumulated at St. Antoine by the first of December. Three days later, Riedesel wrote a private letter to the governor, expressing astonishment that General Carleton had sent him no news in his recent correspondence other than some friendly answers to inquiries about his family. Quebec was gasping for intelligence of the broader conflict, but dispatch after dispatch from New York revealed nothing of significance. On a personal note, the baron mentioned a painful operation that his wife had just undergone. Typically, that courageous lady made no mention of it in her personal journals.[53]

———————

On December 9, Justus Sherwood wrote a plaintive letter to Captain Mathews regarding problems with his agents:

> Too much has been said in public of the Vermont affairs, and it gives me the greatest concern to find that Mr Stevens and Mr Pritchard in particular and I fear too many others have[,] notwithstanding every precaution[,] pretended in the Country to a perfect knowledge of his Excellency's most secret thoughts[. B]y this kind of finesse they have drawn too many secrets from some of Gen A[llen']s second hand confidants, who with the same views of making themselves appear consequential, have told those gentlemen all they really knew or could conjecture.... [Stevens is] a brave soldier, zealous for his Majesty's service, and from his former services, deserving of his Excellency's notice, but ...[54]

In a private letter, the governor informed Riedesel that the Royal Artillery commander, Colonel Forbes Macbean, had been ordered to Sorel, as he had committed a professional indiscretion at headquarters. He warned Riedesel of Macbean's personality quirks and advised the baron to restrain the man from making unjust claims to authority. Riedesel knew Forbes and considered him the most conspiring and dangerous man in Canada and wished he had been sent elsewhere, as he truly feared the fellow. He noted that Sorel had hitherto been the happiest post in Canada, but now he fully expected Macbean to try to turn him against the governor and, when that failed, to carp over trifles and complain both publicly and in his correspondence. The governor replied, offering assurances that there was no reason to fear Macbean's machinations, either in Quebec or with the king.[55]

Early in December, word was received at Niagara that a force under the rebel general, George Rogers Clark, had destroyed the Shawnee town of Chillicothe in Ohio territory. The Iroquois were extremely anxious and sent a delegation to Detroit to "spirit up" the Lakes' and Ohio nations. The delegates carried "strings of wampum ... to deliver to the Shawnee to encourage them not to be cast down on this melancholy occasion or to lose courage, but to take example from them who had lost all their villages, which misfortune had made them more daring and desperate, and set their resolve to act like men to be revenged on so cruel and wicked a people."

A formal council was held at Niagara on December 11 with many prominent persons in attendance: Onondaga sachem/war captain Teaqwanda; Mohawk war captains Aaron Hill Kanonraron and Joseph Brant Thayendanegea, and Oneida "chief" Oscononda. The Europeans attending were the Indian Department's deputy agents, Lieutenant-Colonel John Butler and Dr. John Dease with their captains, Gilbert Tice and John Powell, and lieutenants William Ryer Bowen, John Docksteder, and Frederick Young. The military was represented by Brigadier Allan Maclean, Lieutenant-Colonel Alexander Dundas, and an artillery officer and three officers of the 34th Regiment.

The Iroquois were renowned orators, as Teaqwanda demonstrated when he opened the council:

> Our Brothers, the Shawnee, informing us of their late misfortune, their lower town having been cut off by the perfidious cruel rebels at a time when they and we were forbidden to go to War and directed to cease hostilities by the Great General of our Brother, the King of England. Upon our agreeing to obey the orders of the General, the perfidious rebels have taken advantage of our inactivity and have come like thieves in the night when the Shawnee warriors were out at their hunting grounds, surrounded one of their towns and murdered all the women and children.

We therefore think it proper to acquaint you that you may let the Great General know that we shall no longer remain idle and see our Brethren and people destroyed by these cruel rebels, since the fate they have met with may be ours next if we do not go to War and prevent it. Therefore we desire that you will request the Great General in our name to assist us heartily in sharpening our axe.

We have already mentioned unto you the cruelties committed by the rebels, whose unparalleled cruelty lately destroyed the poor Moravian Indians, their near neighbours, who never went to war against them or any other people. Under the cloak of friendship[,] they murdered them in cold blood and reduced their bones to ashes that the murder might not be discovered.

In the year 1779, when the rebels attacked the villages of the Six Nations, their cruelty was equally great, for at the Onondaga Town, they put to death all the women and children except some of the young women whom they carried away for the use of their soldiers and were afterwards put to death in a most shameful manner. Yet these rebels call themselves Christians. We have been so often deceived by the rebels that we can no longer trust to their words, and we find by sad experience that the enemy profit by our laying still and following the advice of the General.

We are, therefore, resolved that in the future we will act upon our own principles and show them no lenity or mercy; and we hope for assistance from the Great General and that he will not find fault with us for following the example of the rebels. Though we have hitherto in general refrained from retaliating [against] their cruelties, except in the instance of Colonel Crawford, the principal agent in the murder of the Moravians. He was burned with Justice and according to our custom. Yet make no doubt that the rebels will imagine that our not going to war proceeds from fear.

> We therefore propose to send a Flag to them to
> acquaint them that we in future follow the example set
> by themselves, seeing it is in their intention to destroy
> the Indians and possess themselves of their country.

A more eloquent description of the natives' war could not have been
delivered. As was traditional, the council adjourned until the next day
when Maclean gave his response. His speech showed that he had absorbed
a great deal of native diplomacy, no doubt through John Butler's coaching.
Typical of such messages, it held a blend of genuine sympathy, good
intentions, promises and half-truths, strongly leavened with self-interest.

> Brothers, you acquainted me yesterday with your great
> uneasiness on account of the misfortune of your younger
> Brothers, the Shawnee ...
>
> Your being desired to cease from going to war by
> your Brother, the General, was for very good reasons
> which tended to your advantage. But he repeatedly
> requested that you should send out frequent scouts
> to be upon your guard and not allow yourselves to be
> surprised, and had the Shawnee followed that good
> advice, the enemy would not have surprised them.
>
> The reason His Excellency had for wishing you not
> to go to war was fully explained to you at his desire by
> Lieutenant Colonel Butler. I shall again repeat them.
> Last fall there were certain accounts that great numbers
> of the rebel inhabitants were dissatisfied with Congress
> for refusing such generous offers as were made them by
> your Father, the King, and many of them refused to pay
> their taxes on that account. And His Excellency, knowing
> that would be the first people you might hurt in going to
> war, he therefore desired you to cease hostilities and keep
> out scouts to watch the motions of the enemy which he
> has repeatedly recommended to you (well knowing the
> treachery of your enemies) in order that they might be

discovered before they get into your country....

Brothers, had the Shawnee kept out scouts as they were advised to do, they could not have been surprised and I recommend it to your particular care that you will keep out scouts to watch the motions of the enemy. There will be no danger of your being in the same situation with your younger Brothers, the Shawnee, and should the rebels attempt to come into your country, in that case I have orders to sharpen your axe and not permit it to become dull.

Brothers, I shall endeavour to supply you with your wants as much as possible and it is my orders to do so. I can assure you that it is not the General's fault or any neglect of mine that you have not been supplied as usual. The presents intended for you arriving so late from England, made it impossible for His Excellency to order them up sooner, and that nothing but the contrary winds has prevented the two vessels which I had ordered to return from Carleton Island with the remainder of the presents destined for you could prevent me from being able to supply all your wants.

With respect to your situation being worse than ours, in some respects it is very true, but in general it is not so. There are now men on this ground whose situation is exactly similar to yours with respect to the rebels, and in some degree worse. Many of their friends have been put to death and they have been obliged to take banishment for sake of their country and leave all their property behind them.

Brothers, your situation now is as good as it has been for some time past. You are still strong and I have orders to tell you that you shall be well supported, provided you don't allow yourselves to be surprised. The enemy cannot come into any of your villages easily without being discovered. They live at a great distance from you and if you act agreeably to the character you have hitherto supported[,] it is not in their power to proceed two day's march with a body of troops without your discovering them. In that case, I doubt not, but with our mutual strength we shall be able to make them pay dear for the attempt.

Brothers, I must request and entreat that you will not follow the examples of barbarity and cruelty committed by your enemies on your women and children as I am sure it would be very displeasing to your great Father, the King, and to your Brother, the General. And I believe that your great success against the enemy must convince you that the humanity shown by most of your warriors to their women and children, hundreds of whom you have brought in prisoners, is much more pleasing to the Great Spirit above than the cruelty committed by your enemies, who improperly call themselves Christians. And it has constantly been recommended to you by your great Father, the King, not to bring a blush in his face by acting contrary to his method of fighting by killing women and children. I therefore hope you will still continue to act with the same humanity.

I shall certainly let the Commander-in-Chief know your desire of having a number of red coats to join you early in the spring in order to carry the war into the enemy's country and prevent them from coming into yours. And I doubt not that I shall have his answer before the spring of the year will admit of any movement of that kind to take place and I shall acquaint you with his sentiments.

Brant was thoroughly dissatisfied with the council's outcome. In particular, he was upset that the confederacy had deferred its decision to attack the rebels to hear the governor's views. Maclean heard that Joseph had expressed the hope that Haldimand would have the humanity not to tie their hands, and declared that the natives' situation was altogether different from that of the loyalists.

Two weeks after the council, Brant wrote to his boyhood friend, Sir John Johnson, who, significantly, had been sidestepped by the League's message to Haldimand.

> I have been very uneasy since we had the News of the Shawanese misfortune who fell in the hands of the white Savage Virginians and did alarmd the five Nations greatly and made them to hold Councils about the matter & made Speeches to the General but badly translated into English. Wee the Indians wishes to have the blow Return'd on the Enemy as early as possible, but I am afraid it will again [be considered] but [a] trifling affair when our Speech gets below which is too often the case, which will be [a] very vexatious affair, because we think the Rebels will ruin us at last if we go on as we do one year after another doing nothing only Destroying [he means, consuming] Government goods & they [the government] Crying all the while for the great Expences[,] so we are in[,] as it were[,] between two Hells. I am sure you will assist all you can to Let us have an Expedition Early in the spring[.] Let it be [a] great or small one, let us not hang our heads between our Knees and be looking there — I beg of you dont tell us to go Hunt Deer & find you selves Shoes because we shall soon forget the War that Ways[,] for we are gone too far that way already against the Rebels to be doing other things.[56]

On December 15, Regimental Orders at Fort Rensselaer noted that "the Situation of the Regim't renders it necessary to introduce the Small pox at this post, the Doctor will Inoculate such of the Inhabitants and others who dwell within the Vicinity of the Garrison as choose to have that Operation performed upon them." Any soldier who had not had smallpox was to be inoculated the following Tuesday, including men of Cannon's company at Johnstown, who were to be marched to Rensselaer.

The post-mutiny angst continued. Several men had deserted and their locations were known. If they were allowed to get away with being absent, the morale of the rest would be badly affected, so, on Christmas Eve, Captain Job Wright sent a corporal's squad to collect them. Twenty-six of his company were to march to Fort Herkimer, leaving behind nineteen with smallpox. The captain closed his note to Pliny Moore with, "I wish you a mery Crismus and a hapy New Year."

In the face of these tidings of good cheer, Willett's serjeant-major, John Myers, was found guilty of insolence and disobedience two days after Christmas and was awarded eighty lashes and reduced to a private sentinel, although the whipping was forgiven because of his previous good behaviour. Two days later, another serjeant was found guilty of disobedience while on duty as a guard commander and was reduced to the ranks.[57]

In a friendly note of December 11, Haldimand regretted being unable to hear of Baroness Riedesel's progress, as the river was blocked with ice. He hoped that the baron's headaches had subsided. As for himself, he was buried under a mass of paperwork, which he resolved to put in order by springtime. The next day, Riedesel acknowledged receiving the report from New York that the thrusts against the upper posts had been abandoned and that the French fleet was proceeding to the West Indies. He was quite unable to fathom the enemy's designs. On immediate military business, he reported more desertions from Yamaska and that he had instructed that every man from Fort St. John's downward be issued a pair of snowshoes, as they might be called out at any moment.[58]

In Montreal, the John Prenties's affair reached its climax. Major Gray sent a sheaf of documentation to headquarters, including a pleading letter from the culprit addressed to his fellow officers:

I have committed great errors and indiscretions, and am free to confess that [the] great part of my conduct warrants but too justly your selection from my society, and disinclinations to share the duties of our profession with me…. Convinc'd and repenting of my imprudencies, [I] ask pardon, of the whole Regiment for the discredit and trouble, I may have brought on them by my irregular sallies, dictated merely by the folly of youth and inexperience of the world, and not, I trust I may be believed, proceeding from a bad Heart.

This remorseful confession had elicited a memorial from his fellow officers that Gray also forwarded. "At the same time in consideration of his long confinement[,] his youth, his contrition, his earnest desire to make every reparation and his promise to behave better in future, we request you please to signify to His Excellency that we would wish to shew him lenity and not bring him to trial." These appeals were sufficient and Prenties was returned to duty, which he must have performed to everyone's satisfaction, as he held a first lieutenancy when the battalion was reduced in December 1783.[59]

Although many were in despair over the endless grind of the war, some men kept light hearts by submerging themselves in mind-numbing revelry. James Hunter, who had left the Royal Yorkers to take a lieutenant's commission in the Artillery, replied to a letter from his friend Malcolm McMartin, the senior lieutenant of his old battalion. McMartin had written that the winter quarters at Ile Jesu were much more agreeable than the town of St. John's. Hunter agreed:

In My Opinion, St. Johns was Made at half Past Eleven o'clock of a Saturday night & Likewise hard Frost, when the Almighty was Either Afraid of breaking Sunday Or Getting his fingers frost bitt. As for Doctor Pillbox[,] he Has Got a house In the Fort And Notwithstanding the Intense Coldness of the Weather, I Once Every Day Make it as hot as hell. I make it my Particular Study to Salt that Dear Countryman of Yours, & [take] him By the Ears, to the Infinite Diversion of the Mess ...

By God, McMartin, I have Not Been Eight Nights Sober Since You Left St. John's. On Saturday Last the Officers of the Navy In Company with Several other Gentlmn to the Amount of Twenty Dined at one Robbinson's[.] In the Toasting[,] I Hunter[,] had the honour of Being President. As for Doctor Pierce[,] About Six Oclock he Got out of a Back Window & ran all the Way up to the Garrison, & for Old Thompson he Could Not Keep his Course but Ran into the Rappids, & for Chisholm I Got him Into One Corner of the Room with two Sticks & Made him Play the fiddle for the rest to Dance to, And Certainly, it was an agreeable Sight to any Person to have seen us About twelve o'clock at Night.[60]

Haldimand reacted immediately to the new desertions from Yamaska by advising Riedesel to adopt the method employed by Ross at Oswego and Butler at Niagara — which was to send Indians to run down and scalp the culprits. For the purpose, five or six natives might be stationed near the blockhouse under Fraser's orders. Although he had not put this idea in public orders, he assured the baron that he would justify any consequences that might attend its execution. Once again, the war appeared far from over.[61]

On December 23, Wasmus recorded the death of four Prinz Ludwig dragoons whose sleigh had broken through the Richelieu River ice. This was just one of several fatal winter accidents that befell the Brunswick troops during their time in Canada.[62]

The year ended on a sour note for the King's and Loyal Rangers. Haldimand had habitually cautioned his loyalist regimental commanders about recruiting rebel deserters and prisoners, as so many of these types enlisted simply to collect intelligence for the enemy, which the recent desertions confirmed. Riedesel was instructed to warn Jessup and Rogers that they would be held responsible for the conduct of their corps and were to send any men about whom there was the slightest doubt to Quebec City, where a close eye could be kept on them. Although there was undeniably much truth in the governor's observation, his chiding instructions must have been very difficult for Jessup and Rogers to swallow after working so hard to build up their battalions.[63]

On New Year's Eve, two New Hampshire men returning from a secret meeting with Governor Haldimand visited Captain Sherwood at the Loyal Blockhouse. In friendly conversation, they revealed that Vermont brigadier Roger Enos, Ira Allen's father-in-law, was willing to raise a regiment for the British if he was granted the rank of full colonel and if his regiment was placed on the British regular establishment. (Imagine Sir John's reaction if this had been allowed!) Enos's posturing was so very typical of the fantasies woven into the Vermont negotiations.[64]

Balthasar Friedrich Leizelt, circa 1775.
(Library of Congress, LC-USZ62-45387.)

The busy harbour of Quebec City.

9

*D*espite Colonel Marinus Willett's erratic performance in the summer, his reputation as a decisive, successful officer remained intact in late 1782 and led to his final adventure of the war.

After setting the winter quarters for his troops, Willett travelled to Fishkill in late November to bring his wife, Mary, back to his Albany lodgings for the winter. As Fishkill was across the Hudson from General Washington's headquarters at Newburgh, he crossed the river to pay his respects and was invited to dinner. After the meal, the C-in-C took him into his office to discuss a secret plan to destroy Fort Ontario at Oswego.

Some say that Willett did not immediately rise to the challenge, as he was looking forward to a quiet winter with his lady, but, because of his

James Peale after Charles Wilson Peale, circa 1788. (Independence National Historical Park Collection, Philadelphia.)

General George Washington, commander-in-chief of the United States Continental Army.

intense loyalty to Washington, he embraced the task. If that remark were true, such hesitancy would have been entirely out of character for a man, who in the past had seized every opportunity for fame. In any event, when Marinus returned north, it appears that Mary had been left behind.[1]

On November 29, he wrote to Washington about the project from Albany:

> I have thought much about your Excellencies plan since I left you and the more I think of it the more I like it. Perhaps no design was bid fairer to succeed. Indeed from every circumstance it appears to me that without some very crass Intervention it must terminate successfully — For my own part I can only assure your Excellency that I shall be supremely happy in the execution of a Scheme with such promising advantage, and that nothing which can be done by me shall be wanting to give it a happy accomplishment. The prosspect is truly pleasing and I find myself possessed of as much anxiety as is necessary to see it brought to a desirable finish.
>
> Your Excellencies observation of secrecy being an essential Ingredient in the performance of this business makes the first and most Important article, and your remark of the danger of having even a third person let into the knowledge of it shews how much value ought to be set on this arcanum [secret] of the business. This being the case all the measures proper to be taken shuld be formed in such a way as will best lend to keep the design concealed, and this is the work that commands a considerable proportion of my thoughts. In making the necessary preparations so as to prevent Suspicion of the design particular attention is necessary and in order to direct the preparation, the necessary materials must be inquired after, and here I beg leave to mention to your excellency such as appear to me, I should suppose five hundred men proper to be employed on this service. The men ought to be well Clothed

as well as accoutered. If it should be agreeable to your Excellency I could wish one half of the men were taken from our state troops and the other half from such other Corps as your excellency may choose to direct. But our troops are not yet clothed … I am therefore compeled most earnestly to wish that their Clothing may be forwarded as soon as possible[,] for without Clothing it will not be possible for them to participate in the business which to be deproved of would be cause of extreem regret. If they could be procured I should think it would be well for every man who may go in this service to have a Coat, a Vest a pair of Woolen overhalls a pair of Stockings a Shirt, a Blanket, a Woolen Cap a pair of Mittens and in the place of the Common Shoes, It would be best for them to have either Indian or Canadian Shoes and Socks; The shoes and socks cannot cost as much as the Common Shoes and are much better for a bad Country, Besides where snow shoes are used the Common Shoe will not do and I think if they could be procured it would be well for every man to have a pair of Snow Shoes For notwithstanding the March is to be performed in Shoes something may turn up to make it necessary to manuver the whole party on foot in which case Snow Shoes would be essential. The cost of snow shoes can be but trifling especially if we should procure hides and get the Indians to make them. At any rate some snow shoes must be provided for the troops this Quarter, as it is not possible to keep out Scouts without them and should your excellencys plan be carried into execution, it would be of great service to send a party of smart men on Snow Shoes a day before hand to trace the Path And the marching a few men on snow shoes is the best way that I know of to break a road for Slays were the snow is deep. Now Sir permit me to remind you that such of these things as your Excellency may join with me in conceiving ought to be procured it will be necessary for your Excellency to give directions about in such a way as you may conceive best calculated to conceal the design.

Whether it would be proper to direct the Quarter Master to assist in procuring Slays, or whether this part of the business may not be left with me I beg to submit to your Excellencies consideration. If the Quarter Master should receive orders to perform this business any time before hand the door of discovery will be open. I have thought whether it may not do to have the troops when they become detached for the expedition ordered to different places (in Companies) along the Mohawk river and having previously procured the names of such persons as are know[n] to have good horses and slays, let each officer Commanding a Company be furnished with the names of such persons whose Slays are intended to transport his Company with orders to take those Slays with a Driver to each and as many days forage as may be thought necessary and repair to the German flatts at which ... place it would perhaps be best to have the whole Detachment Victualed that being our advanced post and will be much convenient for a general Rendezvous. These orders may be given to each officer Commanding a Company separately, and executed in such a way as will not discover the strength of the party and the design may be kept out of sight by giving out to the officers commanding companies respectively that they are going to Fort Schuyler to bring down stores that were left at that place when it was [destroyed.] And it is a truth pretty well known that when that place was abandoned [there were] a number of shot left in the woods about a mile or two below the Fort —

Towards the last of January [would] be a good time I humbly conceive to carry your excellencies plan into execution and not before, as the Ice is hardly ever good previous to that time. I mention this that Your

Excellency may not be at a loss about the proper time in which the materials ought to be furnished.[2]

Washington responded on December 18:

I am glad to find you enter so readily into a measure which appears very practicable in my eyes, provided the Troops for the Enterprise can be properly accommodated. I have again written to the Secretary at War respecting clothing for the York State Troops, and desired Colo. Tilghman, who left this on Sunday last for Philadelphia to enforce it, not only on him, but on the Clothier General also; that, if it can be had, it may be sent up without delay. From the Deputy Clothier's Store at this place, I could furnish Vest and Woolen hose enough for the State Troops, and Woolen Caps, Socks, and Mitts sufficient for the whole party. Indian Shoes or Moccasons, I must depend upon you to procure; as also the Snow Shoes, of which I do not see the necessity for each Mans having a pair; tho' some may be indispensably necessary I well remember to have directed (two years ago) a number of Snow Shoes to be made; and if I mistake not it was done; but I do not suppose any dependence is to be had on them at this time. It may not be amiss however, to enquire of General Schuyler (to whom I think I wrote on this subject) the Qr Master, or any other who may be likely to give information, whether they are yet in being. To provide [and] carry Scaling Ladders from the Settlement would at once announce your design, and more than probably defeat the Enterprise; at any rate they would be troublesome to transport, and must impede the rapidity of your movement, on which every thing depends. It appears to me therefore that the attempt would be improper, and that the difficulty may be surmounted by carrying a few Tools (to wit Axes,

Saws, Augers and a Gouge) with which at a convenient time and place, a sufficient number of Ladders might soon and easily be made.

The mode your propose for obtaining the Sleighs, and assembling the Troops, I approve of preferably to the Qr Masters having any Agency in the business as I do of the time named for the execution if the Clothing can be got to you in Season, but having doubt on this head I should be glad to know to how late a period can be delayed with safety, on Acct. of the Ice on the Oneida Lake, and goodness of the Sleighing. If there is a *necessity* for a Party to preceed the Sleighs a day or two, to mark the rout, it ought to consist of picked men of tried fidelity; and even then, the chance of discovery is great than it otherwise wd. be.

The strength of your Party should be proportioned to that of the Garrison you attempt, for which reason every possible means should be used to obtain the most accurate acct. of it. If you have men to set the enemy at defiance, in case of their discovering you previous to the Assault, or miscarriage therein, it is all that is necessary; more than these would render your movements unwieldy and slow; consequently more liable to discovery in your preparation and on the March.

I should be glad to hear from you again on this head by some safe conveyance; and if matters can be properly prepared for the Enterprise, and nothing more than I know of at this time to hinder it, I will be at Albany when you March, that I may be at hand to remove difficulties if any should occur …

PS. It will be essentially necessary to fix your Eyes upon some one or more persons (deserters or otherwise) who have been in and are well acqd. with the Enemies works, and seize them at the moment they are wanted that you may have them as guides.[3]

On December 22, Willett wrote to Washington from Fort Rensselaer, expressing concern about the possibility of insufficient ice on the rivers that were the best line of advance. Undaunted, he added: "Dificulties however which … I humbly conceive ought not to superseed the attempt — An attempt which I am very desirous of making." He provided details of the works at Fort Ontario, which he had gleaned from various sources.

> The Fort is a regular built fortification Lying on the North Side of the river Consisting of Five angles with a Bastion to each angle[. T]he Angles are all of one length supposed about 100 paces — The Ditch is about 30 feet wide and Nine feet deep[. F]rom the bottom of the Ditch to the top of the Paraput is about 30 feet except the Angles w[h]ere the Sally port is fixed … w[hich] is 20 feet — Ther is a row of pickets in the center of the Ditch and a row of Horisontal Pickets /sharpened ends/ along the wall about for … 6 feet above the Berm — The Gate way secured by a Draw bridge. At the entrance of the Gate on one Side is the Guard house and on the other side a house for the Commandant[.] Within one of the Bastions is placed the Magazine in the other four Bastions and Curtains are filed with Barraks … All of the buildings are said to be Bum proof[.] Three of the Angles of the Fort front the Lake a[nd] the River And in some places lay very near to those waters. It is not Improbable but the Ditch may be nearly … filled with Snow — the most familiar way however to assend the wall it appears to me would be to Lay boards from the Paraput of the Glacis to the top of the … Pickets which are placed in the Ditch and on top of those boards the feet of the Ladders of about 14 feet I think would answer the purpose — I should suppose a helf dosen of those Ladders would not be too many — And that might be easly placed together with a few boards in the Bottom of the Slays.

The season at present in this Quarter is remarkably open — I have been thinking about the 12 or 13th of Febry would be sufficiently early to put the affairs in execution and I would pitch on one [of] those days on account of Benefiting by the moon which will then sett between 3 & 5 oC in the morning so that we may profit by its Light in our march & execute the business Just after it has withdrawn its light at which time it is Generally darkest so that we may hope to approach the river undiscovered.[4]

On January 18, Washington's headquarters ordered the assistant clothier general to "issue five hundred Woolen Caps, five hundred Socks and five hundred pr of Mits to Capt Ten Eyck Pay Mastr of Col Willets Regt. for the use of that and Col Olneys Regt; also such other Articles as you may have in store, which are wanted by sd Regt; the same to be delivered on account, and proper vouchers Recd. for the whole, when the Cloathing is issued to them which is daily expected from Philadelphia."[5]

Two days later, Washington sent a letter to Willett. "Your Pay Mastr will inform you that besides the usual proportion of cloathing, a Number of Articles have been issued, ostensibly for the use of Olney's and your Regt; but in reality, they are designed only for the object you have in contemplation[. U]nless it is attempted, I would not have any of the Woolen Socks, Caps, or Mitts distributed among the Troops, I have ordered them all therefore to be addressed to you and to await your Orders."[6]

Two days later, he again wrote to Willett:

I informed you that besides the usual proportion of Clothing I had sent to your orders Woolen Caps, Socks, and Mitts for the intended Enterprise, to be made use of or not according to the circumstances. I have also written to Mr. Duer who is now at Albany, to lay in a Months Provisions for a hundred men at each of the Posts of Fort Renselaer and Herkimer. And, till farther orders[,] have placed the Rhode Isld. Regiment under your direction.

For the reasons you assign, I approve of the time proposed for the Attack, and suppose it will be necessary for you to begin your March from Fort Herkimer at the time you mention, viz. on the 8th or 9th of next Month. If the Sleighing should be good, and business does not prevent it[,] I will endeavour to be at that place, or Fort Renselaer by that time; but of this you will take no notice to *any body* nor suffer it to have any influence on your preparations or conduct before or at the time as many things may intervene to detain me.

All that remains to be done is now with you to do, and as the matter is between ourselves and you have better information of the situation of the enemy and difficulty in getting them than I; I have only to request you to act from your best judgment under a firm perswasion that [if] the enterprise in contemplation was even better known than it is[,] no imputation could fall on you for having laid it aside if the difficulties in the way, or a want of information should be greater than appeared at first view.[7]

On January 23, the secretive preparations for the stroke against Oswego began at Fort Rensselaer with the arrival of the first sleighs, ostensibly to be used for drawing firewood. As this was a valid requirement, the presence of several of the conveyances passed unremarked. Four days later, orders were given to the company commanders to have all their men join by February 1, and further, that no man was to be absent a single day until all the clothing was issued. This was another believable pretence. Further, no liberty would be granted until inspections were held between February fifth and eighth. "A Soldier appearing without a bayonet or having … his arms not Clean in the Best possible Manner as well as the Musket & Barrel adequately Pollished and the acrutiments Brush'd, Cleaned & Pollished in the best Manner will receive particular (censure)."[8]

Washington was strongly focused on the coming adventure and saw fit to address two issues that had hitherto been ignored. On February 1, he instructed that two or three hogsheads of rum or other spirits be sent to the outposts on the Mohawk River. Further, he noted that it had somehow been omitted to make provision for the subsistence of Willett's officers and ordered that they be supplied with provisions consistent with their ranks.

Next day, he wrote to Willett:

> One hundred and fifty Blankets (all that are in the Clothiers Store at this place) and twenty five Axes are now packing to be sent to you; and the Qr Master Genl will endeavor, if possible, to have them at Albany on the 4th.; from whence you must take measures to get them to Fort Herkimer in time. If any of Olneys Men (on the Enterprise you are going) should be in greater need than yours, they must be supplied out of this parcel, that the whole may be as comfortable as it is in my power to make them.
>
> I do not send Medicines, Bandages and Instruments because it would take some time to procure them, and not a moment is to be lost in dispatching the Sleighs with the Blankets, that they may arrive in time; and because (tho's I wish you not to be unprovided) it is to be remembered, and I wish to impress it upon you, that, if you do not succeed by Surprise the attempt will be unwarrantable. The Wounds received in the former [i.e. the surprise], more than probable, will be trifling.
>
> Every plausible deception should be used to mask the object of your Expedition to the latest moment. Your movements afterwards should be quick, and pains must be taken to discover, by tracts or otherwise, whether intelligence has out gone you. If you should be fully convinced of this, the further prosecution of the Enterprise would not only be fruitless, but might prove injurious.

To an Officer of your care, attention and foresight, I shall not dwell upon circumspection and caution. The consequence of a Surprize (not only to the party you command, but to your own reputation) is too serious and self evident, to stand in need of illustration. A Vast deal depends upon having good Guides to Oswego; and every thing, in a manner, upon persons who can carry you without hesitation or difficulty, to the points of Attack when you arrive there. How far a few Indians would be useful to you for the purpose; and how far they are to be confided in, you, from a better knowledge of them than I possess, must judge and act accordingly.

Guides who are pressed into the Service must be well secured, lest they desert from you in a critical moment.

From having recourse to the Almanack I am led to Wish that the Night for the Attack may not be delayed beyond the 12th Instt.; as I find that the sitting of the Moon (even at that time) approaches so near day light, that the intervening space is short; and consequently must be very critical; as accidents unforseen, and consequently unprovided for, may embarrass your movements towards the Works and retard the Attack of them beyond the hour designed, to the entire disappointment of the plan. Let me caution you therefore against being too exact in your allowance of time for your last Movement; reflect that you can always waste time, but never recover it. Halts, or slow Marching will accomplish the first, but nothing can effect the latter, consequently in such an Enterprise as yours want of time will be certain defeat.

Let your disposition be such, that in any circumstance your retreat to your Sleigh[s], and afterwards with them, may be secure.

If success should crown your endeavors, let your first object be to secure your Prisoners, whom you will treat with lenity and kindness; suffering no Insult or abuse to be offered to them with impunity. Your next object must be to destroy the Works, Vessels (if any should be found there), and every thing else that cannot be brought away. Such Works as cannot be consumed by Fire, nor easily razed by the labor of the Soldiers, must be, if practicable, blown up. In a Word they are to be effectually demolished, if it is within the Compass of your power to do it.

Whatever is found in, or about the Works belonging to the Enemy, and is agreeable to the Rules and Customs of War, humanity and generosity; shall be given to the Party as the reward of their Gallantry and fatigue; to be distributed in proportion to their pay; the drivers of Sleighs, if Countrymen, should receive a part as an extra encouragement for their Services.

Make me the earliest report (if successful from the Scene of Action, at any rate on your return) of your progress, and the Issue of the Expedition. The Inclosed Letter will shew you what I have done respecting Spirits and Subsistence for your officers. Seal it before delivery, and make your own arrangements with the Contractor. I begin to doubt the practicability of my being up. My sentiments however you are possessed of, as well as all the Aid I can give. Your own judgment must govern where my Instructions are deficient. I heartily wish you honor and success, and am etc.[9]

As can be seen from Washington's intense concentration on Oswego, Fort Ontario had become a most serious threat to the rebels. It was viewed not only as a base in Indian Territory from which raids could be mounted against the frontiers, but as a lynchpin in the system of posts along the boundary with Canada that would impede the United States'

Unknown artist. (Collection of Fort Ontario New York State Historic Park.)

The mouth of the Oswego River and Ross's Fort Ontario.

westward expansion when the war was over and prevent their gaining a substantial share of the lucrative fur trade.

There are scant details about the fortress as it appeared in late 1782 and early 1783 that have not already been mentioned; however, Captain John Enys, 29th Regiment, left an excellent description when he began a tour of duty there three and a half years after Willett's expedition.

He noted that the fort had not been built on top of old Fort Oswego, but rather on the opposite side of the Onondaga River on top of the ruins of the works that Haldimand had built late in the Seven Years' War. Enys spoke of a bar across the mouth of the river that shifted without pattern from one season to another and made the river unnavigable and that the ground around the fort was extremely broken. A number of small redoubts had been erected at convenient places to command the different ravines.

> Ontario itself is a handsom well built Earthfort of a Pentagonal form, the exterior Pollegon if which is about Ninty Yards. The Bastions are all full, each of which contains a Block house with Bomb proofs under it. Four of these were designed for the men, the fifth as the residence of the commanding Officer. On the

curtains are also Buildings which were designed for Officers quarters, Storehouses, and Kitchens for the Blockhouses, which have no Chimneys in them except the Commanding Officers house. On the Parade are two Wells of water and in one of the Bastions is a third but it is but very indiffent so that the Lake water is in general made use off. There is a very good Bomb proof Maggazeen. It has a Ravlin toward the land side, a Line of Pikets entirely Round in the Ditch and some part of the Covertway.... The soil is very good in general, and was it not for the Wind the Gardens might be extremely forward, but of all the places I was ever at this is the most subject to hard Gales of Wind particularly in the fall of the Year, when it is seldom a boat can go out of the River, without danger, which makes it very difficult to supply the place with fuel for the Winter. The River Abounds with good fish of all kinds, and the co[u]ntry Rownd except just near the fort, with Beaver, Bear, Otter, and all kinds of Game, so much so that Indians come from a great distance to hunt near it.... It is about ... 150 [miles] East of Niagara & 140 W by N of Albany.[10]

In early February, a report was received in Quebec that a body of one thousand Continentals was being prepared for an attack upon the British outposts near Lake Champlain as soon as the ice was firm enough. This word had come from a reliable source, but Haldimand was unpersuaded and thought "the object scarce worth the danger and difficulties" attending such a venture, although he ordered a body of Light troops to occupy positions near the targeted posts "under the Pretext of practicing Snow Shoeing and Hutting."

Sir John was secretly ordered to raise all the natives available to cut off the retreat of this rebel force if it approached:

I cannot think of alarming the Province by any Preparation or Movement of consequence on so trivial an occasion, you will always have it in your power to take with you a fine Detachment of the flank companies and most active men of your own Battn., and should the Alert take place, it will be necessary that you shew this Letter to Brigadr. General St. Leger which he will consider as a Regular Order thro' him but if it does not you will please never to shew or mention it to any Person whosoever.

After the fact, it became clear that the threatened attack on the Champlain posts was intended to mask the thrust against Oswego. Haldimand had also heard of the possibility of an attack on Fort Ontario in a message from Castleton, Vermont, but felt it to be even more unlikely due to the season of the year. Yet, he noted that, as the report was "affirmed by a person of reputed veracity and Fidelity, some credit must be given to it," although he strangely failed to send a warning to Major Ross.[11]

In further preparation for the Oswego expedition, orders were issued at Fort Rensselaer on February 2:

All the Men belonging to the Regiment at this Fort except Shoemakers & Blacksmiths will parade for Inspection precisely at Seven O Clock to morrow morning with their Packs ..., Kettles, Axes etc. ... Those men of Capt. Wright's, Harrison's & Cannons Companies will fall in with Capt. Newells Company[.] It is expected the men will appear Neat & Clean Their Cartouch Boxes polished & Regularly Strung, their Hair properly cut[,] Hatts in Uniform, their Kettles cleaned without the fire Line.[12]

Matthew Calkins of Tierce's company recalled leaving Fort Plain under Lieutenant Thornton's command and marching to Fort Herkimer.

Snow had fallen to a depth of four feet and the company was ordered to break a road through to Lake Oneida, a strenuous, grinding task. The men marched two abreast on snowshoes to stamp down a track. The front pair was regularly rotated. Branches and whole trees that had fallen into the road had to be chopped up and cleared away. At night, the men camped in the deep snow around a gigantic fire, using hemlock bows for bedding. The job took four long, fatiguing days.[13]

Over several days, seven Rhode Island companies under the command of senior captain John Holden were secretly and expeditiously staged forward on snow-packed roads from Saratoga to Fort Herkimer. The regiment's Light Company was commanded by Captain William Allen and the six line companies by Captains Holden, Zephaniah Brown, Eben Macomber, David Sayles, and Benjamin Peckham. New Yorker David Perry took particular note of the large number of Rhode Island's black soldiers.

Similarly, the six companies of New York's State Troops under Major-Commandant Elias Van Benschoten's command concentrated at the fort. By the first week of February, five hundred troops and 120 horse-drawn sleighs and militia drivers from Tryon, and likely Albany County, as well, were ready for the movement.

To assist in choosing the route, Willett had taken Washington's advice and brought together four unnamed British deserters who had absconded from Oswego since August and "several [other] men ... who were well acquainted with Oswego & were other ways Intelligent."[14]

Henry Glen, deputy quartermaster general at Schenectady, wrote to Willett on February 6. The colonel had asked him to select two Oneida guides and his letter sheds some light on his choices.

> The moment I Recd yours I whent for the Incampment [where] my Regiment Lys[.] I Got Jonjost & Captain John[,] a Very prudent savage & a man that Can [be] dependd on[,] Ready for the ... Randevous You had orderd which is F Renselier who I now send to You & Flatter my self will Answer.... [T]hey are both Trouble

some when in Liquor perticuler Jonhost....

Glen then revealed that he had correctly divined from circumstantial evidence what was afoot and this must have given Willett fresh concerns about local Tory spies.

> [There] are ... Conjectures since you have past this City & the More so since a Number of slays with Armed men Past Likewise[.] As the matter of the troops marching from the North to the westward Gives a large field for Conjecture I must think[,] tho. No Great thinker my self[,] if their was Some thing in the wind[.]
>
> Should that be the Cause[,] No men shell be more happyier to learn the Success of this Expedition then your truly friend if its not Connected with the duty you owe your Country to tell me by a line before you Department & Conveyed me by a save hand I am Equally Contented[. S]hall pray our save Return to one who is Near & dear who in Mrs Willott & more friends I must Conclued with my Best wishes for you save Return if you Go & at all times my wishes will Attend you ware Ever you Go I will all most Insure you Success should you to the part of O. If you Carry your Slays as far as west End of ondia Leake & no forther — three days after that will do the Job & two back too the slays.

Ultimately the letter was given into the hands of the natives to deliver, but even before the warriors set out, Glen had to add a postscript. "Since writing this Letter Jonjost Got in the Frowlking [Frolicking] ... & unfit to Go for which I have optained a[n]other one in his place whos name is Peter[,] St[r]ongly Recommand[ed] by the Sesham [Sachem]." From where and when Willett's third Oneida guide was obtained has not been discovered.[15]

Willett reported to Washington prior to leaving Fort Herkimer on February 8:

> After a Variety of Dificulties [we] are furnished with
> every thing necessary to proceed in our march[.] I
> expect we shall encamp this night ten or fifteen Miles
> above this. If too many horses don't give out nor any
> other Insurmountable obstacle occur I hope to be able
> to execute the business at the time mentioned in your
> Excellencies letter of the 2d Instant.

As an afterthought, he applied to the C-in-C for a press warrant for
the sleighs, as he had discovered that acting without one laid him open
to legal prosecutions by outraged owners. The dispatch complete, Willett
ordered the expedition to mount the sleighs and the long column headed
west along the track beaten down by Thornton's men.

The bitter, cold weather took its toll even before the sleighs arrived
at Lake Oneida. The young Yorker, Ray Guile, who was certainly no
shirker, and three or four others were so badly frostbitten they could not
proceed. Willett ordered them to make their way back to the ruins of
Stanwix and find shelter there.

According to one participant, the force crossed the lake on the ice that
night. After a six-mile ride, they arrived at the ruins of Fort Brewerton,
where Willett decided that the sleighs would be an encumbrance on
the river. He also worried that the horses's neighing would betray their
presence, so he ordered the sleighs left and their drivers to camp and
await the expedition's return.[16]

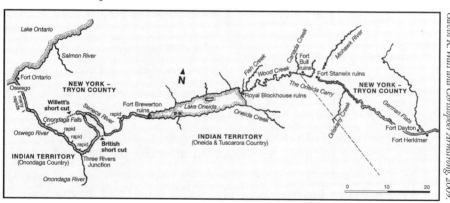

Route of Willett's expedition against Fort Ontario.

The men marched along the frozen Seneca River. When close to the river's northernmost tip where its course turned sharply south, the expedition set off overland on a twelve-mile detour to avoid the twenty-four-mile-long bend and emerged onto the Oswego River just south of Onondaga Falls. At 2:00 p.m. on February 12, they halted at the falls to construct nine twenty-foot-long siege ladders. Apparently, Willett had decided against his original idea of fourteen-foot ladders, which he had intended the troops would rest on boards to reach the appropriate height. Perhaps he had concluded there would be too much danger of the ladders slipping and sliding and had them built six feet longer to compensate.

While that task was underway, Willett held an orders group to instruct each company commander about his particular role in the storming of the fort. Final adjustments to arms, accoutrements, and clothing were made in the knowledge that the fort lay only seven miles from the falls and that the assault would be made in the dark hours of the next morning.

As a precaution, Willett ordered the killing of a dozen or so dogs to prevent their barking from alerting the fort's garrison and had their carcasses piled in a heap. Understandably, this seemingly callous action shocked the owners of those faithful canines that had shared the journey.

Early in the evening, the march resumed on the frozen river. The ladders had been made from green timber and were heavy and awkward, although the sixteen men carrying each one experienced fairly easy marching while on the ice. Their strenuous ordeal would come later.

The troops were "within four or five miles of Oswego between ten & Eleven oClock" when the ice was found too thin to proceed any farther on the river. Private John Pettit recalled that some men had their feet soaked by seeping, ice-cold water before the decision was made to go cross-country through the woods.

The three Oneida guides, "all of high estimations with respect to their fidelity," were brought forward to lead the way. The principal scout was Captain John Otaawighton, who had been commissioned by Congress on June 1, 1779. His "behaviour has been uniform & upright in all the changes of our affairs" and the other two had earlier "submitted to [his] superior skill." After predicting to the colonel that the force would be within striking distance of the fort by midnight, Otaawighton took the lead and set off.

The cross-country venture began just before 11 o'clock with a struggle to climb the river's steep bank. Then the men wallowed through deep snow, over hills, and across frozen swamps. The ladders were an agonizing burden to lug over the uneven ground and they frequently had to be wrenched free of tree trunks and branches. Despite these tribulations, Willett recalled that the men moved with briskness and cheerfulness.

After tramping nearly three hours in "Zig Zag movements" without seeing any sign of the fort, the colonel became intensely worried. Private Calkins recalled that the plan had been to advance close to the fort before midnight and lay up for some time to recharge everyone's strength for the assault and to allow the moon to set. It was not to be.

Willett advanced to the head of the column and spoke to the Oneidas, who appeared confused and entirely lost. He halted the troops and snowshoed ahead for a distance on his own, but was no more successful. "The moon had set and the day was dawning." He returned to the column and placed the three natives under guard. In the meantime, some soldiers had their feet frozen into potholes where the marching had churned up water; in Willett's later words, many men were already "badly frosted."

As the sun rose, Fort Ontario appeared three quarters of a mile off. Willett dramatically recalled, "we was Just within View of the Fort undiscovered whilst every breast was filled with ardor and the most animated determination."

In reality, a disaster loomed. A daylight attack was out of the question and there was no hope that five hundred men could escape discovery while hunkered in the woods so close to the fortress while waiting for another night. In bleak foreshadowing, it was discovered that one of Olney's black soldiers and one of the State Troops who had left the ranks during the night, had lain down in the snow and frozen to death. And, the troops had no provisions, as the incredibly overconfident Willett had assumed his men would be enjoying the fort's supplies. Such a rash presumption!

The Oneidas and their guards were sent down the back trail. Willett ordered the ladders jettisoned and a tired, crestfallen expedition began to retrace its steps. The temperature was falling and the men guarding the Oneidas grew disgruntled and let them drift away. In any event, Willett was convinced they were innocent of deception.[17]

Williams Avery of Newell's remembered marching about five miles when a party of British and natives fired on his company and raised fears of an attack. He was sent atop a high log as a lookout and his motionless feet became badly frozen, but no threat developed and the retreat continued.

Somewhere along the route, other men in the column met and spoke with some British Indians, offering them friendship. These natives were shocked to discover such a large body of rebels deep in their country and, as Ross reported later, they returned the words of friendship.

Every man knew it would take at least a day to get back to the sleighs and at least another to arrive at Fort Herkimer. The spectre of severe privation loomed; indeed, the very fate that Willett had predicted for Ross's raiders — with such great relish sixteen months before — now confronted his own force, all due to his overweening hubris.

The rebels were unprepared, mentally or physically, to face a retaliatory sally and retreated as fast as conditions allowed. When they arrived at the falls where the dead dogs had been piled, their hunger, magnified by near panic, drove many to fall upon the carcasses. Some furiously hacked at the frozen bodies and wolfed down hunks of raw meat. The more fastidious built fires, but fighting broke out and half-burned flesh was snatched back and forth. Of course, a handful of dead dogs was not enough to feed five hundred men and most went without. When the column marched, Calkins saw one fellow gnawing a dog's hind leg, more from the joy of

Colonel Marinus Willett, commander of the strike against Fort Ontario.

Unknown artist. (William M. Willett. A Narrative of the Military Actions of Colonel Marinus Willett... New-York: G. & C. & H. Carvill, 1831.)

having something than deriving nourishment.[18]

On the morning of February 14, Fort Ontario's garrison received its first indication that it had narrowly missed being attacked. Ross reported:

> The first information I had of their approach was by a deserter picked up by some Workmen going out into the Woods the 14th in the morning, who informed me that they had been misled by their Guides the night before but that we might expect them the succeeding night. I immediately got the Garrison under Arms and called in the working Parties, some of which were several miles up the River, the Troops were most spirited on the occasion. This deserter was young and unintelligent. I could not put much Confidence in his assertions, every means was used to take a Prisoner but could not succeed, we had some Indians here but they would not make the attempt. In the afternoon our working Parties and those who were sent to cover them got into the Fort and informed me that the Enemy had retreated some miles up the River, at the same time another deserter came from them confirming the same and informing me that as the Rebels were misled by their Guides the preceding night, they despaired of success and were making the best of their way to their Sleighs at Fort Bruington.[19]

Moses Nelson, a rebel who had been captured earlier in the year, was serving as a waiter for the Indian Department officers in the garrison. He noted that two of Willett's badly frozen men entered the fort the morning after the failure and told the story of the attempt. Accordingly, a party of British soldiers went out to find the abandoned ladders and brought them to the fort. Moses recalled, "[T]he longest of them when placed against the walls inside the pickets reached only about 2/3 of the way to the top." He went on to say that the post was strongly garrisoned and, in his opinion, "the accident or treachery which misled the troops was most providential, tending to save Colonel Willett from defeat, and most of his men from certain death."[20]

Returning to the retreating rebels — Calkins had fallen while carrying a ladder and was lamed as a result. He found marching too difficult and got permission to fall out of the column, as did three other men in similar condition. Oddly enough, when they were free of having to march in formation, they found easier routes around drifts and obstacles and soon were well ahead of the expedition.

Distraught with hunger and blinded by the need to keep moving, the four missed the turnoff for the overland shortcut that bypassed the big bend in the river. Unwittingly, they now faced a much longer route. They limped on until it grew too dark, and took shelter in a thick wood on the riverbank. Calkins was ravenous. He had failed to get any dog meat and it was days since he had eaten a morsel of food. After building a fire, the men wrapped in a blanket and fell asleep on the snow. By daybreak, the snow had shrunk with their body heat and the fire and they were almost on the ground.

They climbed out of the four-foot hole and resumed their march. They worried they had missed the turnoff, but were heartened at finding many tracks going upriver and thought that part of the expedition had taken the long route and passed them as they slept. They tramped on for more than an hour before coming up to a point of land jutting out from the shore. Looking through the leafless trees, they were shocked to see thirty whites and natives in "British and Canadian" clothing breakfasting on the ice.

Now they knew they had missed the shortcut and they struck off overland, but were so weak from lack of food and their struggle through the deep snow that it was impossible to keep going. They backtracked onto the frozen river, and, with hunger nibbling at their resolve, they almost looked forward to surrendering so they could get something to eat, but when they arrived at the jutting point, the enemy party had gone.

Ross continued his report:

> [B]eing now pretty certain of their strength which did not amount to 600 men, under Willett, I immediately dispatched an Officer and 30 men with orders to try

and pass the Enemy and cut off their Sleighs at Fort
Bruington which were said to be near 200 with drivers
unarmed, and the same night I sent a Detachment from
the Garrison with orders not to come to a General
conflict on account of the disparity of numbers but to
hang on the rear of the Enemy and to Harrass them
the more to facilitate the cutting off the Sleighs, but
the Rebels fled too precipitately for either[. The
detachment's] want of Snow Shoes was a mortifying
Circumstance and exceeding favourable to the Enemy
on this occasion.

Obviously, Ross's thirty-man party was the British force seen by
Calkins and his mates at the jutting point in the river. Being fresh and
well supplied, the British must have reasoned to bypass the expedition
by taking an alternate route.

When Calkins's group came to where the enemy had breakfasted,
one fellow found a small rind of cheese and, wolfing it down, proclaimed
it "a true Cheshire," as it was "so good and rich." Close to nightfall, they
saw that the enemy had put on snowshoes and headed cross-country,
taking an alternate shortcut to bypass a different bend in the Seneca
River. The four remained on the river and soon came to the turnoff point
that the expedition had used in its advance downriver. Although it was
now only twelve miles to the sleighs, two of the men gave up, saying it
was impossible to continue.

The four had finished collecting hemlock boughs for a bed when
Calkins suddenly became sharply aware of their great peril, but he could
not persuade the two men to march, so he and the fourth fellow started
off. They had gone just a short distance when they heard shouting and
stopped to wait for the two laggards to catch up.

The foursome stumbled on through the dark, their eyes swimming
and their limbs wobbly. About 2:00 a.m., they heard neighing horses
and the voice of a driver preparing to set out. If they had been just a few
minutes later, the sleighs would have been gone. Willett's column had
outstripped the British patrol and the drivers and sleighs were safe.

By pure chance, Calkins met up with his company commander and asked him for something to eat, but was told there was nothing. The captain gave them his part-full canteen of whiskey to share with the other three. The slug of liquor and a handful of oats and peas that Calkins filched from a horse's nosebag were all the nourishment he had until the sleighs were at the fort sixty miles later. As the sleighs were so overburdened with men, not a single horse had been sacrificed for food, an indication that a very deep sense of danger lay across the force, either that, or the iron hand of discipline.

The expedition arrived at Fort Herkimer just after dark on February 19. The men had gone five days without food, except for the few fortunate enough to get scraps of dog carcass. Calkins recalled that two-thirds were severely frostbitten, mostly on their feet. The Rhode Islanders were particularly affected, perhaps through lack of experience or preparation. First Serjeant Immanuel Deake of Wright's Company said that a great many of the expedition died, including two Oneida guides, and that one Rhode Island company, primarily of blacks, mostly died. Although Deake overstated the case, over 130 Rhode Islanders had suffered frostbite and Major Coggeshall Olney reported to Washington that forty were in danger of losing their limbs. Two years later, fourteen men invalided by the Oswego campaign applied for compensation. Most had lost all the toes of one foot and some on the other. One man continued to have open sores that refused to heal.

Tryon militiaman John Roof said that "numbers of Col. Willett's men [were] destroyed by cold, some with hands and feet frozen, [and were] totally deprived of their limbs, and ... remained helpless for ever thereafter." Seth Rowley, the orderly serjeant of Harrison's Company, recalled that many men froze to death with only about thirty to forty of the regiment being fit for duty upon their return." Although many of the troops had escaped frostbite while marching, the cold struck deep when they sat immobile on the sleighs. Calkins had been alert enough to move his limbs about and avoided being struck. Whatever the numbers, the event was a severe trial for all participants and a disaster for rebel arms.[21]

One of Willett's biographers wrote that the colonel was met by a letter from Washington on his return. If so, it must have been with a heavy heart that he read the C-in-C's opening lines. "I sincerely hope this will meet you returning successful from your Expedition." He replied:

> I can't help feeling great regret at the disappointment whilst I reflect with gratitude at the honor Confered in me by your Excellency in affording me an opportunity of atchieving so much at so small a risk. I pretend not to say that the work has been performed as well as it might have been done, perhaps I have been deficient in points of discernment. But I am sure I have not been so in points of Integrity & exertions. These have been stretched to the Utmost. Yet I have unfortunately failed.

Not long after Adjutant Pliny Moore returned to his post, he wrote his father about the escapade:

> We return from our unsuccessful expedition to Oswego the 18th at evening after as fatiguing a March I believe as has been since the War.[W]e were nine nights in the woods without seeing a House, marched Thirty Six Hours without one hours intermission & as long at another item with but about three Hours Halt for Refreshment & to compleat our disappointment when our hopes were most Sanguine after marching all day & all night Cold fatiguid & many of us frozen.... By the perfidy or ignorance of one Savage, the former of which is most probable, the Continent is at more than a thousand pounds expense besides the loss of several good Men, a number of Toes & a quantity of good health.[22]

Calkins's account continued with a tale about a British deserter named Mortimer, who told the rebel troops that the British were at "full strength at Oswego," which Calkins surmised had been unknown to Willett. From the deserter's advice, the troops concluded that had "the expedition ... persevered in the attempt[,] the men would have been cut to pieces."

In fact, the garrison had the same number of troops as the expedition. If surprise had been attained, there might have been some chance of overpowering an equal number; however, Mortimer also revealed that the ladders had been six feet too short. Even the doziest of sentries would have been alerted to the expedition's struggles to erect the ladders and their confusion and muttered curses once they were found too short. Truly, an even greater disaster had been averted by the accident of getting lost.

First Serjeant Deake made another interesting claim, to wit, that a British serjeant (Mortimer?) and a fifer had deserted. Deake had spotted the British thirty-man patrol when he was setting out guards at Fort Brewington, but chose not to shout a warning for fear of prompting an attack. The British serjeant claimed he had spotted the expedition at the same time and hid behind an elm tree and said nothing to the troops in his detachment, presumably because he already planned to desert. Deake also said that Major Ross later sent a party to claim the two deserters, but Willett refused. As neither Ross nor Willett reported these events, one has to wonder if Deake had an overactive imagination.

The British patrol that had been sent to cut off the sleighs at Fort Brewington returned to the fort (presumably less two deserters) with two Rhode Island Continentals they had captured at Three Rivers. The pair must have become separated from the expedition's main body when it took the overland shortcut bypassing that well-known meeting place.[23]

Ross's report to Haldimand continued:

> I cannot help observing to your Excellency that there never was a more ridiculous Expedition.... Between 5-600 men (most of them from Saratoga) came and laid down nine Scaling Ladders within two miles of this Place and retreated with the utmost precipitation without so much as even having seen the Fort or taking a single Prisoner. Nothing but a frantic zeal or a misinformation of our situation could have induced them to have undertaken so ridiculous an enterprise, and I believe I may add a professional Ignorance in whoever planned the expedition, to think of succeeding at any

time, and particularly at the fullest time of the moon, when every object was as discernible as at noonday.

I should have counted this the most fortunate event of my life had matters been pushed to Extremities even with numbers much superior to theirs, and will venture to affirm to your Excellency that without any considerable loss on the part of His Majesty's Troops, the whole of this Party would have fallen a sacrifice. They have some merit in the secrecy and dispatch with which it was carried on, as they performed the Expedition in Eight days unknown before their departure to any person on the Mohawk River, and although I never had at any Juncture so many Scouts out as at that time[,] yet [I] had no information of their approach[. T]hey came across the Lake in five hours and marched in two days from Ft Bruington to this place.

The Six Nations Indians covering our Wood Cutting Parties were with them on the morning of their Retreat, the Rebels bespoke them Friendship, in which I think they were successful[,] for on their arrival I found the rest more obstinate than ever, and was obliged to threaten them hard before I could get them … to join the Troops in pursuit … they were about ten in number, the Rebels had only five Indians.

The Rebels have only left five men behind them, viz. two deserted, two taken Prisoners, and one found dead in the road, the Garrison has not lost a Single man so that the Rebels are ignorant as ever of our Situation, however, I think I may venture to inform your Excellency that the more the Enemy know of this place, the less hopes they will have of succeeding in such enterprises and every day adds to our strength.[24]

Moses Nelson, the rebel prisoner serving in 6NID, later wrote that the expedition had "certainly added no laurels to the chaplet of the brave Willett." Yet, there was much to admire in the thoughtful, detailed planning of this effort. As Ross said, the great secrecy and sheer audacity in the face of winter was admirable. Contrary to Ross's derisive comments about the full moon, its light had allowed the troops to navigate through the woods and, as has been seen, there was no intention to attack before the moon set. Yes, there had been a risk of being seen before the force was in position, but that was a recognized gamble.

There were two major planning errors. First, the short ladders, an error that may have been the result of relying upon historical information regarding the height of the works during the Seven Years' War; however, as Ross had reported on June 26, "The Works in General are about Thirty feet Perpendicular which exceeds the plan by one-third." The second, and far less forgivable failing, was Willett's infatuated decision not to carry provisions in case of failure.[25]

Washington reported Willett's attempt to the president of Congress on February 26:

> I am sorry to have to acquaint your Excellency, for the information of Congress, that a project which I had formed for attacking the Enemys Post at Oswego, as soon as the Sleighing should be good, and the Ice of the Oneida Lake should have acquired sufficient thickness to admit the passage of the Detachment, has miscarried. The report of Colol. Willett, to whom I had entrusted the Command of the Party (consisting of a part of the Rhode Island Regiment and the State Troops of New York, in all about 500 Men) will assign reasons for the disappointment.[26]

When Washington wrote Willett to acknowledge the news of the failure, his words were characteristically gracious.

I have been favoured with your Letter of the 19th of Febry. announcing the failure of your Attempt against Oswego.

Unfortunate as the Circumstance is, I am happy in the persuasion that no Imputation or reflection can justly reach your Character, and that you are enabled to derive much Consolation from the animated Zeal, fortitude and Activity of the Officers and Soldiers who accompanied you. The failure, it seems, must be attributed to some of those unaccountable Events, which are not within the controul of human Means and which tho' they often occur in military life, yet require not only the fortitude of the Soldier, but the calm reflection of the Philosopher, to bear.

I cannot omit expressing to you the high Sense I entertain of your persevering Exertions and Zeal on this Expedition; and begging you to accept my warm Thanks on the Occasion; And that you will be pleased to communicate my Gratitude to the Officers and men under your Command, for the Share they have taken in that Service.[27]

Despite Washington's warm and forgiving words, this last offensive action of the rebellion is said to have ended in a great public outcry over the misadventure's casualties. One veteran of the expedition claimed that Willett had made the attempt simply "for the purpose of getting a great name" and that he quickly escaped to Albany to avoid the wrath of his troops.

After Ross's news of his unexpected and bloodless victory was received at headquarters in Quebec City, the governor wrote a detailed, flattering reply:

I read with great Satisfaction your account of Mr. Willett's romantick and fruitless attempt to surprize the Post you Command. I heartily regret with you that it was not carried into Execution from the firm Persuasion that the Result would have procured to you and your Garrison much Honor. You and the Troops have not however less Merit from your Exertions to cut off the Enemies Retreat in which you would have probably Succeeded had you been better Supplied with Intelligence. This Detachment had been in Motion since the first week in February and it was industriously reported that a Surprize of our advanced Posts of Lake Champlain or Subduing the Vermonters was their Object, which was so confidently affirmed by different Messengers from the Rebel Country as to Occasion my taking some Precaution, (tho' I never gave Credit to the former part of the Report) and I much less suspected they would have undertaken a march to Oswego, upon the vain Presumption of surprising a Post and Garrison so considerable as they now are.

Finding they did not advance by the Lake [Champlain,] it was surmised about Ten Days ago that they had dispersed or taken the Road to Oswego. I should not have been under the least apprehension had I known the Fact. Satisfied of your Vigilance and unremitting Attention to your Duty in a Situation that will not admit of the smallest Relaxation in either of which, the Enemy's rapid and undiscovered Advance is the most convincing Proof. It is to be regretted that you had not a good Party of Indians with you unless they might have been so ill-disposed to support you as the few you had, they were so small in number that in the discontented Mood the Indians in General seem upon being restrained from War, I am of opinion that your rebuking them yourself may have a better effect than my taking notice of it ...

At present we are entirely without Intelligence but from what can be gathered out of News Papers and the pressing Desire of the Americans to encroach as far as possible upon the upper Country to secure the Fur Trade, it would appear that a Peace is at hand. Upon this Principle

I am convinced they will make a vigorous Effort to obtain
Oswego, it being a Post of such Consequence to the Trade
from Albany upwards, I therefore strongly recommend to
you a Continuance of the Diligence you have hitherto
exerted in making yourself as Strong as possible.

After basking in such praise, Ross sent a second dispatch, giving
more detail and admitting that his confidence in his scouting parties had
been grossly misplaced:

I did not in my letter specify the number of Scouts I had
in my Front when the Enemy made their undiscovered
march, being too sensible of your Excellency's generosity
in my behalf to think that I had relaxed in that essential
Duty, at the same time on the arrival of all those Scouts,
which had not taken place when I had the honor to
write your Excellency, I found that the same security is
not to be expected from them that I imagined. Being
somewhat apprehensive of the Enemy's intentions of a
Winter Expedition from a Scout of theirs having been
discovered on Wood Creek, I sent out four different
Scouts, one to Johnstown for Intelligence, and the other
three towards Fort Stanwix on both sides of Oneida
Lake, yet the Enemy passed all those undiscovered, one
excepted, which saw their Sleighs at Fort Bruington when
too late. They lay within a mile of another for half a day,
and the third brought me news that they had retreated
three days after. The Rebels in their Sleighs so far exceed
our Scouts in Travelling that altho' they had discovered
them it would have availed nothing. The fourth returned
from Johnstown on the 26th of March … informed me
that Mr. Willett arrived at the German Flatts the third
day after he left this, but notwithstanding the rapidity
of his Flight, most of his men (particularly the Rhode
Island Continentals) were frost bitten, some drowned,

and some dying daily, the purport of their Expedition was said to be planned with a view of securing Oswego to the Congress before a peace should take place, which in that case was to belong to the United States.

The weather has been favorable of late altho' the frost is still in the ground. The Block Houses leaked exceedingly whenever it rained by which means the men were very uncomfortable, they are all now raised upon and make excellent Barracks. The Fort is riveted [revetted] half way up with Timber and does not appear in the least to give way. The Glacis and Redoubts are now our principal object, which I hope will be soon completed.[28]

For all those who thought the war must surely be over now and that the gallant, long-suffering Continentals could at last enjoy the fruits of their victory, the shocking results of a court-martial at Washington's headquarters were announced the same day as the C-in-C's letter was written to Willett. A Massachusetts soldier was awarded one hundred lashes for desertion and, for the same offence, an accomplished Massachusetts soldier had his merit badges stripped off by the drum major at the head of his regiment and was awarded fifty lashes.[29]

On April 13, Sir Guy Carleton, C-in-C America, sent an overland express directly to Ross from New York City, warning that 1,200 Continentals were at Newburgh preparing for an expedition, possibly against Oswego. In some astonishing manner, the message reached Fort Ontario in three days. Ross immediately warned Niagara and Carleton Island and advised Quebec headquarters that he had taken every precaution against attack, but was short of ammunition.

It was April 25 before Carleton's advice reached General Haldimand; however, the terms of the official peace had preceded the warning, which prompted the governor to write a private letter to Ross full of doom and gloom.

> An Express arrived from N. York with the Proclamation mentioned in my Letter accompanying this. I have also received the preliminary Articles [of peace] but they are so unfavourable to this Province that I shall if possible avoid disclosing them in the Hope that some Provision will appear in the Particulars for the Six Nations and our other Indian Allies, of whom I cannot learn that any mention has been made in the Provisional Articles. They will soon … become acquainted with this unpleasant information and the Effect it will have upon them may be easily conceived. It will therefore be highly necessary that you narrowly watch the Conduct of the Indians and[,] without seeming to suspect them[,] tak[e] every Precaution against their surprizing any small Posts or Detachments you may have abroad for there is no saying what their Resentment may tempt them to do. Their Conduct at the close of the last War was an example of this. Use also your best Endeavours to Console them & continue your Attention to them in very Respect.[30]

After peace became a reality months later, neither the British nor the Americans had any reason to be proud of their treatment of their native allies. The British, who had encouraged and enjoyed so much more native support than the Americans, were particularly ignorant in their negotiations, disregarding the many treaties they had entered into with the various nations. Native aspirations were cast aside like a pair of dirty stockings.

At the end of April, Haldimand wrote to his friend and confidant,

Captain-General Frederick Haldimand, governor of Canada, 1718–1791. "I am heartily ashamed, and wish I was in the interior of Tartary."

Friedrich Riedesel, "My soul is completely bowed down with grief at seeing that we (with no absolute necessity) have humbled ourselves so much as to accept such humiliating boundaries. I am heartily ashamed, and wish I was in the interior of Tartary."[31]

The next month, Brigadier Maclean held a council at Niagara with six principal Six Nations' chiefs, who found it impossible to believe that Britain had not secured their territories for them and angrily exclaimed that the king had no right to give up to the rebels what was not his to give. Maclean reported:

> I would by no means answer for what they may do when they see us evacuate these Posts.... [Brant] is much better informed and instructed than any other Indian, he is strongly attached to the interest of his Countrymen, for which I do honor him, but he would be so much more sensible of the miserable situation in which we have left this unfortunate People, that I do believe he would do a great deal of mischief here at the Time. I do from my soul Pity these People, and should they commit outrages at giving up these Posts, it would by no means surprize me.[32]

Ultimately, it was Frederick Haldimand, that fastidiously correct, foreign-born governor, who had the wisdom, compassion, and courage to recognize Britain's obligations and make provisions to resettle the Six Nations and their affiliates in western Quebec. In tiny part, this

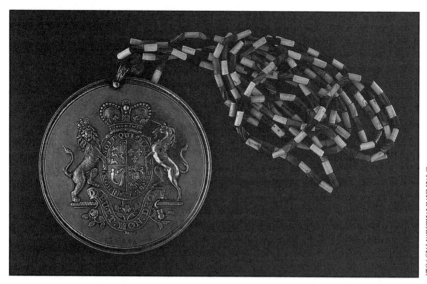

© McCord Museum M5932.

Medal and wampum. A typical medal awarded to principal warriors and war captains of the Eastern Woodlands Indians to encourage their sustained support, *circa* 1763–89.

addressed the wrongs done to the natives who had been one of Britain's most significant allies during the war. The constant, loyal Mississaugas were persuaded to give up their sovereignty in two key geographic areas in favour of their more politically astute Iroquoian associates; however, nothing was done for the Lakes' and Ohio Nations. It was simply hoped that their isolation from the rapacious United States would save their societies, which proved a very faint hope indeed!

It was also Haldimand who refused to surrender the upper posts, as such an action would have laid Canada bare to American aggression and thoroughly enraged the natives over their abandonment.[33]

Nor were his sympathies confined to the natives. While the British peace negotiators had insisted on provisions in the treaty's articles for American loyalists, Haldimand saw the futility of these insipid measures. He well knew that the passions of the rebels' northern inhabitants, whose families and properties had been subjected to mayhem over the past seven years, were at an unforgiving pitch. Accordingly, without instructions or approval from Britain, he made preparations to settle the loyalist families in western Quebec and, immediately prior to their relocation, appointed Sir John Johnson as the Superintendent General of Refugee Loyalists.[34]

Haldimand's Army in Canada, 1782

Regiment	Strength	Where Stationed
Artillery		
Royal Artillery[1]	289	Throughout Quebec
Combined German[2]	108	Lower Quebec
Subtotal	**397**	
Infantry — British		
King's (8th) Regiment[3]	674	Upper Posts[4]
29th Regiment[5]	434	Lower Quebec
31st Regiment[6]	474	Lower Quebec
34th Regiment[7]	532	Lower Quebec and mid-Upper Posts[8]
44th Regiment[9]	429	Lower Quebec
53rd Regiment[10]	519	Lower Quebec[11]
1Bn, 84th (RHE) Regiment[12]	550	Throughout Quebec
Subtotal	**3612**	
Infantry — German		
Anhalt-Zerbst Regiment[14]	697	Lower Quebec

Dragoon Regiment Prinz Ludwig[15]	255	Lower Quebec
Regt Prinz Friedrich[16]	635	Lower Quebec
Regiment von Riedesel[17]	367	Lower Quebec
Regiment von Rhetz[18]	311	Lower Quebec
Regiment von Specht[19]	368	Lower Quebec
Brunswick Light Infantry Regiment[20]	403	Lower Quebec
Hesse-Hanau Free Jäger Corps[21]	602	Lower Quebec
Hesse-Hanau Erbprinz von Hessen Regiment[22]	290	Lower Quebec
Regiment von Lossberg[23]	391	Lower Quebec
Subtotal	**4319**	
Infantry — American Provincial		
1st Battalion, King's Royal Regiment of NY[24]	545	Lower Quebec[25]
2nd Battalion, King's Royal Regiment of NY[26]	468	Lower Quebec and the mid-Upper Posts[27]
Butler's Rangers[28]	525	Upper Posts[29]
Loyal Rangers[30]	482	Lower Quebec[31]
2nd Battalion, King's Rangers[32]	200	Lower Quebec
Herkimer's Bateaux Company[33]	25	Coteau-du-Lac and mid Upper Posts
Subtotal	**2245**	
Grand Total	**10573**	

Note: The mid upper posts were: Oswegatchie, Fort Haldimand on Carleton Island, Fort Ontario at Oswego, Fort Niagara and its dependencies — Forts Schlosser and Erie. The far upper posts were Detroit and Michilimackinac.

APPENDIX II

Haldimand's Native Allies and His Indian Departments, 1782

Native Alliance	Strength	Located
Canada Indians[1]	680	Lower Quebec[2]
Fort Hunter Mohawks[3]	55	Lachine, Lower Quebec[4]
Six Nations & Affiliates[5]	1600	Indian Territory and Niagara[6]
Mississaugas[7]	250	Across the north shore of Lake Ontario[8]
Total Lower Quebec and Mid Upper Posts	**2500**	
Lakes' Nations[9]	5400	Upper Great Lakes and river system below[10]
Ohio/Western Nations[11]	1100	Ohio River Valley[12]
Total High Upper Posts	**6500**	
Quebec Indian Department	105	Throughout Quebec[13]
Six Nations' Indian Department	110	Montreal/Niagara[14]

It should be noted that strength numbers for the native nations are "soft" and compiled from an amalgam of sources cited below. Native populations were in a constant state of flux with men being off on the hunt and others at war, and, in some cases, villages moving from one site to another. Written records were not kept by the natives themselves and only rarely by the Indian Departments.

Sources

PRIMARY — PUBLISHED

Bloomfield, Joseph. *Citizen Soldier: The Revolutionary War Journal of Joseph Bloomfield*, Mark E. Lender and James Kirby Martin, eds. Newark: New Jersey Historical Society, 1982.

Captain Dalton, Superintendent of Indian Affairs for the United States "Number of Indian Warriors Employed [by the British] in the Revolutionary War," published at Philadelphia, August 5, 1783. Cited in William W. Campbell, *Annals of Tryon County or the Border Warfare of New York During the Revolution*. Cherry Valley: The Cherry Valley Gazette Print, 1880, 285.

Lajeunesse, Ernest J., ed. *The Windsor Border Region, Canada's Southernmost Frontier: A Collection of Documents.* Toronto: The Champlain Society, 1960.

Penrose, Maryly B., ed. *Indian Affairs Papers, American Revolution* (Franklin Park, NJ: Liberty Bell Associates, 1981).

The Sullivan-Clinton Campaign in 1779, Chronology and Selected Documents. Albany, NY: The University of the State of New York, 1929.

SECONDARY — BOOKS AND THESES

DePeyster, John Watts. *The Life, Misfortunes & the Military Career of Brig. General Sir John Johnson Bart.* New York: Chas. H. Ludwig, 1882.

Frazier, Patrick. *The Mohicans of Stockbridge.* Lincoln and London: University of Nebraska Press, 1992.

Graymont, Barbara. *The Iroquois in the American Revolution.* Syracuse: Syracuse University Press, 1972.

Stevens, Paul L. "His Majesty's 'Savage' Allies: British Policy and the Northern Indians During the Revolutionary War — The Carleton Years, 1774–1778." Ph.D. diss., State University of New York at Buffalo, 1984.

Watt, Gavin K., and James F. Morrison, *The British Campaign of 1777: The St. Leger Expedition — The Forces of the Crown and Congress*, 2nd ed. Milton, ON: Global Heritage Press Inc., 2003, 74–100.

APPENDIX III

Rebel Casualties at the Destruction of Ellice's Mill, Little Falls, July 21, 1782

Killed	Unit
Private Daniel Petri	4TCM

Wounded	Unit
Gersham Skinner	Miller

Prisoners	Unit
Captain Frederick Getman	4TCM, Company CO
Ensign Jacob Petri	4TCM
Serjeant Peter Orendorf	2NH, Dustin's Company
Serjeant Christian Edick/Ely/Chris'r Ittic	4TCM
Private Stephen Ames	2NH, Dustin's Company
Private James Bailey	2NH, Dustin's Company
Private Samuel French	2NH, Dustin's Company
Private Bartholomew Gayor/McGuire	2NH, Dustin's Company
Private Lawrence Harter/Hatter/Herter	4TCM
William Martin	N/A
Private Andrew Piper	4TCM
Marks Rosbach	N/A
Private Edward Sawyer/Sayer	2NH, Dustin's Company

Private Oliver Smith	2NH, Dustin's Company
Private Thomas J./T. Shoemaker	4TCM
Peter Wolleaver	N/A

Taken and Released	**Unit**
Elizabeth Petri	N/A
Mrs. Skinner	N/A

Note: 4TCM — it is unknown how many of these militiamen were performing duty as the convoy's escort and how many were simply at the mill doing business as farmers.

Sources

Benton, Nathaniel S. *A History of Herkimer County, including the Upper Mohawk Valley, from the earliest period to the present time.* Albany, J. Munsell, 1856, Chapter 5, *passim*.

French, Samuel, *NH Rolls & Documents*, 465.

Lovejoy, John M. "A Study of letters and rolls relating to the 2nd New Hampshire Regiment in 1782." J.F. Morrison collection.

McHenry, Chris, compiler. *Rebel Prisoners at Quebec 1778-1783.* Author, 1981.

NYSL, Special Collections and Manuscripts, Audited Accounts, Vol. A, 265.

Petri, Elizabeth, widow of Daniel. Pension Application, NYSL, Special Collections and Manuscripts, Audited Accounts, Vol. A, 288.

Simms, Jeptha R. *Frontiersman of New York Showing Customs of the Indians, Vicissitudes of the Pioneer White Settlers and Border Strife in Two Wars with a Great Variety of Romantic and Thrilling Stories Never Before Published* [hereafter *FNY*], Vol. 2 (2 vols.) Albany: Geo. C. Riggs, 1883, 523–25.

NOTES

CHAPTER ONE —THE AFTERMATH OF THE 1781 CAMPAIGN

1. Sir Henry Clinton to Frederick Haldimand, New York City August 2, 1781. General staff (Historical section) ed., "The War of the American Revolution, the Province of Quebec Under the Administration of Governor Frederic Haldimand, 1778–1784," in *A History of the Organization, Development and Services of the Military and Naval Forces of Canada From the Peace of Paris in 1763 to the Present Time With Illustrative Documents* [hereafter *HSGS*] Vol. 3 (2 vols.) (Ottawa: King's Printer, n.d.), 208, from LAC, HP, B147, 331–32, Lieutenant James M. Hadden, *A Journal Kept in Canada and Upon Burgoyne's Campaign in 1776 and 1777*, Horatio Rogers, ed. (Albany: Joel Munsell's Sons, 1884), 38fn, and HQ, Quebec City, September 13, 1781, LAC, HP, AddMss21744; **Riedesel's Early Career:** Max von Eelking, *Memoirs, Letters and Journals of Major General Riedesel during his Residence in America*, [hereafter *Memoirs*] Vol. 1 (2 vols.), William L. Stone, ed. and trans. (Albany: J. Munsell, 1868), Stone's biographical sketch, 1–17. Stone reports that Riedesel was promoted to lieutenant-general in 1787 and, in 1788, commanded the Brunswick contingent that was sent to Holland. He retired to his Hessian ancestral castle in 1793, but was recalled the following year as commandant of the city of Brunswick. He died in 1800 at the age of sixty-two; When Riedesel was exchanged to New York City in 1781, General Sir Henry Clinton promoted him to lieutenant-general and gave him command of Long Island, but this must have been a local rank only. Captain, later major, Georg Pausch, Hanau Artillery, referred to Riedesel as a major-general. See, George Pausch, *Georg Pausch's Journal and Reports of the Campaign in America*, Bruce E. Burgoyne, tr. and ed. (Bowie, MD: Heritage Books, Inc., 1996), 117, and Haldimand referred to Riedesel as a major-general in his dispatch to Shelburne, August 17, 1782, *HSGS*, Vol. 3, 225.

2. Friedrich Riedesel to George Germain, October 10, 1781, LAC, HP, AddMss21811; Max von Eelking, *The German Allies in the American Revolution, 1776–1783*, [hereafter *German Allies*] J.G. Rosengarten, trans. (Albany: Joel Munsell's Sons, 1893 – reprinted,

Kessinger Publishing, n.d.), 247. Von Eelking writes that Riedesel arrived with nine hundred soldiers including five Brunswick staff officers, sixteen captains, twenty-four, and four hundred men. The rest were Hesse-Hanau and Anhalt-Zerbst recruits. Just before Riedesel arrived, Captain von Schlagenteuffel arrived with seventy Brunswick soldiers who had bought their own release; **Sorel, a Major Defensive Installation**: *HSGS*, Vol. 3, 24, and Jean N. McIlwraith, "Sir Frederick Haldimand," *The Makers of Canada*, Vol. 3 (11 vols.) (Toronto: Morang & Co., Limited, 1911), 125, 132–35. In 1780, Haldimand purchased the seigniory of Sorel to avoid ownership squabbles, *ibid.*, 183, and Haldimand to Germain, Quebec City, October 15, 1778, CO42/37, 198; **Fifty Barracks**: Julius Friedrich Wasmus, Helga Doblin, tr., Mary C. Lynn, ed., *An Eyewitness Account of the American Revolution and New England Life: The Journal of J.F. Wasmus, German Company Surgeon, 1776–1783* (New York: Greenwood Press, 1990), 253; **Haldimand's Intimacy with Riedesels**: Riedesel had been warned that he would find Haldimand "a sour looking and morose man, and of a very unsocial disposition ... [Haldimand] was in truth somewhat morose, [but] soon grew more friendly and talkative. [They] parted, each well pleased with the other." Eelking, *Memoirs*, Vol. 2, 108, and Eelking, *Allied Troops*, 247. See also, Baroness Frederike Charlotte Louise von Riedesel, *Letters and Journals Relating to the War of American Independence and the Capture of the German Troops at Saratoga* (Toronto: German-Canadian Museum of Applied History, n.d.), 155–70. Specific quote, 157, and McIlwraith, 296–304; **House**: Baroness Riedesel, 155–56. This house is extant and presently known as the "Maison des Gouverneurs." See also, Eelking, *Memoirs*, Vol. 2, 108–09; **Haldimand's Room**: *Ibid.*, 112; **Hesse-Hanau Recruits**: Pausch, 117.

3. Jean-Pierre Wilhelmy, *German Mercenaries in Canada* (Beloeil, QC: Maison des Mots, 1985), 183, from von Eelking, *The German Allied Troops*, 247; Riedesel to Haldimand, October 19, 1781, Dresler, Horst, *Henry & John Ruiter, 1742–1819* (Woodstock, VT: Anything Printed, 2005), 30–31.

4. John Stuart to the Society for the Propagation of the Gospel, Montreal October 13, 1781. "Letters of the Rev. John Stuart," [hereafter *Stuart Letters*} James J. Talman, ed., *Loyalist Narratives from Upper Canada* (Toronto: The Champlain Society, 1946), 342–43.

5. Ernst de Speth to Haldimand, Montreal, October 16, 1781, LAC, HP, AddMss21789, 262; Wilhelmy gives the brigadier's full name as Ernst Ludwig W. von Speth. However, the name constantly appears in the Haldimand Papers in the French version "de Speth" and I have followed that lead. Wilhelmy, 256.

6. **Coteau-du-Lac Garrison**: James Gray to William Twiss, Montreal, October 16, 1781, LAC, HP, AddMss21789, 265; Joseph Anderson to Gray, Coteau-du-Lac, October 30, 1781. *Ibid.*, 267.

7. Pausch to the Hereditary Prince of Hesse-Kassel, reigning Count of Hanau [hereafter Prince of Hesse-Hanau], Charlesbourg, October 17, 1781, Pausch, 119–20; **Black Drummers**: *Ibid.*, 111–12. This entry describes the drummers' uniforms in considerable detail.

8. Haldimand to Germain, Quebec City, October 20, 1781, CO42/42, 20–21.
9. **Niagara Scandal**: Isabel Thompson Kelsay, *Joseph Brant, 1743–1807: Man of Two Worlds* (Syracuse: Syracuse University Press, 1984), 323, and Colin G. Calloway, *The American Revolution in Indian Country, Crisis and Diversity in Native American Communities* (Cambridge: Cambridge University Press, 1995), 146–47.
10. Henry Watson Powell to Haldimand, Niagara, October 20, 1781, HP, AddMss21765. Lieutenant-Colonel William A. Smy, tr. and ed. "The Butler Papers: Documents and Papers Relating to Colonel John Butler and his Corps of Rangers 1711–1977" [hereafter *Smy Transcripts*] (u.p., 1994); Lieutenant-Colonel William A. Smy, *An Annotated Nominal Roll of Butler's Rangers 1777–1784 with Documentary Sources* [hereafter *Annotated Roll*] (St. Catharines, ON: Friends of the Loyalist Collection at Brock University, 2004), 183; Wilkinson's memorial dated October 20, 1781, requesting a captaincy is found in LAC, HP, AddMss21876, 20; **DePeyster**: After the war, he retired to Dumfries, Scotland, and assisted in raising a company of Gentlemen Volunteers during the French Revolution in the process befriending fellow poet, Robert Burns, whose final poem was written to his friend, DePeyster.
11. *Public Papers of George Clinton, First Governor of New York, 1777–1795, 1801–1804* [hereafter *PPGC*] Vol. 7 (9 vols.) (New York and Albany: State of New York, 1902), 434; Marinus Willett to George Clinton, Fort Rensselaer, October 22, 1781, *ibid.*, 434–35; Clinton to Willett, Poughkeepsie, October 29, 1781, *ibid.*, 457–58; Clinton's speech to State Assembly, October 23, 1781, *ibid.*, Vol. 8, 162–63.
12. Haldimand to Germain (No.97), Quebec City, October 22, 1781, LAC, HP, AddMss21715, 21–23,35; Haldimand to Germain (Secret), Quebec City, October 23, 1781, *ibid.*, 35–36; Haldimand to Germain (most private), Quebec City, October 23, 1781, *ibid.*, 36–40 and CO42/42, 38–39; Haldimand to Germain (No. 102), Quebec City, October 23, 1781, *ibid.*, 101–02; Haldimand to Germain (No.59), Quebec City, October 23, 1781, LAC, CO42/40, 123–25.
13. Jeptha R. Simms, *History of Schoharie County, and Border Wars of New York; Containing also a Sketch of the Causes Which Led to the American Revolution; etc. ...* [hereafter *Schoharie*] (Albany: Munsell & Tanner, 1845), 467–68, and Jeptha R. Simms, *Frontiersman of New York Showing Customs of the Indians, Vicissitudes of the Pioneer White Settlers and Border Strife in Two Wars with a Great Variety of Romantic and Thrilling Stories Never Before Published* [hereafter *FNY*], Vol. 2 (2 vols.) (Albany: Geo. C. Riggs, 1883), 523–25.
14. **Crysler Raid**: Simms, *Schoharie*, 481–86, and Simms, *FNY*, Vol. 2, 739–40. Simms erroneously named Brant as the war captain. He also claimed Isaac was Peter's father, but the sire had died a decade earlier according to Jeff O'Connor's research. Also, "The Journal of Adam Crysler" in *Loyalist Narratives From Upper Canada*, James J. Talman, ed. [hereafter *Talman*] (Toronto: The Champlain Society, 1946), 59–60; **Militiaman**: Pension Application [hereafter "PA"] R730 of John Bellinger; **Date of Raid**: Crysler claimed November 28, 1781, yet John Sacket of Hale's Company, was killed on November 10, 1781, according to Willett and PA W25748, widow of Joseph Hager, which stated that he was wounded in the head on November 10, 1781.

See also, PA S12193 of Barent Becker and pension deposition of David Freemoyer, "The Indian Frontier," in *The Revolution Remembered, Eyewitness Accounts of the War for Independence* [hereafter *Freemoyer*], John C. Dann (Chicago: The University of Chicago Press, 1980), 302; **Double-Barreled Rifle**: PA W16971, widow of Major Cornelius Eckerson, 15th Albany County Militia [hereafter 15ACM]; **Hale**: He had served in four major battles as a lieutenant. Later, he had been a captain in the Connecticut Continental Line and was recommended by Colonel Van Ness, 9ACM, to command a company of Levies. Jeff O'Connor's research and Clinton to Van Ness, July 18, 1781, *PPGC*, Vol. 7, 92, 96. The governor wrote to Van Ness about Hale, who, in addition to serving in the Connecticut Line, had been a 3rd New York [hereafter 3NY] company commander on the Sullivan Expedition. Clinton explained that Willett and Lush were responsible for collecting the names and ranks of supernumerary Levies officers and other gentlemen with prior service who wanted an appointment in the new levies. Without this list he could not say whether Hale might be appointed for fear of disappointing someone with seniority. That said, Hale could have a lieutenancy and, if it later appeared that he was entitled to a company, justice would be served. He then wrote to Lush, "[I]t will answer to give Mr. Hale a company, as he is an Old Officer well recommended and appears to be a decent man."

15. **Proposals**: LAC, HP, MG13, WO28/5, (No.53), 171–74,182, and LAC, HP, MG21, B166, 184–88.

16. **Peters's Complaints**: Mary Beacock Fryer, *King's Men, the Soldier Founders of Ontario* (Toronto: Dundurn Press, 1980), 228; **Jessup's Son**: Peters must have been referring to Edward Jessup Jr., who, on the 1783 final role of officers, was credited with six-and-a-half years' service. See J.F. Pringle, *Lunenburgh or the Old Eastern District* (Belleville: Mika Silk Screening Limited, 1972), 361–62, and William D. Reid, *The Loyalists in Ontario, The Sons and Daughters of the American Loyalists of Upper Canada* (1973; reprint, Genealogical Publishing Co., 1973), 163. These sources advise that Edward Jr. was born in 1766. So, he was fifteen in 1781 and eight and a half when he started his six-and-a-half years' service. Peters's complaint was justified; **Zadock Wright**: John Nairne to Robert Mathews, October 24, 1781. LAC, HP, AddMss21821, 340.

17. Wasmus, 249.

18. Haldimand to Arent DePeyster, Quebec City, November 1, 1781. *Smy Transcripts*, Found in HP, AddMss21781.

19. Mathews to John Butler, Quebec City, November 1, 1781, *ibid.*; While the governor emphasized that Butler's Rangers lacked officers who had been "brought up in the army," it is not difficult to understand the frustration of twenty-eight-year-old Walter, as he may have been aware that Francis Lord Rawdon had been appointed lieutenant-colonel of the Volunteers of Ireland at age twenty-four and Banastre Tarleton had been appointed lieutenant-colonel of the British Legion at age twenty-seven, and John Graves Simcoe had been appointed major-commandant of the Queen's Rangers at age twenty-five.

20. Mathews to Powell, Quebec City, November 1, 1781, *ibid.* Found in HP, AddMss21764; Mathews to Butler, Quebec City, November 2, 1781, *ibid.* Found in HP, AddMss21765.
21. **Ox/12-pdr**: PA W12099, widow of Peter Flagg. J.F. Morrison research; Marinus Willett, "Col Marinus Willett's Letter and Orderly Book, Fort Rensselaer 1781," [hereafter *Willett OB*] Charles Gehring, tr. Document No.15705, New York State Library, Albany, Archives and Manuscripts, 34–35.
22. Haldimand to Stuart, Quebec City, November 3, 1781, LAC, HP, B159, 165; **Protestant**: This was interesting terminology on Stuart's part, as Anglicans consider themselves Catholic, not Protestant, although not Roman.
23. Gray to Richard Lernoult, Montreal, November 4, 1781, LAC, HP, MG13, WO28/5, No.24, 78; **Richard Berringer Lernoult**: Born in England, 1732. Ranked as captain, July 15, 1767. Acting commandant of Niagara after the death of Colonel Caldwell in 1777 and breveted major on November 10, 1782. Appointed major, 8th Regiment, September 13, 1783. John A. Houlding, "The King's Service: The Officers of the British Army, 1735–1792" (u.p., n.d.).
24. Surgeon Austin's report, November 5, 1781, LAC, HP, B158, 243; inquiry into Thompson's beating, n.d., *ibid.*, 244.
25. **Yamaska**: Riedesel to Haldimand, November 5, 1781. LAC, HP, AddMss21796.
26. Haldimand to Powell, Quebec City, November 5, 1781. *Smy Transcripts, HP*, AddMss21764 and Butler to Lernoult, Niagara, November 4, 1781, *ibid.* Found in WO28/4.
27. John Ross to Haldimand, Oswego, November 6, 1781, LAC, HP, MG21, B124, 32–33; **Secord**: Solomon was recommended as a second lieutenant, which was at first refused and then granted prior to disbandment. Smy, *Annotated Roll*, 163.
28. Smyth to Mathews, November 7, 1781. Hazel C. Mathews, *Frontier Spies* [hereafter *Spies*] (Fort Myers: self-published, 1971), 81. Found in HP, B176, 331.
29. **German Rreorganization**: Wilhelmy, 183–84, and Eelking, *Memoirs*, Vol. 2, 109–10, 119, and Eelking, *Allied Troops*, 248; Haldimand to Germain, No.94, Quebec City, October 20, 1781. CO42/42, 20–21; **von Barner's Given Name**: Claus Reuter, *History of the Brunswick Light Infantry Battalion "von Barner" in North America from 1776 to 1783* (Toronto: self-published, n.d.).
30. John Stark to William Heath, Saratoga, November 6, 1781. *Memoir and Official Correspondence of Gen. John Stark, with Notices of Several Other Officers of the Revolution*, Caleb Stark, tr. and ed. (Concord, MA: G. Parker Lyon, 1860), 289–90.
31. Clinton to Willett, Poughkeepsie, November 8, 1781. *PPGC*, Vol. 7, 493–94.
32. Heath's General Orders, Continental Village, November 9, 1781, Stark, 290–91.
33. Mathews to Jacob Maurer, Quebec City, November 11, 1781, *Smy Transcripts, HP*, AddMss21721.
34. William Morison to Gray, Point Clair, November 11, 1781, LAC, HP, B158, 246.
35. Gilbert Tice to Guy Johnson, Niagara, November 15, 1781, transcribed in Ernest Green, "Gilbert Tice, U.E." *Ontario Historical Society's Papers and Records, Vol. 21*

(1924): 186–97.

36. **Officer Appointments**: General Orders, Quebec City, November 12, 1781. "The Orderly Book of the King's Loyal Americans and the Loyal Rangers," dated from September 4, 1780 to October 23, 1783, "Edward Jessup Papers" [hereafter *Jessup OB*], Archives of Ontario, Ms521(1). In order of seniority, the four lieutenants from Leake's were, William McKay, Henry Young, William Fraser, and John Howard.

37. Gray to Mathews, Montreal, November 12, 1781, LAC, HP, B158, 248.

38. Riedesel to Haldimand, Sorel, November 12, 1781. Correspondence of General Riedesel, *State Library of Virginia, Richmond*, The Lidgerwood Collection, HZ-1(2), [hereafter *Riedesel Correspondence*] Lewis Biegigheiser, tr.; Eelking, *Memoirs*, Vol. 2, 115. Von Eelking noted that Riedesel maintained a regular correspondence with Cornwallis during the fighting in the south due to his concerns over the fate of the Convention Army.

39. **Prisoners**: LAC, HP, AddMss21789, 276.

40. Powell to Haldimand, Niagara, November 13, 1781. *Smy Transcripts*, HP, AddMss21761; Robert Kerr to John Campbell, Carleton Island, November 14, 1781, LAC, HP, AddMss21772, 112. Kerr's submission was very odd, as the treatments he listed occurred from May 30 to August 26, 1781, and were unrelated to Ross's expedition.

41. Haldimand to Riedesel, November 15, 1781, *Riedesel Correspondence*.

42. Two letters from Haldimand to Powell and one Haldimand to Ross, Quebec City, November 16, 1781, *Smy Transcripts*, HP, AddMss21764. This is the only instance I have found where a comparative rating of Indian Department and Provincial officers' ranks was so clearly stated.

43. **Girty Wound**: DePeyster to Alexander McKee, November 11, 1781, Kelsay, 315, 321; Phillip W. Hoffman, *Simon Girty, Turncoat Hero, The Most Hated Man on the Early American Frontier* (Franklin, TN: American History Imprints, 2008). There is no evidence of Girty wounding Brant in Hoffman's biography. However, that Brant grievously wounded Simon Girty in August 1781 is dealt with in detail.

44. Journal entry of November 12, 1781,Wasmus, 252–53.

45. **300 Stand of Arms**: Mathews to Ross, Quebec City, November 16, 1781, LAC, HP, AddMss21788, 110, and Ross to Haldimand, Carleton Island, March 6, 1782, LAC, HP, B127. Ross was "sorry that Indian fusils are the only arms; it is a great diminution of our strength"; Ross to Mathews, November 22, 1781, *Smy Transcripts*, HP, AddMss21784.

46. Heath to Clinton, Continental Village, November 13, 1781, and Clinton to Heath, Poughkeepsie, November 15, 1781, *PPGC*, Vol. 7, 502–03; Heath to Stark, Continental Village, November 14, 1781, Stark, 292.

47. Willett to Clinton, Fort Rensselaer, November 16, 1781, *PPGC*, Vol. 7, 504–05.

48. Chittenden to Denker/Dencker, Arlington, November 20, 1781, *ibid.*, 512; Clinton to New York's delegates, November 23, 1781. *ibid.*, 515.

49. Haldimand to Charles Jenkinson, secretary at war, Quebec City, November 20,

1781, *Smy Transcripts, HP*, AddMss21720; Haldimand to Riedesel, November 20, 1781, *Riedesel Correspondence*; Haldimand to Germain, Quebec City, November 23, 1781, LAC, HP, AddMss21715, 55–59.

50. Journal entries of November 23, 24, and December 22, 1782, Wasmus, 253, 254 respectively; Eelking, *Memoirs*, Vol. 2, 119.

CHAPTER TWO — INVASION FEARS AROUSED

1. Haldimand to Germain, (Most Secret) Quebec City, November 23, 1781. *HSGS*, Vol. 3, 215–16 from Q19, 268–74.

2 General Orders, HQ Quebec City, November 25, 1781. *Jessup OB*; **Five Nations**: Originally, five nations comprised the Iroquois Confederacy or League and the grouping was frequently referred to as such long after the Tuscaroras joined as non-voting members in 1732.

3. Haldimand to Germain, (most private) HQ Quebec City, November 26, 1781. LAC, HP, AddMss21715, 72–74.

4. Ross to Mathews, Carleton Island, November 27, 1781. LAC, HP, B127; Natives had a thorough understanding of the medicinal and nutritional value of many plants. For an account of a young woman captured by the Indians in 1779, who returned to European society after the war and used her knowledge of native foods and medicines to feed and doctor settlers in the St. Lawrence "Royal" Townships during the difficult early days, see Elizabeth L. Hoople, *Medicine Maid — The Life Story of a Canadian Pioneer* (Belleville: Mika Publishing Company, 1977); Naturally-harvested ginseng continued to be a substantial export crop after the Revolutionary War.

5. **Pensioners' Company**: *Jessup OB*.

6. Daniel Claus to Mathews, Montreal, November 29, 1781, LAC, HP, AddMss21774, 208.

7. **Germain/North**: Piers Mackesy, *The War for America 1775–1783* (Lincoln, NE: University of Nebraska Press, 1992), 434–35.

8. Clinton to Heath, Poughkeepsie, November 27, 1781, *PPGC*, Vol. 7, 526–27; Washington to Heath, Philadelphia, November 28, 1781, in *The Writings of George Washington from the Original Manuscript Sources, 1745–1799* [hereafter *Washington Writings*], John C. Fizpatrick, ed., Vol. 23 (39 vols.) (Washington, D.C.: United States Government Printing Office, 1937), 362–63; Stark to Heath, Saratoga, November 29, 1781, Stark, 293–94; Heath to Clinton, November 30, 1781, *PPGC*, Vol. 7, 529–31; Clinton to Peter Gansevoort and Robert Van Rensselaer, Poughkeepsie, December 3, 1781, *ibid.*, 537–39; Clinton to Heath, December 4, 1781, *ibid.*, 541–42.

9. Robert Leake to Mathews and Gray to Mathews, November 29, 1781, LAC, HP, B158, 249; Leake ended the war as 2KRR's major and Gumersall as the senior captain.

10. Butler to Mathews, Niagara December 1, 1781, *Smy Transcripts*, HP, AddMss21765.

11. Gray to de Speth, Montreal December 3, 1781, LAC, HP, MG13, WO28/5, No.24, 79; Ross to Haldimand, December 7, 1781, LAC, HP, AddMss21787, 291; Mathews to Gray, Quebec City, December 3, 1781, LAC, HP, B159, 166.

12. Twiss to Haldimand, December 3, 1781, in "Blockhouses in Canada, 1749–1841: A Comparative Report and Catalogue" [hereafter *Blockhouses*], *Canadian Historic Sites: Occasional Papers in Archaeology and History* by Richard J. Young, (Ottawa: Parks Canada, 1980), 90. Found in LAC, HP, G1, B154, 302–03; **Twiss**: Born in England, 1745. A practitioner engineer, November 19, 1763; a subaltern engineer, April 1, 1771; An engineer extraordinary and brevet captain, December 12, 1778. A captain, March 23, 1786; a brevet major, March 1, 1794; a lieutenant-colonel, June 1, 1794; a brevet colonel, January 1, 1800; a colonel, April 18, 1801; a major-general October 30, 1805; colonel-commandant, June 24, 1809; a lieutenant-general, January 1, 1812; and a general, May 27, 1825. Twiss died on March 14, 1827. Houlding, *King's Service*; *The Dictionary of Canadian Biography* [hereafter *DCB*], Vol. 6 (1821–1835) offers these details. Thirty-one-year-old Twiss landed in Quebec in early June 1776 and became aide-de-camp to Colonel William Phillips. Governor Carleton appointed Twiss the controller of works for the building of the fleet on Lake Champlain, which defeated a rebel fleet in the battle of Valcour Island. Under Burgoyne in 1777, Twiss was instrumental in the capture of Ticonderoga. After the surrender, Twiss was exchanged to Canada where he was promoted to captain (local) and was given responsibility for all posts in Canada except the fortress of Quebec. In 1781, he was appointed chief engineer in Canada and became responsible for all works. Riedesel was particularly impressed with Twiss's capabilities. He had "solved questions which seemed impossible." He had a hand in developing the naval yards on Carleton Island, the building of Fort Haldimand, the locks and canals at Coteau-du-Lac and hospitals, windmills, storehouses, barracks, fortifications, roads, bridges, prisons, dams, etc. at Quebec, Sorel, Isle aux Noix, St. John's, and Montreal.

13. John Van Rensselaer to Gansevoort, Sancoick, December 4, 1781, and Gansevoort to Henry Van Rensselaer and Robert Yates, Albany, December 5, 1781, *PPGC*, Vol. 7, 553–55; **Rouse Affidavit**: *ibid.*, 609–10.

14. Heath to Stark, December 5, 1781, Stark, 295–96.

15. Clinton to John McKinstry, Poughkeepsie ,December 5, 1781, *PPGC*, Vol. 7, 551–52.

16. Gansevoort to Clinton, Albany, December 6, 1781, *ibid.*, 552–53; Solomon Pendleton to Clinton, Albany, December 7, 1781, *ibid.*, 557–59; **Pendleton**: see James Sullivan and Alexander C. Flick, eds., *Minutes of the Albany Committee of Correspondence, 1775–1778*, Vol. 2 (2 vols.) (Albany: State University of New York, 1923 and 1925), 1032, 1048, 1052, 1059–60. See also, Willis T. Hanson, *A History of Schenectady During the Revolution to which is appended a Contribution to the Individual Records of the Inhabitants of the Schenectady District During that Period* (self-published, 1916), 200–01.

17. Job Wright to Clinton, Ballstown, December 8, 1781, *PPGC*, Vol. 7, 568–69.

18. Clinton to Willett, Poughkeepsie, December 9, 1781, *ibid.*, 569–71.

19. Stark to Robert Yates, Saratoga, December 8, 1781, *ibid.*, 569.

20. Clinton to Robert Yates, Poughkeepsie, December 11, 1781, *ibid.*, 572–73; Clinton

to Robert Van Rensselaer and Gansevoort, Poughkeepsie, December 11, 1781, *ibid.*, 573–74.

21. McIlwraith, 228–31.

22. Mathews to Leake, Quebec City, December 10, 1781, LAC, HP, B159, 169. One would expect that the rank of full captain was senior to captain-lieutenant, but there must have been some complication with command of an independent company versus line command; *Jessup OB*.

23. General Orders, HQ, Quebec City, December 11, 1781, *Smy Transcripts*, HP, AddMss21743; **Godefroy de Tonnancoer (Godefroi de Tonnancourt) Family**: Gustave Lanctot, *Canada & the American Revolution, 1774–1783*, Margaret M. Cameron, trans. (London: George G. Harrap & Co. Ltd, 1967), 69, 81, 147, 153, 172, 177, 198; **Tonnancoer's 1777 Service**: MG21/WO28/10, Part 1.

24. Stark to Heath, Saratoga, December 12, 1781, Stark, 297–98; **Abbot/Abbet**: Abbet is shown as a captain on a 14ACM master roll. *New York in the Revolution as Colony and State*, [hereafter *NY in Rev War*] Vol. 1 (2 vols.) (Albany: State of New York, 1904), 125; Heath to Stark, December 12, 1781, Stark, 299–300; Yates to Gansevoort, Sancoick, December 12, 1781, and Phelps Affidavit, December 12, 1781, Cambridge, *PPGC*, Vol. 7, 575–76, 579–80; Clinton to Heath, Poughkeepsie, December 12, 1781, *ibid.*, 577–79.

25. Moodie to Clinton, West Point, December 12, 1781, *ibid.*, 580–81; Robert Benson to Henry K. Van Alstyne, Poughkeepsie, December 15, 1781, *ibid.*, 582–83; Stark to Yates, Saratoga December 14, 1781, Stark, 300–01; Stark to Weare, Saratoga, December 14, 1781. *ibid.*, 301–02; Chittenden to Stark, Arlington, December 15, 1781. *ibid.*, 302; Abbott to H.K. Van Rensselaer, December 16, 1781. *PPGC*, Vol. 7, 585.

26. Willett to Governor Clinton, Albany, December 16, 1781, *ibid.*, 587–90; Willett to Clinton, Albany, December 17, 1781, *ibid.*, 596–97.

27. Handbill, Schaghticoke, December 15, 1781, and two notes from Walbridge to H. Van Rensselaer, Mapletown, December 17, 1781, *ibid.*, 591–92; Gansevoort to the officer commanding the Vermont troops, Schaghticoke, December 18, 1781, *ibid.*, 602; **Ebenezer Walbridge**: Born in Norwich, Connecticut, in 1783, and moved to Bennington in 1765. He was an officer in Warner's Green Mountain Boys in 1775 and served as a regimental adjutant during Arnold's expedition to Quebec in 1776. In 1777, he fought in the battle of Bennington. He was one of the few, beyond the original eight conspirators, who were privy to the negotiations with Haldimand. In 1778, he was a lieutenant-colonel of the Bennington militia regiment, replacing Samuel Herrick. In 1782, he commanded Vermont's troops who opposed Gansevoort's brigade in the Sancoick confrontation. He was promoted to brigadier in 1782.

28. Willett to Clinton, Albany, December 18, 1781. *ibid.*, 600–02.

29. **Loyal Rangers**: *Jessup OB*; Stuart to Haldimand, Montreal, December 17, 1781, LAC, HP, B158, 257; **Lonas Lovelace**: *Jessup OB*; **Sutherland**: LAC, HP, B158, 274.

30. Heath to Clinton, HQ, Highlands Department, December 19, 1781, *PPGC*, Vol. 7, 604–05.

31. Judges R. Morris and R. Yates to Clinton, Albany, December 20, 1781, including two affidavits, *ibid.*, 606–07; **Jonas Fay**: Born in Hardwick, MA, 1737. Educated as a physician. Served as a Massachusetts Provincial at Fort Edward in 1756 and moved to Bennington in 1766. Became prominent in the NH Grants and acted as a Grants agent to Governor Tryon in 1772. Was a clerk of the convention of March 1774, which resolved to defend Ethan Allen and others who had been outlawed by New York Province. Fay was a surgeon under Ethan at Ticonderoga in 1775 and then in Warner's Regiment. He was a member of the convention that declared Vermont an independent republic in 1777, assisted to draw up Vermont's constitution, a member of the Council of Safety, and a member of the State Council from 1778 to 1785. He was very involved in the Vermont negotiations with Haldimand's administration.

32. Stark to Washington, Albany, December 21, 1781, Stark, 303–05.

33. Gansevoort to Clinton, December 21, 1781, *PPGC*, Vol. 7, 617–19; Clinton to New York delegates, December 24, 1781, *ibid.*, 623–24.

34. Robert Van Rensselaer and Gansevoort to Clinton, Albany, December 21, 1781, *ibid.*, 619–20.

35. Stark to Heath, December 22, 1781, Stark, 305–06; **Reid**: Edward L. Parker, *The History of Londonderry, comprising the towns of Derry and Londonderry, N.H.* (Boston, 1851), 231 and the State of New Hampshire, Part 1, *Rolls and Documents relating to Soldiers in the Revolutionary War*, Isaac W. Hammand, ed. (Manchester, NH: State of New Hampshire, 1889); Reid to Stark, Stark, 306.

36. Indian Council, Niagara. HP, AddMss21779, 406.

37. Mathews to Campbell, December 21, 1781, LAC, HP, AddMss21773, 158.

38. **Prison Island:** Twiss to Haldimand, December 3, 1781, *Blockhouses*, 90, from LAC, HP, G1, B154, 302–03; **Yamaska:** *ibid.*, 32,100. Twiss to Haldimand, December 22, 1781, LAC, HP, G1, B154, 365.

39. Powell to Haldimand, Niagara, December, 1781, *Smy Transcripts*, HP, AddMss21761; **Wemple:** Smy, *Annotated Roll*, 195. Smy shows his rank as second lieutenant. Wemple died on July 27, 1782; **Silas Secord**: As Solomon Secord had been recognized for his service under Ross in 1781, one could suspect that Silas was being confused for Solomon, however, Smy reports that Silas had been recommended for his service with Sir John Johnson [hereafter SJJ] in October 1780.

40. William Fraser to Riedesel, Yamaska, December 25, 1781, LAC, HP, MG21, B136, f.255; William Fraser to Riedesel, Yamaska, December 29, 1781, *Riedesel Correspondence, HZ-1.*

41. Mathews to Justus Sherwood, Quebec, December 27, 1781, Mary Beacock Fryer, *Buckskin Pimpernel, the Exploits of Justus Sherwood Loyalist Spy* [hereafter *Pimpernel*] (Toronto: Dundurn Press, 1981), 159; Haldimand to de Speth, Quebec, December 27, 1781, LAC, HP, AddMss21791, 144.

42. Heath to Stark, HQ, December 25, 1781. Stark, 307.

CHAPTER THREE — TO TAKE POST AT OSWEGO

1. **Putnam's Company:** PA S13497 of Samuel Hubbs. Transcribed in Ken D. Johnson, Fort Plank Historian, *The Bloodied Mohawk, The American Revolution in the Words of Fort Plank's Defenders and Other Mohawk Valley Partisans* (Rockport, MA: Picton Press, 2000), 444–45; PA S13013 of William Feeter; PA S19272 of John M. Dake, *ibid.*, 356.

2. Washington to Chittenden, January 1, 1782, *Washington Papers, Library of Congress, 1741–1799: Series 3C Varick Transcripts*, ff.267–70.

3. Chilton Williamson, *Vermont in Quandary 1763–1825* (Montpelier: Vermont Historical Society, 1949), 113; Thomas Johnson to Washington, April 30, 1782, Frederic P. Wells, *History of Newbury, Vermont, From the Discovery of the Coös Country to Present Time* (St. Johnsbury, VT: The Caledonian Company, 1902), 399.

4. Charles H. Lesser, ed. *The Sinews of Independence: Monthly Strength Report of the Continental Army* (Chicago: The University of Chicago Press, 1976), 212.

5. Germain to Haldimand, London, January 2, 1782, LAC, HP, CO42/42, f.1–26.

6. Ten Broeck court martial, January 1782, *Smy Transcripts*, AddMss21743.

7. Edward Jessup to Mathews, Verchère, January 2, 1782, LAC, HP, AddMss21821, 362.

8. E.J. Devine (S.J.), *Historic Caughnawaga* (Montreal: Messenger Press, 1922), 296–97, 302fn, 303; **Oratoskon:** written as Oghradonshon by Claus; **Claus Report:** Ernest A. Cruikshank, "The Coming of the Loyalist Mohawks to the Bay of Quinte," *OHSPR, 26* (1930): 396 from LAC, HP, B114, 224–25.

9. Diary entries for January 6, 7, and 18, 1782, Wasmus, 259.

10. Johann August von Loos to Riedesel, Quebec City, January 7, 1782, Eelking, *Memoirs*, Vol. 2, 220–21; Despite von Loos's obvious troubles with Haldimand, Eelking noted, "The German officers, Papet and others, spoke highly of Haldimand in their letters home," Eelking, *Allied Troops*, 247, and despite Haldimand's lack of faith in von Loos, Eelking maintained that the brigadier gained the affection of both German and English soldiers, *ibid.*, 250.

11. Walter Sutherland to Patrick Langan, Mill Bay, January 7, 1782, *Hugh McMillan Collection*, researched and transcribed by Heather Devine and Barbara Rogers, [hereafter *Sutherland Papers*] LAC, HP, B114, 215–6; Ernest A. Cruikshank, "The Adventures of Roger Stevens, A Forgotten Loyalist Pioneer in Upper Canada," *OHSPR* 33 (1939); Claus to Mathews, Montreal January 14, 1782, *Sutherland Papers*, LAC, HP, B114, 218–21; **Miller:** Most likely Jonathon Miller, KR, who at times served in the Secret Service. He was returned in the Major's Company, KR, at St. John's on January 27, 1784, H.M. Jackson, *Rogers' Rangers: A History* (Toronto: self-published, 1953), from LAC, HP, B160, 153–56; **Ailsworth:** Perhaps this was Francis Ailsworth, who was with a woman at Niagara in 1785 and had taken an oath of allegiance.

12. LeMaistre, Deputy Adjutant General, General Orders, Quebec City, January 7, 1782, *Jessup OB*; Christian Wehr to Mathews, Montreal, January 7, 1782, LAC, HP, B158, 265.

13. Leake to Mathews, January 10, 1782, *ibid.*, 266.

14. January 11, 12, and February 1, 1782, *Jessup OB* and Mathews to Edward Jessup, January 12, 1782, LAC, HP, AddMss21823, 75.

15. William Fraser to Riedesel, Yamaska Blockhouse, January 13 and 25, 1782, *Riedesel Correspondence HZ-1*.

16. Claus to Mathews, Montreal January 14, 1782, *Sutherland Papers*, LAC, HP, B114, 218–21; **Claus's Men:** This phrase suggests that soldiers from 1KRR had been attached to Claus to act as Indian Department rangers; Mathews to Claus, Quebec January 14, 1782, *ibid.*, 221.

17. **Trial results:** Report of J. Burke, Clerk of the Peace, enclosed in Gray to Mathews, January 24, 1782, LAC, HP, B158, 268; **Thompson's Earlier Imprisonment:** H.C. Burleigh, *Deforests of Avesnes and Kast, McGinness* (self-published, n.d.), 6.

18. Gray to Mathews, Montreal, January 24, 1782, LAC, HP, B158, 268.

19. Tench Tilghman to Heath, Philadelphia, January 8, 1782, *Washington Writings, Vol. 23*, 433–34.

20. Chittenden to Washington, Arlington, January 15, 1782, *Washington Papers, Series 4*.

21. *Orderly Book of Capt. Moses Dusten 2nd New Hampshire Regiment — December 15, 1781–July 24, 1783* [hereafter *Dusten OB*], New York State Library, Department of History and Archives, Albany, NY. Mss11391, V.2. Schenectady, January 19, 20, 23, 24, 1782. Merrow was also spelled Muroin, Murroin.

22. **Oswegatchie Return:** WO28/6, 106.

23. Ross's State of Garrison, Carleton Island, February 1, 1782, WO28/6, 107; Powell's State of the Garrison of the different Posts upon the upper Lakes, February 1, 1782, *ibid.*, 108.

24. Diary entry, February 1, 1782, Wasmus, 260.

25. Terence Smyth report, February 6, 1782. Mathews, *Spies*, 62, from LAC, HP, B177, Part 1, 28, and Cruikshank, *Stevens* and Fryer, *Pimpernel*, 166.

26. **Clark Tour:** *Jessup OB*; Von Loos to Riedesel, Quebec City, February 14, 1782. He mentions that Clark had departed on February 11.

27. Edward Jessup to Mathews, Verchère, February 14, 1782, LAC, HP, AddMss21821, 355; **Ranging Suits:** From a survey of the DQMG Stores, I have concluded that these suits were brown jackets, waistcoats, and breeches; **St. Francis Scout:** William Fraser to Freeman, Yamaska Blockhouse, February 14, 1782, and Fraser to Riedesel, February 15, 1782, *Riedesel Correspondence HZ-1*.

28. William Parker to Haldimand, February 16, 1782, LAC, HP, AddMss21874, 241.

29. Von Loos to Riedesel, St. Agnace, February 17, 1782, Eelking, *Memoirs*, Vol. 2, 222–23.

30. Cruikshank, *Stevens*; **Abel Stevens:** Mathews, *Spies*, 95–96, from Sherwood to Mathews, January 30, 1782, LAC, HP, B177-1, 23; Fryer, *King's Men*, 288; Ernest A. Cruikshank and Gavin K. Watt, *The History and Master Roll of The King's Royal Regiment of New York* [hereafter *KRR NY*] (1984; reprint, Campbellville: Global Heritage Press, 2006), 85.

31. **Schuyler's Warning:** *Smy Transcripts*, From LAC, MG11, Q14; **Brehm's Report:** Dietrick/Didrick Brehm to Haldimand, Niagara, May 8, 1779, K.D. Johnson research. HP, AddMss21759, 36. Brehm, a Swiss artillery bombardier in 1756, had been recruited as a subaltern for the Royal Americans. J.A. Houlding, research.

Brehm was serving as the Canadian Department's Barrack Master General on December 25, 1783; **Native Deputations**: *Ibid.*, LAC, CO42/37, 225; Gilbert Tice to Claus, Carleton Island, February 18, 1780, LAC, Claus Family fonds, MG19, F1, Vol. 2, (26 vols.) [hereafter *Claus Papers*], 173.

32. **Carleton Council**: Paul L. Stevens, "His Majesty's 'Savage' Allies: British Policy and the Northern Indians During the Revolutionary War — The Carleton Years, 1774–1778" (Ph.D. diss., State University of New York at Buffalo, 1984). Apparently from HP, AddMss21779. Stevens transcribed a speech given by the Mohawk Aaron Hill in 1779 that recalled the details; Haldimand to Mason Bolton, Quebec, City April 8, 1779, *Smy Transcripts*, HP, AddMss21764; Tice to Claus, Carleton Island, February 18, 1780, *Claus Papers, Vol. 2*, 173; Germain to Haldimand, May 17, 1780, CO42/40; Haldimand to SJJ, April 27, 1780, LAC, HP, AddMss21819, 97; Mathews's Report, September 21, 1780, *Claus Papers, Vol. 2*, 251.

33. Haldimand to Ross, February 18, 1782, Cruikshank and Watt, *KRR NY*, 85–86; Haldimand to Powell, February 18, 1782, *Smy Transcripts*, HP, AddMss21764.

34. Riedesel to Haldimand, Sorel, January 18, 1782, LAC, HP, B137, 11.

35. Powell to Haldimand, Niagara, February 19, 1782, *ibid.*, HP, AddMss21761.

36. Ross to Haldimand, Carleton Island, February 20, 1782, cited in C.C.J. Bond, "The British Base at Carleton Island" *OHSPR* 52 (1960) from LAC, HP, B127, 296.

37. Sir Henry Clinton to Haldimand, New York City, February 22, 1782, *HSGS*, Vol. 3, 217–18, from LAC, HP, B48, 98–99.

38. Mathews to Gray, Quebec City, February 23, 1782, LAC, HP, B159, 176.

39. "Narration of Hesse–Hanau Jäger Corps in America," [hereafter *Kreutzbourg Narration*] John C. Zuleger, tr. Hessian Papers (Morristown, NJ: Morristown National Historic Park), 130.

40. An order of February 24, 1782, La Prairie. "Orders of the Field Jaeger Corps from May 7, 1777 to April 30, 1783," Virginia Rimaldy, tr. (u.p., n.d., 182).

41. Andrew Finck to Clinton, Stone Arabia, February 20, 1782; John Zeillie was delivered to the Commissary of Prisoners in New York City on October 9, 1782. John, Henry, and William Shultes were exchanged from Quebec City in October 1782. Philip Bellinger appears on the Quebec lists of prisoners, but I have found no record of his exchange. His two boys were likely held in Niagara or by the Indians. Chris McHenry, compiler, *Rebel Prisoners at Quebec 1778–1783* (self-published, 1981), 41, 55, 60.

42. **Dissolution of Unions**: Williamson, 113; **Tichenor**: A member of Vermont's house of representatives, 1781–1784. Vermont's agent to Congress in 1782. A state councillor, 1787–1792. A commissioner for the arrangement of the territorial dispute with New York in 1791, *www.famousamericans.net/isaactichenor* (accessed January 16, 2009).

43. **Clothing**: *Dusten OB.*

44. Sutherland to Langan, Loyal Blockhouse, February 24, 1782, LAC, HP, B112, 118–19; Sutherland to Langan, Loyal Blockhouse, February 25, 1782, and Stevens's report. LAC, HP, AddMss21837-1, 81, 85.

45. Riedesel to Haldimand, Sorel, February 25, 1782, LAC, HP, B137, 16; **Rochambeau**: General Jean-Baptiste Donatien de Vimeur Comte de Rochambeau, C-in-C of the French army in America.
46. Entry of February 26, 1782, *Jessup OB*.
47. Cruikshank, *Stevens*; Sherwood to Mathews, Loyal Blockhouse, February 24, 1782. From LAC, HP, AddMss21837-1, 79.
48. Haldimand to Riedesel, March 1, 1782. *Riedesel Correspondence HZ-1(2)* and *Sutherland Papers* from LAC, HP, B137, 32–33.
49. Sherwood report, February 28, 1782, LAC, HP, B177, Part 1, 85.
50. Diary entry of March 1, 1782, Wasmus, 260.
51. Haldimand to Ross, March 2, 1782, Cruikshank and Watt, *KRR NY*, 86–87.
52. Two letters from Riedesel to Haldimand, Sorel, March 4, 1782, LAC, HP, B137, 21, 25; Eelking, *Memoirs*, Vol. 2, 121–22; **Fire Details**: Baroness Riedesel, 163–64. The baroness erroneously reported the fire in November; **Ages**: Glenn A. Steppler, "Regimental Records in the Late Eighteenth Century and the Social History of the British Soldier," *Archivaria* 26 (Summer 1988): 14–15. Steppler makes the point that the British regiments that had been in America for six years or longer were starved for recruits and the men had simply grown old in the service. This, of course, was true for the German regiments, as well. However, 28 percent of the 590 other ranks of 1KRR, who had been recruited in America, were over forty (although 95 percent of fifty-eight Grenadiers were under forty). Cruikshank and Watt, *KRR NY*, 164, from LAC, WO28/10, part 4, 489.
53. Haldimand to Sir Henry Clinton, March 5, 1782, *HSGS*, Vol. 3, 218, from LAC, HP, B148, 16–19.
54. William Fraser to Riedesel, Yamaska Blockhouse, two letters of March 7, 1782, *Riedesel Correspondence. HZ-1*.
55. Riedesel to Haldimand, Sorel, March 7, 1782, LAC, HP, B137, 29.
56. Riedesel to Haldimand, Sorel, March 9, 1782, *Sutherland Papers* from LAC, HP, B137, 32–33.
57. **Ellice's Mill**: LAC, HP, AddMss21780.
58. **Rebel Scouting Parties**: H.M. Jackson, *Justus Sherwood: Soldier, Loyalist and Negotiator* (Toronto: self-published, 1958), 40.
59. Luc Schmidt to Riedesel, St. Francis, February and March, 1782, *Riedesel Correspondence, HZ1–4*; **Vassal de Monviel**: Ensign François-Xavier Vassal de Monviel had served under Captaine Hertel de Rouville on the St. Leger expedition against Fort Stanwix in 1777. All of de Rouville's officers were kept on strength after the 1777 disaster. In 1796, de Monviel was listed as a lieutenant in the 7th Regiment and was a captain in the Royal Canadian Volunteers from 1797 to 1802, *DCB*, Vol. VII (1836–1850), *www.biographi.ca/*.
60. Gray to Lernoult, March 11, 1782, LAC, HP, MG13, WO28/5, No. 23, 85.
61. William Ellice to Haldimand, Whitehall, March 15, 1782, *Smy Transcripts*, HP, AddMss21705.

62. William Parker report, March 16, 1782, LAC, HP, AddMss21874, 305.
63. Von Loos to Riedesel, La Prairie, March 16, 1782, Eelking, *Memoirs*, Vol. 2, 223.
64. Mackesy, 466–70; Piers Mackesy, "Could the British Have Won the War of Independence?" A transcript of the Bland-Lee Lecture (1975), at Clark University, Worcester, Massachusetts.
65. PA W13941, Elisabeth, widow of Peter Suts; **Sawyer**: McHenry, 66.
66. James Lovell to Washington, Boston, March 11, 1782, cited in Wells, 396.
67. **French and Gros**: PA S11376 of Henry Shaver, Johnson, 182.
68. **Franklin's Propaganda**: Francis Whiting Halsey, *The Old New York Frontier, Its Wars with Indians and Tories, Its Missionary Schools, Pioneers and Land Titles* (New York: Charles Scribner's Sons, 1917), 313–14, and a Dutchess County newspaper article containing a supposed letter from Albany dated March 7, 1782, enclosing Craufurd to Haldimand, Tioga, January 3, 1782. William W. Campbell Jr., *Annals of Tryon County; or the Border Warfare of New York* (Cherry Valley: The Cherry Valley Gazette Print, 1880), 273–77.
69. PA R4920 of Daniel Herrick and PA R4017 of Ray Guile, J.F. Morrison research.
70. **Finck**: John B. Koettertiz, "Andrew Finck, Major in the Revolutionary Wars." An address delivered to The Herkimer County Historical Society, 1897, 11.
71. PA S13013 of William Feeter; Christopher P. Yates to Henry Frey, March 22, 1782, Simms, *Schoharie*, 498; **McFees**: As we shall see later, Alexander was serving in Guy Johnson's Foresters and it appears that the parents were reunited with the children at Niagara or in Lower Canada. See the list — "Return of American Prisoners forwarded from Ticonderoga to their respective States, July 18, 1783 by order of His Excellency General Haldimand"— Alexander, 31; Elloner, 31; Andrew, 7; Barbary, 9, and William, 5. McHenry, 71; PA W19497, widow of Conrad Getman, Johnson, 416.
72. *New York in Revolutionary War*, Vol. 1, 12, [hereafter *NY in Rev War*] and Vol. 2, 199–202; Records for the New York State Comptroller's Office Revolutionary War Accounts and Claims are found in *www.archives.nysed.gov/a/research/fa/A0200.shtml* (accessed January 17, 2009). A preamble states, "In 1781, the continuing lack of funds led to compensation for war service in land rights. Officers and privates were granted bounty rights to unappropriated lands (a "right" being five hundred acres) according to rank. In 1782, each "class" (fifteen- or thirty-five-man subdivision of a Militia regiment) was granted a two-hundred-acre bounty for furnishing one man for service in the Levies (drafts from Militia regiments who could be called on to serve outside the state for the entire term of their service) as required by law. The man enlisted for service in the Levies received a five-hundred-acre bounty right. The two-hundred-acre bounty granted to the class could be assigned to the enlisted man or any other person." This is notably at variance with what was stated in Vol. 2, 199–202, noted above.
73. Tyler was out from March 10 to 17, de Monviel from March 11 to 24, and Tegers from March 15 to 21. Reports were made by Luc Schmid to Riedesel and Riedesel to Haldimand on March 28 and 29, 1782, respectively, LAC, HP, B137, 35, 41, 48, 50, 56.

74. Von Loos to Riedesel, Fort St. John's, March 28, 1782, Eelking, *Memoirs*, Vol. 2, 223; Diary entry for March 30, 1782, Wasmus, 261.

CHAPTER FOUR — NOTHING BUT CURSED HYPOCRISY AND DECEIT

1. Stevens to Sherwood, Onion River Falls, March 17, 1782, Cruikshank, *Stevens*, from LAC, HP, AddMss21837-1, 138, and Mathews, *Spies*, 134.

2. **Land Bounties**: Papers of Lieutenant Pliny Moore, Hugh McLellan, ed., *Captain Job Wright's Company, Colonel Marinus Willett's Levies at Ballston, New-York 1782* (Champlain: Moorsfield Press, 1928), 61 and *NY in the Rev War*, Vol. 2, 199–201; **Newall**: PA S11226 of John Pettit.

3. **John Parker**: Likely a brother of William Parker, 1KRR. His capture is described in Simms, *FNY*, Vol. 2, 586–88.

4. **Bettys's Capture**: Simms, *ibid.*, 589–91, and Mathews, *Spies*, 116–17, and Katherine Q. Briaddy, *Ye Olde Days, A History of Burnt Hills-Ballston Lake* (Ballston Spa, NY: Women's Club, 1974), 32–33, and William L. Stone, *Life of Joseph Brant — Thayendanegea including the Indian Wars of the American Revolution* [hereafter *Brant*] Vol. 2 (2 vols.) (1838; reprint, St. Clair Shores, MI: Scholarly Press, 1970), 212–13. Stone named Corey and Perkins as being involved in Bettys's capture; *NY in Rev War*, Vol. 1, 120–21 shows a Lieutenant John Corey, 12ACM, but no one named Perkins. The only Philmore this source lists in the regiment was Sirus. A Richard Filmore was in Willett's, *ibid.*, 89; PA W1499. Lydia was the widow of Thaddeus Scribner and her deposition named Miller's companion as VanderBogert. Her account of Bettys's capture claims he was taken only after a "desperate struggle"; **Van Camp**: The son could have been Jacob, twenty-five, Tunis, twenty-two, John, eighteen, all in John Jones' Company, LR, or Jacob, thirty-nine, in 1KRR, who was from the Saratoga area; **Gordon**: His given name was given as Kenathy. An Ensign Kenneth Gordon is listed in *Documents Relating to the Colonial History of the State of New York, XV*, State Archives, V.1, Fernow, Berthold, ed., [hereafter *V.XV, SA1*] (Albany, NY: Weed, Parsons and Company, Printers, 1887), 271.

5. Powell to Haldimand, Niagara, March 23, 1782, *Smy Transcripts*, HP, AddMss21762; Indian Department Nominal Roll, Niagara March 24, 1782, *ibid.* and Norman K. Crowder, *Early Ontario Settlers, A Source Book* (Baltimore: Genealogical Publishing Co., Inc., 1993).

6. Riedesel to Haldimand, Sorel, March 26 and 29, 1782, LAC, HP, B137, 48, 60 respectively.

7. Fryer, *Pimpernel*, 163.

8. **Hanging**: Briaddy mentions only Bettys's hanging. No date for Parker's execution has been found and I have presumed that it occurred the same day (Briaddy, 33); **Haldimand's Reaction**: Mathews, *Spies*, 117, and Fryer, *Pimpernel*, 164; **Snetsinger**: Sherwood to Snetsinger, April 30, 1782, LAC, HP, AddMss21837-1, 237.

9. *New York State Library, Special Collections and Manuscripts, Audited Accounts*, Vol. A, 67.

10. **Congress**: Williamson, 116–17; **Abel Stevens**: Roger Stevens's report, April 5, 1782, Cruikshank, *Stevens*, 21–22.

11. Riedesel's order, April 1, 1782, *Jessup OB*; Riedesel to Haldimand, April 1, 1782, LAC, HP, B137, 64.

12. **1KRR**: LAC, HP, MG13, WO28/5, No.23, 89.

13. Gray to Claus, Montreal April 2, 1782, LAC, HP, B158, 270; Sutherland to Mathews, Montreal June 30, 1783, *ibid.*, 306–07. At the time he wrote in 1783, he had been paid no more than £10 Halifax for twenty-four days of various missions for St. Leger, 125 days for Claus, and thirty-nine directly for Haldimand.

14. Diary entries for April 3 and 7, 1782, Wasmus, 261; Von Loos to Riedesel, Quebec City, April 3, 1782, Eelking, 224. This cache of funds was likely the regimental chest; **Holland**: D. Peter MacLeod, *Northern Armageddon: The Battle of the Plains of Abraham — Eight Minutes of Gunfire that Shaped a Continent* (Vancouver: Douglas & McIntyre Ltd., 2008). His extensive service is detailed throughout this book. See index.

15. **Crowfoot**: Mathews, *Spies*, 132, LAC, HP, B177-1, 175.

16. Riedesel to Haldimand, Sorel, April 6, 1782, LAC, HP, B137, 85.

17. Chambers to Mathews, St. John's, April 6, 1782, LAC, HP, B142, 145.

18. Cruikshank, *Stevens*; **Ziba Phillips**: Mary B. Fryer and Lieutenant-Colonel William A. Smy, *Rolls of the Provincial (Loyalist) Corps, Canadian Command American Revolutionary War Period* (Toronto: Dundurn Press, 1981), 97, from LAC, HP, B160, 203–07; Houghton to Riedesel, Kahnawake, April 7, 1782, *Riedesel Correspondence HZ1–2*.

19. **Snowshoes**: Entry for April 8, 1782, *Jessup OB*; Intelligence extract, Montreal, April 8, 1782, *Riedesel Correspondence. HZ-1*.

20. Cruikshank and Watt, *KRR NY*, 87; Powell to Haldimand, Niagara, April 14, 1782, *Smy Transcripts*, HP, AddMss21762.

21. Gideon Adams Report, Yamaska Blockhouse, April 15, 1782, *Riedesel Correspondence, HZ-1.*

22. Diary entries for April 17 to 24, 1782, Wasmus, 261.

23. Powell to Haldimand, Niagara, April 18, 1782, *Smy Transcripts*, HP, AddMss21762; **Clowes**: Born in England, 1753. An ensign in the 8th, September 14, 1770. A lieutenant, 8th, March 16, 1776, and a captain, 8th, January 27, 1786. Houlding, *King's Service*.

24. Chambers to Mathews, St. John's, April 19, 1782, LAC, HP, B142, 151.

25. Riedesel to Haldimand, April 19, 1782, LAC, HP, B137, 96.

26. Haldimand to Powell, Montreal, April 20, 1782, *Smy Transcripts, HP*, AddMss21756; Hendrick Nelles to Butler, Pine Creek, April 20, 1782, *ibid.* Found in HP, AddMss21762; Ebenezer Allen to Butler, Chenussio, April 21 and 22, 1782, *ibid*; **John Abeel/Abiel**: This was most likely the Seneca War Chief, Cornplanter/ Gayentwahga, the son of the white Indian trader John Abeel. At times, Cornplanter called himself "John Abeel," or "Captain Abeel," or simply "Abeel." See Maryly B. Penrose, ed., *Indian Affairs Papers, American Revolution* (Franklin Park, NJ: Liberty Bell Associates, 1981), 286, and Simms, *FNY*, Vol. 1, 369–73.

27. DePeyster to Powell, Detroit, April 21, 1782, Kelsay, 322; Joseph Anderson to Mathews, Coteau-du-Lac, April 22, 1782, LAC, HP, B158, 272; David Abeel

affidavit, December 20, 1781, *PPGC*, Vol. 7, 607.

28. Bayley to Washington, Newbury, April 10, 1782, Wells, 397.

29. **Miller**: LAC, HP, AddMss21875, Part 2. His application to Dr. Smyth for expenses was refused; Riedesel to Haldimand, April 22, 1782, LAC, HP, B137, 100; **Lernoult's Order**: Entry for April 24, 1782. *Jessup OB*.

30. Haldimand to Riedesel, April 25, 1782, *Riedesel Correspondence, HZ-1*.

31. State of the Garrison of Oswego, April 23, 1782, WO28/6, 113; Ross to Haldimand and Ross to Powell, Oswego, April 24, 1782, Cruikshank and Watt, *KRR NY*, 87.

32. A.S. Hamond to Haldimand, Halifax, April 25, 1782. *HSGS*, Vol. 3, 220, LAC, HP, B149, 238–41.

33. Gray to Lernoult, St. Vincent, April 25, 1782, WO28/5, No. 23, 92, 94.

34. Riedesel to Haldimand, Sorel, April 26, 1782, *Smy Transcripts*, HP, AddMss21797.

35. Brehm to Chambers, Montreal, April 28, 1782, LAC, HP, B142, 154.

36. Trumbull to Washington, Newburgh, April 24, 1782, *Washington Writings*, Vol. 24, 159–60.

37. PA W17353 Anna Brookman, widow of John, and PA W16548 Christina Cramer, widow of John C. See Johnson, 321–22, 351–52, respectively; **Shively/Whitmosure**: *ibid.*, 97; John Brookman was captured on Mohawk River and John Gramer (Creamer) was taken at Conegehany (Canajoharie). McHenry, 48, 59, respectively; PA S13341 of George Lighthall, which included the testimony of Baltus Dillenbeck.

38. Haldimand to Sir Henry Clinton, Montreal, April 28, 1782, *HSGS*, Vol. 3, 220–22, from LAC, HP, B148, 24–29.

39. Powell to Haldimand, Niagara, April 30, 1782, *Smy Transcripts, HP*, AddMss21762; **Secord**: This could be Silas or Solomon. Smy, *Annotated Roll*, 163; **Servos**: Could be either Daniel or Jacob, both 6NID lieutenants.

40. **Pritchard**: Cruikshank, *Stevens*, 23.

41. **Cough, etc**: Simms, *FNY*, Vol. 2, 608–12; George Coe (Cough) and two boys of the same surname, aged fourteen and twelve, were taken on April 19, 1782. McHenry, 38.

42. PA W15789 of Margaret Meyer, widow of Daybold. Johnson, 489; **Plain**: PA S13119 of Jacob Garlock and PA W18543, widow of Henry Murphy. Johnson, 97; **Johnson's Mill**: PA R6461 of Dietrick Loucks, *ibid.*, 477 and PA W13941 of Elizabeth Suts; **Stoner**: Fernow, *V.XV, SAI*, 550.

43. Riedesel to Haldimand, Sorel, April 24, 30, and May 4, 5, 1782, LAC, HP, B137, 107, 114, 116, 119 respectively; Haldimand's appreciation of the importance of fresh produce was renowned. His country house, Montmorency, near the falls of that name east of Quebec City, had a substantial orchard of fruit trees. This concern even extended to the Riedesel's departure, at which time he organized the planting of salad seeds in a box of soil on the deck of their vessel. McIlwraith, 299, 304.

44. State of Carleton Island Garrison, May 1, 1782, LAC, WO28/6.

45. Diary entry for May 1, 1782, Wasmus, 261.

46. Sherwood to Mathews, Loyal Blockhouse, May 2, 1782. He refers to Seth Warner and Samuel Herrick. Mathews, *Spies*, 132, and LAC, HP, AddMss21837,

Part 1, 254; **Warner**: Walter S. Fenton, "Seth Warner," *Proceedings of the Vermont Historical Society*, Vol. 8, No.4 (1940); **Herrick**: George H. Jepson, *Herrick's Rangers, Bennington Museum Series #1* (Bennington, VT: Hadwen, Inc., 1977).

47. Winney report, Nanticoke, May 3, 1782, *Smy Transcripts*. HP, AddMss21762, and Smy, *Annotated Roll*, 199.

48. State of 2KRR in Canada, May 3, 1782, LAC, MG13, WO28/5, No.53, 193.

CHAPTER FIVE — A MAJOR STRIKE IN THE MOHAWK

1. Cruikshank and Watt, *KRR NY*, 87–88, and Cruikshank, *Loyalist Mohawk*, 396, and Haldimand to Ross, Montreal, May 7, 1782, *Smy Transcripts*, HP, AddMss21784.

2. Diary entries for May 8 and 15, 1782, Wasmus, 261–62.

3. William Johnston report, May 9, 1782, *Smy Transcripts*, HP, AddMss21762.

4. A.G. Bradley, *Lord Dorchester: The Makers of Canada* Vol. 3 (11 vols.) (Toronto: Morang & Co., Limited, 1911), 195, and Preface, *PPGC*, Vol. 7, xv.

5. Gray to Lernoult, May 10, 1782, LAC, MG13, WO28/5, No.23, 96–97.

6. **Communicating with Sir Henry Clinton**: Haldimand's biographer wrote:

> With Sir Henry Clinton … he could have worked in harmony had the difficulties of communication been less. Haldimand sent him a 'trial Letter' by each new route to see if it would reach him safely, and all epistles had to be duplicated, even triplicated, if there was to be any likelihood of their delivery. For six months of one year the Canadian governor did not hear from Clinton at all, though he sent him nineteen letters; and during that time he had to rely upon scraps of information from the rebel newspapers that occasionally found their way to Quebec (McIlwraith, 131).

Arnold's Information: James Robertson to Haldimand, New York City, October 31, 1781, and Sir Henry Clinton to Haldimand, November 12, 1781, received at Quebec City, May 14, 1782, *HSGS*, Vol. 3, 214, LAC, HP, B147, 381, 388; For an indication of how Arnold's information was used, see McIlwraith, 280–83.

7. **Brant**: Kelsay, 322; Guy Johnson to Haldimand, May 17, 1782. LAC, HP, AddMss21768, Part 3, 45; **Carleton Island**: Cruikshank and Watt, *KRR NY*, 88.

8. **Rogers**: Wells, 98, 397; Johnson to Washington, May 14 and 21, 1782. *ibid.*, 400.

9. Mathews to Butler, Quebec City, May 16, 1782, *Smy Transcripts*, HP, AddMss21765; Haldimand to Powell, Quebec City, May 16, 1782. *ibid*, HP, AddMss21764.

10. Ross to Haldimand, Oswego, May 18, 1782, Cruikshank and Watt, *KRR NY*, 88.

11. Sherwood to Mathews, May 19, 1782 transcribed in Mathews, *Spies*, 135 from LAC, HP, B177, Part 1, 303; Fryer, *Pimpernel*, 167 from WO28/5, 168.

12. Gray to HQ, May 22, 1782. WO28/5, No. 23, 98–99 and Gray to Lernoult, Montreal May 26, 1782. *ibid.*, 102.

13. Diary entry of May 22 and 24, 1782. Wasmus, 262; **Punishments**: *ibid.*, 270fn6.

Editor Helga Doblin states that typical penalties in the Brunswick regiments included "80 blows on the shirt for insubordination to a non-commissioned officer; running the gauntlet 10 times through 100 men for getting drunk on outpost, running the gauntlet 32 times over two days for desertion. Other deserters were court-martialled and shot."

14. Riedesel to Haldimand, (most private) Sorel, May 24, 1782, LAC, HP, B137, 146; Diary entry of May 26, 1782, Wasmus, 262.
15. Ross to Lernoult, Oswego May 25, 1782, WO28/8, 290.
16. Smyth to Mathews, Fort St. John's, May 26, 1782, Mathews, *Spies*, 77.
17. Gray to HQ, May 26, 1782, LAC, HP, MG13, WO28/5, No.23, 100.
18. Chambers to Mathews, Fort St. John's, May 31, 1782, LAC, HP, B142, 185.
19. Lernoult to Edward Jessup, Montreal, May 30, 1782. A copy of this order is in the author's collection without citation, although the handwriting matches that of Jessup's Orderly Book. In an odd clerical quirk, the two promotions appear in the Orderly Book dated November 4, 1782, following an entry dated March 11, 1782, and followed by one dated April 1, 1782.
20. **Kentfield**: General Court Martial, Albany, May 6, 1782, *Washington Writings*, Vol. 24, 279, and Benjamin Tupper to Washington, Albany, May 23, 1782, *ibid.*, 280fn; **The Scheme**: The men chosen to destroy the ship were John Lindsay and William Amesbury of Sherwood's Company, Loyal Rangers (Mathews, *Spies*, 98–102), and Willett to Washington, Albany, May 27, 1782, *Washington Papers, Series 4, General Correspondence*.
21. Willett to Washington, Albany, May 27, 1782, *ibid*.
22. Ross to Lernoult, Oswego, May 28, 1782, WO28/8, 292.
23. Haldimand to Powell, HQ, May 28, 1782, *Smy Transcripts*, HP, AddMss21764.
24. Haldimand to DePeyster, HQ, May 31, 1782, *ibid.*, HP, AddMss21781; Barbara Graymont, *The Iroquois in the American Revolution* (Syracuse: Syracuse University Press, 1972), 252. Graymont considers the Moravian atrocity to be "the most brutal act of the entire war."
25. Wehr to Mathews, May 31, 1782, LAC, HP, AddMss21821, 426.
26. Jonathon Trumbull Jr. to Tupper, HQ, May 29, 1782, *Washington Writings*, Vol. 24, 302.
27. Bayley to Washington, Newbury May 30, 1782, Wells, 397.
28. *Sinews*, 212.
29. WO28/5, No.23, 130–31; **1KRR Grenadiers**: The other ranks in John McDonell's Company ranged between 5' 9½" and 6' 1½" in height and were between twenty to forty-five years of age with forty-two of them between twenty-five and thirty-five. LAC, WO28/10, part 4, 489.
30. Two letters, Butler to Mathews, Niagara, June 1, 1782, *Smy Transcripts*, HP, AddMss21765; **Foresters**: This is one of the few incidents that I have seen of the Foresters going on active campaign; Butler to Mathews, Niagara, June 12, 1782, *ibid*; Jacob Servos to Butler, Canagawara, June 13, 1782, *ibid*. Found in HP, AddMss21762; **Great Tree**: Also known as, Big Tree. Originally, pro-rebel, he

changed his allegiance when Indian Territory was invaded in 1779 and his town of Kanaghsaws was destroyed. Graymont, 180,216.

31. Claus to Mathews, June 13, 1782. Cruikshank, *Loyalist Mohawk*, 396, LAC, HP, B114, 243.

32. Riedesel to Haldimand, Sorel, June 5 and Montreal, June 9, 1782, LAC, HP, B137, 157, 159 respectively.

33. Chambers to Mathews, Fort St. John's, June 9, 1782, LAC, HP, B141, 190.

34. Diary entries of June 10 and 11, 1782, Wasmus, 263; Von Loos to Riedesel, Quebec, June 13, 1782, Eelking, 227.

35. Ross to HQ, Carleton Island, June 11, 1782, WO28/8, 294; **Crawford's Subaltern**: Possibly Lieutenant Henry Young (formerly LIC) or Lieutenant Alexander McKenzie (formerly 1KRR). Seventeen-year-old William Crawford Jr. was promoted to ensign in August 1782, perhaps as a result of this successful raid; **Serjeant**: Likely Thomas Cavan (formerly 1KRR) or John McIntire. From a roll of Crawford's Company dated October 25, 1782, LAC, MG23, B23.

36. Colonel Isaac Clark to the officer commanding ships on Lake Champlain, Skenesborough, June 9, 1782, LAC, B142, 192; Chambers to Mathews, St. John's, June 13, 16, and 21, *ibid.*, 193, 194, 196.

37. De Speth to HQ, June 17 and 24, 1782, LAC, HP, AddMss21790, and Gray to Lernoult, June 1782, MG13, No.23, 118–19; Despite Chief Engineer Twiss's prediction to the governor in December that "your Excellency will not hear of any making their Escape from thence," escapes from Prison Island were a constant occurrence throughout the year. De Speth reported the escape of five men on July 15 while McAlpin's court martial was underway. On August 22, Captain Joseph Anderson reported that two men had escaped and then another two on September 5. Four days later, three men attempted an escape and two were immediately caught. On September 12, some paroled prisoners had run off and four were recaptured at St. John's. On October 3, de Speth reported that ten prisoners had escaped, but all were recaptured and put in irons. Then, they discovered how to remove the irons and threw them into the river. For the various letters on the above occurrences, see LAC, HP, B130, 14, 33, 41, 43, 46, 56, 63.

38. **Brant at Oswego/His Complaints**: Kelsay, 324–25.

39. **Hazen's Road**: Schmid to Ried, St. Francis, June 16, 1782, *HSGS*, Vol. 3, 222–23, LAC, HP, B137, Part 2, 163, Wells, 401–03, and Calloway, 79; **Portuguese Coins**: A Moidores coin was valued at twenty-seven shillings sterling. See, Douglas R. Cubbison, "The Coins of the British Private Soldier in the American Revolution," *www.csmid.com/files/coins.html* (accessed January 18, 2009).

40. Jonathon Trumbull Jr. to Bayley, June 13, 1782. *Washington Writings*, Vol. 24, 337–39; **Thomas Johnson/Bayley Attempt**: Wells, 99–102, Mathews, *Spies*, 73–76; Dow to Weare, Haverhill, June 16, 1782, Wells, 401–03; Pritchard to Mathews, Fort St. John's, June 21, 1782, LAC, HP, B177, Part 2, 367; **Vermont Prisoners**: Of interest, Bayley's son was not listed among the rebel prisoners in Quebec, but a Samuel Torry/Tarrey, aged twenty-nine, was noted as being taken in Cöos on June 15 (McHenry, 36, 60).

41. Washington to Reid, June 15, 1782, *Washington Writings*, Vol. 24, 345–46.
42. Papers of Lieutenant Pliny Moore, Hugh McLellan, ed., "In the Mohawk Valley in 1782, Col. Marinus Willett's Regiment of Levies" in *Moorsfield Antiquarian*, Vol. 2 (2 vols., 1938 and 1939) (Champlain: Moorsfield Press), 9; **Fort Edward Prisoners**: Henry and John Bitely, Silas Bristol, Levey Crocker, Abram Crooker, Thomas Durkey, Morris Kieth, Dan Sealey, and Ezra Swain (McHenry, 36).
43. Ethan Allen to Haldimand, June 16, 1782, LAC, HP, AddMss21837, Part 1, 354, and Mathews, *Spies*, 135–36.
44. A letter of July 15, 1782, from an officer stationed at Fort Rensselaer printed in the *Pennsylvania Gazette* of August 7, 1782. William B. Efner, city historian, "Warfare in the Mohawk Valley — Transcriptions from the *Pennsylvania Gazette*, 1780–1783" [hereafter Efner] (Schenectady: 1948); Claus to Mathews, Montreal, August 5, 1782, LAC, HP, AddMss21774, 285–86, *The New York Packet and American Advertiser, August 1, 1782*; Claus to Haldimand, July 1, 1782, Cruikshank, *Loyalist Mohawk*, 396, LAC, HP, B114, 245; Claus to Mathews, Montreal, August 5, 1782, provides many details of Deserontyon's activities during this raid, LAC, HP, AddMss21774, 285–86.
45. **Ambush**: Claus to Mathews, Montreal, August 12, 1782, LAC, HP, AddMss21774, 287–88; **Honyery's Sons**: His two eldest sons were Jacob and Cornelius. Joseph T. Glatthaar and James Kirby Martin, *Forgotten Allies — The Oneida Indians and the American Revolution* (New York City: Hill and Wang, 2006), 149.
46. **Calkins**: "A True History of the Feats, Adventures and Sufferings of Matthew Calkins in the Time of the Revolution," *Magazine of History, V. XVIII*, Extra No. 70 (1920). Calkins's memoir identified Willett as the commander of the pursuit and claimed that 1,500 men were sent on this duty, which would have been more Continentals, Levies, and militiamen than were available in the Valley.
47. Deserontyon's report in Claus to Mathews, Montreal, July 1, 1782, LAC, HP, AddMss21744, 269.
48. Willett to Washington, Fort Rensselaer, July 17, 1782, *Washington Papers*, Series 4, Reel 86.
49. **Ellice's Mill**: Richard Buckley, *Early Entrepreneurs of Little Falls, New York: John Porteous, Alexander Ellice and Edward Ellice* (Little Falls, NY: Little Falls Historical Society, 1996), 72–74.
50. **Wedding**: Simms, *FNY*, Vol. 2, 616–17.
51. Robertson to Brehm, Oswego, June 20, 1782, LAC, HP, AddMss21780, 161. The date of Robertson's letter is at odds with other sources.
52. **Mutilation**: A letter from an officer at Fort Rensselaer, July 28, 1782, printed in the *Pennsylvania Gazette*, August 14, 1782, Efner, 13. The officer wrote the man's name as Peters, but it should have been Petri; **Petri**: The name Elizabeth is found in the New York State Library, Special Collections and Manuscripts, Audited Accts, Vol. A, 288; Betsy Voorhees, "The Attack on the Old Mill," *www.rootsweb. com/~nyherkim/littlefalls/littlemill.html* (accessed January 28, 2005).
53. Nathaniel S. Benton, *A History of Herkimer County, including the Upper Mohawk Valley,*

from the earliest period to the present time (Albany, J. Munsell, 1856), Chapter 5, *passim*.

54. **Isaac Hill**: Claus to Haldimand, July 10, 1782, Cruikshank, *Loyalist Mohawk*, 396, LAC, HP, B114, 245.

55. **Fort Herkimer**: Simms, *FNY*, Vol. 2, 618.

56. **Frey's Mills**: The *New York Packett* and *American Advertiser*, August 1, 1782. Transcribed Johnson, 97–98. Two females were taken at Freybush in June — Elizabeth Strawberry, 14, Nancy Platson, 28. See McHenry, 67.

57. A letter from an officer at Fort Rensselaer, July 28, 1782, printed in the *Pennsylvania Gazette*, August 14, 1782, Efner, 13.

58. Chambers to Mathews, Pointe-au-Fer, July 13, 1782, LAC, HP, B142, 202.

59. **Robertson's Son**: LAC, HP, AddMss21780, 155, 157, 162, and Brian Leigh Dunnigan, *King's Men at Mackinac, The British Garrisons, 1780–1796* (Mackinac Island, MI: Mackinac Island State Park Commission, 1973), 34.

60. Washington to the president of Congress, July 9, 1782, partially transcribed, Simms, *FNY*, Vol. 2, 625–26; **Raid's Prisoners**: According to Claus's report, these were the NH Continental, William Martin, and militiamen, Frederick Hess, Christian Ittik, Andrew Piper, and Thomas Shoemaker. Claus to Mathews, Montreal, July 1, 1782, LAC, HP, AddMss21744, 269. McHenry lists the following (page numbers in brackets) — Stephen Ames (61), Christian Ely (58), Samuel French (62), George Nellis (65), Edward Sayer (58), and Oliver Smith (61). And possibly Peter Duncal and Bartholomew McGuire (66).

61. Ross to HQ, Carleton Island, June 29, 1782, WO28/8, 296.

CHAPTER SIX — AN END TO ACTIVE OPERATIONS

1. Carleton to Haldimand, New York City, June 20, 1782. Cruikshank and Watt, *KRR NY*, 90. The exact date of this letter is in doubt.

2. Haldimand to his post commanders, June 21, 1782, *Smy Transcripts*, HP, Add Mss21753.

3. (Most Secret) Shelburne to Haldimand, Whitehall, April 22, 1782, CO42/42, ff. 174–80. The date of receipt of this dispatch is found in the transcript, LAC, HP, B50, 164–73; **Shelburne**: *http://en.wikipedia.org/wiki/William_Petty,_2nd_Earl_ of_Shelburne* (accessed December 16, 2008); No. 1 — Shelburne to Haldimand, Whitehall, April 22, 1782, CO42/42, 275–93; Mackesy, 471–73.

4. **47th**: *Jessup OB*; **Watts**: Return of the 8th (King's) Regiment, August 1, 1782, WO17/1576; Smyth to Mathews, June 26, 1782, *Sutherland Papers*, LAC, HP, B177, 373–35; Ross to Mathews, June 26 and 27, 1782, Cruikshank and Watt, *KRR NY*, 89.

5. Powell to Haldimand, Niagara, June 27, 1782, *Smy Transcripts*, HP, AddMss21762; Butler to Lernoult, Niagara, June 27, 1782, *ibid.*, WO28/4; Butler to Mathews, Niagara, June 29, 1782, *ibid.*, HP, AddMs21765.

6. Mathews to Nairne, Quebec City, June 28, 1782. *Jessup OB*.

7. Washington to the city of Albany, June 27, 1782, *Washington Writings*, Vol. 23, 388; **Ballstown**: *Moore Papers*, Vol. 2, 9–11; **Washington at Albany/Saratoga/Schenectady**:

Hanson, 121–23, Glatthaar and Martin, 284–85, Simms, *Schoharie*, 522–23, *FNY*, Vol. 2, 625, and J.F. Morrison, "Biography of Frederick Visscher," *Tryon County Militia Newsletter*; Washington to the Dutch Reformed Church, Schenectady, June 20, 1782, *Washington Writings*, Vol. 23, 389–90; Leonard Gansevoort to Bronck, Albany, June 30, 1782, in Raymond Beecher, ed., *Letters from a Revolution 1775–1783, A Selection From the Bronck Family Papers*. (Albany, NY: The Greene County Historical Society and the New York State American Revolution Bicentennial Commission, 1973), 41–42.

8. PA S11226 of John Pettit; Patrick Frazier, *The Mohicans of Stockbridge* (Lincoln, NE: University of Nebraska Press, 1992), 232, 276; **Rolls**: Document No. 11105, Descriptive Book No. 4, 1782–83, Special Collections and Manuscripts, New York State Library, Albany; **Bingham/Rangers**: PA S28755 of Amos Hamlin, a private in Newell's Company. K.D. Johnson research, see *www.fort-plank.com/Additional_Partisans*.

9. **Stoner**: Jeptha Simms, *Trappers of New York: or, A Biography of Nicholas Stoner and Nathaniel Foster; together with Anecdotes of other Celebrated Hunters and some account of Sir William Johnson and his style of living* (1871; reprint, Fleischmanns, NY: Harbor Hill Books, 1980), 83–85; PA R4017 of Ray Guile.

10. "A Return of the N Hamp'r Troops & where Station'd," July 1, 1782, *State of New Hampshire, Rolls and Documents*, 442; *Willett OB*; **Captain's Given Names**: J.F. Morrison research; **Colonel**: PA W1525, widow of Marinus Willett; **State Troops**: This reference is one of the first I have found that refers to the two- and three-years' men in this fashion. Many more are to follow.

11. **Veeder**: Hanson, 152–53, 256.

12. **Schoharie**: Simms, *FNY*, Vol. 2, 593–94; **Adam Vrooman**: Identified in deposition of Josias E. Vrooman in support of PA S12338 of Joseph Brown. See *Morrison's Pensions*; Freemoyer Narrative, 303–05.

13. **Rockingham/Shelburne/Townshend**: Mackesy, 474, and *www.historyhome.co.uk/c-eight/ministry/rocky2s.htm* (accessed October 10, 2008).

14. Haldimand to Powell, Quebec City, July 1, 1782, *Smy Transcripts*, Add Mss21764; Powell to Haldimand, Niagara, July 1, 1782, *ibid.*, HP, AddMss21762; **Moravian Massacre**: Hoffman, 161–66, and Alan Fitzpatrick, *Wilderness War on the Ohio — The Untold Story of the Savage Battle for British and Indian Control of the Ohio Country During the American Revolution* (Benwood, WV: self-published, 2003), 489–90, 497–98, and Graymont, 252–53.

15. **Oswego Garrison**: Return of July 1, 1782, WO28/6, 123. It is odd to see two ensigns assigned to the grenadiers, as usually grenadier subalterns were first and second lieutenants; **Maclean**: Mary Beacock Fryer, *Allan Maclean, Jacobite General, The Life of an Eighteenth Century Career Soldier* (Toronto: Dundurn Press, 1987), 183.

16. Kim Stacey, "No One Harms Me with Impunity — The History, Organization, and Biographies of the 84th Regiment of Foot (Royal Highland Emigrants) and Young Royal Highlanders, During the Revolutionary War 1775–1784" (Manuscript in progress, 1994), 116. Stacy commented, "The 84th had an excessive number of convicted officers.... Of the total of 83 convicted officers in the army, the 84th

contributed 10%. It is also recorded that over half a dozen officers were allowed to resign or sell out, in lieu of being court martialled for their misconduct."

17. Diary entries for July 1 and 7, 1782, Wasmus, 264.

18. Ross to Mathews, Oswego, July 7, 1782, and Captain George Singleton's journal of the last foray into the Mohawk Valley, July 5 to 15, 1782 [hereafter *Singleton's Journal*]. Cruikshank and Watt, *KRR NY*, 90–92; **Oriskany**: Gavin K. Watt, *Rebellion in the Mohawk Valley, the St. Leger Expedition of 1777* (Toronto: Dundurn Press, 2002), 136–94.

19. Sutherland to Mathews, Montreal, July 7, 1782, *Sutherland Papers*, LAC, HP, B112, 127–29; Sutherland's expense account. *Ibid.*, LAC, HP, B158, 274.

20. Pausch to the prince of Hanau, July 16, 1782, Pausch, 123; *Kreutzbourg Narration*, 122–24.

21. Haldimand to Ross, Quebec City, July 8, 1782, LAC, HP, B125, 41.

22. *Singleton's Journal*; Kelsay, 324, HP, AddMss21765; Powell to Haldimand, Niagara, July 10, 1782, *Smy Transcripts*, AddMss21762.

23. Washington to Reid, Newburgh, July 10 and 11, 1782, *Washington Writings*, Vol. 24, 417–18, 426, 429–30; **Montour**: Washington's letter did not provide his given name. Penrose, *Indian Affairs*, 281, index. She suggests that this fellow was Rowland Montour, a nephew of Jacob Reed, an Oneida interpreter. If so, Rowland had switched sides, as he had been a British ally in 1779 and 1780. Reed's petition of August 30, 1782, to Congress stated that his nephew was "commander of the Oneida tribes." Calloway, 280fn. A John Montour held a captain's commission in the U.S. Army and served with a contingent of Delaware native soldiers in 1781. Calloway cites "Pay Roll of the Delaware Indians in service of the United States," June 15, 1780 to October 31, 1781 found in U.S. National Archives, Revolutionary War Rolls, 1775 to 1783, Microfilm M246, reel 129.

24. Washington to John Laurens, HQ, July 10, 1782. *Washington Papers*, Series 3b, Varick Transcripts, 321–22; **John Laurens**: Washington's aide-de-camp in 1777. A South Carolinian, he promoted the idea of arming black slaves and giving them freedom after the war was won. While Congress approved the concept, he was unable to pass it through his home state's legislature on three attempts: 1779, 1780, and 1782. He commanded an infantry regiment in the 1779 attack on Savannah, was taken at Charlestown in 1780, and paroled in November. In December 1780, Congress named him special minister to France and he was sent by Washington to Paris in March 1781, where he laid the plan of attack on Canada before the court. See *http://en.wikipedia.org/wiki/John_Laurens.* (accessed August 15, 2008); **Admiral Robert Digby**: For some information on his activities, see *www.fullbooks.com/American-Prisoners-of-the-Revolution7.html* (accessed January 25, 2009).

25. Haldimand to Powell, Quebec City, July 11, 1782, *Smy Transcripts*, HP, AddMss21764.

26. **Crown Point**: Diary entry of July 12, 1782, Wasmus, 265; **Swiss Birth**: Diary entry, July 21, 1782, *ibid.*

27. WO28/5, No.23, 120–23; Prenties's distress over his arrest. LAC, HP, AddMss21875, 9–10.

28. **Ross**: Cruikshank and Watt, *KRR NY*, 90, and Singleton Journal, *ibid.*; **2NH Casualties**: Lovejoy, "2NH 1782." J.F. Morrison collection.

29. PA S11226 of John Pettit.

30. *Singleton Journal*; **Garrison's Sally**: PA W19032, widow of Christopher Shoemaker; **Motivation of Indians**: Kelsay, 327.

31. Willett to Clinton, Fort Rensselaer, July 17, 1782, *Washington Papers*, Series 4, Reel 86.

32. *Pennsylvania Gazette* of August 7, 1782, printed a letter from Fort Rensselaer dated July 15, Efner; Matt Nelson research. *The Pennsylvania Packet*, Vol. XI, Issue 920, Philadelphia, August 6, 1782; **Raid's Prisoners**: According to McHenry (page numbers in brackets), Peter Curtner (58), Cunrad/Conrad Fretcher/Frilcher (61), Peter Gardner (55), Adam Garlock (55), Nathan Foster (72) are possibilities; PA R3917 of Adam Garlock Jr. Morrison explains in a footnote to this transcript that Adam Sr., aged fifty-two, and Conrad Fritcher and Peter Geotner, aged fifty-six, all of Captain Roof's Company, TCM, were taken prisoner on July 11, 1782. See, *Morrison's Pensions*.

33. **Schoharie**: *Pennsylvania Gazette* issue of August 7, 1782, printed a letter from Fort Rensselaer dated July 15 (Efner, 12); Entry of July 16, 1782, "Diaries of John Barr, 1779–1782 and Samuel Tallmadge, 1780–1782," in *Orderly Books of The Fourth New York Regiment, 1778–1780 — The Second New York Regiment, 1780–1783 with Diaries*, Almon W. Lauber, ed. and tr. (Albany, NY: University of the State of New York, 1932), 853.

34. PA W20648, Sarah, widow of Robert Ayres; *Moore Papers*, 2, 12.

35. Willett to Washington, Fort Rensselaer, July 24, 1782, *Washington Writings*, Series 4.

36. Clinton to Washington, Poughkeepsie, July 24, 1782, *ibid.*

37. Pausch to the prince of Hanau, Point Levis, July 16, 1782, Pausch, 124–25; Surgeonmate Moerschell's case dragged on for some time. As all involved said Moerschell knew the details of the entire plot, he was reduced to the ranks and ultimately punished by running a two-hundred-man gauntlet, sixteen times in one day. See, Pausch to the prince of Hanau, Point Levis, July 1, 1783. *ibid.*, 139; **German Punishments**: The British punishment of flogging with a cat of nine tails was not a German practice. Very common was the running of the gauntlet, which was a misnomer, as the man was not given free rein to run, but instead was walked between the two lines with a junior officer at his head preventing him from speeding his pace. Another punishment was to strike the man's hands with fifty or one hundred blows of a cane. Yet another, which was considered the equivalent of the gauntlet, was to beat a man's bare buttocks, which had the additional feature of humiliation (*Kreutzbourg Narration*, 120–21).

38. **Flax**: *Pennsylvania Gazette* of August 14, 1782, printed a letter from an officer at Fort Rensselaer dated July 28, 1782 (Efner 13).

39. Clinton to J.M. Scott (Secretary of State), July 29, 1782, *PPGC*, Vol. 81, 16–17.

CHAPTER SEVEN — STUMBLING TOWARD PEACE

1. Riedesel to Haldimand, Sorel, July 12, 1782, LAC, HP, B137, 191.
2. General Orders, Quebec City, July 15, 1782, LAC, HP, AddMss21743, ff.195,97; Entry of July 22, 1782, *Jessup OB*; **Prison Conditions**: J. Fraser, *Skulking for the King, A Loyalist Plot* (Erin, ON: Boston Mills Press, 1985), 60–61 from the Fitch Papers, items, 261, 275, 500.
3. De Speth to Haldimand, Montreal, July 15, 1782, HP, AddMss21790; **Joseph Anderson**: Resigned December 24, 1782, WO28/5, 102.
4. Haldimand to Shelburne (Most Secret), Quebec City, July 17, 1782, *HSGS*, Vol. 3, 223–24 from Q20, 163–67.
5. Butler to Mathews, Niagara, July 17, 1782, *Smy Transcripts*, HP, AddMss21765.
6. De Speth to Haldimand, Montreal, July 18, 1782, and Haldimand to de Speth, Quebec City, July 22, 1782, LAC, HP, B130, 16, and B131, 154 respectively.
7. Ross to Haldimand, Oswego, July 28, 1782, Cruikshank and Watt, *KRR NY*, 90–91; Ross to Haldimand, Oswego, August 3, 1782, LAC, HP, B125, 46.
8. **Klock's Orders**: The *Pennsylvania Gazette* issue of August 28, 1782, printed a letter from Albany dated August 17 (Efner, 13); **Klock's Scout**: Ted Egly Jr., *History of the First New York Regiment* (Hampton, NH: Peter E. Randall, 1981), 154; Testimony of Jacob J. Klock, August 10, 1782, *Willett Papers, Miscellaneous Manuscripts*, New York Historical Society; Jacob C. Klock, Johnson, 462.
9. Washington to Clinton, July 30, 1782. *Washington Writings*, Vol. 24, 443–44.
10. **Vermont's Message**: Fryer, *Pimpernel*, 171.
11. **Sequestered**: New York State Library, Special Collections and Manuscripts, 163; **Victims**: PA W13941 of Elizabeth Suts. Philip Empie and the boy were taken. John Reed and his wife killed and Joseph Davis was also killed; **Report**: *Pennsylvania Gazette* of August 7, 1782, citing a letter of August 1 from Fishkill (Efner, 11).
12. **Guy Johnson/Taylor & Forsyth**: Judge Thomas Dunn to Haldimand, July 24, 1782, HP, AddMss21770, and Bruce Wilson, "The Struggle for Wealth and Power at Fort Niagara 1775–1783," *Ontario History*, Vol. 68 (1976). Guy Johnson's suspension was mentioned in Haldimand to Townsend, Quebec City, October 22, 1782.
13. Judge Thomas Townshend to Haldimand, July 31, 1782, *HSGS*, Vol. 3, 224–25 from Q19, 93–95; **Townshend**: He was in Shelburne's cabinet beginning in July 1782, Mackesy, 476.
14. August Return, Niagara, WO28/6, 125.
15. Kelsay, 328–29, HP, AddMss21785, Part 2, 54–55; Ross to Haldimand, Oswego, August 3, 1782, Cruikshank and Watt, *KRR NY*, 92.
16. Smyth to HQ, Fort St. John's, August 3, 1782, Cruikshank, *Stevens*, LAC, HP, B177, Part 2, 417.
17. Thomas Man to HQ, Sorel, August 4, Riedesel to Haldimand, Sorel, August 5, William Fraser to Riedesel, Yamaska Blockhouse, August 6, and Riedesel to Haldimand, Sorel, August 12, 1782, LAC, HP, B137, 209, 214, 216, 220 respectively; Haldimand to Riedesel, Quebec City, August 8, 1782,. LAC, HP, B139, 177.

18. **Nellus**: Captain Hendrick Nelles and his son Robert were in the 6NID, not the Royal Yorkers. I have not been able to identify George Nellus's father-in-law. Claus to Mathews, Montreal. August 5, 1782. LAC, HP, AddMss21774, 285–86.

19. **Payfer**: De Speth to Haldimand, Montreal, August 3, 1782. LAC, HP, B130, 22 and examination of Antoine Payfer by Town Major James Hughes, August 17, 1782, *ibid.*, 25–26, and Haldimand to de Speth, Quebec City, August 22, 1782, *ibid.*, B131, 158.

20. Haldimand to Riedesel, Quebec City, August 5, 1782, LAC, HP, B137, 212, and Riedesel to Haldimand, Sorel, August 5, 1782, Eelking, *Memoirs*, 125–26.

21. Butler to Mathews, Niagara, August 5, 1782, HP, AddMss21765, f.294.

22. **Hanna's Town**: *http://en.wikipedia.org/wiki/Hannastown* (Pennsylvania) (accessed February 24, 2009).

23. Affidavit of Eve Oury, Westmoreland County, Pennsylvania, December 4, 1846. For her extensive services to the state in the fort's defence during and after the attack, Oury was awarded a $100 gratuity on March 17, 1838. Research by Starlene Oary. *http://files.usgwarchives.net/pa/westmoreland/bios/ourye0001.txt*

24. "Joseph Brownlee and the Destruction of Hannastown," *www.mcn.org/2/NOEL/ Westmoreland/WestHistory.htm#JOSEPH%20BROWNLEE* (accessed February 24, 2009). This source gives Brownlee's given name as Joseph or John. Other sources refer to him as Jack.

25. Thomas Lynch Montgomery, ed., "The Frontier Forts of Western Pennsylvania — Hannastown," Volume 2 (2 vols.) (Harrisburg: Report of the Commission to Locate the Site of the Frontier Forts of Pennsylvania, 1896), 290–332. Includes transcripts of several detailed contemporary letters written by participants. After the attack it was found that Judge Hanna's house was reasonably intact and it continued to be used as a courthouse, but the town no longer flourished. Three years after the war, the county seat moved to Greensborough and Hannastown fell into ruin.

26. Washington to the secretary at war and Washington to Willett and Washington to Reid, HQ, August 6, 1782, *Washington Writings*, Vol. 24, 470, 476–77, respectively; **Wolf and Savage**: Washington to James Duane, September 7, 1783. Glatthaar and Martin, 294 from Washington's Writings, 27:133, 140.

27. Haldimand to Powell, Quebec City, August 8, 1782, *Smy Transcripts*, HP, AddMss21764; **Alexander Dundas**: Born in Scotland, 1731. A captain in Drumlanrig's regiment of the Scots-Dutch Brigade, April 5, 1748. A captain in Halkett's Regiment, Scots-Dutch Brigade. A captain, 72nd Regiment, March 24, 1761. A captain, 34th Regiment, August 25, 1762. The major, 34th Regiment, January 6, 1776. The lieutenant-colonel, 8th Regiment, November 1, 1780. Retired, September 13, 1783. Houlding, *King's Service*.

28. Haldimand to Riedesel, (private) Quebec City, August 18, 1782, LAC, HP, B139, 182.

29. **Dead Kahnawake**: Claus to Mathews, Montreal, August 12, 1782, LAC, HP, AddMss21774, 287–88, and Mathews to Claus, Quebec City, August 15, 1782, *ibid.*, 289, and Haldimand to John Campbell, Quebec City, August 15, 1782, LAC, HP, B113, 168.

30. **Secret Treaty**: Haldimand to Carleton, Quebec City, August 11, 1782, Williamson, 122–23.
31. Haldimand to Chittenden, Quebec City, August 8, 1782, CO42/43, 130.
32. Jessup to Riedesel, Parson's Point, August 7, and Riedesel to HQ, Sorel, August 15, LAC, HP, B137, 207, 222, respectively, and Haldimand to Riedesel, August 17, 1782. LAC, HP, B139, 181. Jessup to Riedesel, Crown Point, August 24, 1782, LAC, HP, B137, 241.
33. Haldimand to Shelburne (Most Secret), Quebec City, August 17, 1782 (two letters) *HSGS*, Vol. 3, 225–27 from Q20, 213–15, 199–204.
34. **Sir John's Arrival**: The *Quebec Gazette* and Earle Thomas, *Sir John Johnson, Loyalist Baronet* (Toronto: Dundurn Press, 1986), 97.
35. Clinton to Willett, Poughkeepsie, August 16, 1782, Johnson, 99–100.
36. **Oswego Prisoners/Deserters**: Ross to HQ, Oswego, August 24, 1782, Cruikshank and Watt, *KRR NY*, 93. The prisoners, Emanuel Humphries and Henry Smith, returned to duty before the peace and settled in Canada. The deserter, John Clark, may have been recaptured, as he was court martialled at Niagara and sentenced to one thousand lashes on February 4, 1783. In November, this was commuted to service on board a "Ship of War." The fate of Robert Reynolds is uncertain, although a man of that name applied for land at Amherstburg in 1796. WO28/6 and Smy, *Annotated Roll*. Humphrey and Smith, 111, 172, respectively. Clark and Reynolds, 66, 153, respectively.
37. **Sir John's Tour**: Cruikshank and Watt, *KRR NY*, 93, and Kelsay, 329–30.
38. **Blue Licks**: Butler to Powell, Niagara, August 27, 1782, *Smy* Transcripts, HP, AddMss21762. For a thorough account of the action, see Fitzpatrick, 547–49, 555–66, and Hoffman, 183–85.
39. Riedesel to Haldimand, Sorel, August 21 and 22, 1782, LAC, HP, B137, 233, 235, respectively. Perhaps the von Retz regiment's commander, Lieutenant-Colonel Johann von Ehrenkrook, was in ill health, as he died on March 22, 1783, Wilhelmy, 259; Haldimand to Riedesel, Quebec City, August 24, 1782, LAC, HP, B139, 185; Baroness von Riedesel, 163. She recalled that her husband went to Isle aux Noix in the fall, but evidence is that the order to prepare the new works was given in August; Riedesel to Haldimand, Nicolet, August 23, 1782, LAC, HP, B137, 235.
40. Haldimand to Riedesel, Quebec City, August 22, 1782, LAC, HP, B139, 184.
41. Diary entries for August 24, 27, and 28, 1782, Wasmus, 267.
42. Butler to Powell, Niagara, August 27, 1782, *Smy Transcripts*, HP, AddMss21762; Haldimand to SJJ, November 25, 1782, *ibid*, AddMss21775; SJJ to Haldimand, Montreal, November 28, 1782, *ibid*.; Haldimand to SJJ, Quebec City, December 5, 1782, *ibid*.; Maclean's Brigade Order, Niagara, December 10, 1782, *ibid*., HP, AddMss21762; **Dease**: Stevens, *Savage Allies*, Vol. 5, 296. He was considered, "a good natured man … very fond of Entertainments." As such, he would have been a perfect crony for Guy; David Armour, Dease's biographer in the *DCB* contends that Guy Johnson recognized Butler's greater competence and indicates that Dease had confronted Butler with his claim to greater seniority. See *www.biographi.ca*.

43. Duane to Clinton, Philadelphia, August 20, 1782, *PPGC*, Vol. 8, 33–36.
44. Willett to Washington, Fort Rensselaer, August 21, 1782, *Washington Papers*, Series 4, General Correspondence.
45. **Organization of the State Troops Battalion**: PA R1661 of James Cannan/Cannon and PA S12020 of Williams Avery, who deposed, "near after the discharge of the nine months men we were formed in to a Battalion called the New York State Battalion, commanded I believe by Major Benscouten."
46. Washington to Clinton, August 21, 1782. *Washington Writings*, Vol. 25, 56.
47. Washington to Stirling, Newburgh, August 29, 1782, *Washington Writings*, Vol. 25, 89–90.
48. Washington to Benjamin Lincoln, Verplank's Point, September 2, 1782, *Washington Papers*, Series 4, General Correspondence.
49. DePeyster to Powell, Detroit, August 27, 1782, *Smy Transcripts*, HP, AddMss21783.
50. Riedesel to Haldimand, Sorel and Isle aux Noix, August 29 and 31 and September 1, 1782, LAC, HP, B137, 244, 246, 251, respectively; Riedesel eventually had detachments from eight British, German, and Provincial regiments working on the island. Eelking, *Memoirs*, 211–12.
51. Certificate of Dr. H.A. Kennedy, Quebec City, August 29, 1782, LAC, WO28/4.
52. Return of Fort Ontario, September 1, 1782, WO28/6.
53. Fraser to Riedesel, Yamaska, August 30 and court findings, Yamaska, September 9, 1782, LAC, HP, B137, 245, 269, respectively; Riedesel to Haldimand, Isle aux Noix, September 8, 1782, *ibid.*, 260.
54. Riedesel to Haldimand (private), Isle aux Noix September 3, 1782, LAC, HP, B137, 255.
55. Haldimand to Ross, September 9, 1782, Cruikshank and Watt, *KRR NY*, 93–94.
56. Haldimand to Dundas, Quebec City, September 9, 1782, *Smy Transcripts*, HP, AddMss21764.
57. Gray to LeMaistre, Montreal, September 9, 1782, WO28/5, No.23, 107.
58. Kreutzbourg to the Prince of Hesse-Hanau, La Prairie, September 10, 1782. On October 12, he informed the prince that he had just received his dispatch of April 15, 1781, a year and a half after it was written. *Kreutzbourg Narration*, 125, 132 respectively; **Blankets and Clothing**: *ibid.*, 128.
59. Haldimand to Riedesel, Quebec City, September 10 and 15, 1782, LAC, HP, B139, 197, 200, respectively.
60. **Wheeling**: Ernest A. Cruikshank, *The Story of Butler's Rangers and the Settlement of Niagara* (1893; reprint, Owen Sound, ON: Richardson, Bond & Wright Ltd., 1975), 109, and Hoffman, 187. Fitzpatrick, 522–40 provides a highly detailed account.
61. Sherwood to Mathews, Fort St. John's, September 11, 1782, Cruikshank, *Stevens*, LAC, HP, B177, Part 2, 483.
62. Riedesel to Haldimand (private), September 12 and 13, 1782, LAC, HP, B137, 271, 275 respectively; Haldimand to Riedesel, Quebec City, September 16, 1782, LAC, HP, B139, 202; Kreutzbourg referred to Twiss building "three great redoubts."

Obviously, these were major works. *Kreutzbourg Narration*, 131; **Casemented Stone**: Eelking, *Allied Troops*, 250.

63. William Ancrum to Haldimand, Fort Haldimand, September 13 and 18, 1782, LAC, HP, B127, 307, 310, respectively.

64. Diary entry for September 15, 1782, Wasmus, 267. Editor Mary Lynn notes that the French disease was known medically as *Morbus Gallicus*. The common name, "syphilis," did not come into use until 1850.

65. Haldimand to Riedesel, Quebec City, September 16, 1782, Eelking, 129–30.

66. McIlwraith, 244–45; "Horatio Nelson's Account Of His Services, Port Mahon October 15, 1799" found at *http://ourcivilisation.com/smartboard/shop/nelsonh/myself.htm* (accessed February 2, 2009); **Albermarle**: A description found at *www.ageofnelson.org/MichaelPhillips/liste.php?char=A#0090* (accessed February 2, 2009).

67. Pausch, 128.

68. Haldimand to Carleton, September 18, 1782, Kelsay, 334. From Indian Affairs, Michigan Historical Collections, 20: 57–58.

69. "A Plan of the Camp and Manoeuvres at Point Levis, September 18, 1782," prepared by Lieutenant Michael Bauch, Hesse-Hanau Artillery. Digitales Archiv Marburg, HStAM WHK 29/88; Von Loos to Riedesel, Point Levis, September 26, 1782, Eelking, 228.

70. Ross to Haldimand, September 29, 1782, LAC, HP, B125, 71.

71. **SJJ at Niagara**: Haldimand to SJJ, September 9, 1782, LAC, HP, B115, 8, and SJJ to Haldimand, Niagara, October 14, 1782, *ibid.*, 13; Kelsay, 333–34; Dundas to Haldimand, Niagara October 5, 1782, *Smy Transcripts*, HP, AddMss21762 and Graymont, 255.

72. Pausch to the prince of Hesse-Hanau, Point Levis, October 20, 1782, 133; Kreutzbourg to the prince of Hanau, La Prairie, October 10, 1782, *Kreutzbourg Narration*, 131; Wilhelmy, 265; Diary entry of September 30 and October 8, 1782, Wasmus, 268.

73. **Liberty Pole**: Williamson, 122–23.

74. *Moore Papers*, Vol. 2, 310–11.

CHAPTER EIGHT — OBSESSED WITH OSWEGO

1. General Orders of Major-General Lord Stirling, HQ, Albany, September 16, 1782, *Washington Papers*, Series 4, General Correspondence, 164; Stirling to Washington, Albany, September 18, 1782, and Willett to Stirling, Albany, same date, and an undated clothing return signed by lieutenant and paymaster, Abraham Ten Eyck, and Colonel Willett, *ibid.*

2. Stirling's General Orders and Stirling to Reid and Stirling to Willett, Albany, September 20, 1782, *ibid.*, 190–92.

3. Bayley to Washington, Newbury, September 19, 1782, Wells, 401.

4. Washington to Clinton, October 19, 1782, *PPGC*, Vol. 8, 47fn; Clinton to Washington, Poughkeepsie, October 20, 1782, *ibid.*, 47–48.

5. Schuyler to Washington, Albany, September 21, 1782, *Washington Papers*, Series 4, General Correspondence.

6. **Fort Plain**: PA S10589 of Marcus Dusler. Johnson, 376–77; **Fort Herkimer**: *ibid.*, 182; **Scout**: See John V. Van Ingen, 2ACM, Hansen, 240.

7. Stirling to Washington, Albany, October 23, 1782, *Washington Papers*, Series 4, General Correspondence, 373.

8. Washington to Clinton, *ibid.*, Series 3c, Varick Transcripts, 374.

9. **Rhode Island Regiment's (RIR) History**: Robert K. Wright, Jr., *The Continental Army* (Washington: Army Lineage Series, Centre of Military History, United States Army, 1989), 227–29, and the following websites: *www.firstrhodeisland. org* (accessed January 28, 2009); *www.earlyamerica.com/review/2004_summer_ fall/soldiers.htm* (accessed January 28, 2009); *http://americanrevolution.org/firstri. htm* (accessed January 28, 2009); *http://revolution.h-net.msu.edu/essays/adams2. html;*(accessed September 14, 2008); **RIR Strength**: Lesser, 236.

10. Washington to Stirling, HQ, October 30, 1782, *Washington Papers*, Series 3b, Varick Transcripts.

11. Diary entry of October 23, 1782, Wasmus, 268.

12. General Orders, HQ, Quebec City, October 21, 1782, *Jessup OB*.

13. **Upper Posts**: Return of October 21, 1782, WO28/6, 137.

14. Lernoult to Maclean, October 20, 1782, *Smy Transcripts*, HP, AddMss21741, part 2.

15. Maclean to Haldimand, Oswego, October 1782, Cruikshank and Watt, *KRR NY*, 95.

16. Haldimand to Townshend, Quebec City, October 19 and 21, 1782. Kelsay, 334–35. Kelsay drew from two sources, CO42/43 and Indian Affairs, Michigan Historical Collections, 10: 663,668–69.

17. Carleton to Haldimand, New York City, October 26, 1782, CO42/43, 278.

18. Riedesel to Haldimand, Isle aux Noix, October 27 and two letters, October 30 and same to same, Sorel, November 11 and 21, 1782, LAC, HP, B137, 310, 312, 314, 344, 363.

19. Haldimand to Riedesel, Quebec City, October 27, 1782, LAC, HP, B139, 214; Haldimand to Ross, Quebec City, November 2, 1782, Cruikshank and Watt, *KRR NY*, 96.

20. Riedesel to Haldimand, n.d., Eelking, *Memoirs*, Vol. 2, 141–42; Riedesel to Haldimand, October 30, 1782, *ibid.*, 143–44; Eelking, *Allied Troops*, 251.

21. SJJ to Haldimand, Quebec City, October 28, 1782, LAC, HP, B115, 19, and Thomas, 101.

22. Order of October 30, 1782, at La Prairie. *Field Jaeger Corps Orders*, 196–96.

23. Ross to Haldimand, November 1, 1782, LAC, HP, B125, 78.

24. Baroness Riedesel, 164–65; **Godfather**: Riedesel to Haldimand, Sorel, November 5, 1782, LAC, HP, B137, 336; McIlraith, 296; Von Loos was asked to be the child's second godfather. Von Loos to Riedsel, Point Levis, September 26, 1782, Eelking, *Memoirs*, 228.

25. Two letters, Haldimand to Riedesel, Quebec City, November 4, 1782, LAC, HP, B139, 218, 221 respectively; Fryer, *King's Men*, 291–92.

26. General Orders, Quebec City, November 4, 1782, *Jessup OB*; Von Loos to Riedesel, Cape St. Ignace, November 4, 1782, Eelking, 229.

27. Haldimand to Riedesel, November 5, 1782, LAC, HP, B139, 225.
28. Fryer, *Maclean*, 186–89; Haldimand to Maclean, Quebec City, November 4, 1782, *Smy Transcripts*, HP, AddMss21765.
29. St. Leger to Lernoult, November 7, 1782, WO28/2, 24. In this exchange, St. Leger puts paid to the conventional wisdom that spirits were on constant issue to all troops in Canada; Riedesel to Haldimand, Sorel, November 7 and 11, 1782, LAC, HP, B137, 339, 344 respectively.
30. Diary entry of November 7, 1782, Wasmus, 269.
31. Ross to Maclean, November 10, 1782, Cruikshank and Watt, *KRR NY*, 96–97.
32. **Bingham's Scout**: S11226 of John Pettit.
33. **RIR Arrival**: A report from Albany dated November 4, 1782, published in the *Pennsylvania Gazette*'s issue of November 20; **Logging**: Simms, *FNY*, Vol. 2, 455.
34. *Moore Papers*, Vol. 2, 313–14, and Lieutenant Pliny Moore, "Adjutant Pliney Moore's Orderly Book, Fort Rensselaer 1782–1783" [hereafter *Moore OB*], Wayne Lenig, tr., J.F. Morrison, typescript. New York State Library, Document, No.8174, 1–3.
35. Gray to Mathews, St. Vincent, November 13, 1782, LAC, HP, B158, 279.
36. Haldimand to Maclean, Quebec City, November 14, 1782, *Smy Transcripts*, HP, AddMss21764; **McDonell**: Although the captain's given name was not noted in Haldimand's dispatch, Captain James McDonell signed the October 1, 1782, return of the Carleton Island garrison. WO28/6, 135, and James McDonell wrote to Haldimand from the island on October 4, 1782, LAC, HP, AddMss21787, 312. Also, Ross to Haldimand, Oswego, October 31, 1782, LAC, HP, B125, 76; St. Leger to Lernoult, October 2, 1782. A request that Lieutenant Wingrove, 34th, be allowed to come down from Oswego to rejoin his company, which had left Carleton Island, WO28/2.
37. Haldimand to Townshend, Quebec City, November 14, 1782, CO42/44, 17.
38. **Bateaux Return**: Conductor's names were: LaFontasie, LaPensée, Chenier, Hubert LeRoux, Pennienville, Augé, and Gabriel LeRoux, LAC, HP, AddMss21849, 190.
39. DePeyster to Maclean, Detroit, November 21, 1782, *Smy Transcripts*, HP, AddMss21783.
40. Ross to Haldimand, Oswego, November 25, 1782, LAC, HP, B125, 85.
41. Sherwood to Mathews, November 26, 1782, and proceedings of a court martial, December 3, 1782. See, Fryer, *King's Men*, 291–92; Haldimand to Riedesel, December 5 and 23, 1782, LAC, HP, B139, 240, 258, respectively.
42. Weare to Washington, Hampton Falls, November 25, 1782, *Washington Papers*, Series 4, General Correspondence; An unnamed agent to Sherwood, October 3, 1782, LAC, HP, B177/2, 517–18.
43. Wells, 102–03.
44. *Moore OB*, 3–7.
45. **Willett's Company Returns**: *Moore Papers*, Vol. 2, 316.
46. SJJ to Haldimand, Montreal, November 20 and 28, 1782, and Haldimand to SJJ, Quebec City, December 5, 1782, LAC, HP, B115.
47. **Oswego Return**: November 27, 1782, LAC, WO1/11.

48. "Return of His Serene Highness the Duke of Brunswicks Troopes (Rank and File only) that are present in Canada ...," *circa* November 1782, *ibid*; "General Return of the Country, Age, Size, & Time of Service of the Men of the 1st Battalion of the King's Royal Regiment of New York ... Terre Bonne January 11, 1783.," LAC, WO28/10, part 4, f489.

49. Macksey, 505–06.

50. Sherwood to Riedesel, Loyal Blockhouse, November 29, 1782, LAC, HP, B137.

51. St. Leger to Lernoult, Montreal, November 28 and December 2, 1782, WO28/2, 34, 38 respectively.

52. Congressional representatives to Clinton, Philadelphia, December 9, 1782, *PPGC*, Vol. 8, 56–57.

53. Diary entry of December 1, 1782, Wasmus, 269; Riedesel to Haldimand, December 4, 1782, LAC, HP, B137, 377.

54. Sherwood to Mathews, December 9, 1782, Cruikshank, *Stevens*.

55. **Macbean**: Haldimand to Riedesel (private), December 12, 1782, LAC, HP, B139, 243, and Riedesel to Haldimand (private), December 16, 1782, *ibid.*, B137, 403, and Haldimand to Riedesel (private), December 19, 1782, *ibid.*, B139, 253.

56. Proceedings of the Councils at Niagara, December 11 and 12, 1782, *Smy Transcripts*, HP, AddMss21756, and Kelsay, 335–36; *Ibid.*, 336 from LAC, HP, B115, 47.

57. *Moore Papers*, Vol. 21, 321–22; *Moore OB*, 8.

58. Haldimand to Riedesel, December 11, 1782, LAC, HP, B139, 246; Two letters, Riedesel to Haldimand, December 12, 1782. *ibid.*, B137, 388, 394.

59. WO28/5, No. 23, 118–31.

60. James Hunter to Malcolm McMartin, St. John's, December 18, 1782, *Elizabeth Blair Papers*. Hunter was an excellent artist and left a body of work that provides many important images of early Canadian life.

61. Haldimand to Riedesel (private), December 19, 1782, LAC, HP, B139, 255.

62. Diary entry of December 23, 1782, Wasmus, 262.

63 Haldimand to Riedesel, December 30, 1782, LAC, HP, B139, 262.

64. Fryer, *Pimpernel*, 176–77 from Sherwood to Nairne, LAC, HP, B161, 474.

CHAPTER NINE — SO RIDICULOUS AN ENTERPRISE

1. William M. Willett, *A Narrative of the Military Actions of Colonel Marinus Willett, Taken Chiefly from his Own Manuscript* (New York: G.&C.&H. Carvill, 1831), 90–91; George M. Clark, "Washington's Last Expedition: Capture Fort Ontario!" [hereafter *Clark*] from *http://fortontario.com/History/George2/Willett.html* (accessed January 27, 2009).

2. Willett to Washington, Albany, November 29, 1782, *Washington Papers, Series 4, General Correspondence*, 183–85.

3. Washington to Willett, Newburgh, December 18, 1782, *Washington Writings*, Vol. 25, 449–51.

4. Willett to Washington, Fort Rensselaer, December 22, 1782, K.D. Johnson research.

Willett Family Papers, New York State Library, SC16670, Box 1, Folder 15.

5. Orders to assistant clothier general David Brooks, HQ, January 18, 1783, *ibid.*, Vol. 26, 47–48.

6. Washington to Willett, January 20, 1783, *ibid.*, 52.

7. Washington to Willett, Newburgh, January 22, 1783, *ibid.*, 57–58.

8. General Orders, Fort Rensselaer, *Moore OB*, 9–10.

9. Washington to Willett, Newburgh, February 2, 1783. *Washington Writings*, Vol. 26, 90–93.

10. Journal entry of September 22, 1786. John Enys, *The American Journals of Lt John Enys*, Elizabeth Cometti, ed. (Syracuse: The Adirondack Museum and Syracuse University Press, 1976), 109–12.

11. **Lake Champlain Outposts**: Cruikshank and Watt, *KRR NY*, 97.

12. Entry of February 2, 1783, *Moore OB*.

13. Calkins, 89. After the Oswego expedition, it seems that Calkins had had enough excitement, as he is shown as a deserter on an undated return prepared by Adjutant Pliny Moore, entitled, "A Roll of Deserters from Col. Willett's New York State Regiment of Two and Three Years Troops and the Battalion Commanded by Major Elias Van Benschoten."

14. PA W4189, widow of Gideon Elliot of Pierce's Company, WL; PA R4017 of Ray Guile; PA W2064, widow of Robert Ayres of Wright's Company, WL; **Rhode Island Regiment**: PA W25362, widow of Samuel Ashman of Wright's Company, WL; **Captain Holden**: Willett to Washington, Fort Herkimer, February 19, 1783, *Washington Papers, Series 4, General Correspondence*, and Holden's given name — J.F. Morrison research; PA W2643, widow of David Perry; **Rhode Island Companies**: list found in Daniel M. Popek's website: *http://freepages.genealogy.rootsweb.ancestry.com/~smithandyoung/Chillson.htm* [hereafter *Popek*]; **Benschoten**: Willett to Washington, February 19, 1783, *Washington Papers, Series 4, General Correspondence*; **Four Deserters**: Their identity has not been found. Perhaps the two Klocks and Forbes were amongst them; **Three Oneida Guides**: *ibid.*; **500 Men**: Washington to President of Congress, February 26, 1783, *Washington Writings*, Vol. 26, 165.

15. Glen to Willett, Schenectady, February 6, 1783, K.D. Johnson research. Willett Family Papers, New York State Library, SC16670, Box 1, Folder 15.

16. **Prosecution**: Willett to Washington, Fort Herkimer, February 8, 1783, K.D. Johnson research. Willett Family Papers, New York State Library, SC16670, Box 1, Folder 15; **Expedition Departs**: Willett to Washington, February 19, 1783, *ibid*.

17. Willett to Henry Glen, February 19, 1783. Throop Wilder, "The Glen Letters — That We May Remember," *New York History, Vol. XXVI*, No.3 (July 1945), and Glatthaar and Martin, 287, and Willett to Washington, Fort Herkimer, February 19, 1783, *Washington Papers, Series 4, General Correspondence*. I have viewed these sources as the most accurate accounts of the expedition. Willett informed Washington that the expedition left the river on the night of the February 12. Ross told Haldimand that the attempt took place on February 13; **Oswego Falls**: Often referred to as Onondaga

Falls; **Ladders**: Elmer D. Lince, "The Last Expedition of the Revolutionary War: Fort Oswego," *Journal of the Johannes Schwalm Historical Association, Inc.,* Vol. 5, No. 1 (1993*)*; **Dogs**: Calkins mentions the owners' grief. See also, the recollections of John Roof from Simms, *FNY*, Vol. 2, 646; **Identity of the Primary Guide**: Glathaar and Martin (287), identify the guide as Captain John Onondiyo (Silversmith). They do not list Otaawighton as one of the Oneidas commissioned as Continental Army captains (236), but do list Tewagtahkotte (The Standing Bridge), which, by process of elimination, may be the same man; **Otaawighton's Commission**: Graymont, 197; Otaawighton and two other Oneida captains and three lieutenants petitioned the U.S. Senate for a pension. "Indian Officers Petition New York for Payment," February 5, 1785, Penrose, *Indian Affairs*, 314, 349. Penrose lists Otaawighton as Willett's guide in 1783. He received three hundred acres in 1792; **Frozen Feet**: Willett, 92, and Willett to Washington, Fort Herkimer, February 19, 1783, *Washington Papers, Series 4, General Correspondence*; **Fired Upon**: PA S12020 of Williams Avery.

18. **Natives Shocked**: Lieutenant Andrew Thompson to his brother, Fort Rensselaer, January 24, 1783, transcribed in *The Historical Magazine, and Notes and Queries Concerning the Antiquities, History, etc....* Vol. 3 (Series 1, 10 vols.) New York: Charles B. Richardson, 1859; **Dog Carcasses**: PA W4189, the widow of Gideon Elliot and Matthew Calkins.
19. Ross to Haldimand, Oswego, February 17, 1783. Cruikshank and Watt, *KRR NY*, 97–98.
20. **Nelson**: Simms, *FNY*, Vol. 2, 646.
21. **Frozen Limbs**: PA S11226 of John Pettit, Newell's Company, WL. He was so badly frostbitten and in other ways disabled as to be unfit for any duty and deserted March 31, 1783. He also recalled that many men were invalids for life and PA R9985 of Orange Spencer of Florida, Harrison's Company, WL, had feet frozen and PA W4189 of Gideon Elliot mentioned that many men froze and PA R2245 of Abraham Conyne, 3TCM, Harrison's Company, WL, had his feet frozen and Samuel Joy received a third of a full invalid's pension as a result of having frozen feet in Willett's expedition, as did John Smith, who deposed that he "was frozen in his feet to such a degree as to lose sundry parts of his toes which partly deprives him of obtaining a subsistence." See, K.D. Johnson, Additional Partisans and PA S13125 of Benjamin Gaus of Cannon's Company states he froze his toes. *Ibid.* and PA W2643, widow of David Perry of Pierce's Company, WL, who deposed that his "feet were frozen en route and he has yet to recover from the injuries," *ibid.*, and the papers of Terry and Hazel Glasier. "The Ancestors of My Daughters." A study of the (De) Kalb family in America mentions that John Kalb, WL, lost some toes to frostbite and John Malone of Canajoharie, Pierce's Company, WL, had his feet frozen and lost some toes. J.F. Morrison research; PA S24101 of David Campbell, a MA farmer in Pierce's Company, WL, had one foot severely frozen; PA S16105 of Immanuel Deake, first serjeant of Wright's Company, WL. He deposed that "a great number were frozen considerably" Andrew Thompson, Fort Rensselaer,

January 24, 1783. Thompson recalled that 130 men were frostbitten, "some very dangerously"; **Rhode Island Injuries**: Transcripts of the "Records of the State of Rhode Island and Providence Plantations," 162–67, found in *www.rootsweb.ancestry.com/~rigenweb/articles* and *Popek*. Of the forty-seven men who sought compensation for wartime injuries, fourteen were from the Oswego debacle and six of these were apparently black; C. Olney to Washington, Saratoga, February 27, 1783, *Washington Papers, Series 4, General Correspondence*; PA S14371 of John Roof; PA S12020 of Williams Avery. He deposed, "my feet were so badly frozen that I have been decrepid by turns ever since"; **Rowley:** PA W24777, widow of Seth Rowely.

22. PA W20648, widow of Robert Ayres, Wright's Company, WL; Washington to Willett, HQ, February 13, 1783, *Washington Papers, Series 4, General Correspondence*; Moore to his father, February 18, 1783. As Willett wrote Washington from Fort Herkimer on February 19, the date of Moore's correspondence is in question. The text of this letter is in part found in *Moore Papers*, Section 2, 323, and possibly March 23, 1783, *ibid.*, Section 3.
23. John Garner and Abraham Whatson, RI men, taken at Three Rivers, McHenry, 67.
24. Ross to Haldimand, Oswego, February 17, 1783, Cruikshank and Watt, *KRR NY*, 97–98.
25. **Nelson:** Simms, *FNY*, Vol. 2, 646; Ross to Haldimand, Oswego, June 27, 1782, *ibid.*, 89; The deserter may have been Peter Hendricks of Cannon's Company, WL, who surrendered to the garrison. J.F. Morrison research. Hendricks appears on Pliny Moore's undated roll of deserters.
26. Washington to president of Congress, Newburgh, February 26, 1783, *Washington Writings*, Vol. 26, 165.
27. Washington to Willett, HQ, March 5, 1783, *ibid.*, 190.
28. **Angered at Willett:** PA S16076 of Heman Chapman; Ross to Haldimand, Oswego, February 17, 1783, Cruikshank and Watt, *KRR NY*, 97–99; Haldimand to Ross, Quebec City, March 11, 1783, *ibid.*, 99; Ross to Haldimand, Oswego, March 1783, *ibid.*, 100; **Revetment:** A strong wall, built on the outside of the rampart and parapet, to support the earth, and prevent its rolling into the ditch. Captain George Smith, inspector of the Royal Military Academy at Woolwich, *An Universal Military Dictionary, A Copious Explanation of the Technical Terms &c. — Used in the Equipment, Machinery, Movements, and Military Operations of an Army* (1779; reprint, Ottawa: Museum Restoration Service, 1969), 225.
29. General Orders, Newburgh, March 5, 1783, *Washington Writings*, Vol. 26, 191.
30. Haldimand to Ross, Quebec City, April 25, 1783, Cruikshank and Watt, *KRR NY*, 101.
31. Haldimand to Riedesel, Quebec City, April 26, 1783, Kelsay, 341, from Riedesel Memoirs, 2, 168–69.
32. Kelsay, 341 and Fryer, *Maclean*, 201, HP, AddMss21714, 118–19.
33. **Fate of the Rebel and Loyal Indians:** Glatthaar and Martin, 289–323; Taylor, 106–395; Graymont, 259–291; Charles M. Johnston, ed., *The Valley of the Six Nations — A Collection of Documents on the Indian Lands of the Grand River* (Toronto: The

Champlain Society, 1964), xxxiii–xcvi; Cruikshank, *Coming of the Loyalist Mohawks to the Bay of Quinte.*

34. Brigadier-General E.A. Cruikshank, *The Settlement of the United Empire Loyalists on the Upper St. Lawrence and Bay of Quinte in 1784* (Toronto: Ontario Historical Society, 1934).

APPENDIX ONE — HALDIMAND'S ARMY IN CANADA, 1782

1. When Burgoyne launched his 1777 expedition, Carleton was left with an artillery company of forty-two other ranks to defend Quebec Province. Christian Rioux, "The Royal Regiment of Artillery in Quebec City 1759–1871," *History and Archaeology 57* (Ottawa: Parks Canada, 1982): 29; After Burgoyne's surrender, this number was increased by the return of the forty-two other ranks who had been with St. Leger and the artillerists who had manned Ticonderoga. Lieutenant James M. Hadden, *A Journal Kept in Canada and Upon Burgoyne's Campaign in 1776 and 1777* (Albany, NY: Joel Munsell's Sons, 1884), 46; Although reinforcements must have been received from Britain over the years, details have not been found, yet returns of August 1 to October 1, 1782, show a total of 235 all ranks at Quebec City, Sorel, Chambly, Fort St. John's, and Isle aux Noix, and a total of fifty-four all ranks at Carleton Island, Oswego, Niagara, Detroit, and Mackinaw. WO17/1576, 136, 156, 161, respectively.

2. In 1778, Haldimand formed a Hesse-Hanau company of artillery by combining the small remnant of men who had escaped Burgoyne's surrender with Hanau infantrymen who had been left behind with Carleton. Historical Section of the General Staff, ed., Volume 3, "The War of the American Revolution, The Province of Quebec under the Administration of Governor Frederic Haldimand, 1778–1784," in *A History of the Organization, Development and Services of the Military and Naval Forces of Canada From the Peace of Paris in 1763 to the Present Time With Illustrative Documents* [HSGS] (Ottawa: King's Printer, n.d.), 69, 70 from LAC, HP, B54, 25–30; The company was reorganized in July 1782 under Major Georg Pausch of the Hesse-Hanau Artillery. For guns, Pausch had his four Hesse-Hanau light English 3-pdrs; two Hesse-Cassel light English 6-pdrs, and two light 3-pdrs of Anhalt-Zerbst. This new formation was attached to Major-General von Loos's brigade; Wilhelmy reports the Hanau manpower at sixty and Cassel's at twenty-four. Assuming the Anhalt strength would match Cassel, this would give Pausch a total strength of 108. Bruce E. Burgoyne, tr. and ed., *Georg Pausch's Journal and Reports of the Campaign in America* (Bowie, MD: Heritage Books, Inc., 1996).

3. The King's (8th) came to Canada in 1768 and, in 1774, was sent to the Upper Posts to replace the 10th Regiment, which had been ordered to Boston. Alan Kemp, "Notes on each Regiment in America," in *British Army in the American Revolution* (London: Almark Publications, 1973), 62, and George F.G. Stanley, *Canada Invaded 1775–1776* (Toronto: Samuel Stevens Hakkert & Company, 1977), 126, and Paul L. Stevens, *A King's Colonel at Niagara 1774–1776* (Youngstown, NY: Old Fort Niagara Association, 1987), 9; The Light Company and a line company, totalling

ninety-four other ranks, served with St. Leger during the Fort Stanwix siege in 1777, *WO17/1571*, 245. Detachments were on active service in the Mohawk Valley and Indian Territory until 1781 and, in the west, from 1778 to 1782.

4. The returns of December 1, 1782, show 279 men at Niagara; 321 at Detroit and seventy-four at Mackinac, WO28/6, 138,139,142; The 8th's unusual size was due to the drafting of two companies and a detachment of the 47th Regiment in June, HQ Order, Quebec, June 25, 1782, HP, AddMss21743, 192; As an indication of how many men were added by this 1782 draft, in November 1778, the 47th had a total of 152 rank and file at Carleton Island, CO42/39, 72.

5. The 29th Regiment arrived at Quebec City on May 6, 1776. George F.G. Stanley, *For Want of a Horse* (Sackville, NB: Tribune Press, 1961,) 69; In 1777, Burgoyne left the 29th's line companies behind to defend Canada, enigmatically commenting that the regiment was not brigaded. Lieutenant-General John Burgoyne, "Thoughts for Conducting the War from the Side of Canada," *A State of the Expedition From Canada as Laid Before the House of Commons By Lieutenant-General Burgoyne ...* (London: J. Almon, 1780), Appendix 6; In the ensuing years, the 29th became one of the most active British regiments in Canada; The flank companies were reconstituted in Canada on October 1, 1780, and the Light Company went with St. Leger on his Lake Champlain venture in 1781. John Enys, Elizabeth Cometti, eds., *The American Journals of Lt John Enys* (Syracuse: The Adirondack Museum and Syracuse University Press, 1976), 53; From August to October, 1782, the regiment was headquartered at Terrebonne with detachments at La Chenaye, Mascouche Le Chenaye, Montreal, and Lachine. It averaged a total strength of 434 over that time period, with six drummers and 136 other ranks wanting to complete, WO17/1576, 133, 153, 164, respectively. The regiment was assigned to garrison Fort St. John's over the winter of 1782–83.

6. The 31st Regiment arrived at Quebec City from Ireland on May 29, 1776. The flank companies served under Burgoyne in 1777 and were part of the surrender, but were reconstituted in Canada prior to 1781 (Hadden, lxvii); When Burgoyne left the line companies behind to defend Canada, he damned the 31st by noting that the regiment was "not equally in order with the other regiments for services of activity," John Burgoyne, "Thoughts"; During the following years, the 31st was quite active on the frontiers and, in the fall of 1781, the Light Company supported St. Leger's demonstration on Lake Champlain, Gavin K. Watt, *A dirty, trifling piece of business — Volume 1: The Revolutionary War as Waged from Canada in 1781* (Toronto: Dundurn Press, 2009); From August to October 1782, nine companies were headquartered at Quebec City, a forty-two-man detachment was at Spanish River and the Light Company was a Fort St. John's. The regiment's average strength in those months was 474 all ranks with ninety-six wanting to complete, WO17/1576, 132, 151, 152, respectively; Over the winter of 1782/83, the Grenadier Company garrisoned Quebec City, the Lights were located on two outlying islands in the St. Lawrence, and the line companies in four small settlements.

7. Like the 31st, the 34th arrived in Quebec from Ireland on May 29, 1776. The regiment's flank companies served under Burgoyne in 1777 and were part of the surrender. They were reconstituted in Canada prior to 1781 (Hadden, lxvii); About 120 line infantry served under St. Leger at Stanwix and Ticonderoga in 1777. In the ensuing years, the 34th was the most active Regular regiment in Haldimand's army. In 1778, a detachment under Captain Ross raided the Mohawk River and in 1779, 140 all ranks went with Sir John on his abortive relief expedition to the Six Nations. A company went with Sir John to Johnstown in May 1780 and the Lights and a line company with Johnson to the Schoharie and Mohawk Valleys in October 1780. Simultaneously, 115 all ranks went with Major Carleton on his Lake Champlain expedition. In 1781, the Light Company and seventy-five line infantrymen went with Ross to the Mohawk Valley and one hundred line infantry with St. Leger to Lake Champlain; The 34th was the principal instrument used for training Sir John Johnson's King's Royal Yorkers, supplying many staff and command officers to both battalions of that regiment.

8. From August 1 to September 1, 1782, the regiment had five companies at Fort St. John's, two at Isle aux Noix, one at Chambly, one at Carleton Island, and one not reported. On October 1, eight companies were at St. John's, one at Chambly, and one unreported. The latter was likely Captain Ancrum's company coming down from Carleton Island. Total strength averaged 532 over those three months with 108 wanting to complete, WO17/1576, 131, 150, 167, respectively; On December 1, the regiment had fourteen men on Carleton Island; forty-seven at Oswego; 171 at Niagara, and 110 at Detroit for a total of 342, WO28/6, 138, 139, 142. There is no indication that detachments of the 34th had remained behind in winter quarters in lower Quebec, so I have not been able to reconcile the December total of 342 with the strength of 532 reported two months earlier.

9. The 44th was the only British regiment to reinforce the Canadian army after 1776, arriving from New York City on June 29, 1780, after heavy service in lower New York and New Jersey in 1776 and at Brandywine and Germantown in 1777; In 1781, the Light Company served with St. Leger's demonstration on the Lake Champlain frontier, which may have been the regiment's only active service while in Canada (Watt, *Dirty, trifling*); The August 1 to October 1, 1782, returns indicated that all the companies were stationed in Quebec City. The average total strength was 429 all ranks with three drummers and 142 other ranks wanting to complete, WO17/1576, 130, 149; the 44th garrisoned Quebec City over the winter of 1782/83.

10. The 53rd Regiment arrived in Quebec from Ireland on May 29, 1776, and served with Burgoyne (Hadden, lxvii); Five weak companies were assigned to garrison Ticonderoga and in October, they "suffered the disgrace of a surprise" at the hands of rebel militia and lost thirteen officers and 143 other ranks as prisoners, which left only 106 men to withdraw to Canada after Burgoyne's surrender. Gavin K. Watt, *Rebellion in the Mohawk Valley — The St. Leger Expedition of 1777* (Toronto: Dundurn Press, 2002), 287, 307; Although the sick men left behind in Canada were

absorbed into this remnant, reinforcements from Britain must have been received in the intervening years, as the regiment paraded over 500 men in 1782.

11. In 1778, thirty men of the 53rd joined Major Christopher Carleton on a raid into Vermont. Ida H. and Paul A. Washington, *Carleton's Raid* (Canaan, NH: Phoenix Publishing, 1977), 16; In May 1780, thirty-four men served on the Johnstown raid with Sir John Johnson, and, in the fall of that year, 113 all ranks served under Major Carleton in the expedition against Forts Ann and George. Gavin K. Watt, *Burning of the Valleys — Daring Raids from Canada Against the New York Frontier in the Fall of 1780* (Toronto: Dundurn Press, 1997), 77, 95; A return dated August 24, 1782, showed seven companies at Isle aux Noix, one at Sorel, and two unreported. By October 1, ten companies were on Isle aux Noix and a thirty-six-man detachment was at Three Rivers. Average total strength was 519, with 191 wanting to complete, WO17/1576, 138, 174; Over the winter of 1782/83, the regiment garrisoned Pointe-au-Fer and Isle aux Noix.

12. The Highland Emigrants was originally a Provincial corps raised across America, primarily from Scots and Irish immigrants from Massachusetts, New York, Quebec, Newfoundland, Ile St Jean (PEI), Cape Breton, Nova Scotia, and the lower provinces as far south as Georgia. Latterly, the regiment was permitted to recruit in Britain. The RHE was very significant during the 1775 rebel siege of Fort St. John, during the defence of Quebec City, and particularly in the repulse of the rebel attack on December 31, 1775. During the siege of Quebec, its strength was 192, all ranks. Carleton to Germain, May 14, 1776, *HSGS*, Vol. 2, 147; On December 24, 1777, the RHE mustered 508 all ranks; On April 10, 1779, the regiment was elevated to the British establishment and numbered the 84th. Germain to Haldimand, Whitehall, *ibid.*, 103, HP, B43, 113; Detachments of the 1st Battalion, 84th RHE were on active service on the frontiers from 1779–81. The regiment's establishment was increased on September 7, 1781, to twelve companies of three serjeants, four corporals, two drummers, fifty-six privates, and two fifers in the Grenadiers, HP, AddMss21743. This authorization could have increased its strength to 814 all ranks, but nothing like that strength was recruited. See, a new Beating Order for the 84th Regiment dated August 30, 1779, and a Hand Bill, *HSGS*, Vol.3, 124, 125; Although only a handful of Canadiens served in the various loyalist corps, an exception was the 84th, which boasted a "French" company in 1779, although, for administrative reasons, the Canadien officers and men were dispersed throughout the battalion in later years. (A 2nd battalion was raised in and defended Nova Scotia and had detachments serving in the 1781 southern campaigns.)

13. On August 1, three companies of 1/84 were reported at regimental HQ at Batiscan, two at St. Anne, one at Lake Champlain, two at Carleton Island, one at Oswego, and one at Oswegatchie, for a total of 476 all ranks, with eighty-four wanting to complete (not remotely near to 814). By September 1, the companies and detachments were spread from Quebec City, to Sorel, Oswegatchie, Carleton Island, Oswego, and Mackinac and six companies were on the march. That month, there were 479 all ranks with eighty-one wanting to complete. By October 1, six companies were in

Montreal, three in Oswego, one at Oswegatchie, and sizeable detachments were at Lachine and Mackinac. That month, the regiment's total strength was 472, with eighty-eight wanting to complete, WO17/1576, 129, 148, 175, respectively.

14. **Anhalt-Zerbst**: The Princess of Anhalt's two-battalion regiment arrived at Quebec in May 1778. In a fit of petulance, Governor Carleton kept the men aboard their vessels for three months until official word of their coming was received from Britain. In October 1779, 174 recruits arrived. During the following June, the regiment worked on rebuilding the citadel at Quebec City. Jean-Pierre Wilhelmy, *German Mercenaries in Canada* (Beloeil, QC: Maison des Mots, 1985), 167, 168, 180, 266; When the corps was inspected by Haldimand in 1779, he noted they were in an excellent state, although composed primarily of raw recruits. Haldimand to Germain, September 13, 1779, CO42/39, 261; The regiment was never employed on active campaign during the whole of its service in Canada.

15. **Brunswick**: Prinz Ludwig's Dragoon regiment arrived at Quebec in June 1776. Although appropriately uniformed and accoutred for its role, the regiment had arrived without horses on the erroneous assumption that sufficient animals could be found in Canada. Prinz Ludwig's served with Burgoyne's expedition and its commanding officer, Lieutenant-Colonel Baum, led the ill-fated excursion to Bennington (in part to find mounts), which resulted in the virtual destruction of his regiment. When reformed in 1781, Prinz Ludwig's was substantially under strength and commanded by a senior captain. In 1782, a detachment of dragoons and Brunswick Light Infantry went on patrol to Crown Point.

16. **Brunswick**: Musketeer Regiment Prinz Friedrich arrived in Quebec June 1, 1776, as part of the large Brunswick contingent commanded by Major-General Riedesel and supported Burgoyne in 1777. Wilhelmy, 253, and Hadden, 37fn; After Ticonderoga fell to Burgoyne, the regiment was assigned to garrison that fortified complex with the British 53rd and, as a result, was saved from the surrender and able to return to Canada intact (Watt, *Rebellion*, 287–309); When the von Retz regiment was rebuilt in October, 1781, a company of Prinz Friedrich's was transferred to it (Wilhelmy, 184); After 1777, the regiment was not employed on active campaign.

17. **Brunswick**: Musketeer Regiment von Riedesel arrived in Quebec on June 1, 1776. In 1777, the regiment saw action at Hubbardton, Freeman's Farm, and Bemis Heights, and was reformed in 1781 with a blend of the sick and lame men left behind in 1777, many exchanged soldiers of the Convention Army, and recruits from Brunswick. The regiment saw no active service after 1777.

18. **Brunswick**: Musketeer Regiment von Rhetz arrived at Quebec in September 1776. In 1777, it saw action at Hubbardton, Freeman's Farm, and Bemis Heights, and suffered major losses before the surrender and could only be reconstituted when Riedesel brought exchanged troops from New York City in September 1781 and combined them with the regiment's sick and lame left behind by Burgoyne in 1777. Even then, he had to add a company of von Breymann's grenadiers and one from Prinz Friedrich's to bring up its strength. After 1777, the regiment saw no more active campaigning.

19. **Brunswick**: Musketeer Regiment von Specht came to Quebec in September 1776. During Burgoyne's expedition, the regiment fought at Hubbardton, Freeman's Farm, and Bemis Heights. Using sick and lame men left behind in 1777 and exchanged troops of the Convention Army and Brunswick recruits, the regiment was reconstituted in 1782. The regiment saw no further active campaigning after 1777.

20. **Brunswick**: Von Barner's Brunswick Light Infantry regiment arrived in Canada on September 17, 1776. It was composed of a company of Jägers and four Musketeer companies and was often referred to as the "combined battalion." Claus Reuter, *History of the Brunswick Light Infantry Battalion "von Barner" in North America from 1776 to 1783* (Toronto: German-Canadian Museum of Applied History, n.d.); In 1777, the battalion served under Burgoyne and fought at Hubbardton and was heavily engaged at Bennington and Freeman's Farm. The battalion was commanded by Major Friedrich Albrecht von Barner, who when grievously wounded at Bennington, was evacuated to Canada. William L. Stone, ed. & tr., *Letters of Brunswick and Hessian Officers During the American Revolution* (New York: Da Capo Press, 1970), 109; The remnant of this battalion, many of whom were recovered wounded men from early actions under Burgoyne, was combined in 1778 with new recruits from Brunswick and men from Prinz Ludwig's Dragoon Regiment, von Breyman's Grenadier Battalion, and the Musketeer regiments of von Rhetz, Riedesel, and Specht and was temporarily named Regiment von Barner. In November 1781, Riedesel re-established the original regiments. Von Barner's Light battalion was reconstituted by combining men from the Regiment von Barner and von Lucke's detachment of 231 Brunswickers that had just arrived in Canada. It mustered 413 all ranks. Reuter, 13, 14 and Wilhelmy, 194, 263; Haldimand to Germain, October 15, 1778, NAC, CO42/37, 203; In 1782, a mixed detachment of von Barner's and Prinz Ludwig's dragoons went on patrol to Crown Point.

21. **Hesse-Hanau**: Von Kreutzbourg's Jäger Free Corps (Chausseurs) was assigned to St. Leger for the 1777 campaign. Only one company arrived in time to join in his attempt against Fort Stanwix and fought at Oriskany on August 6, 1777. Three additional Jäger companies joined St. Leger after he had withdrawn to Oswego and went with him to Ticonderoga in a vain attempt to reinforce Burgoyne. After Burgoyne's surrender, the regiment returned to Canada intact (Watt, *Rebellion*, 92, 158, 265); In August 1778, a dispute arose over the Jägers refusing to labour in the works at Niagara and they were sent to Carleton Island where they again exerted their treaty right to perform strictly military duties. Although Haldimand agreed with von Kreutzbourg's interpretation of the treaty, he was not pleased, as he needed troops who were willing to perform all types of duties. This disagreement continued until 1782 when the count of Hanau wrote in support of his colonel, although Kreutzbourg relented when he discovered that fellow Hanau officers were allowing their men to perform construction work. Whilhelmy, 178, 179; In 1779, an additional company arrived from Hanau. Haldimand was unimpressed, commenting that "so far from being experienced Woods, and Marks Men (as they are in general

conceived to be) there are perhaps a few in each company who may be considered as such[,] the rest are, in both respects, far inferior to the worst of our Troops who have been any Time in this Country" (CO42/39, 261); A platoon of Hanau Jägers served under Sir John on Mohawk Valley raids in May 1780 and again in the fall. (Watt, *Burning*, 77,164); In 1781, a section of twelve Jägers went on the Ross expedition to the Mohawk Valley and several companies went up Lake Champlain with their colonel as part of St. Leger's demonstration (Watt, *Dirty, trifling*, 363–402); A lieutenant and sixty-two recruits arrived in 1782. Max Von Eelking, *Memoirs, Letters and Journals of Major General Riedesel during his Residence in America*, Vol. 1 (2 vols.) William L. Stone, ed. and tr. (Albany, NY: J. Munsell, 1868), 219.

22. **Hesse-Hanau**: Hesse-Hanau Grenadier Regiment arrived in Quebec on June 1, 1776, and went with Burgoyne in 1777 and saw action at Freeman's Farm and Bemis Heights. A detachment commanded by Captain Frederich von Schoell managed to return to Canada sometime after the surrender. In 1782, the regiment was reformed into six companies of line infantry by incorporating Schoell's detachment and exchanged Convention troops and recruits. Prince Wilhelm of Hanau named the new formation the first battalion of Erbprinz von Hessen (Wilhelmy, 264, 265 and Pausch, 122).

23. **Hesse-Cassel**: Fusilier Regiment alt von Lossberg arrived in New York City in August 1776 and fought at Fort Washington and White Plains. On December 26, 1776, it was surprised and mauled by the rebels at Trenton, New Jersey, and the survivors were folded into the Regiment von Loos for the 1777 Philadelphia campaign. That December, von Loos's regiment was divided into two elements at New York City, one of which resumed the name von Lossberg early next year. The latter was sent to Quebec in 1779, but suffered tragic losses because of storms and was forced to return to New York. The regiment finally arrived in Canada at the end of June 1780 and by August was at work on the fortifications of Quebec City (Wilhelmy, 180–81, 267). The regiment saw no further campaigning.

24. The beating order for the 1st Battalion, Royal Regiment of New York (King's Royal Yorkers), was dated June 19, 1776. In 1777, it was the largest unit serving under St. Leger with three hundred all ranks. During the campaign, it recruited its strength to 390. In May 1780, Lieutenant-Colonel Sir John Johnson led an expedition to Johnstown, New York, which included 150 of his Royal Yorkers and he returned with sufficient recruits to complete the first battalion and begin a second. In October that year, the 1KRR fielded 357 all ranks in a second invasion of New York. During 1781 and 1782, 1KRR was in lower Quebec maintaining the communications with the upper posts, garrisoning various posts, and providing scouting parties and Secret Service agents. News that the battalion was raised to the American Establishment was received in Quebec on March 21, 1782. Ernest A. Cruikshank and Gavin K. Watt, *The History and Master Roll of The King's Royal Regiment of New York*, revised edition (Campbellville: Global Heritage Press, 2006); However, this later proved to be only an elevation to the Provincial Establishment in America, not at all the same status enjoyed by five of the loyalist regiments in the Central Department as anticipated by Sir John.

25. On August 1, 1782, 1KRR was headquartered on Ile Jesu, north of Montreal, with seven of its companies. Duncan's company was at Rivière du Chêne; Alexander McDonell's at Quinze-Chênes and Vaudreuil and Joseph Anderson's at Coteau-du-Lac. Little changed in September, but, by October, Duncan's and Archibald McDonell's companies were posted at Carillon and the Lights were on Isle aux Noix. The first battalion's total strength averaged 545 over those three months with fifteen wanting to complete, WO17/1756, 126, 144, 166, respectively.

26. A second battalion was conditionally approved in Sir John's original beating order in 1776. After the May 1780 Johnstown raid, Johnson organized his surplus recruits into provisional second battalion companies. On July 13, 1780, official permission was received to proceed with the new battalion and Grenadier Captain John Ross, 34th, was appointed the major-commandant. On November 30, 1780, Ross arrived at Carleton Island with one hundred 2KRR soldiers and took command of the post. A great many of Ross's men remained in lower Quebec, attached to 1KRR for training. Forty of Captain Robert Leake's Independent Company, which, from 1778–80 had been operating as a *de facto* 11th Company of 1KRR, joined Ross and 155 all ranks of 2KRR on an arduous raid into the Mohawk Valley in October 1781. On November 12, 1781, 2KRR's officers were officially appointed and Leake and his company were absorbed into the battalion, as were some men from Peters's, Adams's, and McAlpin's units. On January 1, 1782, 272 other ranks of 2KRR were at Carleton Island. In April 1782, two hundred other ranks of 2KRR reoccupied Oswego and, with detachments of other regiments, began to rebuild the works. On May 1, 1782, seventy other ranks were still at Carleton Island and, by June, this had been increased to eighty-eight by the arrival of reinforcements from the lower province (Cruikshank and Watt, *KRR NY* and WO28/6). When Sir John received word that 1KRR was — he thought — raised to the American establishment, the Crown advised that Governor Haldimand would decide whether 2KRR would also be so recognized. No confirmation, one way or the other, has been found, although, like all provincial officers in Canada, both battalions' officers were granted half-pay for life after disbandment.

27. By August 1, 1782, the majority of the battalion was headquartered at Fort Ontario, Oswego, although there were several detachments at other posts. Two serjeants and forty other ranks were serving as marines on Lake Champlain; five serjeants and fifty-six other ranks were at Coteau-du-Lac; one serjeant and twenty rankers were at The Cedars; sixteen rankers at Isle aux Noix; fifteen rankers at Carleton Island; nine rankers at Fort St. John's, eight at Sorel, and five at Lachine. The return of August 1 showed a total strength of 455, which increased to 476 on September 1 and dropped to 473 on October 1, WO17/1576, 124, 125, 142, 143, 177, 179.

28. Major John Butler received his beating warrant for an eight-company regiment of rangers on September 15, 1777, following the failure of the siege of Fort Stanwix. He immediately filled two companies with Six Nations' Indian Department rangers who had served with him at Stanwix. One company was specifically designated to serve among the natives and the other companies were to act in co-operation with

them. The rates of pay were different in these two distinct capacities and, in both cases, higher than regular infantry, which caused Butler much difficulty later. Butler's Rangers became as much of a scourge to the rebel frontiers as the natives. The battalion was the widest-ranging of all British regiments, raiding across New York, western Pennsylvania, into New Jersey, and Virginia. Butler had three companies complete by July 1778 and two more by November 1779. A seventh was added before July 1780 and, a year later, the eighth was complete. Approval was then given for two more companies and, by September 17, 1781, they were complete. Butler's Rangers's raids against New York, western Pennsylvania, and New Jersey were managed from HQ at Fort Niagara and by employing outstations in Indian Territory. By August 1780, a company was sent to Detroit and, from this point on, the Rangers also operated in the far west out of Detroit and several outposts in various native towns. By 1782, the regiment's presence in central New York was rare. Lieutenant-Colonel William A. Smy, *An Annotated Nominal Roll of Butler's Rangers 1777–1784 with Documentary Sources* (St. Catharines, ON: Friends of the Loyalist Collection at Brock University, 2004), 32, and Ernest A. Cruikshank, *The Story of Butler's Rangers and the Settlement of Niagara* (1893; reprint, Owen Sound, ON: Richardson, Bond & Wright Ltd., 1975).

29. In April 1782, Butler's Rangers supplied 194 other ranks to work on the rebuilding of Oswego and had 234 at Niagara, seventy-three at Detroit, and twenty-one in Indian Country for a total of 521. Returns from August 1 to October 1 averaged a total strength of 525 all ranks with an average of 315 at Niagara, 118 at Detroit, and ninety-two at Fort Ontario, WO17/1756, 138, 159, 184, respectively. On August 19, 1782, Captain William Caldwell and his company, assisted by Indian Department officers and a body of Lakes' warriors, defeated a large force of mounted Kentucky militia at a river crossing known as Blue Licks. The final British action of the war was fought by Captain Andrew Bradt's company and natives at Wheeling, (West) Virginia, on September 11, 1782.

30. The regiment of Loyal Rangers was established on November 12, 1781, under the command of Major-Commandant Edward Jessup. This was accomplished by amalgamating his brother Ebenezer's King's Loyal Americans, John Peters's Queen's Loyal Rangers, Daniel McAlpin's "American Volunteers," (which earlier had absorbed Samuel Adams's company of rangers), a remnant of Van Pfister's/ Mackay's "Loyal Volunteers" and the Independent Companies of Captains Peter Drummond and William Fraser. "The Orderly Book of the King's Loyal Americans and the Loyal Rangers, dated from September 4, 1780 to October 23, 1783," *Archives of Ontario, Ms521(1), Edward Jessup Papers*; In 1780, a KLA detachment participated in Major Carleton's expedition against Forts Ann and George while Captain William Fraser's Independent Company raided Ballston in conjunction with two 1KRR companies. In October 1781, the KLA and other loyalists under Major Edward Jessup went with St. Leger to Ticonderoga and penetrated south of Lake George. After the amalgamation of November 1781, the Loyal Rangers saw no active service as a battalion. In May 1782, a ninth company was created by

incorporating Captain John Walden Meyers's Independent Company as a nucleus and a tenth was created with Thomas Fraser promoted to captain as its commander and, apparently, absorbing the balance of Peters's invalid company.

31. The return for September 1, 1782, showed the Loyal Rangers headquartered at Verchère and its largest contingent, consisting of three lieutenants, nine serjeants, and 206 other ranks, was serving in the engineering department under Captain Jonathon Jones. Captain Sherwood had two ensigns, four serjeants, and fifty-seven other ranks garrisoning the Loyal Blockhouse in addition to a lieutenant, two ensigns, a serjeant, and seven other ranks under him in the Secret Service. Captains William and Thomas Fraser had one lieutenant, five serjeants, one drummer, and seventy-seven other ranks garrisoning the two Yamaska blockhouses. Major Jessup had one captain, two lieutenants, one ensign, four serjeants, and thirty-seven other ranks cutting hay along Lake Champlain. There were twenty-nine other ranks in the barrack master's department, six in the quartermaster's department, and seven as marines on Lake Ontario. By October 1, Major Jessup had returned to Verchère and had four captains, seven lieutenants, three ensigns, the adjutant, seven serjeants, and eighty-one other ranks there. Captain Jonathon Jones had three lieutenants, ten serjeants, and 180 other ranks in the engineers' department. The garrisons at the Loyal and Yamaska blockhouses and the men serving in the barrack master's and quartermaster's departments were almost unchanged. Only Ensign Thomas Sherwood and two serjeants continued in the Secret Service and the marines had come off the lake. On September 1, the battalion returned a total strength of 478 all ranks and a month later, 487. On this latter date, the battalion was overstrength by five serjeants and ten rank and file — the only British formation to show an excess. The eight original companies established in November 1781 had included one of pensioners, nominally commanded by Lieutenant-Colonel Eben Jessup as captain, and another of invalids nominally commanded by Lieutenant-Colonel John Peters as captain. On October 1, 1782, Ebenezer Jessup's Company of Pensioners was specifically returned with the three officers at regimental headquarters and sixty-two other ranks widely spread at other posts and cantonments. There was no return made of the invalid company and it had likely been converted into Thomas Fraser's 10th company.

32. Major James Rogers endured two years of limbo in Quebec, attempting to recruit his 2nd battalion, King's Rangers, and, in the process, created much controversy with fellow loyalist officers. In the fall of 1780, the King's Rangers accompanied Major Christopher Carleton on his expedition against Forts Ann and George and was pre-eminent in the action at Bloody Pond (Watt, *Burning*, 95, 103, 104); In April 1781, Rogers and Lieutenant-Colonel John Peters were unsuccessful in gaining approval to amalgamate the King's Rangers with the remnants of the Queen's Loyal Rangers, HP, AddMss21874, 205, 212; In the fall of 1781, the King's Rangers accompanied St. Leger to Ticonderoga to make a demonstration (Watt, *Dirty, trifling*, 369, 376, 392, 398); For most of 1781 and 1782, the majority of the King's Rangers were occupied in Secret Service and scouting activities in Vermont, garrisoning their head-

quarters at Fort St. John's and serving as marines on Lake Champlain. On November 25, 1781, the three-company 2nd Battalion of King's Rangers (2KR) was finally accepted by Haldimand into his Northern Department as a distinct corps, MG13, WO28/5, 171; With Sir John Johnson's blessing, Rogers again sought amalgamation in April 1783, this time with 2KRR, perhaps in an attempt to be included on the American establishment, perhaps in hopes of a Lieutenant-Colonelcy. He was unsuccessful (Sir John Johnson to James Rogers, Montreal April 28, 1783, *Archives of Ontario, Ms522 Rogers' Papers*); It appears from Provincial regimental returns that the King's Rangers was ranked senior to the Loyal Rangers. See "State of the Provincial Troops in Canada Serving under His Excellency General Frederick Haldimand, Head Quarters Quebec 1st November 1782 and 1st January 1783," WO1/11.

33. This company of bateauxmen was established in September 1780 under the command of Captain Han Jost Herkimer, formerly of the Six Nations' Indian Department. Mary Beacock Fryer, *King's Men, the Soldier Founders of Ontario* (Toronto: Dundurn Press Limited, 1980), 32. A number of blacks, who had come to Canada to earn their freedom by serving in the military, were incorporated, as were a handful of natives; While strictly not infantry, the bateauxmen were armed with long Indian fusils and given scalping knives to whittle down to make plug bayonets, HP, AddMss21773, 177; Although Herkimer had demonstrated his competence in the management of boats and pioneering duty on the St. Leger Expedition, he seems to have been either quite stupid or dishonest. On October 12, 1780, the governor severely chastised him for carrying seventy-two persons on his roster when his company was only able to crew two bateaux. Haldimand wrote, "Your company being intended for Service and not as Invalids or a nursery for women and children." Lieutenant-Colonel William A. Smy, tr. and ed., "The Butler Papers: Documents and Papers Relating to Colonel John Butler and his Corps of Rangers 1711–1977," (u.p., 1994), from HP, AddMss21788, and AddMss21848, 110, 112; A return of August 24, 1782, showed twenty-five all ranks, HP, AddMss21752.

APPENDIX TWO — HALDIMAND'S NATIVE ALLIES AND HIS INDIAN DEPARTMENTS, 1782

1. The Canada Indians (Seven Nations of Canada) had been settled by the French as Roman Catholic converts in satellite towns in lower Quebec to protect the European settlements. The major groupings were: 1. the Hurons at Lorette. 2. the Abenakis at St. Francis (Odanak) and Bécancour. 3. the Kahnawakes at Sault St. Louis, who were mixed Abenakis, Mohawks, and Oneidas. 4. At Lake of the Two Mountains (Lac de Deux Montagnes) there were three communities — the primarily-Mohawk Kanehsatakes (Oka), the Algonquins and the Nippisings. 5. the Akwesasnes at St. Régis were Abenakis, Mohawks, and Onondagas. 6. A small allied community of Onondagas and Cayugas was located at Oswegatchie and were known by that place name.

2. "Return of the Several Indian Nations and Equipment given agreable to their respective Classes belonging to Lieut Colo Campbells Department in the Districts of Quebec," Montreal, 1780, HP, AddMss21770. This listed fifty-seven "Chiefs,"

sixty-five "Escabias" (presumably principal Warriors), and 560 "Warriors."

3. The Six Nations' Mohawk town of Fort Hunter in the Mohawk Valley had been abandoned in 1777 and, after Burgoyne's surrender, the people settled temporarily at Lachine, near Montreal, to be closer to their hunting territory than they would have been at Niagara.

4. "Return of the Officers and Rangers attached to the Six Nations Indian Department under the immediate Direction of Daniel Claus Esqr Agent for the Six Nations in Canada ... together with the Number of Indians now in the Mohawk Village" signed by Claus and dated Montreal August 4, 1782, AO, HP, Ms622, Mf Reel 51. The return showed a total of fifteen officers and rangers and fifty-five "Indians bearing Arms."

5. The Six Nations or Iroquois Confederacy (League of the Iroquois) was an alliance of Mohawks, Oneidas, Tuscaroras, Onondagas, Cayugas, Genesee, and Allegheny Senecas. As the Tuscaroras joined in 1732, well after the Confederacy's founding, they did not have a vote in council, although their opinions were heard through their sponsoring brothers, the Oneidas. A large proportion of the Oneidas and Tuscaroras supported the rebel cause; In an attempt to offset its dwindling numbers, early in the eighteenth century the Confederacy had encouraged small groups of affiliated Indians to settle near to, or interspersed amongst, their towns. These were: Delawares/Munsees, Shawnees, Mohicans/Stockbridges, Brothertons, Squakies, Tuteloes, Saponis, Nanticokes, and Conoys. These affiliates and the Schoharies (said to be an offshoot of the Mohawks) supported the loyalists of the Six Nations throughout the conflict.

6. "General State of the Corps of Indians and Department Of Indian Officers ..." signed by John Butler, Niagara, September 2, 1782, HP, AddMss21770. This return showed 355 warriors at Niagara and 1,258 "at their towns." Although some of the original western Seneca towns had been reoccupied by 1782, in the main, the loyal Iroquois and their affiliates were settled in new villages near to Fort Niagara and, presumably, it was these latter towns that were referred to in Butler's report.

7. The Mississaugas lived in fishing communities along the north shore of Lake Ontario where major rivers flowed into the lake. Although they lived in Quebec Province, they were close friends of the Senecas and consequently were administered by the Six Nations' Indian Department; For evidence of the alliance of the Mississaugas with the Iroquois as early as 1700, see Percy J. Robinson, *Toronto During the French Régime* (Toronto: University of Toronto Press, 1965), 59, 60.

8. "Return of Indian stores given to the Missesagey Nation of Indians as a payment for the Lands at Toronto & the communication to Lake Huron relinquished by them to the Crown" signed P[atrick] Langan, 1788, *ibid.*, 250. At that time, Langan noted that the Mississaugas' male strength was 287.

9. The Lakes' Nations were the Wyandots, Ottawas, Potawatamis, Chippeways, Menominees, Winnebagos, Sauks and Foxes, and Santee Sioux.

10. In 1781 and 1782, the Winnebagos and Santee Sioux were active in the far west in modern Michigan and Indiana while the other nations supported their Ohio brothers in the Ohio, Illinois, and Kentucky countries.

11. The Ohio Nations were the Allegheny Seneca, Delawares/Munsees, Shawnees, and Mingos (the latter made up of mixed Iroquoian peoples).

12. Some of these Indians remained in the Ohio River valley during the conflict and others moved closer to Detroit and yet others to Niagara. These nations were very active against rebel incursions out of Virginia and Kentucky territory, and Pennsylvania in 1781 and 1782 (Alan Fitzpatrick, *Wilderness War on the Ohio*).

13. A "Return of the Officers[,] Interpreters and others in the Indian Department," dated Montreal, December 25, 1781, showed forty-two men of all ranks and included six men posted to Detroit and Mackinac; A "List of Officers and Others employed during the Rebellion in the Department of the Seven Nations in Canada ... 24th December 1783," AO, HP, Mss622, Mf Reel 113. Shown were Superintendent Lieutenant-Colonel John Campbell and Deputy Superintendent Captain Alexander Fraser, plus one captain, nineteen lieutenants, eleven interpreters, three assistant interpreters, five commissaries, two storekeepers, three conductors of presents, five labourers, and one accountant for a total of fifty-two; Then, returning to the far west — a "List of Officers and other employed during the Rebellion in the Indian Department at Detroit ..." sent to Britain on February 13, 1784, AO, HP, Mss622, Mf Reel 113, showed a principal agent, four captains, two lieutenants, thirty-four Volunteers, six militia serjeants, three interpreters, and one secretary, for a total of fifty-one.

14. An undated return entitled "List of Officers and others Employed during the Rebellion the Department of the Indian Six Nations at Niagara ..." enigmatically included Daniel Claus, who at no time served at Niagara. Listed were Superintendent and Colonel Guy Johnson, with three deputy superintendents (Daniel Claus, John Dease, and John Butler), six captains, sixteen lieutenants, eleven Volunteers, two serjeants, and thirty-seven Foresters with staff officers — secretary, clerk, storekeepers, commissaries, gunsmith, and six interpreters, AO, HP, Mss622, Mf Reel 113; As to Claus's sub-department at Montreal/Lachine, a "Return of Mens Names employed as Rangers with the Mohawk Indians ..." signed by Dan Claus dated Montreal, April 8, 1782, listed eleven men, *ibid.*, Mf Reel 51; The above returns showed that Six Nations' officers and interpreters were also at times stationed at Detroit.

BIBLIOGRAPHY

PRIMARY SOURCES — ARCHIVAL

Archives of Ontario

Ms521(1), Edward Jessup Papers.

   The Orderly Book of the King's Loyal Americans and the Loyal Rangers,
   dated from September 5, 1780 to October 23, 1783.

British Library

Haldimand Papers

   AddMss21705, Letters from the English Ministers to General Haldimand.

   AddMss21710, Letters from the English Admiralty 1777–84.

   AddMss21714, V.1, Ministerial Letters of Appointment to Various Commands
      Held by General Haldimand, 1778–80.

   AddMss21715, Letters to the Ministry (Vol. 2) 1780–82.

   AddMss21720, Letters from General Haldimand to the Secretary at War, the
      Ordnance Office, the Admiralty, and the Board of Trade.

   AddMss21721, Letters from the Secretaries of General Haldimand as Commander
      in Chief, 1778.

   AddMss21734, V.3, Letters from Various Persons to Haldimand, 1781–82.

   AddMss21741, Part 2, Register of Letters from the Adjutant General's Office at
      Quebec, 1781–1783.

   AddMss21743, General Orders issued by Carleton and Haldimand, 1776–83.

   AddMss21744, General Orders by General Haldimand, 1783–84.

   AddMss21753, V.5 Register of Warrants for the Extraordinary Service of the Army.

   AddMss21756, Correspondence with Officers Commanding at Mackinac and
      Niagara, 1777–82.

   AddMss21759, Letters and Drafts Relating to the Upper Posts, n.d., 1778–1782.

   AddMss21761, Letters from Officers Commanding at Niagara, 1781.

   AddMss21762, Letters from Officers Commanding at Niagara, 1782.

AddMss21764, Letters to Officers Commanding at Niagara, 1779–83.

AddMss21765, Correspondence with Officers at Niagara, 1777–84.

AddMss21768, Part 3 of above, 1782–83.

AddMss21770, V.2, ditto, n.d., and 1782–87.

AddMss21772, V.2, Letters from Lieutenant-Colonel J. Campbell and Others, n.d., 1782–87.

AddMss21773, Letters to Lieutenant-Colonel J. Campbell and Others, 1779–82.

AddMss21774, Correspondence with Lieutenant-Colonel Daniel Claus, n.d. and 1777–84.

AddMss21775, Correspondence with Colonel Sir J. Johnson, n.d., 1777–84.

AddMss21779, Reports on Indian Meetings, Treaties, etc., n.d. and 1778–84.

AddMss21780, Correspondence with Officers Commanding at Oswegatchie, 1778–84.

AddMss21781, Register of Correspondence with Offices Commanding at Detroit, 1776–83.

AddMss21783, V.2, Correspondence with Lieutenant Governor Hamilton and Papers relating to Detroit, n.d., 1778–84.

AddMss21784, Register of Correspondence with Officers Commanding at Carleton Island, Oswego, Cataraqui, 1781–83.

AddMss21785, Correspondence with Major John Ross at Oswego, etc., 1782–84.

AddMss21786, Correspondence with Major John Ross and Others at Carleton Island, Cataraqui, n.d. and 1783–86.

AddMss21787, Letters from Officers Commanding at Carleton Island, 1778–84.

AddMss21788, Letters to Officers Commanding at Carleton Island, 1779–83.

AddMss21789, V.1, Letters from Officers Commanding at Montreal, 1778–81.

AddMss21790, V.2, as above, 1782–84.

AddMss21791, Letters to Officers commanding at Montreal, 1778–84.

AddMss21796, V.1, Letters from Officers commanding at Sorel, n.d., 1778–81.

AddMss21797, V.2, as above, n.d., 1782.

AddMss21811, Letters from Officers of the German Legion (Vol.1).

AddMss21819, Letters to Officers of the KRR NY, 1779–83.

AddMss21821, V.1, Letters from Officers of the Loyalists, 1777–82.

AddMss21823, Letters to Officers of the Loyalists, 1779–83.

AddMss21837, Part 1, Letters from Captain Sherwood and Dr. Smyth, n.d., 1782.

AddMss21837, Part 2, Letters from Captain Sherwood and Dr. Smyth, 1782.

AddMss21849, Returns and Papers relating to the Quartermaster General's Department at Quebec, n.d., 1778–82.

AddMss21874, Part 1, Memorials from Provincial Corps and Loyalists, n.d. and 1777–82.

AddMss21875, Part 2, as above, n.d., 1783–84.

AddMss21876, Memorials from the Indian and Naval Departments, n.d. and 1777–84.

Library and Archives Canada

Claus Family fonds, MG19, F1, vols. 25 and 26.

MG21

B50, Letters from the English Admiralty, 1777–1784.

B112, Vol. II of Letters from Lieutenant-Colonel J. Campbell and Others, 1780–1783.

B113, Letters to Lieutenant-Colonel D. Claus, n.d., 1777–84.

B114, Correspondence with Lieutenant-Colonel D. Claus, 1777–1784.

B115, Correspondence with Brigadier-General Sir John Johnson, 1782–84.

B124, Register of Correspondence with Officers Commanding at Carleton Island, Oswego, Cataraqui.

B125, Correspondence with Major Ross at Oswego, 1782–84.

B127, Letters from Officers Commanding at Carleton Island, 1778–84.

B130, Letters from Officers Commanding at Montreal, 1778–84.

B131, Copies of Letters to Officers Commanding at Montreal, 1778–84.

B136, V.1, Letters from officers Commanding at Sorel, n.d. and 1782.

B137, V.2, as above, 1778–1784.

B139, Copies of Letters to Officers commanding at Sorel, 1778–1783.

B154, Correspondence with Officers of the Engineers, 1771–1784.

B158, Letters from Officers of the Royal Regiment of New York with Returns, etc. 1776–84 (AddMss21818).

B159, Copies of Letters to Officers of the Royal Regiment of New York, 1779–83 (AddMss21819).

B161, V.1, Letters from Officers of the Loyalists, 1777–82.

B166, Returns of Loyalists in Canada, n.d., 1778–87.

B177, Part 1, Letters from Captain Sherwood and Dr. Smyth, n.d., 1782.

B177, Part 2, as above, 1782.

Colonial Office Records

CO42 (Canada, Original Correspondence).

42/37 (Q14), 1777, Burgoyne's expedition and Surrender.

42/40 (Q17), Dispatches and Miscellaneous, 1779–80.

42/42 (Q19), January 2, 1782–June 19, 1782.

42/43, as above, July 16, 1782–October 20, 1782.

42/44, as above, November 10, 1782–August 20, 1783.

War Office Papers

WO28/4, Butler's Rangers, 1775–83.

WO28/5 (MG13), Royal Regiment of New York, 1776–83; Roger's King's Rangers, 1781–83.

No.23, R. Regiment New York. Field Officers Letters for 1781 and 1782.

No.24, R. Regiment New York. Field Officers Letters for 1778 to 1788. Provincial.

No.53, Papers concerning the 2d B.RR. New York. 1780.

WO28/10, Miscellaneous Returns, 1776–85.

War Office Records
WO1/11, Carleton War Office, In-Letters, North America, 1755–85.
17/1576, British, Provincial, and German Troops serving in Canada 1782.
28/2, Letters from Field officers, 34th Regiment, 1778–83
28/10, Part 4, Headquarters Records and Returns, America, 1775–95.
28/6, Headquarters Records and Returns, Upper Posts, 1782–83.
28/8, Letters, Returns, etc. …, (including) Carleton Island, Cataraqui, Oswego, 1779–83.

Library of Congress
Washington, George. Papers of George Washington.
Series 4, General Correspondence.
Papers of George Washington, 1741–1799: Series 3C, Varick Transcripts.

New York Historical Society (Collections)
Willett, Marinus, Papers of: Miscellaneous Manuscripts.

New York State Library
Special Collections and Manuscripts, Audited Accounts.

Nieders, Staatsarchiv, Wolfenbuettel, Braunschweig, Germany
Archivbezeichnung — 237 N 96.

State Library of Virginia, Richmond
The Lidgerwood Collection.
HZ-1 (2). Correspondence of General Riedesel. [Riedesel Correspondence] Transcribed by Lewis Biegigheiser.

U.S. National Archives and Records Center
Pension Applications
Key: S — survivor; W — widow of; R — rejected.
Ashman, Samuel, widow of, W25362.
Ayres, Robert, widow of, W20648.
Avery, Williams, S12020.
Becker, Barent/Barnet, S12193.
Bellinger, John, R730.
Brookman, John, widow Anna, W17353.
Brown, Joseph, S12338.
Campbell, David, S24101.
Cannan/Cannon, James, R1661.
Conyne, Abraham, R2245.
Cramer, John C., widow Christina, W16548.

Dake, John M., S19272.

Deake, Immanuel, S16105.

Dusler, Marcus, S10589.

Eckerson, Cornelius, widow Catherine, W16971.

Elliott/Eliot, Gideon, widow Hannah, W4189.

Feeter/Vetter, William, S13013.

Flagg, Peter, widow of, W12099.

Garlock, Adam, R3917.

Garlock, Jacob, S13119.

Gauss, Benjamin, S13125.

Getman, Conrad, widow of, W19497.

Gile/Guile, Ray/Rea, R4017.

Hager, Joseph, widow of, W25748.

Hamlin, Amos, S28755.

Herrick, Daniel, R4920.

Hubbs, Samuel, S13497.

Lighthall, George, S13341.

Loucks, Dietrick/Richard, R6461.

McGregor, David, S42959.

Meyer, Daybold, widow Margaret, W15789.

Murphy, Henry, widow of, W18543.

Perry, David, widow of, W2643.

Pettit, John, S11226.

Roof, John, S14371.

Rowley, Seth, widow Innocent, W24777.

Scribner, Thaddeus, widow Lydia, W1499.

Shaver, Henry, S11376.

Spencer, Orange, R9985.

Suits/Suts, Peter, widow Elizabeth, W13941.

Willett, Marinus, widow Margaret, (NY) W1525.

Wisconsin, State Historical Society
"Captain John Deserontyon's Services," 14F49.

PRIMARY SOURCES — PUBLISHED

Newspapers and Periodicals
New York Packett and American Advertiser, August 1, 1782.
The Pennsylvania Packet, Vol.XI, Issue 920, Philadelphia, August 6, 1782.

Published Documents, Maps, and Contemporary Works
Barr, John (1779–1782) and Samuel Tallmadge (1780–1782), et al. Diaries thereof.
   Orderly Books of The Fourth New York Regiment, 1778–1780 – The Second New York

Regiment, 1780–1783 with Diaries. Edited and transcribed by Almon W. Lauber. Albany, NY: University of the State of New York, 1932.

Clinton, George. *Public Papers of George Clinton, First Governor of New York, 1777–1795, 1801–1804.* 6 vols. New York and Albany, NY: State of New York, 1902.

Crowder, Norman K. *Early Ontario Settlers: A Source Book.* Baltimore: Genealogical Publishing Co., Inc., 1993.

Dann, John C. *The Revolution Remembered: Eyewitness Accounts of the War for Independence.* Chicago and London: The University of Chicago Press, 1980.

Fernow, Berthold, ed. *Documents relating to the Colonial History of the State of New York.* [V.XV, SAI] Albany, NY: Weed, Parsons and Company, Printers, 1887. XV, State Archives, V.1.

Fryer, Mary B. and Lieutenant-Colonel William A. Smy. *Rolls of the Provincial (Loyalist) Corps, Canadian Command American Revolutionary War Period.* Toronto: Dundurn Press, 1981.

General Staff, Historical Section of, ed. "The War of the American Revolution, The Province of Quebec under the Administration of Governor Frederic Haldimand, 1778–1784," in *A History of the Organization, Development and Services of the Military and Naval Forces of Canada From the Peace of Paris in 1763 to the Present Time With Illustrative Documents [HSGS].* 2 vols. Canada, King's Printer, n.d.

Johnston, Charles M., ed. *The Valley of the Six Nations: A Collection of Documents on the Indian Lands of the Grand River.* Toronto: The Champlain Society, 1964.

McHenry, Chris, compiler. *Rebel Prisoners at Quebec 1778–1783.* Author, 1981.

Penrose, Maryly B., ed. *Indian Affairs Papers, American Revolution.* Franklin Park, NJ: Liberty Bell Associates, 1981.

Pringle, J.F. *Lunenburgh or the Old Eastern District.* Belleville, ON: Mika Silk Screening Limited, 1972.

Reid, William D. *The Loyalists in Ontario: The Sons and Daughters of the American Loyalists of Upper Canada.* 1973. Reprint, Baltimore, MD: Genealogical Publishing, 1993.

Roberts, James A., comptroller. *New York in the Revolution as Colony and State.* 2 vols. Albany, NY: State of New York, 1904.

Smith, Captain George, Inspector of the Royal Military Academy at Woolwich. *An Universal Military Dictionary, A Copious Explanation of the Technical Terms &c. — Used in the Equipment, Machinery, Movements, and Military Operations of an Army.* 1779. Reprint, Ottawa: Museum Restoration Service, 1969.

Stark, Caleb, tr. and ed. *Memoir and Official Correspondence of Gen. John Stark, with Notices of Several Other Officers of the Revolution. Also, A Biography of Capt. Phineas Stevens, and of Col. Robert Rogers.* Concord, ON: G. Parker Lyon, 1860.

State of New Hampshire. *Part 1. Rolls and Documents Relating to Soldiers in the Revolutionary War.* Edited by Isaac W Hammand. Manchester, NH: State of New Hampshire, 1889.

Sullivan, James and Alexander C. Flick, eds. *Minutes of the Albany Committee of Correspondence, 1775–1778.* 2 vols. Albany, NY: State University of New York, 1923 and 1925.

Von Eelking, Max. *Memoirs, Letters and Journals of Major General Riedesel During his Residence in America.* 2 vols. William L. Stone, translator and editor. Albany, NY: J. Munsell, 1868.

———. *The German Allies in the American Revolution, 1776–1783.* Transcribed by J.G. Rosengarten. Albany, NY: 1893. Reprint, Kessinger Publishing, n.d.

Washington, George. Washington Papers, Library of Congress, 1741–1799: Series 3C, Varick Transcripts.

———. *The Writings of George Washington from the Original Manuscript Sources, 1745–1799.* [*Washington Writings*] Edited by John C. Fizpatrick. XXXIX vols. Washington: U.S. Government Printing Office, 1937.

PRIMARY SOURCES:

UNPUBLISHED TRANSCRIPTS, LETTERS, DOCUMENTS, AND JOURNALS

Barr, John. *Diary of, 1779–1782.* Orderly Books of The Fourth New York.

Dusten, Captain Moses. *Orderly Book of Capt. Moses Dusten 2nd New Hampshire Regiment: December 15, 1781–July 24, 1783.* (Mss.11391, V.2.) Albany, NY: New York State Library, Department of History and Archives.

McMillan, Hugh (collection of). *Letters from and related to Lieutenant Walter Sutherland, KRR NY.* [*Sutherland Papers*] Researched and transcribed by Heather Devine and Barbara Rogers from the Haldimand Papers.

Moore, Lieutenant Pliny. *Adjutant Pliney Moore's Orderly Book Fort Rensselaer 1782–1783.* [*Moore OB*] Transcribed by Wayne Lenig. Typescript by James F. Morrison. New York: New York State Library, Document, No.8174, n.d.

Morrison, James F. Unpublished study of the NYSL, Mss and Special Collections, Audited Accounts, Vol. A., n.d.

Rimaldy, Virginia, transcriber. "Orders of the Field Jaeger Corps from May 7, 1777 to April 30, 1783," n.d.

Singleton, Captain George. Journal of the last foray into the Mohawk Valley, July 5–15, 1782.

Smy, Lieuenant-Colonel William A., tr. and ed. "The Butler Papers: Documents and Papers Relating to Colonel John Butler and his Corps of Rangers 1711–1977." [*Smy Transcripts*] u.p., 1994.

Tallmadge, Samuel. *Diary of 1780–1782. Orderly Books of The Fourth New York Willett, Marinus. Col Marinus Willett's Letter and Orderly Book, Fort Rensselaer 1781.* [*Willett OB*] Transcribed by Charles Gehring. Typescript by James F. Morrison. Document No. 15705. Albany: New York State Library, Archives and Manuscripts.

———. *The Examinations of Jacob James and Jacob Conrad Klock taken at Fort Rensselaer, August 10, 1782.* New York: Papers of Marinus Willett, Miscellaneous Manuscripts, New York Historical Society.

PUBLISHED MEMOIRS, DEPOSITIONS, DIARIES, JOURNALS, POEMS, AND CORRESPONDENCE
American (See Also Pension Depositions Noted Above)
Beecher, Raymond, ed. *Letters from a Revolution 1775–1783, A Selection From the Bronck Family Papers*. Albany, NY: The Greene County Historical Society and the New York State American Revolution Bicentennial Commission, 1973.
Freemoyer, David. Pension Deposition thereof. "The Indian Frontier," in [hereafter *Freemoyer*] *The Revolution Remembered, Eyewitness Accounts of the War for Independence*, John C. Dann (Chicago: The University of Chicago Press, 1980), 288–306.
Glen Family and Throop Wilder. "The Glen Letters — That We May Remember." *New York History*, Vol. XXVI, No. 3 (July 1945).
Lesser, Charles H., ed. *The Sinews of Independence: Monthly Strength Report of the Continental Army*. Chicago: The University of Chicago Press, 1976.
Moore, Lieutenant Pliny (papers of). Hugh McLellan, ed. *Captain Job Wright's Company, Colonel Marinus Willett's Levies at Ballston, New-York 1782*. Champlain, NY: Moorsfield Press, 1928.
———. Hugh McLellan, ed. "In the Mohawk Valley in 1782, Col. Marinus Willett's Regiment of Levies." *Moorsfield Antiquarian Vols. I & II*. Champlain, NY: Moorsfield Press, 1938–39.
———. *Adjutant Pliney Moore's Orderly Book Fort Rensselaer 1782–1783*. [*Moore OB*] Transcribed by Wayne Lenig. Typescript by James F. Morrison. New York: New York State Library, Document No. 8174.
Thompson, Lieuteant Alexander. Letter to his brother, Fort Renssealaer, January 24, 1783. *The Historical Magazine, and Notes and Queries Concerning the Antiquities, History, etc....* Vol. 3 (Series 1, 10 vols.) New York: Charles B. Richardson, 1859.
Washington, George. *Papers of George Washington*. [*Washington Papers*] Library of Congress, n.d., *http://gwpapers.virginia.edu*.
———. *The Writings of George Washington from the Original Manuscript Sources, 1745–1799*. [*Washington Writings*] Edited by John C. Fizpatrick. XXXIX vols. Washington: U.S. Government Printing Office, 1937.

British, German, and Canadian
Crysler, Adam and James J. Talman, eds. "The Journal of Adam Crysler." In *Loyalist Narratives From Upper Canada*. Toronto: The Champlain Society, 1946.
Enys, John and Elizabeth Cometti, eds. The *American Journals of Lieutenant John Enys*. Syracuse: The Adirondack Museum and Syracuse University Press, 1976.
Hadden, Lieutenant James M. *A Journal Kept in Canada and Upon Burgoyne's Campaign in 1776 and 1777*. Edited by Horatio Rogers. Albany, NY: Joel Munsell's Sons, 1884.
Von Riedesel, Baroness Frederike Charlotte Louise. *Letters and Journals Relating to the War of American Independence and the Capture of the German Troops at Saratoga*. Toronto: German-Canadian Museum of Applied History, n.d.

Hesse Hanau Jäger Battalion

Pausch, Georg. *Georg Pausch's Journal and Reports of the Campaign in America.*. Transcribed and edited by Bruce E. Burgoyne. Bowie, MD: Heritage Books, Inc., 1996.

Rimaldy, Virginia, transcriber. *Orders of the Field Jaeger Corps from May 7, 1777 to April 30, 1783.* u.p., n.d.

Stuart, John. James J. Talman, eds. "Letters of the Rev. John Stuart." *Loyalist Narratives From Upper Canada.* Toronto: The Champlain Society, 1946.

Sutherland, Lieutenant Walter. *Letters from and Related to Lieutenant Walter Sutherland, 2KRR NY.* Researched and transcribed by Heather Devine and Barbara Rogers from the Haldimand Papers. Collection of Hugh McMillan.

Talman, James J. ed. *Loyalist Narratives from Upper Canada.* Toronto: The Champlain Society, 1946.

Tice, Captain Gilbert (Six Nations' Indian Department). Letter to Guy Johnson, dated Niagara, November 15, 1781, NAC, HP, B107, 312.

Von Kreutzbourg, Lieutenant-Colonel Carl. "Narration of Hesse Hanau Jäger Corps in America." [Kreutzbourg's Narration] Transcribed by John C. Zuleger. Hessian Papers. Morristown, NJ: Morristown National Historic Park.

————. "Letterbook of Lieutenant-Colonel Carl von Kreutzbourg, March 31, 1777 to October 31, 1783.

Von Riedesel, Major-General Friedrich Adolphus. Correspondence of General Riedesel 1776–87. Letters HZ-1(1–5). Lidgerwood Collection. Hessian Papers. Morristown, NJ: Morristown National Historic Park.

Wasmus, Julius Friedrich. *An Eyewitness Account of the American Revolution and New England Life — The Journal of J.F. Wasmus, German Company Surgeon, 1776–1783.* Transcribed by Helga Doblin and edited by Mary C. Lynn. New York, etc: Greenwood Press, 1990.

Zuleger, John C., tr. "Narration of Hesse Hanau Jäger Corps in America." Hessian Papers. Morristown, NJ: Morristown National Historic Park, NJ.

Zuleger, John C., tr. Von Kreutzbourg Letterbook — Letter Q. Lidgerwood Collection. Hessian Papers. Morristown, NJ: Morristown National Historic Park.

SECONDARY SOURCES — BOOKS

Benton, Nathaniel S. *A History of Herkimer County, including the Upper Mohawk Valley, from the earliest period to the present time.* Albany, NY: J. Munsell, 1856.

Bradley, A.G. "Lord Dorchester." *The Makers of Canada.* Vol. 3, 11 vols. Toronto: Morang & Co., Limited, 1911.

Briaddy, Katherine Q. *Ye Olde Days, A History of Burnt Hills-Ballston Lake.* Ballston Spa, NY: Women's Club, 1974.

Buckley, Richard. *Early Entrepreneurs of Little Falls, New York: John Porteous, Alexander Ellice and Edward Ellice.* Little Falls: Little Falls Historical Society, 1996.

Calloway, Colin G. *The American Revolution in Indian Country: Crisis and Diversity in Native American Communities.* Cambridge: Cambridge University Press, 1995.

Campbell, William W. Jr. *Annals of Tryon County; or the Border Warfare of New York.* Cherry Valley: The Cherry Valley Gazette Print, 1880.

Cruikshank, Ernest A. *The Story of Butler's Rangers and the Settlement of Niagara.* 1893. Reprint, Owen Sound, ON: Richardson, Bond & Wright Ltd., 1975.

Cruikshank, Ernest A. and Gavin K. Watt. *The History and Master Roll of The King's Royal Regiment of New York.* Revised edition. 1984. Reprint, with the additions of an index, appendices, and a Master Muster Roll. Campbellville: Global Heritage Press, 2006.

Cruikshank, Ernest A. *The Settlement of the United Empire Loyalists on the Upper St. Lawrence and Bay of Quinte in 1784.* Toronto: Ontario Historical Society, 1934.

Devine, E.J. (S.J.) *Historic Caughnawaga.* Montreal: Messenger Press, 1922.

Dresler, Horst. *Henry & John Ruiter, 1742–1819.* Woodstock, VT: Anything Printed, 2005.

Dunnigan, Brian Leigh. *King's Men at Mackinac, The British Garrisons, 1780–1796.* Mackinac Island, MI: Mackinac Island State Park Commission, 1973.

Egly, T.W. Jr. *History of the First New York Regiment.* Hampton, NH: Peter E. Randall, 1981.

Fitzpatrick, Alan. *Wilderness War on the Ohio: The Untold Story of the Savage Battle for British and Indian Control of the Ohio Country During the American Revolution.* Benwood, WV: Author, 2003.

Fraser, J. Skulking for the King: *A Loyalist Plot. Erin, Ontario.* The Boston Mills Press, 1985.

Frazier, Patrick. *The Mohicans of Stockbridge.* Lincoln, Nebraska, and London: University of Nebraska Press, 1992.

Fryer, Mary Beacock. *Loyalist Spy, The experiences of Captain John Walden Meyers during the American Revolution.* Brockville, ON: Besancourt Publishers, 1974.

———. *Buckskin Pimpernel: The Exploits of Justus Sherwood Loyalist Spy.* Toronto: Dundurn Press, 1981.

———. *Allan Maclean, Jacobite General: The Life of an Eighteenth Century Career Soldier.* Toronto: Dundurn Press, 1987.

———. *King's Men: The Soldier Founders of Ontario.* Toronto: Dundurn Press, 1980.

Glatthaar, Joseph T. and James Kirby Martin. *Forgotten Allies: The Oneida Indians and the American Revolution.* New York City: Hill and Wang, 2006.

Graymont, Barbara. *The Iroquois in the American Revolution.* Syracuse, NY: Syracuse University Press, 1972.

Halsey, Francis Whiting. *The Old New York Frontier, Its Wars with Indians and Tories, Its Missionary Schools, Pioneers and Land Titles.* New York: Charles Scribner's Sons, 1917.

Hanson, Willis T. *A History of Schenectady During the Revolution to which is appended a Contribution to the Individual Records of the Inhabitants of the Schenectady District During that Period.* The author, 1916.

Hoffman, Phillip W. Hoffman. *Simon Girty: Turncoat Hero, The Most Hated Man on the Early American Frontier.* Franklin, TE: American History Imprints, 2008.

Houlding, J.A. "The King's Service: The Officers of the British Army, 1735–1792." u.p., n.d.

Jackson, H.M. *Rogers' Rangers: A History.* Toronto: self published, 1953.

———. *Justus Sherwood: Soldier, Loyalist and Negotiator.* Toronto: author, 1958.

Jepson, George H. *Herrick's Rangers*. Bennington, VT: Hadwen, Inc., 1977.

Johnson, Ken D., *Fort Plank Historian*. *The Bloodied Mohawk, The American Revolution in the Words of Fort Plank's Defenders and Other Mohawk Valley Partisans*. Rockport, MA: Picton Press, 2000.

Kelsay, Isabel Thompson. *Joseph Brant 1743–1807: Man of Two Worlds*. Syracuse, NY: Syracuse University Press, 1984.

Lanctot, Gustave, Margaret M. Cameron, trs. *Canada & the American Revolution, 1774–1783*. London, Toronto, Wellington, Sydney: George G. Harrap & Co. Ltd, 1967.

Mackesy, Piers. *The War for America 1775–1783*. 1964. Reprint, Lincoln and London: University of Nebraska Press, 1992.

Mathews, Hazel C. *Frontier Spies*. Fort Myers: self-published, 1971.

McIlwraith, Jean N. "Sir Frederick Haldimand." *The Makers of Canada*. Vol. 3 (11 vols.) Toronto: Morang & Co., Limited, 1911.

Montgomery, Thomas Lynch, ed. "The Frontier Forts of Western Pennsylvania — Hannastown." Vol.2 (2 vols.) Harrisburg, PA: Report of the Commission to Locate the Sites of the Frontier Forts of Pennsylvania, 1896.

Parker, Edward L., *The History of Londonderry, comprising the towns of Derry and Londonderry, N.H.* Boston, 1851.

Reuter, Claus. *History of the Brunswick Light Infantry Battalion "von Barner" in North America from 1776 to 1783*. Toronto: self-published, n.d.

Simms, Jeptha R. *Frontiersman of New York Showing Customs of the Indians, Vicissitudes of the Pioneer White Settlers and Border Strife in Two Wars with a Great Variety of Romantic and Thrilling Stories Never Before Published*. 2 vols. Albany, NY: Geo. C. Riggs, 1883.

———. *History of Schoharie County, and Border Wars of New York; Containing also a Sketch of the Causes Which Led to the American Revolution; etc....* Albany, NY: Munsell & Tanner, 1845.

———. *Trappers of New York*: or, *A Biography of Nicholas Stoner and Nathaniel Foster; together with Anecdotes of other Celebrated Hunters and some account of Sir William Johnson and his style of living*. 1871. Reprint, Fleischmann's, NY: Harbor Hill Books, 1980.

Smy, Lieutenant Colonel William A. *An Annotated Nominal Roll of Butler's Rangers 1777–1784 with Documentary Sources*. [*Annotated Roll*]. St. Catharines, ON: Friends of the Loyalist Collection at Brock University, 2004.

Stone, William L. *Life of Joseph Brant: Thayendanegea including the Indian Wars of the American Revolution*. 2 vols. 1838. Reprint, St. Clair Shores, MI: Scholarly Press, 1970.

Thomas, Earle. *Sir John Johnson, Loyalist Baronet*. Toronto: Dundurn Press, 1986.

Watt, Gavin K. Research assistance by James F. Morrison. *Rebellion in the Mohawk Valley, the St. Leger Expedition of 1777*. Toronto: Dundurn Press, 2002.

———. Research assistance by James F. Morrison and William A. Smy. *A dirty, trifling, piece of business — Volume I: The Revolutionary War As Waged From Canada in 1781*. Toronto: Dundurn Press, 2008.

Wells, Frederic P. *History of Newbury, Vermont, From the Discovery of the Coös Country to Present Time.* St. Johnsbury, VT: The Caledonian Company, 1902.

Wilhelmy, Jean-Pierre. *German Mercenaries in Canada.* Beloeil, QC: Maison des Mots, 1985.

Willett, William M. *A Narrative of the Military Actions of Colonel Marinus Willett, Taken Chiefly from his Own Manuscript.* New York: G.&C.&H. Carvill, 1831.

Williamson, Chilton. *Vermont in Quandary 1763–1825.* Montpelier, VT: Vermont Historical Society, 1949.

Wright, Robert K. Jr. *The Continental Army.* Washington: Army Lineage Series, Centre of Military History, United States Army, 1989.

Young, Richard J. "Blockhouses in Canada, 1749–1841: A Comparative Report and Catalogue." [Blockhouses] Canadian Historic Sites: Occasional Papers in Archaeology and History. Ottawa: Parks Canada, 1980.

SECONDARY SOURCES:

ARTICLES, MONOGRAPHS, BOOKLETS, NEWSLETTERS, CATALOGUES, AND THESES

Beacraft, ___. "A True History of the Feats, Adventures and Sufferings of Matthew Calkins in the Time of the Revolution." *Magazine of History*, Vol. XVIII Extra No. 70 (1920).

Bond, C.C.J. "The British Base at Carleton Island." *OHSPR*, Vol.52 (1960).

Burleigh, H.C. *Deforests of Avesnes and Kast, McGinness.* Self-published, n.d.

Cruikshank, Ernest A. "The Coming of the Loyalist Mohawks to the Bay of Quinte." *OHSPR*, 26 (1930).

———. "The Adventures of Roger Stevens: A Forgotten Loyalist Pioneer in Upper Canada." OHSPR, 33 (1939).

Efner, William B., "Warfare in the Mohawk Valley — Transcriptions from the *Pennsylvania Gazette*, 1780–1783." Schenectady, 1948.

Fenton, Walter S. "Seth Warner," *Proceedings of the Vermont Historical Society*, Vol. 8, No.4 (1940).

Glasier, Terry & Hazel (papers of). "The Ancestors of My Daughters." In *A study of the (De) Kalb family in America.* u.p., n.d.

Green, Ernest. "Gilbert Tice, U.E." *OHSPR*, Vol.21 (1924).

Koettertiz, John B. "Andrew Finck, Major in the Revolutionary Wars." An address delivered to The Herkimer County Historical Society, 1897.

Lince, Elmer D. "The Last Expedition of the Revolutionary War: Fort Oswego." *Journal of the Johannes Schwalm Historical Association, Inc.*, Vol. 5, No.1 (1993).

Lovejoy, John M. "A Study of letters and rolls relating to the 2nd New Hampshire Regiment in 1782." James F. Morrison collection.

Mackesy, Piers. "Could the British Have Won the War of Independence?" A transcript of the Bland-Lee Lecture (1975), at Clark University, Worcester, Massachusetts.

Morrison, James F. "Biography of Frederick Visscher." TCMN, Vol. I, No.1 (1983).

Stacey, Kim. *No One Harms Me with Impunity — The History, Organization, and Biographies of the 84th Regiment of Foot (Royal Highland Emigrants) and Young Royal Highlanders, During the Revolutionary War 1775–1784.* Manuscript in progress, 1994.

Steppler, Glenn A. "Regimental Records in the Late Eighteenth Century and the Social History of the British Soldier." *Archivaria* 26 (Summer 1988).

Stevens, Paul L. "His Majesty's 'Savage' Allies: British Policy and the Northern Indians During the Revolutionary War — The Carleton Years, 1774–1778." Ph.D. diss, State University of New York at Buffalo, 1984.

Wilson, Bruce. "The Struggle for Wealth and Power at Fort Niagara 1775–1783." *Ontario History*, V.68 (1976).

SECONDARY SOURCES — WEBSITES

Clark, George M. "Washington's Last Expedition: Capture Fort Ontario!": *http://fortontario.com/History/George2/Willett.html* (accessed March 2005).

Bach, Lieutenant Michael. "A plan of the camp at Point Levis and the manoeuvres of September 18, 1782." DigAM Digitales archive marburg, no. 88, *www.digam.net/index.php?dok=2037&h%5B0%5D=sorel.*

Brownlee, Joseph (John/Jack). "Joseph Brownlee and the Destruction of Hannastown": *www.mcn.org/2/NOEL/Westmoreland/WestHistory.htm#JOSEPH%20BROWNLEE* (accessed March 12, 2009).

Cubbison, Douglas R. "The Coins of the British Private Soldier in the American Revolution": *www.csmid.com/files/coins.html* (accessed January 18, 2009).

Dictionary of Canadian Biography Online: *www.biographi.ca.*

Digby, Admiral Robert. *www.fullbooks.com/American-Prisoners-of-the-Revolution7.html* (accessed January 25, 2009).

"Hanna's Town." *http://en.wikipedia.org/wiki/Hannastown* (accessed February 24, 2009).

HMS Albermarle: *www.ageofnelson.org/MichaelPhillips/liste.php?char=A#0090* (accessed February 2, 2009).

Johnson, Ken D: *www.fort-plank.com/Additional_Partisans.*

Laurens, John. *http://en.wikipedia.org/wiki/John_Laurens* (accessed August 15, 2008).

Nelson, Horatio: *http://ourcivilisation.com/smartboard/shop/nelsonh/myself.htm* (accessed February 2, 2009).

Oury, Eve, affidavit of, Westmoreland County, Pennsylvania. December 4, 1846. Research by Starlene Oary. (accessed February 24, 2009) *http://files.usgwarchives.net/pa/westmoreland/bios/ourye0001.txt.*

Popek, Daniel M. "The Rhode Island Regiments in the Revolutionary War": *http://freepages.genealogy.rootsweb.ancestry.com/~smithandyoung/Chillson.htm.*

Revolutionary War Accounts and Claims: *www.archives.nysed.gov/a/research/fa/A0200.shtml* (accessed October 2008).

Revolutionary War Pensions. Morrison, James F. and A.J. Berry Enterprises. *http://morrisonspensions.org.*

Rhode Island Continental Regiments' histories:
www.firstrhodeisland.org (accessed January 28, 2009).
www.earlyamerica.com/review/2004_summer_fall/soldiers.htm (accessed January 28, 2009).

http://americanrevolution.org/firstri.htm (accessed January 28, 2009).

http://revolution.h-net.msu.edu/essays/adams2.html (accessed September 14, 2008).

"Records of the State of Rhode Island and Providence Plantations": *www.rootsweb. ancestry.com/~rigenweb/articles.*

Rockingham Ministry: *www.historyhome.co.uk/c-eight/ministry/rocky2s.htm* (accessed October 10, 2008).

Shelburne, Earl of: *http://en.wikipedia.org/wiki/William_Petty,_2nd_Earl_of_Shelburne* (accessed December 16, 2008).

Tichenor, Isaac. Biographical notes: *www.famousamericans.net/isaactichenor* (accessed July, 2008).

Voorhees, Betsy. "The Attack on the Old Mill": *www.rootsweb.com/~nyherkim/littlefalls/ littlemill.html* (accessed March 24, 2009).

INDEX

1. All page entries in bold indicate that the subject is in an image or on a map.
2. A native's affiliation is designated by a two- or three-letter abbreviation after his/her name, e.g. Abenaki (Ab); Delaware (De); Kahnawake (Kah); Tuscarora (Tu).

ALSO BY GAVIN K. WATT

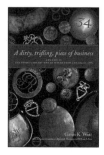

A dirty, trifling, piece of business
Volume I: The Revolutionary War as Waged from Canada in 1781
978-1-55488-420-9 / $35.00

By 1781, the sixth year of the American rebellion, British strategic focus had shifted from the northern states to concentrate in the south. Canada's governor, Frederick Haldimand, was responsible for the defence of the Crown's largest colony against the threat of Franco-American invasion, while assisting overall British strategy. He cleverly employed his sparse resources to vigorously raid the rebels' frontiers and create anxiety, disruption, and deprivation. Haldimand flooded New York's Mohawk and Schoharie valleys with Indian and Loyalist raiders and, once the danger of invasion passed, he dispatched two coordinated expeditions south. The rebels effectively countered both expeditions.

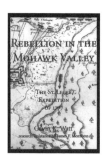

Rebellion in the Mohawk Valley
The St. Leger Expedition of 1777
978-1-55488-005-8 / $20.50

In the summer of 1777, while the British and the Americans were engaged in the bitter American Revolution, a massive campaign was launched from Canada into New York State. Brigadier Barry St. Leger led a crucial expedition from Lake Ontario into the Mohawk Valley. The goal was to travel by waterways to join Lieutenant General John Burgoyne in the siege of Albany. But Leger encountered obstacles along the way. While laying siege to Fort Stanwix, he received word that Benedict Arnold was leading a massive relief column that was headed their way. Leger and his men retreated, and despite a later attempt to carry on, were never able to help Burgoyne. The Americans then destroyed the British-held Fort Ticonderoga, marking the end of the campaign. The results of the failed St. Leger expedition were historic.

Burning of the Valleys
Daring Raids from Canada Against the New York Frontier in the Fall of 1780
978-1-55488-312-7 / $20.99

In the fifth year of the War of Independence, while the Americans focused on the British thrust against the Carolinas, the Canadian Department waged a decisive campaign against the northern frontier of New York. Their primary target was the Mohawk River region, known to be the "grainbowl" that fed Washington's armies. Without benefit of modern transportation, communications, or navigational aids, four coordinated raids, each thoroughly examined in this book, penetrated deeply into American territory. The raiders fought skirmishes and battles, took hundreds of prisoners, burned forts, farms, and mills, and destroyed one of the finest grain harvests in living memory. *The Burning of the Valleys* details the actions of both sides in this exciting and incredibly effective British campaign.